Sword Unsheathed

A Battle of the Bibles and Bible History Manual

Written & Compiled by Dallas P. Roberts

© 2022 Dallas P. Roberts
All rights reserved – worldwide

This book may be copied for the purpose of *freely* sharing with others who may not have resources to purchase their own copy. However, it may only be copied, provided it is copied in a full and complete manner and all credits and contact information are included and intact.
Researchers & Reviewers may quote passages for articles & reviews, so long as credit and source information is given.

This book may not to be copied, published, or reproduced in any form or manner whatsoever for marketing or any other type of commercial gain purposes - without first obtaining the written permission of the author.

To contact the author, e-mail at:
biblepathways@hotmail.com

WWW.BIBLEPICTUREPATHWAYS.COM

All Scripture quotations are taken from the
Authorized King James Bible
(unless otherwise indicated)

Printed in the United States of America

ISBN-13: 978-0-9987695-1-6

Dedicated to the Word,

Our Lord and Saviour

Jesus Christ

Who has enabled the compiler to learn
this information for himself, and guided him
to the sources needed for it.

With much grateful appreciation to my wife, Susanna, for her help, encouragement, and support in this project including hundreds of hours spent in editing, layout and formatting

Special thanks to my children
for their support in this project.

To my daughter, Rachel, for taking the time to read the entire book and for her contributions to the Section on Foreign Bibles

To Diana for links and help with the Spanish Bible history

And to my son, Daniel, for the cover design, being our IT guy, and also for reprogramming one of the fonts to include a needed accent mark (é)

Much appreciation to Mr. A. whose gift of several old books inspired and enabled this project to go forward

Table of Contents

Content   **Page**

Foreward --- 1
Introduction --- 5
Definitions and Terms made Simple --- 7
The Beginning of the Christian Church --- 23

The Lineage of the Word of God

First 500 Years --- 31
From 500 AD to 1000 AD --- 87
From 1000 AD to 1600 AD --- 101
The King James Bible (KJV) --- 171
From the KJV to 1870 --- 189
The Revision of the KJV (RV) --- 217
From the RV to 1979 --- 227
The New King James Version (NKJV) --- 253
From the NKJV to Today --- 271
Examples of Modern Bible Changes Affecting Doctrine --- 289
What about Foreign Bibles? --- 315
An Unrelenting Plot --- 323
Conclusion --- 331

Additional Notes

A - Royal Line Compared to Counterfeit Line --- 335
B - The Beauty of Classic Bibles --- 338
C - The "Johannine Comma" - 1 John 5:7,8 --- 339
D - Authenticity of Matthew 28:19 and the Godhead --- 356
E - How to Study the Bible from the Bible --- 358
F - Papal vs. Protestant Bible Study Methods --- 361
G - Miller's Rules --- 366
H - "Christian" Fiction --- 371
I - Law of God vs. Law as Changed by Rome --- 373

Bibliography --- 375
Index --- 384

Dates listed in **Bold** & not specified as BC or AD are all in the Christian Era [AD]
Bible Versions & Translations are shown in this **Font**
Records are listed in Chronological order as much as possible.

FOREWARD
Contending for the Word

"And take the helmet of salvation, and the sword of the Spirit, which is the word of God:" Ephesians 6:17

In the Great Controversy of the ages, God's recommended weapon of offense has always been the Sword of the Spirit, God's Word, the Bible. So it should come as no surprise that from the beginning, Satan's goal has been to take away the Sword, the only offensive armor, from the Christian soldier.

In the book of Genesis, *"Yea hath God said?"* are the first, doubt-ridden words of the subtil serpent. The serpent further continued his stratagem by contradicting the word of God – the result of which was the fall of man. Man was conquered because Satan succeeded in taking away his Sword.

Today, men are still conquered by this plan of Satan. For example, on one occasion, I was able to observe as the writer of this book was led into contact with a man who had totally given up on Christianity (which the man admittedly missed because he stated he "felt safe then"). The man stated that this apostasy from the truth was a direct result of all the contradictions and changes that the modern versions posed to the authority and authenticity of God's Word. How could they all be God's Word when in some cases they were diametrically opposed (distinctly opposite)? The man expressed a desire to be able to read the Greek and Hebrew so that he could see for himself who was telling the truth. Thankfully, through a brief history of the Bibles, similar to that contained in this book, and an assurance that there is indeed a "sure word of prophecy" in English, this man was led back to a renewed study of the Word.

In Matthew 4, we discover another one of Satan's tactics. We again find the tempter, this time disguised as an angel of light, yet still misquoting scripture, taking scripture out of context, and casting doubt on the Word in order to accomplish his evil sword-stealing ends. But instead of dropping His sword, Jesus proved to be equal to the duel, sharpening His sword by use.

"But he [Jesus] answered and said, It is written, Man shall not live by bread alone, but by every word that proceedeth out of the mouth of God." Matthew 4:4

Following the example of his Master, the Christian soldier, to counter those who *"corrupt the word of God"* (2 Corinthians 2:17) must follow the *"every word of God"* method. This will give him an unconquerable advantage.

"For the word of God is quick, and powerful, and sharper than any twoedged sword, piercing even to the dividing asunder of soul and spirit, and of the joints and marrow, and is a discerner of the thoughts and intents of the heart." Hebrews 4:12

Since we are living down in the very "toenails of time," it also would be well to bear in mind that in the *"Revelation of Jesus Christ"* for His last-day people, we find a statement, exposing the tactics of *"the great dragon ... that old serpent, called the Devil, and Satan, which deceiveth the whole world..."* Revelation 12:9. It would be well to consider that recorded here is the fact that Satan's biggest contention is with the Word – he hates those who hold the Sword. *"And the dragon was wroth with the woman, and went to make war with the remnant of her seed, which keep the commandments of God, and have the testimony of Jesus Christ."* Revelation 12:17

John the Revelator recorded having tribulation *"for the word of God, and for the testimony of Jesus Christ."* (Revelation 1:9) Satan is angry because the remnant keep the commandments of God and have the testimony of Jesus Christ. The Bible defines the testimony of Jesus as *"the spirit of prophecy"* (Revelation 19:10) The "sure word of prophecy" is certainly here included, for Jesus wrote. *"Search the scriptures; for in them ye think ye have eternal life: and **they are they which testify of me.**"* John 5:39 The Sword of the Sure Word testifies that Jesus of Nazareth is the Word made flesh. Since the Word exposes Satan and sin, it is thus the object of Satan's greatest wrath. It is this controversy that made plain a need for the details contained in *Sword Unsheathed – A Battle of the Bibles and Bible History Handbook*.

Sword Unsheathed is the culmination of over 40 years of the writer's Sure Word sword use. However, Dallas' most intensive historical research began over seven years ago when he began to study the Royal Line – those who have held, protected, and translated the "sword of the word" throughout the ages. In this volume, the writer brings together for your perusal and consideration, quotations and information from many old and often hard-to-find historical books. Though the writer's primary "Sword language" is English, his research has led him, with the aid of a computer and many language dictionaries, to study Bibles in Hebrew, Greek, French, Italian, German, Dutch, Latin, and many other languages. Indeed, collecting, printing and binding old and foreign Bibles has become one of his favorite hobbies and his most treasured collection.

However, all has not been so pleasant. Throughout history, the serpent has employed many in his service to chop and change, hide, and cast doubt on God's word – seeking by every means to steal the Sword. The writer has observed references in credible history books describing forged manuscripts of the word. Well-translated Bibles that he has looked for were all too often hated, burned, banished, or mysteriously disappeared, some in the matter of a just a few years. Sometimes manuscripts are "locked away" in libraries strangely made inaccessible to the common man. The writer also discovered in the process of his research, that those in what should have been Bible-loving cultural centers were not always happy to help him find copies of what they referred to as the *"so-called... Bible."*

Foreward – Contending for the Word

The writer's quest for truth made evident that unfortunately, the sword-stealing technique of the devil continues, often by pawning off counterfeit "butter-knife" trades to trick people into giving up their real Sword.

In addition, sinister, deep-seated, New Age inroads to dull the Sword, dissolving the true meaning of God's word in an evolutionary manner (a few changes at a time) have come to light. Portions inside many modern Bibles, have also been changed to match New Age theology in choice places. Here we see the devil, again, coming as an angel of light – in this case, in the form of a Bible that has been corrupted.

For example, Matthew 28:20b in the **King James Version** reads *"lo, I am with you alway, even unto the end of the world. Amen."* This has been the standard and Biblically accurate English translation since Wycliffe's Bible in the 1300s. In fact, the word "world" is echoed exactly in all the English Royal Line of Bible translations, from Tyndale and Coverdale to the Matthews' and Bishops' Bibles; from the Geneva Bible even unto Webster's.

So why is it changed in many modern versions? Sadly, even the **New King James Version (NKJV)** reads, *"Lo, I am with you always, even unto the end of the age."* Yet, in other places, such as Mark 4:19 and Luke 16:8, the **NKJV** still translates this very same Greek word as "world." Why? Could this actually be a subtle sword-stealing technique? We needn't search long to see who might profit from this "New" "Age" wording. Would those that are ushering in a New Age of Aquarius with its false Christ (who undermines and reinterprets the word of God) profit from this new interpretation?

Known spiritualist and prolific writer, Alice A. Bailey, writes in her book, *The Reappearance of the Christ*, *"The final words of the Christ to His apostles were, 'Lo, I am with you all the days, even unto the end of the age' or cycle. (Matt. 28.20.)"* Bailey continues by stating that this *"means the end of the time period, with another immediately following after (what would be called the end of a cycle)."*
(*The Reappearance of the Christ*, Alice A. Bailey, PDF pg. 11)

While professing to be within the bounds of "translation," how convenient this retranslation and change is for ushering in a New Age "Christ" who is different from the Jesus Christ recorded in the scriptures. Could sword-stealing and counterfeiting allow Christians to except Satan as Christ? Why does God's word warn those who fear Jehovah to *"meddle not with them that are given to change?"* Proverbs 24:21 In *Sword Unsheathed* the reader will take a deeper look at this question.

Over the past few years, when the writer's friends have asked the writer a history or a Bible version question, inevitably, they get his oft repeated answer – *"It's in my book."* Indeed, the reader will find the book packed full of valuable and often hard-to-find information.

Sword Unsheathed

In this book, the writer has unlocked for the common man hidden histories; he has simplified obscure words and phrases, and paralleled counterfeit "butter-knife swords" with the Sword of the Spirit for comparison. Therefore, it is with the utmost delight that I present to you *Sword Unsheathed* "the book about the Book." I pray you will enjoy its treasures and come to a better understanding of the battle of the Bibles as I have. And may the God of Heaven find you among those that are *"holding fast the faithful word"* and among the remnant that *"keep the commandments of God, and **have** the testimony of Jesus Christ."* – the undiluted, unsheathed Sword of the Spirit.

–Aletheia

"God's Word is full of precious promises and helpful counsel.
***It is infallible**; for God can not err.*
It has help for every circumstance and condition of life,
and God looks on with sadness when His children turn from it
to human aid."
(Signs of the Times, June 26, 1901)

Introduction

It has been said, *"Truth is independent of opinion. By its very definition, truth is intolerant of error, every aspect petitioning the conscience for acknowledgment. The individual however, holds the key to admission or rejection."* This statement correctly portrays the issue that the world is facing when examining the Bible and its role in our lives. In other words, Biblical truth is a one way street, yet the hearer may choose to accept or deny it.

Fundamentally, there are only two streams of Bibles – the Pure Stream and the Corrupt Stream – just as there were two key trees in the Garden of Eden – the Tree of Life, and the Tree of Knowledge of Good and Evil.

Both of these streams, just like a tree, have many branches – but when the branches are followed back to the source root – all of them lead back to only two different original roots. By knowing what the source is, an individual can discern whether the branch is good or evil. *"For if the firstfruit be holy, the lump is also holy: and **if the root be holy, so are the branches**." Romans 11:16*

Satan's goal throughout history has been to try to mix the Evil with the Good, just as he did in Eden. The Tree of Knowledge of Good and Evil was a mixture – some Truth, some Error. But just like rat poison, that small percentage of error brought the "death penalty" on Adam and Eve.

The record of history is the record of the colossal struggle between the forces of Good and the forces of Evil. It is the Great Controversy between Christ and Satan. This battle has always been over the issue of "worship." The two Trees, or the two Streams – the Narrow Way versus the Broad Way – Life or Death – the worship of God or the worship of Satan!

*"Enter ye in at the strait gate: for **wide is the gate, and broad is the way, that leadeth to destruction, and many there be which go in thereat: Because strait is the gate, and narrow is the way, which leadeth unto life, and few there be that find it**. Beware of false prophets, which come to you in sheep's clothing, but inwardly they are ravening wolves. **Ye shall know them by their fruits.** Do men gather grapes of thorns, or figs of thistles?" Matthew 7:13-16*

As one can see from the terms "**Narrow Way**" and "**Broad Way**," the way to Life is the way that is narrowed down – it is basically singular and reformatory in nature – it requires surrender of the will and desires to God; while the way that leads to death is wide and broad – there are many different varieties that oblige the many desires of human nature – it does not require surrender to God but is based on the popular *"Do what thou wilt"* philosophy.

Sword Unsheathed

The Word of God specifically states in 1 Thessalonians 5:21 to *"Prove all things; hold fast that which is good."*

Though many errors had been incorporated into God's church over the centuries, when Christ was here on earth, He would have corrected and pointed out any that had made their way into the record of His Word. One can therefore safely assume that the apostles, who received instruction directly from Him, were teaching the correct doctrines of truth and that their writings which later constituted the New Testament were accurate.

With this being the case, the writer will not take the space, in this condensed work, to travel back much into the 4,000 years before the time of Christ. Instead, this book will mainly focus on the sources of the two streams at the beginning of the Christian era. From there, it will travel down through the 2,000 years of events that have transpired since. In order to understand the issues with all the modern Bible versions of today, one needs to understand just where they came from, what root source they grew out of, and the basic history behind their development.

Sword Unsheathed begins in the first centuries at the time period of the Apostles and early Christian Church, and then proceeds down through the Dark Ages and the time of the Reformation. Finally, it explores the history of the various Bibles in the 19th–21st centuries. However, before beginning this journey, a good foundation must be laid by defining some of the terms that the reader will encounter in the study of the Bible and its surrounding history.

Definitions and Terms made Simple

The **Old Testament** is a collection of **39 books** which were originally written mostly in the Hebrew language (with a little in Aramaic). This is what is known as "the Scriptures" until after the time of Christ! (And among traditional Jews and others who do not recognize the Messiah in the ministry of Jesus Christ – the Old Testament is still the only thing that makes up "the Scriptures.")

These books were written one at a time over the years on sheets of animal skin which were then rolled into separate rolls that were called "scrolls." Whenever a person wanted to read a certain part of scripture, they would have to retrieve whichever scroll contained the particular book that they wanted. Then they would have to scan the text as they rotated through the whole roll to find it. This is evident from the story of Jesus that is recorded in the New Testament scriptures.

"And he came to Nazareth, where he had been brought up: and, as his custom was, he went into the synagogue on the sabbath day, and stood up for to read. ***And there was delivered unto him the book of the prophet Esaias. And when he had opened the book, he found the place where it was written,*** *The Spirit of the Lord is upon me, because he hath anointed me to preach the gospel to the poor; he hath sent me to heal the brokenhearted, to preach deliverance to the captives, and recovering of sight to the blind, to set at liberty them that are bruised, to preach the acceptable year of the Lord."* Luke 4:16-19

The **New Testament** is a collection of **27 books**, written originally in the Greek language; though a few portions were written first in Hebrew or Aramaic and then translated into Greek. The New Testament was added to the Scriptures after the time of Christ by the apostles who were the authors of the various books.

The Greeks made their rolls for their scrolls by cutting up the pith of papyrus into long strips and gluing it together to form sheets which they then glued together to form long rolls. The papyrus was called "biblios" and so they referred to their rolls as "biblion" and when this word passed on into the Latin language it was called "biblia." Thus, "Biblia" is the source of our modern word "Bible."

A **'manuscript'** [often abbreviated as **"MS"** (singular) and **"MSS"** (plural)] is a hand-written document, not one that is typed or printed. Before the invention of the printing press in the 15th century, all copies of the Old and New Testaments were MSS (written by hand).

Manuscripts fall into several categories:

Autographs: Sometimes called 'masters' – these are the ancient original texts written either by the author's own hand or by a scribe under his personal supervision. *There are currently no known original autographs or masters in existence.* They have all long since deteriorated and been replaced by copies.

Copies: These are hand-written copies of the masters or hand-written copies of earlier copies.

Versions: These are *translations* of Scripture made directly from the original languages of Hebrew & Greek. For example: from Hebrew or Greek into Syriac, Latin, German, English or French.

An important fact for the reader to bear in mind is a **translation** from Latin into English, or from English into Chinese, cannot strictly be called a **"version."** It is simply a *translation of a translation*: whereas a **"version"** must be a translation from the original language. However, the common people today have a tendency to use this term interchangeably.

Writings of Church Fathers: These are the early sermons, books, and commentaries written by men who led the Christians in the first few centuries after the New Testament was completed.

Currently there are only a few old manuscripts of the Old Testament in existence, but there are about **5,309** extant (existing) manuscripts of the Greek New Testament or parts of it. There are more than 18,000 copies of those versions in existence.

It is also said that even if mankind did not have the 5,300+ Greek manuscripts or the 18,000 copies of the versions, the text of the New Testament could still be reproduced within 250 years from its composition by searching the writings of the early Christians. In commentaries, letters, etc., these ancient writers quote Biblical text, thus giving another witness to the text of the New Testament.

More than 86,000 citations of the New Testament have been cataloged in the writings of the early church fathers that lived before **AD 325**.

The word **"extant"** means "in being" – in other words "it exists."
An "extant" manuscript is a manuscript that is still in existence today. It can be handled with the hands and seen with the eyes. Manuscripts that are housed in museums and libraries are labeled as being "extant."

Definitions and Terms made Simple

The word **'codex'** simply means 'book' and the plural form of the word codex is **"codices."**

A **"colophon"** is a short note written at the end of a book that tells information about the book – such as who wrote or corrected the book and/or where or when the writing or correction was done.

The term **"eclectic"** means in simple terms to "pick and choose." It is a description of the method of determining the supposed correct reading that is used by the critical scholars when they just "pick and choose" which manuscript or text reading they want to accept that best fits their fancy or particular need.

There are two main types of Bible study methods. These two types can be summarized as the Proof-text method and the Higher Criticism method. There are various branches or sub-methods of these methods, but they all come back to these two sources.

The way a person views the Bible, will determine which method they choose to use to study it.

"The spirit in which you come to the investigation of the Scriptures will determine the character of the assistant at your side. Angels from the world of light will be with those who in humility of heart seek for divine guidance. But if the Bible is opened with irreverence, with a feeling of self-sufficiency, if the heart is filled with prejudice, Satan is beside you, and he will set the plain statements of God's word in a perverted light." (Gospel Workers, 1892, p. 127)

If a person believes that the Bible is just like any other history book written by human authors, then they will choose to study it with one or more of the Higher Criticism methods.

One higher critic stated: *"The text of the Bible…has shared the fortunes of other texts of other literature.* **We find there are errors of transmission. There is nothing divine in the text…"** (Authority of Holy Scripture, p.31)

If a person believes that the Bible is the Word of the Living God, inspired and authored by Him, then they will choose to study it with the Proof-text method.

"Do we receive the Bible as the 'oracle of God'? ***It is as really a divine communication as though its words came to us in an audible voice."***

(Testimonies, vol.5, p. 533)

These two terms are self-defining.

"Proof-text" = using the "text" of the Bible itself to "prove" what the Bible means – allowing the Bible to interpret itself.

"Higher Criticism" = using some other (supposedly "higher" than the Bible) source from outside the Bible, to "critically analyze" the Bible meaning, and define what the Bible means.

True **"Proof-texting"** is what is described by the Bible as how people are to study the Word of God. *"Whom shall he teach knowledge? and whom shall he make to **understand doctrine**? them that are weaned from the milk, and drawn from the breasts. **For precept must be upon precept, precept upon precept; line upon line, line upon line; here a little, and there a little:**"* Isaiah 28:9-10

In other words, if someone wants to learn what God's Word teaches on a certain subject, they must look up and read every verse in the Bible that talks about that subject (*precept upon precept, line upon line, here a little and there a little*). [see Note F] This process is based upon God's word and guidance from the Holy Spirit *"that your faith should not stand in the wisdom of men, but in the power of God."* 1 Corinthians 2:5 The Bible stipulates that the Bible must be interpreted differently than other works of men. Paul wrote, *"Which things also we speak, not in the words which man's wisdom teacheth, but **which the Holy Ghost teacheth; comparing spiritual things with spiritual**. But the natural man receiveth not the things of the Spirit of God: for they are foolishness unto him: neither can he know them, because they are spiritually discerned."* 1 Corinthians 2:13,14

The other method, **"Higher Criticism,"** ignores this biblical directive and, basically, interprets the Bible as one would any other book. It also allows for utilization of outside sources and man's own ability to determine Bible teaching. So "Higher Criticism" refers to the: *"scientific study of literature, and especially the Biblical writings, aiming to ascertain their authorship, dates, and general character, primarily by means of internal evidence (style, historical allusions, dominant ideas, etc.), but <u>also by external evidence</u>. The term is variously used as the equivalent of literary criticism or historical criticism or both.*

"The so-called Higher Criticism which in substance is nothing but a scientific attempt to find out what the Bible did mean literally to those who wrote it.' Walter Lippmann" (Webster's 1946 Unabridged Dictionary)

The "critical" methods originated with the Greek philosophy strongly warned against in the word of God. *"Beware lest any man spoil you through philosophy and vain deceit, after the tradition of men, after the rudiments of the world, and not after Christ."* Colossians 2:8

These "critical" methods are broken down into various subcategories such as the secular type of **Literary criticism** which would be dealing with any secular type of literary work and **Biblical criticism** which would be dealing with specifically the Bible.

Definitions and Terms made Simple

The **Biblical criticism** of higher criticism, virtually rips the Bible apart by putting everything in the Bible into question. Biblical criticism is itself broken down into various subcategories such as textual or lower criticism, literary and historical criticism or higher criticism, linguistic criticism, style criticism, form criticism, and reconstructive criticism.

"One of the methods used by the higher critics is called form criticism developed by Hermann Gunkel (1862-1932). 'Form criticism does not view the literature of the OT as the product of divine-human origin, but as the product of conventional folk memory, evident in folklore in general.' 'Basic to form criticism is both the assumed growth pattern from short to long and the frequently assumed evolutionary movement from primitive to advanced.

"...form criticism is the theory that the various Biblical accounts existed first as 'oral tradition' and then after the passing of many years it was written down. The writers resorted to 'folk memory.' The Scriptures, however, show how bankrupt the theories of form criticism are: 'All scripture is given by inspiration of God.' 2 Timothy 3:16" (Assault on the Remnant, p.72, 73)

In other words, while some of the writers of the Bible did indeed write accounts later, as with Moses writing the book of Genesis, for example, yet the Biblical record is clear that the Bible was inspired by the Holy Spirit, not written by "folk memory."

"For the prophecy came not in old time by the will of man: but holy men of God spake as they were moved by the Holy Ghost." 2 Peter 1:21

Various other terms used to describe these critical methods of Bible study are **"historical-critical," "historical-grammatical," "historical-cultural,"** etc. Higher criticism and its offshoot methods treat the Bible just like any other old history book or book on philosophy, instead of viewing it as it really is, a divine revelation from the living God.

Notice what the stated principle of the historical-grammatical method is:
"That doctrine only is theologically sound which rests upon a strict grammatico-historical interpretation of Scripture, and while <u>all divinely inspired Scripture</u> is profitable for doctrine and discipline in righteousness, <u>its inspiration does not require or allow us to interpret it on any other principles than those which are applicable to uninspired writings</u>. The interpreter is always bound to consider how the subject lay in the mind of the author, and to point out the exact ideas and sentiments intended. It is not for him to show how many meanings the words may possibly bear, nor even how the first readers understood them. The real meaning intended by the author, and that only, is to be set forth." (Biblical Hermeneutics, p.465-466)

Notice that it stated, *"all divinely inspired Scripture"* – instead of the correct reading of *"all scripture"* in 2 Timothy 3:16. By wording it this way, critics enable any scripture that disagrees with their ideas, to be discarded with the excuse that *"Well, that text wasn't divinely inspired."*

Also note, contrary to the higher critical *"scientific attempt to find out what the Bible did mean literally to those who wrote it"* mindset, it is specifically stated that the human writers/authors of the Bible did not always understand what they themselves were recording under inspiration of the Holy Spirit. This can plainly be seen with regards to Daniel.

"And it came to pass, when I, even I Daniel, had seen the vision, and sought for the meaning, then, behold, there stood before me as the appearance of a man. And I heard a man's voice between the banks of Ulai, which called, and said, Gabriel, make this man to understand the vision." Daniel 8:15-16

Now contrast those false principles of "higher critical"/"historical-grammatical" interpretation with these profound Protestant statements:

"The work of the Holy Spirit upon the heart is shrouded in mystery. It can no more be explained than can the operation of the winds. The Lord has never explained to humanity how the soul is impressed by the Spirit of God, affecting the mind and heart of the believer, or how the Spirit puts words into the mouth of the Lord's messengers to give to his people. The prophets, who were especially enlightened by the Spirit of God, <u>often could not understand the meaning of the words they wrote upon the paper, or explain the significance of what they uttered</u> when the Spirit caused them to speak, but the word of the Lord accomplished the very work which he designed that it should, and the fruits of the work testified to its divine character." (Sabbath School Worker, August 1, 1892)

"The Bible has a fullness, a strength, <u>a depth of meaning, that is inexhaustible.</u>" (Education, p.188)

"If we would not have the Scriptures clouded to our understanding, so that the plainest truths shall not be comprehended, we must have the simplicity and faith of a little child, ready to learn, and beseeching the aid of the Holy Spirit. A sense of the power and wisdom of God, and of our inability to comprehend His greatness, should inspire us with humility, and we should open His word, as we would enter His presence, with holy awe. When we come to the Bible, <u>reason must acknowledge an authority superior to itself, and heart and intellect must bow to the great I AM.</u>" (Steps to Christ, p.109)

It is obvious that there is a world of difference between viewing the Bible by man's critical methods and viewing the Bible as the "divine revelation" that it really is!

"The work of higher criticism, in dissecting, conjecturing, reconstructing, is destroying faith in the Bible as a divine revelation. It is robbing God's word of power to control, uplift, and inspire human lives." (Acts of the Apostles, p. 474)

With that detail exposed, it is time to continue with some principles of organization used commonly by Bible researchers. A critical scholar, M. Griesbach (**1745-1812**), classified New Testament readings into groups, and put all manuscripts under these families according to the type of text which they contained. There were three of these families that he came up with, namely, the **Western** family, the **Alexandrian** family, and the **Traditional (Byzantine)** family. Though this method of classification was flawed, in that there are manuscripts that cross and interchange these boundaries, many modern scholars continue to use it.

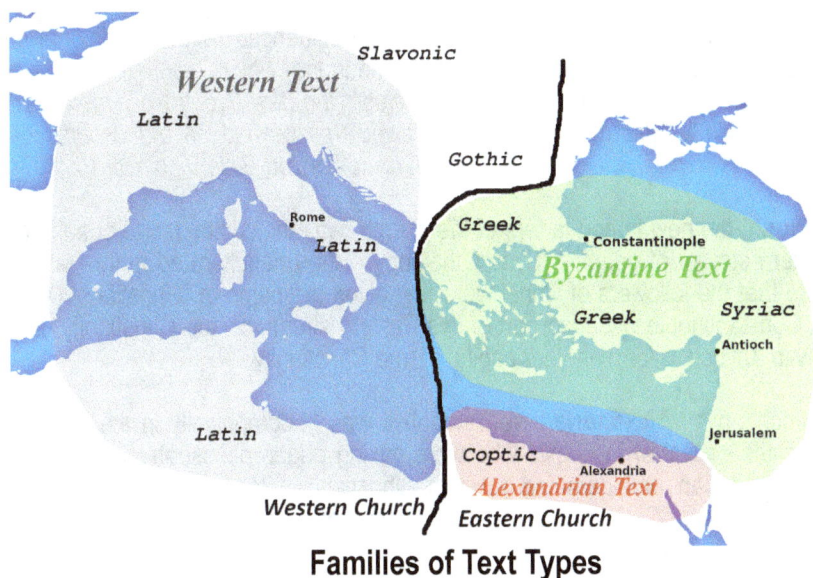

Families of Text Types

Griesbach's **Western** family consists of those New Testament documents which contain that form and style of text found for example in the writings of the Western Church Fathers, like Tertullian and Cyprian. A number of Greek manuscripts contain this text, of which the most important are D and D2. Other witnesses to the Western text are the Diatessaron of Tatian, and the Curetonian and Sinaitic Syriac manuscripts. The western text sometimes tends to gloss and paraphrase, and will usually give the longer reading if a text has both a long and short version.

The **Alexandrian** family consists of those New Testament documents which contain that form of text and style which was used by Origen in some of his writings and also by other Church Fathers who, like Origen, lived at Alexandria. This family includes Papyri 46, 47, 66, 75, B, Aleph, and about 25 other Greek New Testament manuscripts. The Coptic versions also belong to the Alexandrian family of New Testament documents. The Alexandrian text tends to text abbreviation or leaving things out of the copy from the original.

The **Traditional (Byzantine or Eastern)** family includes all those New Testament documents which contain the Traditional (Byzantine) style of text (such as those from the Christian centers at Antioch and Constantinople). The vast majority of the Greek New Testament manuscripts belong to this family. The original Peshitta Syriac version and the Gothic version also belong to the Traditional family of New Testament documents. And the New Testament quotations of Chrysostom and the other Fathers of Antioch and Asia Minor seem generally to agree with the Traditional text.

It is interesting that Griesbach claimed to be influenced by the Traditional or Received Text, yet what he produced was Alexandrian. *"While Griesbach used the Received Text as his measuring rod, nevertheless, the new Greek New Testament he brought forth by this measuring rod followed the Alexandrian manuscripts or, –Origen."* (*Our Authorized Bible Vindicated*, p.107)

Antioch, the new headquarters of the church, was the capital (so to speak) for the Eastern stream of genuine 'Syrian' theology – the unadulterated truth – and it was here that the followers of Christ were first given the name of "Christians" (Acts 11:26). Constantinople was also part of this Eastern stream of true Christianity, and joined with Antioch to form another capital of true Christianity.

Antioch's rival, **Alexandria**, even though it was geographically in the east as well, was the capital of the Jews who were mixing pagan philosophy with gospel truths to make an amalgamated form of Christianity. *"**Woe to the rebellious children**, saith the LORD, that take counsel, but not of me; and that cover with a covering, but not of my spirit, that they may add sin to sin: **That walk to go down into Egypt**, and have not asked at my mouth; to strengthen themselves in the strength of Pharaoh, and to trust in the shadow of Egypt! Therefore shall the strength of Pharaoh be your shame, and the trust in the shadow of Egypt your confusion"* Isaiah 30:1-3

Rome joined with Alexandria, and these two cities formed the capitals of the Western stream of corrupted Christianity. Rome and Alexandria are where it was found that men incorporated into the Word of God, errors that would support their Gnosticism and pagan doctrines.

Some of the commonly heard names for the pure stream from Antioch (Eastern) and the corrupt stream from Alexandria are:

Antioch
Antiochian Text; Byzantine Text; Syrian Text; Majority Text; Koine Text; Universal Text; Reformation Text; Imperial Text; Ecclesiastical Text; Traditional Text; Textus Receptus (Received Text)

Alexandria
Alexandrian Text; Egyptian Text; Neutral Text; Local Text; Hesychian Text; Minority Text

Definitions and Terms made Simple

The two different streams of Bibles are classified into two categories – The Majority Text and the Minority Text.

According to data that was compiled in 1967, the following table illustrates where these terms come from.

Type of Manuscript	Total # of this Type of Manuscript	Number that supports WH*	Number that supports the TR**
		Corrupt Stream	Pure Stream
Papyrus	88	13 (15%)	75 (85%)
Unical	267	9 (3%)	258 (97%)
Cursive	2,764	23 (1%)	2,741 (99%)
Lectionary***	2,143	0	2,143 (100%)

* WH indicates Westcott-Hort Greek Text (Minority Text)
** TR indicates Textus Receptus (Majority Text)
*** A lectionary is a book that contains a collection of scripture readings similar to the responsive readings in the back of our hymnals. Due to the shortage of copies of scripture, lectionaries were used to get Bible texts into the hands of the people.

This means that, as late as **1967**, 99% of the 5,262 extant New Testament MSS discovered by that time, are in agreement with the text known as the **Textus Receptus (Received Text)** which is why the **Textus Receptus** is also sometimes referred to as the **"Majority Text"**. (Note: Be aware that there is also a minority "Counterfeit Majority Text" that shows up in the 20th century. It will be discussed later on.)

Although a few more manuscripts have been discovered more recently (*134 Papyrus, 323 Unical, 2882 Cursive, 2453 Lectionary*), the percentages remain basically identical to the **1967** percentages. The MSS known today as the **Received Text (Textus Receptus)** have by far the vast majority of numbers in agreement with them.

○ Original Autographs
◇ Accurate Copies
◆ Corrupted Copies

Sword Unsheathed

> *"So vast is this majority that the enemies of the received Text admit that nineteen-twentieths and some ninety-nine one-hundredths of all Greek MSS. are of this class; while one hundred per cent of the Hebrew MSS. are for the Received Text."*
> (Our Authorized Bible Vindicated, p.13)

A certain speaker once gave this simple example to illustrate this concept of how the **Majority Text** and **Minority Text** [which is often claimed to be older] came about. It clarifies the concept that older does not always mean better. It went something like this:

Let's say I wanted to start a new worldwide restaurant chain that sells veggie burgers made from my own special recipe. So I hire several thousand managers around the world and open several thousand separate restaurants and I send each manager a copy of my secret recipe. Of course, I speak English and they need the recipe in their own language, so they sit down and translate the recipe into their individual languages so that they can make and sell my burgers. Now there are accurate copies of my recipe in many countries in many different languages. After a few years, the copies of the recipe are beginning to be so covered with flour, fingerprints, and dirt, and the paper is getting so worn out, that they are getting difficult to read, so each of the managers sit down with a new piece of paper and carefully copy the original in detail. Now that they have a new copy of the old worn out original they no longer need the original, so it is discarded. This continues to happen every few years until my restaurant chain is celebrating its 200th anniversary.

Meanwhile, a few years after I opened my restaurants, a very dishonest person decided that they wanted to steal my secret recipe and make it their own. So they copied down the recipe, but they changed several different proportions and took out some of my ingredients and added some of their own. They even get a few friends to join them and they produce several different copies of this counterfeit recipe. Then they announce publicly to the world that they have found the original veggie burger recipe and they even have several copies to prove that it is the original.

But the managers don't believe these false claims because they got the original from me and the counterfeit ones don't match. So they ignore the counterfeits and just leave them lying on the shelf and they continue using the good copies. Over the years, not only do the true recipes go through numerous copies, but the managers die off and so there is nobody who knows first-hand where the originals came from.

Then one day, someone finds the few counterfeit copies that had been rejected and left on the shelf. Now there are two recipes – one that is corrupt and one that is pure – which one is the correct one? Here are some copies found that are written on extremely old paper, much older than the copies currently being used, which would make a person think that they are the originals – but they don't match the recipes that are being used all around the world. Which one is correct?

Definitions and Terms made Simple

*The correct recipe is the one that matches the thousands of copies, in hundreds of languages, from all over the world – the **majority** of witnesses.*

Indeed, it is written *"Where no counsel is, the people fall: but in the multitude of counsellors there is safety."* Proverbs 11:14 Also *"For by wise counsel thou shalt make thy war: and in multitude of counsellors there is safety."* Proverbs 24:6 This is an accurate description of the **"majority text"** – whereas the few corrupted copies which never got used and therefore never wore out, constitute the **"minority text"**.

This is a very important point to remember, *"Older is **not** necessarily always better."* An "older" manuscript just simply means that the manuscript was not used as much – in other words, it laid on the shelf and collected dust, so it didn't "wear out" and "fall apart" as much as the "well-used" copy did!

Another point to realize, is that the term **"Textus Receptus" (Received Text)** and the modern use of the term **"Majority Text"** does not necessarily refer to the exact same thing – although many times people mistakenly use them synonymously.

The **Textus Receptus** is the majority part of what they call the **"Majority Text,"** but it is not the whole **"Majority Text"** as it is sometimes viewed by modern scholars.

Modern scholars view the **"Majority Text"** as the whole family of "Byzantine" manuscripts, including any that may have had changes added to them from corrupt sources. But the term **"Textus Receptus"** is simply the term given to the **uncorrupted correct reading** of all those various Majority texts that trace all the way back to the original text. Here is a picture to illustrate this concept.

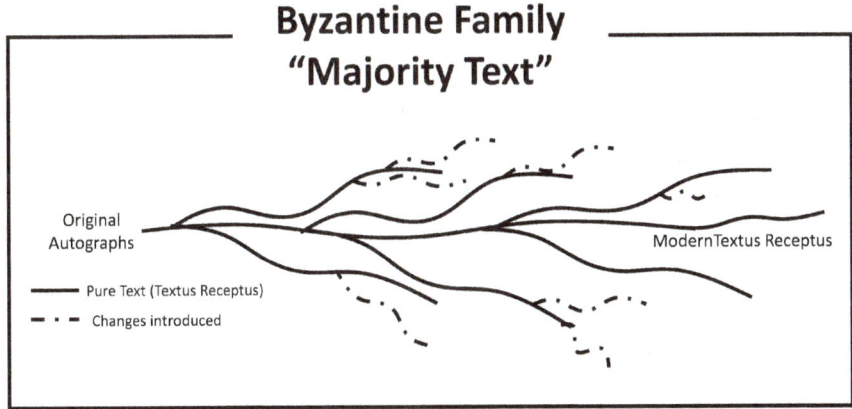

There were commonly two different types of materials used to write the Scriptures on in the first centuries:
- **papyrus** – which was made from the pith of a reed type of plant that grows in the water.
- **vellum** – which was sheets of animal skins (leather), from goats, sheep, calves, or antelopes - always from "clean" animals (Lev.11).

Vellum was also called "parchment." The word parchment gradually developed from Pergamum, because even though people had been using vellum for years, it was the people of Pergamus who turned making vellum manuscripts into a fine art. Even today, the word for parchment in Spanish is pergamino and in the German it is pergament. The parchment sheets (leaves) were then folded together in groups of four, stitched together in the fold, to produce what was called a signature. Then the separate signatures were stitched together to make a book (Codex).

Papyrus was relatively inexpensive compared to **vellum** and therefore was widely used. But it was not very durable and copies would wear out rather rapidly through usage. That is why when papyrus fragments are found, they are usually exactly that – only fragments. The size of papyrus fragments range from a few words or verses to large portions of an entire book.

Papyrus 64 Fragments (Magdalen papyrus)

Papyrus fragments are usually found in Egypt or desert areas. Probably one of the reasons for this is that many of the Byzantine territory used vellum for their Bibles, but another reason is that the northern areas had climates that did not preserve papyrus manuscripts like the hot, dry, desert climates in Egypt would.

As regards the format of the ancient manuscripts, they are often described as one of two types:

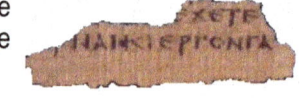

Sample of Unicals or Majuscules

Uncial or Majuscules:
Text written in large, well-separated, carefully written formal letters like our capital letters with no spaces in-between.

Words were abbreviated – in English it would be like the word God was abbreviated "Gd," son was "sn," father was "ftr."

Definitions and Terms made Simple

Cursives or Miniscules:
Text written in small rapidly written letters like our lower case letters with no spaces in-between. Miniscule words were written in a cursive form and were also abbreviated. Later manuscripts placed spaces to separate the words for easier reading.

Sample of Cursives or Miniscules

The earlier Greek Bible texts were written in Uncial format, while the Bible texts in Miniscule format didn't show up until later. The earliest known miniscule text was written in **835 AD**.

Folio, Quarto, Octavo, and Duodecimo are references to the "size" of the book – Folio being the size of two pages from a single sheet of paper or vellum, Quarto being the size of four pages from a single sheet, Octavo being eight pages from a single sheet, and Duodecimo being 12 pages from a single sheet.

The word **"Vulgate"** is where the word "Vulgar" originated. But "vulgate" doesn't necessarily mean *"rude; low; unrefined"* when used in reference to the Bible. It simply means *"common"* or more precisely *"used or practiced by the common people."*

The term **"Latin Vulgate"** is used commonly today, but it should be noted that there are two very different Latin Bibles that are called by that term – one that is from the pure stream and one from the corrupt stream – so it is important to understand which one is being talked about!

Apocrypha: The name means "hidden" and is assigned to the books and chapters that are considered not part of the Bible nor inspired by God. These writings include [but are not limited to] books such as 1 Esdras, 2 Esdras, Tobias (Tobit), Judith, Wisdom, Prayer of Manasseh, Ecclesiasticus, Baruch, Sirach, 1 Maccabees, 2 Maccabees, 3 Maccabees, and 4 Maccabees, Gospel of Peter – as well as the extra 11 verses added to Esther 10 (Esther 10:4-11:1) and the extra two chapters added to Daniel (Daniel 13 & 14). Some of these works are considered to have some historical references, but much of them are considered to be pure fiction. None of them are extant in Hebrew.

"With the exception of the fourth book of Esdras, which is only extant in Latin, they are all written in the Greek language, and for the most part by Alexandrian Jews."
(*An Introduction to the Critical Study and Knowledge of the Holy Scriptures*, vol.1, p.496)

The Apocrypha also teaches doctrines that contradict the doctrines of the canonical scriptures. For example: The book of Tobias teaches that an indiviual can buy his way to heaven – *"Alms deliver from all sin, and from death, and will not suffer the soul to go into darkness. Alms shall be a great confidence before the most high God, to all them that give it."* (Tobias 4:11,12) It also teaches witchcraft in that the angel instructs Tobias to use the heart, gall, and liver of a fish to magically drive away devils. This is nothing but blatant sorcery!

The book of Wisdom teaches the unbiblical doctrines of "purgatory" and an "eternally burning hell." Also out of accordance with the scriptures it also teaches that a child of a harlot or an adulteress cannot be saved.

The Gospel of Peter teaches the unbiblical doctrine that "Sunday" is the "Sabbath!" (see correct doctrine in Gen. 2:1-3, Ex. 20:8-11, Matt. 28:1)

Nobody knows for sure when the apocryphal books were written, but they were never considered by anyone to be authoritative scripture until the Council of Trent in **1546**. Speculations from scholars date their origins to the first and second centuries before Christ (Ironically, the same time period to which the Septuagint is supposedly dated).

"The apocryphal books were not admitted into the canon of Scripture, during the first four centuries of the Christian Church."
(*An Introduction to the Critical Study and Knowledge of the Holy Scriptures*, vol.1, p.497)

The Roman Catholic religion views the Apocrypha as part of the Bible, and they use church "tradition" as their authority to accept the Apocrypha as authoritative. They state, *"It was by the apostolic Tradition that the Church discerned which writings are to be included in the list of the sacred books."*
(*Catechism of the Catholic Church*, IV 120, p.34)

"Apocryphal books added to the Bible (Council of Trent, 1546)"
(*The Fabulous First Centuries of Christianity*, p.474)

The Jews, the early Christians, and the Protestants today all reject the Apocrypha as being non-canonical (not part of the Bible). They do not believe these apocryphal books are inspired by God.

There are also some apocryphal books that were claimed to be part of the New Testament – but they are also not accepted by very many people.

"They are so entirely inferior to the genuine books, so full of nonsensical and unworthy stories of Christ and the apostles, that they have never been regarded as divine, or bound up in our Bibles." (*Smith's Bible Dictionary*, p.45)

Definitions and Terms made Simple

The terms **"rescript"** and **"palimpsest"** means that the manuscript's original writing was erased or scraped off and new writing was written over the erased writing – which then actually forms two or more layers of text, depending on how many times the text was changed.

These multiple layers of erased and rewritten writing are not always visible to the naked eye, but with the development of modern technology, it is now possible to scan the pages and decipher the different layers of text.

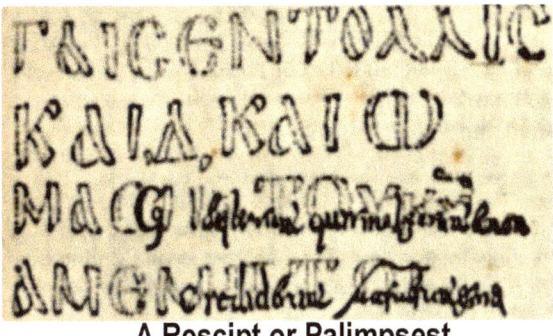

A Rescipt or Palimpsest

In modern times you will also hear the term **"Paraphrase"** – A "Paraphrase" is a writing that is written by someone who reads a Bible and just writes down what **"they think it means."** In other words, it is man's ideas of what God said – as opposed to a direct "translation" that is "word for word."

To give an example of a **"Paraphrase,"** the **KJV** translation of Luke 4:4 says, *"And Jesus answered him, saying, It is written, That man shall not live by bread alone, but by every word of God."*

A "Paraphrase" of this verse might read something like, *"But Jesus replied, 'It is written in the scriptures, 'Other things in life are much more important than bread!'"*
(*The Living Bible Paraphrase*)

The reader will notice that a paraphrase "adds to" and/or "takes away" many details that were not in the original. As a result, it undermines the true meaning of the Word of God. Remember, Proverbs 30:5,6 says, *"Every word of God is pure: he is a shield unto them that put their trust in him. **Add thou not unto his words,** lest he reprove thee, and thou be found a liar."* (Deuteronomy 4:2, Revelation 22:18,19)

Another important thought to keep in mind while examining the following history of the Bible is that Jesus Christ is the **"Word of God"** made Flesh (John 1:1-14); And Jesus also said, *"I am the...Life"* (John 14:6). That means that symbolically speaking, "The Word" of God would represent the "Tree of Life."

"The Word of God is to us the tree of life. Every portion of Scripture has its use." (Letter 3 - February 2, 1898)

If one stops and ponders that concept for a moment, they will find that it is a vast concept that only gets larger the more it is contemplated!

Sword Unsheathed

If the pure Word of God is the "tree of life" then by default any other "word of god," being a contaminated mixture of truth and error, would be a symbolic representation of the tree of knowledge of good and evil – a "false christ" so to speak.

So here again, these two streams can be seen, one stream of purity and another stream that is corrupted by a mixture of truth and error. Consider that Matthew 24:5 says, *"For many shall come in my name, saying, I am Christ [the Word]; and shall deceive many."*

So Jesus Christ Himself foretold that there would be a flood of counterfeit Bibles from the corrupt stream in the last days; but this information was hidden in symbols for the "wise" to search out and understand. In the following chapter, this search commences at the beginning of the Christian Church.

Cutting Edge Facts: Building Faith in God's Word

The Bible has an amazing unity even though it was written...

- **Over a span of roughly 1,500 years**

- **In three different languages** (Hebrew, Greek, Aramaic)

- **By over 40 different writers** of many different occupations (shepherds, kings, priests, scholars, fishermen, and prophets)

- **From 3 different continents** (Europe, Asia, and Africa)

- **Including many different genres** (songs, stories, etc.)

Yet, there is one central message consistently carried by all the writers of the Bible: SALVATION.
God, who created us all, desires a relationship with us.
He calls us to know Him and trust Him.

The Beginning of the Christian Church

Because of the previous Babylonian captivity and the scattering of the Jews throughout the world, by the time of Christ, only a portion of Jews had returned to Jerusalem and Palestine. This scattering had, of course, spread the knowledge of the true God around the world, with groups of Jews living in various countries.

When the Saviour, "God with us" (Jesus Christ), came to earth and became a man and died on the cross to provide salvation for fallen man, His ministry, death, resurrection, and ascension, marked the beginning of the Christian Church. With the ministry and death of Christ and the missionary work of the Apostles, the gospel first went to the Jewish people in Israel (Acts 26:20). Other than the Jews, the first people to accept the gospel were the people of Samaria.

Philip (the Evangelist), the newly elected deacon, was the one who determined to tell the good news to the Samaritans (Acts 8:5). Ethiopia is the second foreign country evangelized by the church at Jerusalem. It is recorded that **Philip** (the Evangelist) witnessed to and baptized the **Ethiopian eunuch** (Acts 8:27-39). Thus began the evangelization of Ethiopia. **Philip** (the Evangelist) also witnessed as far as Carthage, Africa (modern Tunisia).

Philip (the Disciple) is rumored to have taken the gospel to France and Russia.

The apostle **Andrew** took the gospel to Scythia (modern Turkmenistan, Kazakhstan, and lower Russia) and into Asia Minor and Greece.

The apostle **Thomas** was assigned Persia (modern Iraq, Iran, and Afghanistan) but he actually went much farther, taking the gospel all the way into India and some sources say even to China.

Matthew traveled through Persia and then down to Ethiopia.

The apostle **Bartholomew** traveled through India, back to Armenia, and south to Ethiopia and southern Arabia with the gospel message.

Mark went into Egypt and to Rome.

Thaddeus (also called **Judas** or **Jude**) took the message to Persia and Armenia.

James (son of Alphaeus) took the message to Syria & Persia.

James (son of Zebedee) took the message to Spain.

Simon took the message to Persia, then Egypt, Libya and northern Africa all the way to Mauritania (modern Algeria & Morocco), and then on to the British Isles.

Matthias went to Syria as well.

Luke traveled through several countries and made his way to Greece and Rome.

Peter ministered in Babylon, in and around Jerusalem, and later in Rome. His opposition to the sorcerer, Simon Magus, caused Nero to arrest him and have him crucified.

John helped the church in Asia Minor until he was banished to the Island of Patmos. He is the only one of the original apostles who died a natural death (from old age around **100 AD**) – all the rest of the apostles were martyred for their faith.

Paul and **Barnabas** took the gospel to Syria, and **Paul** made several trips into the heart of the Eastern Roman Empire, later known as the Byzantine Empire, taking the gospel across Asia Minor and Galatia (modern Turkey), into Macedonia and Greece, and finally into Italy in the west. *[Some historical sources state that at some point before his captivity, Paul traveled as far as Spain and the British Isles (Romans 15:24)]*

When Jerusalem was destroyed in **AD 70**, the Christians, who had all fled beforehand to Pella in the north, started spreading out and taking the Word of God with them. Antioch in Syria became the new 'capital' or headquarters for the Christian church with Constantinople later becoming a prominent headquarters as well.

The Galatians in Asia Minor were descendants of the Gauls who inhabited the part of Europe that later became known as France, and they carried on extensive trade, both by land and by sea, with their brethren in Western Europe.

Communication between Western Europe and Asia Minor

Thanks to the labors of Paul and others among the Celtic people in Galatia and Constantinople, the message of the gospel spread rapidly across Europe to their Celtic brethren who spoke the same Greek based languages – the Irish, Scotch, British, Welsh, and French.

The Beginning of the Christian Church

"The splendid city of Milan, in northern Italy, was the connecting link between Celtic Christianity in the West and Syrian Christianity in the East. The missionaries from the early churches in Judea and Syria securely stamped upon the region around Milan the simple and apostolic religion. Milan was the rendezvous of numerous councils of clergy from the East, so that the early liturgies of Antioch, Milan, and Gaul were practically identical." (Truth Triumphant, p.67)

Thus, within just a couple centuries, the Word of God had been distributed across the then inhabited world.

However, during this time Satan was not idle. While the early Christians were busy taking the gospel across the globe, Satan was busy building the foundation of his masterpiece of deception.

"Mithraism became the official religion of Rome about the time of Christ" (The Trail of the Serpent, p.9)

Statue of Mithra

Even the Apostle Paul recognized the subtle and sinister inroads that Satan was laying, and he warned the early church to be on guard.

"For the mystery of iniquity doth already work: only he who now letteth will let, until he be taken out of the way. And then shall that Wicked be revealed, whom the Lord shall consume with the spirit of his mouth, and shall destroy with the brightness of his coming: Even him, whose coming is after the working of Satan with all power and signs and lying wonders, And with all deceivableness of unrighteousness in them that perish; because they received not the love of the truth, that they might be saved. And for this cause God shall send them strong delusion, that they should believe a lie: That they all might be damned who believed not the truth, but had pleasure in unrighteousness." 2 Thessalonians 2:7-12

Paul here warns that the mystery of iniquity would be bringing in error and delusion – it would be replacing the truth of God's Word with a lie. As God's Word was making inroads into Satan's kingdom of darkness and paganism, Satan was busy mixing his own errors and corruptions in with the truth and having his agents introduce false doctrines and produce corrupted manuscripts to mislead and deceive souls. He was developing his continued version of the *tree of Knowledge of Good and Evil*.

Not only pagans/heathen persecuted the Christians, but in addition, Christians who compromised and incorporated the elements of paganism into their Christian faith also became persecutors of the true apostolic Christians. Thus, Bible-believing Christians who stayed faithful, not only faced the enemy of paganism, they also faced an enemy of their own brethren who turned against them.

In other words, there are three main groups in this history –
1. **Pagans/Heathen**
2. **Papal/Roman/Alexandrian compromising "Christians"**
3. **True Apostolic/Protestant type of Christians**
with many different branches coming off each of these three groups.

Now it is important to realize, that just because a person claims to belong to one of these groups, does not necessarily mean that they do. Many people do not understand the underlying history or theology of these groups, and are "in the dark" so to speak – therefore, they should not be haphazardly lumped in with the system they claim to follow.

For example, there are individuals who claim to be devout Roman Catholics. They practice, in good faith, all the practices that their religion dictates – yet, they have no realization as to what the foundational doctrines are, nor what takes place behind closed doors in their church's headquarters. The writer has known of several of these dear people who, when given the opportunity to learn the facts of their religion, were appalled and turned with disgust from their former religion to Bible-based Protestantism. Ironically, the writer has also known devout Protestants who, blindly following the teachings of their leaders, ended up ignorantly practicing some of the false teachings of Catholicism, all while believing in good faith, that they were Protestants.

It is the purpose of this book, to examine these and other various systems, doctrines, and historical events (both good and evil), not to denounce or judge the individuals themselves. God loves all people. This is proven by the fact that He sent His Son to die to save humanity. One of the most beautiful texts in the Bible says just this.

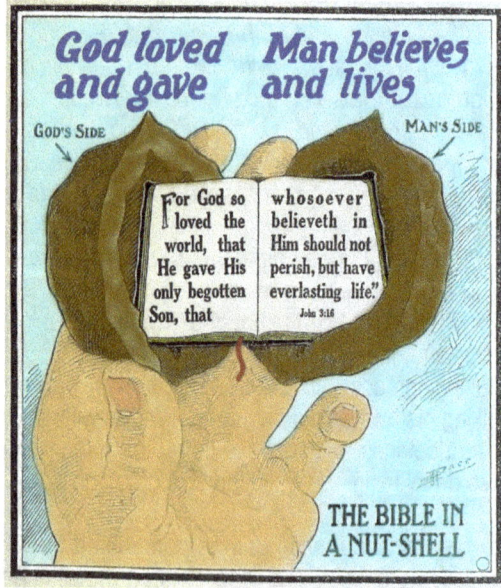

"For God so loved the world, that he gave his only begotten Son, that whosoever believeth in him should not perish, but have everlasting life." John 3:16

It is because of this love for humanity that God gave mankind His Word – to reveal the truth and turn man from his evil ways so that we can be saved. This is the purpose of the

The Beginning of the Christian Church

Word of God – to shed light into people's minds, to reveal what is real Bible truth and to expose the deceptions and errors of man's traditions and false doctrines. That is why the Bible's testimony always supersedes man's testimony. *"It is better to trust in the LORD than to put confidence in man."* Psalm 118:8 *"...We ought to obey God rather than men."* Acts 5:29

"The Bible, with its precious gems of truth, was not written for the scholar alone. On the contrary, it was designed for the common people. The poor man needs it as much as the rich man, the unlearned as much as the learned. It is a great mistake for ministers to give people the impression that they can not understand the teachings of the Word of God, and should be content with the interpretation given by those whose business it is to proclaim the Word of God. Ministers who thus educate the people are themselves in error. To him who loves the truth, the Word of God is as a light shining in a dark place, pointing out the path so plainly that the wayfaring man, tho a fool, need not err therein." (*Signs of the Times*, July 11, 1906)

Again, while the writer's purpose is not to condemn individual people, there are some who have, sadly, enlisted themselves as vicious enemies of God's people and of truth itself. Because of this fact, some unpleasant characteristics will have to be revealed. However, it should be recognized that God, and not man, is the ultimate judge of character, since only God can read the motives, understand the level of knowledge, and recognize true repentance. (Eccl. 12:14, James 4:17, 1 John 1:9) Watchmen on the walls of Zion are only to judge by the fruits and warn others off of dangerous ground.

Now as the enemies of the truth have advanced and grown in power, they have always tried to systematically destroy the records of the true followers of God, in order to erase all record of them and, in essence, to rewrite history in their own favor – even going so far as to create fakes and forgeries of supposedly ancient documents and writings to support their deceptions. History reveals:

"About the close of the eighth century, papists put forth the claim that in the first ages of the church the bishops of Rome had possessed the same spiritual power which they now assumed. To establish this claim, some means must be employed to give it a show of authority; and this was readily suggested by the father of lies. **Ancient writings were forged by monks.** *Decrees of councils before unheard of were discovered, establishing the universal supremacy of the pope from the earliest times. And a church that had rejected the truth greedily accepted these deceptions."* (*Great Controversy*, p.56)

*"**To manipulate ancient writings**, to edit history in one's own favor, did not appear criminal, if the end in view were otherwise just and good."* (*The Roman Catholic Church and the Bible*, p.11)

*"It was a fundamental principle of the order **[the Jesuits]** that **the end justifies the means**. By this code, lying, theft, perjury, assassination, were not only pardonable but commendable, when they served the interests of the church."* (*Great Controversy*, p.235)

"Persecution was not the only way of waging war against the evangelicals. Their records were systematically destroyed. In the empires of antiquity a new conqueror often followed up his purging of the preceding dynasty by the destruction of all writings telling of its past, even to the extent of chiseling annals from stone monuments. In like manner the noble and voluminous literature of the Waldenses, whether of the Italian, French, or Spanish branches, was almost completely obliterated by the rage of the papacy. Only fragments remain. For the rest, one must use the tirades written to vilify them, the accounts of papal inquisitors, the reports of investigators to their prelates, and the decrees and sentences pronounced by emperors, papal councils, and the Inquisition against them to aid in reconstructing their history." (Truth Triumphant, p.240)

Whole libraries have been reduced to ashes and destroyed and Bible manuscripts and historical records have been burned and obliterated by the millions in their attempts to "rewrite history"!

"The history of God's people during the ages of darkness that followed upon Rome's supremacy is written in heaven, but they have little place in human records. Few traces of their existence can be found, except in the accusations of their persecutors. It was the policy of Rome to obliterate every trace of dissent from her doctrines or decrees. Everything heretical, whether persons or writings, she sought to destroy. Expressions of doubt, or questions as to the authority of papal dogmas, were enough to forfeit the life of rich or poor, high or low. Rome endeavored also to destroy every record of her cruelty toward dissenters. Papal councils decreed that books and writings containing such records should be committed to the flames. Before the invention of printing, books were few in number, and in a form not favorable for preservation; therefore there was little to prevent the Romanists from carrying out their purpose." (Great Controversy, p.61-62)

Yet even with all their hellish attempts and partial successes, they have not been able to totally conceal all the details of the glorious lineage of the Word of God. A careful researcher will still be able to find bits and pieces of the true history that they have tried to hide.

"Those who write histories today have more source matter on ancient history, but less on medieval, than historians had four hundred years ago; for after the Reformation had fully aroused the papal church to action, her emissaries, especially the vigilant Jesuits, searched out and destroyed every evidence that was damaging to her...Let no one, therefore, say that statements in older histories are not true because we cannot now find sources to prove them." (Facts of Faith, p.252)

While efforts to hide and rewrite history have been to a large extent successful, God has promised that He preserves His True Word. That means that all the forces of evil will never be able to totally erase the record of Truth – because Truth will last Forever!

The Beginning of the Christian Church

"The grass withereth, the flower fadeth: but the word of our God shall stand for ever." Isaiah 40:8

"Multitudes of Christians were slain in a dreadful manner, because they would preserve the purity of their religion. The Bible was hated, and efforts were made to rid the earth of it. The people were forbidden to read it, on pain of death; and all the copies which could be found were burned. But I saw that God had a special care for His Word. He protected it. At different periods there were but a very few copies of the Bible in existence, yet He would not suffer His Word to be lost, for in the last days copies of it were to be so multiplied that every family could possess it."
(Early Writings, p.214)

All the details of this history of the Word of God are way too extensive to be covered in one small work or even a small library.

The following is just a very brief summary of some of the main details of this fascinating history.

The reader will also want to pay close attention not only to the locations of these historical events but also to the dates of each historical event – because the locations and dates give important details into the "hidden" history that is happening "behind the scenes."

Just a reminder:
Dates listed in **Bold** & not specified as BC or AD are all in the Christian Era [AD]
Bible Versions & Translations may be found easily with this **Font**
Records are listed in Chronological order as much as possible.

> **Cutting Edge Facts – Building Faith in God's Word**
>
> **5 Bible Texts even Athiests cannot Deny**
> **They are Self-Evident**
>
> "Surely the churning of milk bringeth forth butter, and the wringing of the nose bringeth forth blood: so the forcing of wrath bringeth forth strife" Proverbs 30:33
>
> " ... he that cleaveth wood shall be endangered thereby. **If the iron be blunt, and he do not whet the edge, then must he put to more strength:** but wisdom is profitable to direct." Ecclesiastes 10:9b,10
>
> "If the clouds be full of rain, they empty themselves upon the earth: and if the tree fall toward the south, or toward the north, **in the place where the tree falleth, there it shall be.**" Ecclesiastes 11:3
>
> "**If a kingdom be divided against itself, that kingdom cannot stand.**" Mark 3:24
>
> "... **no lie is of the truth.**" 1 John 2:21b

The First 500 Years

God promises that He will preserve His Word for each generation. *"The words of the LORD are pure words: as silver tried in a furnace of earth, purified seven times. Thou shalt keep them, O LORD, thou shalt preserve them from this generation for ever."* Psalm 12:6-7

"Heaven and earth shall pass away, but my words shall not pass away." Also, *"But the word of the Lord endureth for ever..."* Matthew 24:35;1 Peter 1:25

Therefore, no matter how many corruptions the devil brings in to try to undermine God's Word – God will always have a pure text preserved somewhere.

The work of preservation, guarding, and copying of the scriptures (the Old Testament) has always been the job of the Levitical Scribes throughout history. From about **100 BC** to **AD 100** the rabbis and teachers in Palestine, known as the Tannaim, were the ones who faithfully copied them. Then in the early part of the Christian era from about **100–500** it was done by the Talmudists, and then from about **500–1550** the copying and preservation of the scriptures was carried on by the Masoretes. Though, on occasion, a number of writers just label all of these groups as Masoretes.

Vellum Old Testament Scroll

"Soon after the time of Ezra, the celebrated Jewish critics called Masorites, or Mazoretes, began their criticisms and grammatical remarks upon the sacred text. They had their name from the Hebrew word masor, to deliver from one to another, because they professed to deliver the Scriptures to posterity in the state of purity in which they were found previous to the Babylonish captivity. To this end they not only numbered every verse, word, and letter, but even went so far as to ascertain how often each letter of the alphabet occurred in the whole Bible! Thus sacredly did they watch over their records, in order to prevent every species of corruption. These Jewish critics were not a society, but rather a succession of men; and the Masora, or Masoretical criticisms, the work of many critics and grammarians who lived at different periods from the time of Ezra to about the year of Christ 1030..." (*Townley's Biblical Literature*, vol.1, p.54)

The Masorah were families of priests who developed vowel pointing systems to aid in the reading of the Hebrew OT. The original Hebrew text of the Old Testament did not contain vowels, it only had consonants, and each Hebrew was just taught from an early age how to read it correctly. But as time went on, that correct way of reading was being lost, so the Masoretes around the 6th century, determined to preserve the correct reading by inserting the proper vowels into the writing itself.

There were three major schools of Masoretes: the Babylonian school, the Palestinian school, and the Tiberian school, located on the west side of the Sea of Galilee. Each school developed their own vocalization system with a set of vowel symbols and accent marks. The Palestinian and the Babylonian school systems placed their vowel marks above the consonants.

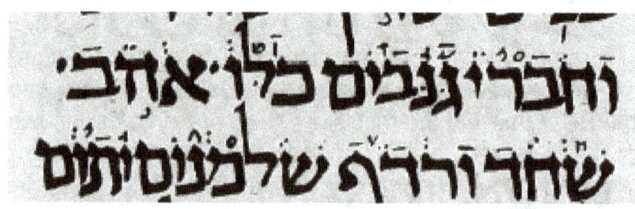
Babylonian Vowel Pointing System

The Tiberian school system placed the vowel marks below the consonants.

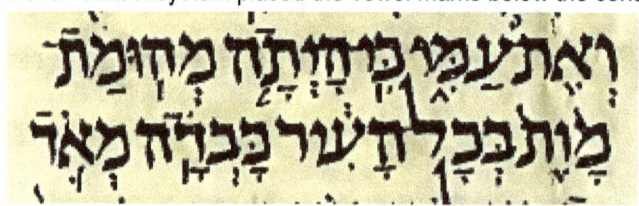
Tiberian Vowel Pointing System

Eventually, the Tiberian school became the standard vowel pointing system for the Hebrew text. The Tiberian school itself, produced two separate families: The Aaron ben Asher and the Moses ben Naphtali families. Each family had a slightly different vowel pointing system.

The Jewish scribes, that had the responsibility of guarding and preserving the text of the Old Testament, were also the ones to copy them. When they copied them, it was done **word for word** and they were so careful when copying the Scriptures, that if they made one single mistake while they were copying, they threw the page away and started over. There were eight rules that the Jewish copyists used in the copying of the texts:

1. The parchment must be made from the skin of a clean animal; must be prepared by a Jew only, and the skins must be fastened together by strings taken from clean animals.

The First Five Hundred Years

2. Each column must have no less than forty-eight, nor more than sixty lines. The entire copy must be first lined.

3. The ink must be of no other color than black, and it must be prepared according to a special recipe.

4. No word nor letter could be written from memory; the scribe must have an authentic copy before him, and he must read and pronounce aloud each word before writing it.

5. He must reverently wipe his pen each time before writing the word for "God" (*Elohim*), and he must wash his whole body before writing the name "Jehovah" (*LORD in all capitals in our King James Bibles*), lest the Holy Name be contaminated.

6. Strict rules were given concerning forms of the letters, spaces between letters, words and sections, the use of the pen, the color of the parchment, etc.

7. The revision (*to correct any errors*) of a roll must be made within thirty days after the work was finished; otherwise it was worthless. One mistake on a sheet condemned the entire sheet. If three mistakes were found on any page, the entire manuscript was condemned.

8. Every word and every letter was counted, and if a letter was omitted, or if an extra letter was inserted, or if two letters touched one another, the manuscript was condemned and destroyed at once.

Because of this carefulness in copying and the fact that the originals were written as consonants only, most of the consonants of the various manuscripts all match each other. The places where there are incorrect renderings in some of the manuscripts is where someone has inserted incorrect vowel markings.

It is also important to understand that because of the high regard that the scribes had for the scriptures as the Word of God; old worn-out and tattered copies were not allowed. This means that whenever there was an old worn-out and tattered copy of the Scriptures, the scribes would painstakingly produce an accurate **word for word** reproduction of it and then bury or destroy the old tattered original. This shows that the scribes placed much more value on the "accuracy" of the "words" of the original manuscript than on the original manuscript itself!

The term **"Septuagint"** is used today to refer to several Greek translations of the Hebrew Old Testament. It is very important to understand, that there are actually three different **"Septuagints"** that are distinct from each other. Two of these are corrupt, but one is from the pure line.

According to a document called the Letter of Aristeas (allegedly written about **96-63 BC**), the Greek version of the Hebrew Bible (Old Testament), which is commonly called today the **Septuagint (LXX)**, was supposedly prepared by 72 Jews (6 from each of the 12 tribes) in Alexandria, Egypt around **285-250 BC**. (LXX is, of course, the Roman numerals for 70. The reason they did not use LXXII is not known).

A Fragment of Habakkuk in the LXX

This **Septuagint** is also the very first time that the books of the Apocrypha were added to the scriptures.

The idea that this **LXX** was written before the time of Christ and that it was the official Greek text in Christ's day, is why many people today are under the false impression that this was the Bible that Christ and the Apostles were using. But this is not true.

It is evident that there were Greek translations done prior to the time of Christ because it is stated:

"For hundreds of years the Scriptures had been translated into the Greek language, then widely spoken throughout the Roman Empire."

(Desire of Ages, p.33)

However, to the thinking mind, this story that the **LXX** is a representation of those translations is highly suspicious for quite a few reasons, among which are:

1. No honest true Jew would have agreed to that translation arrangement, because it was well understood among the Jews that only certain men of the tribe of Levi were allowed to make copies of the Bible – therefore, there would not have been scholars from the other tribes to participate in this forbidden work of preparing a new version.

2. In the last few centuries before Christ (which would be the Hellenistic period in which the **LXX** was supposedly written), before Christ Himself came to correct their prejudice, the official Jews in Palestine considered the Greeks around them nothing more than dogs (ex. Mark 7:26, 27). Therefore, they would not have been even slightly interested in translating their most holy precious possession, the scriptures, into the language used by "dogs."

The First Five Hundred Years

The only "Jews" that would have been interested in making Greek translations, would have been those scattered Jews and those amalgamated Jews that were living in the surrounding Greek-speaking countries – so any Greek translations that would have been done before the time of Christ, would have been varied texts and not considered "official" to the Hebrews in Palestine.

> "Dr. Ginsburg tells how, soon after the publication of the Septuagint, the Jewish authorities declared that the day on which it was made was as calamitous to Israel as the day on which the golden calf was substituted for the true God."
> (All About the Bible, p.25)

Some, in order to promote the BC Greek **LXX** translation concept even go so far as to make the claim that the Hebrew language had become basically extinct by the time of Christ and that the Jews in Palestine only spoke Greek at this point. But this claim is easily proven false by reading the Bible itself.

(Luke 23:38; John 5:2; Acts 21:40; Acts 22:2; Acts 26:14)

3. The text of the **LXX** is a mixture.

> "Moreover, the Greek of the LXX is not straightforward Koine Greek. At its most idiomatic, it abounds with Hebraisms; at its worst it is little more than Hebrew in disguise."   (The Septuagint: A Critical Analysis, p.8)

Also, whereas the official Jewish Scribes were very careful to copy and translate Scripture **word for word** and wouldn't dare to change or alter a single word or letter of the original, the writers of the **LXX** did just that.

> "The translators of the LXX, in marked contrast, are notorious for: Hellenizing and modernizing tendencies, simplifying "difficult" passages, altering the text by deleting what they regarded as apparent "contradictions", and adapting their version to the prevailing opinions of the age so as to commend it to the learning and the culture of the time."   (The Septuagint: A Critical Analysis, p.47)

4. Since this **LXX** translation is the first that has the books of the Apocrypha interwoven into its text, its supposed use by Jesus and the Apostles would imply that they endorsed the Apocrypha.

This would also imply that when Paul wrote *"All scripture is given by inspiration of God..."* 2 Timothy 3:16 – that the inspired books would include the Apocryphal books as well. But Jesus and the Apostles never saw the **LXX**! Besides that fact, the Apocrypha contradicts the teachings of the scriptures.

> "Whatever contradicts God's word, we may be sure proceeds from Satan."
> (Patriarchs and Prophets, p.55)

"...A circumstance that detracts from our faith in the Septuagint is, that it adds idle legends to the inspired word of God." (Analysis of Sacred Chronology, p.222)

The **LXX** adds so many "idle legends" to the Word of God, that it cannot be a trusted source for anything. For example, the **LXX** book of Esther is so embellished with fairy tales that it claims that Esther covered her head in ashes and dung and cut off her hair and scattered it around in her palace. None of the bizarre details of this outlandish story are found in the real Word of God!

5. Another problem with this **LXX** story is that *the letter of Aristeas* is found preserved in the highly spurious non-canonical collection of **FICTION** called *"The Forgotten Books of Eden."* It is believed that the Letter of Aristeas is a later forgery. (See also Hody's 1684 "Contra historiam Aristeae de LXX interpretibus dissertatio")

This forged *letter of Aristeas* appears to be **the sole source** of information concerning the Greek text by 72 men, the origin of the mysterious **Septuagint LXX**. Some supporters claim that there are other sources, such as the historian Josephus, but evidence points to the reality that all other supposed sources, derived their information about the **LXX** from this forged *letter of Aristeas*.

"A member of the Pharisee sect from age 19 until the end of his life, Josephus corroborates the story as related by Aristeas with only slight variations. It is generally agreed that almost certainly, he had access to the letter. Thus, Josephus is not an actual proven independent source." (The Septuagint: A Critical Analysis, p.6)

Because of the evidence of the *letter of Aristeas'* forgery and several of its many other major discrepancies where names and dates and events don't line up correctly with history, many scholars believe that the reference in that letter to a Greek translation of the Bible by 72 scholars was actually just a fictitious story. It is believed that the real **LXX** known today today actually originated with **Origen's Hexapla Bible** in Alexandria in the 3rd century AD, long after the time of the Apostles.

6. There are many details listed in the **Septuagint** that not only contradict the Biblical history from the Hebrew, but they also contradict themselves. A good example is the fact that the **LXX** lists the age and genealogy of Methuselah showing that he didn't die until 14 years after the flood.

"There is nothing wonderful in the fact that Methuselah should have died in the year of, and just previous to, the flood; but by the Septuagint reading, he must have survived the deluge fourteen years!!" (Analysis of Sacred Chronology, p.231)

Some of the **Septuagint** printings today, totally wipe out Bible time-prophecies by changing the original reading of *"two thousand and three hundred days"* in Daniel 8:14 into the incorrect reading of *"2400 days."*

7. Many sources today make the false claim that this **Septuagint** made before the time of Christ is "extant." For example, the introduction to the **1970 LXX** edition published by Zondervan states:

"The earliest version of the Old Testament Scriptures which is extant, or of which we possess any certain knowledge, is the translation executed at Alexandria in the third century before the Christian era: this version has been so habitually known by the name of the Septuagint..." (**1970** LXX edition published by Zondervan)

This is typical of many statements by the modern sources that want to promote the false "Pre-Christian Era" **LXX** concept. But this is nothing but false propaganda used to convince the not-so-careful reader.

There are NO "extant" copies of any "**LXX**" dated earlier than around the middle of the 4th century after Christ!

"The existence of an entire Greek Old Testament predating the life of Christ has no extant documentation." (New Age Bible Versions, p.538)

Also, when the text content of the **LXX** is compared with other earlier Hebrew manuscripts – it does not match much of the text and shows such poor workmanship, that it does appear that it was done by several different translators. Some of the books are not even translations but rather paraphrases of the original. It is stated about this **Septuagint** that:

"...orthodox Judaism either refused to recognize it from an early period or quickly expunged it from among its Scriptures, for there are but few and indirect indications of its existence in any of the rabbinic works."
(Cambridge History of the Bible, vol.2, p.14)

To recap in simple terms, the concept that the **Septuagint (LXX)** was written by 72 Jewish scholars 200+ years before Christ is just a figment of someone's imagination – it is a lie. There is absolutely no solid evidence to support this claim.

The real **Septuagint (LXX)**, that is in existence today, was written by the Gnostic Origen about **240 AD** and then "lost" in the destruction of the Library of Caesarea in the 7th century.

While it was still in existence, it was republished by Eusebius around **350–362 AD** in the 50 Bibles he made for Constantine – and these copies of Eusebius from the 4th century AD, are the only ones that are "**extant**" today.

Some critics will claim that they have "evidence" that can prove the BC existence of the **LXX**. This sole piece of evidence that they refer to is a few tiny scraps of papyrus that are <u>a few words</u> from the book of Deuteronomy written in

Greek – not near enough evidence to base the concept of a whole Old Testament Bible manuscript on.

It is called **Rylands Papyrus 458** and was found in **1917**, by a Quaker manuscript collector named James R. Harris, ironically, while he was in Alexandria, Egypt.

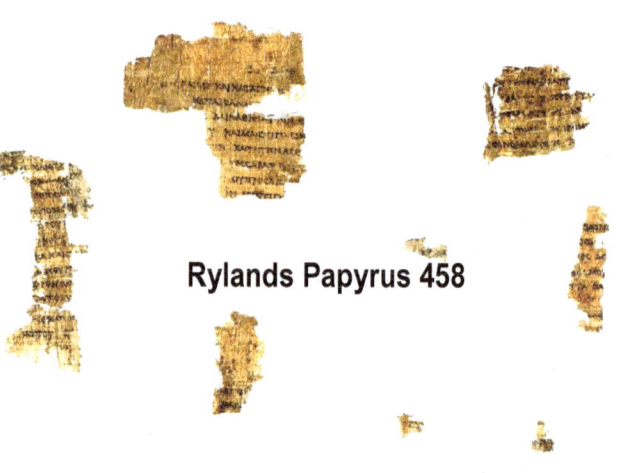

Rylands Papyrus 458

Nobody knows where this papyrus originated, but some suspect it was made in Fayyum, Egypt by some local farmers. Suspiciously, these farmers additionally happened to manage to keep producing "ancient finds" of "old manuscripts" to sell to collectors while keeping out of sight of the authorities. Scholars have assigned it a date in the 2nd century BC. This questionable date is still 50–100 years after the supposed date of the writing of the **Septuagint (LXX)**.

"This piece of papyrus is dated 150 B.C. (date is questioned). However, the existence of a single sheet does not mean that it represents a complete version or an "authorized" translation or the existence of a Greek translation with widespread acceptance and usage prior to and during the time of Christ and the Apostles. It could, for example, be no more than the remains of a private study endeavor or that of an individual practicing his translating skills, etc."
(*The Septuagint: A Critical Analysis*, p.36)

The other two texts that are referred to by modern scholars as **"Septuagint"** were done by Hesychius and by Lucian – which will be covered shortly.

The Samaritans were a sect of amalgamated Jews.

"When the inhabitants of Samaria and of the adjacent country were carried into captivity by Shalmaneser king of Assyria, he sent in their place colonies from Babylonia, Cuthah, Ava, Hamath, and Sepharvaim; with which the Israelites who remained in the land became intermingled, and were ultimately amalgamated into one people."
(*An Introduction to the Critical Study and Knowledge of the Holy Scriptures*, vol.3, p.400)

The **Pentateuch** is the name given to the first five books of the Bible (Genesis-Deuteronomy) also known as the writings of Moses. Both the Jews and the Samaritans possessed copies of these Hebrew writings. The one from Samaria is known as the **Samaritan Pentateuch**.

> "Soon after the Christian era, their version fell into entire oblivion, and no copies of it were known for more than 1000 years, so that its very existence was disputed. How much it may have been corrupted during that time, is unknown."
>
> (*Analysis of Sacred Chronology*, p.196)

Samaritan Pentateuch

The **Samaritan Pentateuch** was not known to the western world until around **1600**. It is claimed by the Jews that the Samaritans have changed parts of the Pentateuch to match their religion and so have corrupted it.

> "The Samaritan inserts in the same place what is wanting in the Hebrew. In other places the same Samaritan copy adds what is deficient in the Hebrew; and what is contained more than the Hebrew seems so well connected with the rest of the discourse, that it would be difficult to separate them."
>
> (*Buck's Theological Dictionary*, p.719)

The **Samaritan Pentateuch** differs from the Masoretic text in some 6,000 places and about 1900 of these differences are in agreement with the **Septuagint (LXX)** and **Jerome's Latin Vulgate**.

Plato, whose real name was Aristocles, was a pagan Greek philosopher who lived from **427–347 BC**.

Plato is the New World Order's first original administrator. His teachings on the mysterious lost civilization of Atlantis (antediluvian civilization) have been the source of all the attempts throughout history to rebuild this "New World Order." Plato's story of this Utopian Atlantis is the motivation underlying the philosophies of Communism, Socialism, Fascism, and even the teachings of the Roman Catholic system. Plato is also one of the most important "high priests" of spiritualism and one of the originators of the philosophies behind the New Age movement and the various secret societies. Many of the pagan philosophies that played a role in the corruption of Bible manuscripts in the Christian era may be traced to Plato and his mystic teachings.

Sword Unsheathed

From about **100 BC** and onward the influences of Greek philosophy started creeping in even among the Jews, especially those Jews that dwelt at Alexandria, Egypt. These amalgamated Christian believers in Alexandria formed what later became known as the Coptic Orthodox Church.

It was here in Alexandria, Egypt, that a renowned Jewish thinker by the name of Philo **(20 BC – 54 AD)** constructed a system of philosophy which attempted to combine the teachings of the Old Testament with the theories of Plato.

"Philo...dabbled deeply in Babylonian astrology and numerology, and taught that the scriptures could not be understood without ascertaining the numerical value of every word and text."
(Trail of the Serpent, p.21)

Philo is suspicioned by some Bible scholars to be the real author of that famous work of fiction called the Letter of Aristeas. Its fictitious story of a Greek Bible translation by 72 Jewish scholars in Alexandria, would later be used by Origen as a basis for his invention of the **Septuagint**.

As time went on, Greek paganism and Roman Paganism began to be "blended" with Christianity and many pagan doctrines began to be given "Christian" endorsement.

"'Christianity was helpless' before the Greek religion. 'The Church did everything it could to stamp out such "pagan"' rites, but had to capitulate and allow the rites to continue with only the name of the local deity changed to some Christian saint's name...From the same popular sources came the Christian use of relics..."
(The Trail of the Serpent, p.7)

Stephen Haskell, in his book, *Story of Daniel the Prophet* (published in **1908**), on page 207-208 gives some interesting insight into the practice of mixing Christianity and Greek philosophy that was done in the early Christian era.

"The history of Greece is the history of physical and intellectual culture. The people admired grace and beauty, and her literary minds worshiped the intellect. Plato, the greatest of Greek philosophers, lived four hundred years before Christ, and his teachings have led the thoughts of writers in' every age since then. The Jews mingled the teachings of the Bible with the philosophy of Plato, and that formed the traditions of men, against which Christ so often warned his followers.

"The false philosophy, and the "science falsely so called" of Paul's time, was Greek teaching, which breathed the spirit of Plato and his students...Here, in

Greek religion and Greek learning, was the most subtle form of that mixture of truth and error which Satan offered at the tree of the knowledge of good and evil, which existed from the days of Eden to the time of Greece. Babylon enslaved the bodies of God's people, Medo-Persia made laws to slay them, but Greece captured their minds, and enslaved them to her ideas. She counterfeited so neatly, so adroitly, the spiritual teachings of the Old Testament; and so quietly, yet so surely, wound her tendrils about God's people, that her slavery was far worse than that of Egypt or Babylon."

Stephen Haskell

On page 261, Stephen Haskell again states: *"Paganism and Christianity met on the battlefield when Constantine contended for the throne of Rome; paganism and Christianity met in more deadly conflict in Alexandria, where Christian and pagan schools stood side by side. Here it was that such men as Origen and Clement, recognized Fathers of the church, adopted the philosophy of the Greeks, and applied to the study of the Bible the same methods which were common in the study of Homer and other Greek writers. <u>Higher criticism had its birth in Alexandria</u>. It was the result of a mingling of the truths taught by Christ and the false philosophy of the Greeks.*

"It was an attempt to interpret divine writings by the human intellect, a revival of the philosophy of Plato. These teachers, by introducing Greek philosophy into the schools which were nominally Christian, opened the avenue for the theological controversies which shook the Roman world, and finally established the mystery of iniquity."   (*Story of Daniel the Prophet*, page 207,208)

Greek philosophy was devoid of Christ. Paul wrote *"For the Jews require a sign, and the* **Greeks seek after wisdom***: But we preach* **Christ crucified***, unto the Jews a stumblingblock, and* **unto the Greeks foolishness***;"* 1 Corinthians 1:22,23

As before stated, in contrast to Greek philosophy and higher criticism, Paul counsels that *"faith should not stand in the wisdom of men, but in the power of God…"* and that *"we speak,* <u>not in the words which man's wisdom teacheth</u>, *but which the Holy Ghost teacheth; comparing spiritual things with spiritual. But the natural man receiveth not the things of the Spirit of God: for they are foolishness unto him: neither can he know them, because they are spiritually discerned."* 1 Corinthians 2:5,13,14

Speaking of the different methods of Bible and textual criticism, the Schaff-Herzog Encyclopedia of Religious Knowledge says: *"The Greeks were the fathers of criticism. No other people of the ancient world employed critical methods; the memory, not judgment, held sway. Judaism was no exception, for the Masorah is text-criticism in a limited sense only. But among the Greeks criticism was the handmaid of interpretation."* (*Encyclopedia of Religious Knowledge*, vol.2, p.427)

The language of the ancient Romans was Latin, and Koine Greek had also become a shared language around the eastern Mediterranean and into Asia Minor as a consequence of the many conquests of Alexander the Great. This made the dominate languages used around Palestine by the time of Christ (**4 BC – AD 31**) to be mostly Hebrew/Aramaic, Greek, and Latin (Luke 23:38).

"Among the Jews, Aramaic was used by the common people, while Hebrew remained the language of religion and government and of the upper class." (*Encylopedia Britannica*, "Aramaic language")

"The Hebrew, Syriac, and Aramaic - the latter, Christ's native speech - were cognate [of the same family, related] *languages."* (*Truth Triumphant*, p.295)

Because most of the apostles were writing to the Greek-speaking believers in various parts of the world, their original autographs of the New Testament were written in the **Greek Vulgate** as were also many of the first copies of those originals within the first couple of centuries.

The copies of the New Testament that were associated with the Constantinople area were also first produced in the Greek language, although the books of Matthew and Hebrews were written first in the Hebrew language and then later translated into the Greek language.

"St. Matthew's Gospel is generally allowed to have been written in the Hebrew or Syro-Chaldaic language, being designed for the immediate use of the inhabitants of Palestine...The Epistle to the Hebrews also appears to have been written by St. Paul in Hebrew..." (*Townley's Biblical Literature*, vol.1, p.72,73)

The apostle John wrote the book of Revelation, the last book of the Bible, somewhere around the year **95**.

The First Five Hundred Years

There is also some evidence that the apostles and their contemporaries were making translations of the Hebrew Old Testament into the Greek language as well. It should not be difficult to comprehend that wherever the Apostles took the Gospel, they also took the pure Word of God to dispel the darkness of heathenism.

However, from the time of the Apostles onward in history, many erroneous doctrines and teachings started creeping into the church and the manuscripts of scripture. Paul warned that there were people who were corrupting the Bible even in his day: *"For we are not as many, which corrupt the word of God…"* 2 Corinthians 2:17

"By the time of Christ, the Old Testament was in a settled condition. Since then, the Hebrew Scriptures had been carried down intact to the day of printing (about 1450 A.D.) by the unrivalled methods of the Jews in transmitting perfect Hebrew manuscripts. Whatever perplexing problems there are in connection with the Old Testament, these have largely been produced by translating it into Greek and uniting that translation to the Greek New Testament. It is around the problems of the Greek New Testament that the battle for centuries has been fought."
(*Our Authorized Bible Vindicated*, p.6)

The Peshitta or Peshitto (meaning "the correct or simple") Bible was the first Syrian translation of the Old and New Testaments from the original languages. It was translated directly from the original into the simple or common Syriac language and there are about 350 copies of it that still exist today.

The Peshitta

The original **Peshitta** was translated around **100 AD**, and it also contains an Aramaic New Testament that was written from about **411–435**.

Sword Unsheathed

"Within the first two centuries of the Christian era, the whole, or parts of the sacred writings, were translated into the Syriac and Latin, two of the most ancient versions of the New Testament, one of which was spread throughout Europe and the north of Africa; the other propagated from Edessa to China. This ancient Syriac translation is usually called the Peshito, or literal, or correct and faithful version; and is thus distinguished from the more modern versions, especially the one made under the patronage of Philoxenus, in A.D. 508, and from him denominated the Philoxenian version." (*Townley's Biblical Literature*, Vol.1, p.80-81)

The original **Peshitta** (made in the 2nd century) *"generally follows the Received Text."* (*Our Authorized Bible Vindicated*, p.25)

However, other versions in the 4th and 5th centuries do not always match the **Received Text**, and since the **1700's**, there have been counterfeit manuscripts and forgeries of the **Peshitta** produced which are corrupted and do not follow the **Received Text** – and many of the modern printings of the **Peshitta** come from these counterfeit manuscripts and forgeries.

Evidence shows that the Biblical Christianity resulting from the missionary work of the Apostles had spread all the way to the British Isles within a dozen years after the time of Christ.

Unmistakably, this Biblical Christianity in Great Britain had not been corrupted by the errors and apostasy which flowed from the apostatizing church at Rome, for it is stated:

"In Great Britain primitive Christianity had very early taken root. The gospel received by the Britons in the first centuries was then uncorrupted by Romish apostasy." (*Great Controversy*, p.62)

As an example of this early Christianity, historic records note Pomponia Graecina, who lived in the British Isles about the year **43**.

"Pomponia Graecina, the wife of Aulus Plautius, the conqueror of Britain,...was probably the first Christian lady of the Roman nobility..." (*History of the Christian Church*, vol.1, p. 374)

Pomponia was a true follower of Jesus Christ, adhering to true Christianity. Though she was the wife of Aulus Plautius, the Roman lieutenant in Britain serving under Claudius, the Roman Emperor, Pomponia was not connected to the Roman Catholic church of Rome. It would not come on the scene until two centuries later.

Polycarp (**69–155**), a 2nd-century Christian bishop of Smyrna, was a personal friend of the apostle John, and it is believed that he is the first one, along with John, who assembled some of the writings of the apostles to form what is now called the New Testament.

As for the various Latin versions, some critical sources state:
"There were a variety of Latin versions before Jerome's day, representing three types of Old Latin text: African, European, and Italian."
(Pictorial Bible Dictionary, p.842)

"The Old Latin Version is consequently one of the most valuable and interesting evidences which we possess for the condition of the New Testament text in the earliest times...it was originally made in the second century, perhaps not very far from a.d. 150, and probably, though not certainly, in Africa. Another version [Itala], apparently independent, subsequently appeared in Europe..."
(Our Bible and the Ancient Manuscripts, p.166)

The old Latin MSS that originated in Africa were called the "**Africana**." The old Latin MSS that were found in Europe and Northern Italy were called the "**Itala**" and they were "independent" from the African MSS. These two streams of "Old Latin" MSS do not match each other. And when the extant examples of these various Latin versions are compared, it is seen that they do not so easily fall into only three classes, but instead that they seem to sporadically come from many sources.

"...the variety of synonyms found in these texts is so great that they could not have arisen except from variety of origin."   (Burgon, Traditional Text Vindicated, p.139)

All these older versions of Latin were classed into the category of "**Old Latin**" called **Vetus Latina** and **Vetus Italica** and they did not originate at Rome.

"One thing is certain, or almost so, that wherever the version or versions originated, it was not at Rome. The language used there in the first two centuries was Greek."   (Making of the English Bible, p.143)

The first translation of the original pure New Testament from the **Greek Vulgate** into the Latin language was made sometime around **100**. This was not the **Africana** MSS but rather the **Itala** MSS and there is evidence that this pure "**Old Latin**" first originated with the church at Antioch before being transported to the Christians in northern Italy.

"Although the evidence has, up to the present time, been regarded as favoring the African origin of the first Latin translation of the Bible, recent investigation into what is called the Western text of the NT has yielded results pointing elsewhere. It is clear from a comparison that the Western type of text has close affinity with the Syrian witnesses originating in the eastern provinces of the empire. The close textual relation disclosed between the Latin and the Syrian versions has led some authorities to believe that, after all, the earliest Latin version may have been made in the East, and possibly at Antioch."
(International Standard Bible Encyclopedia, p.1842)

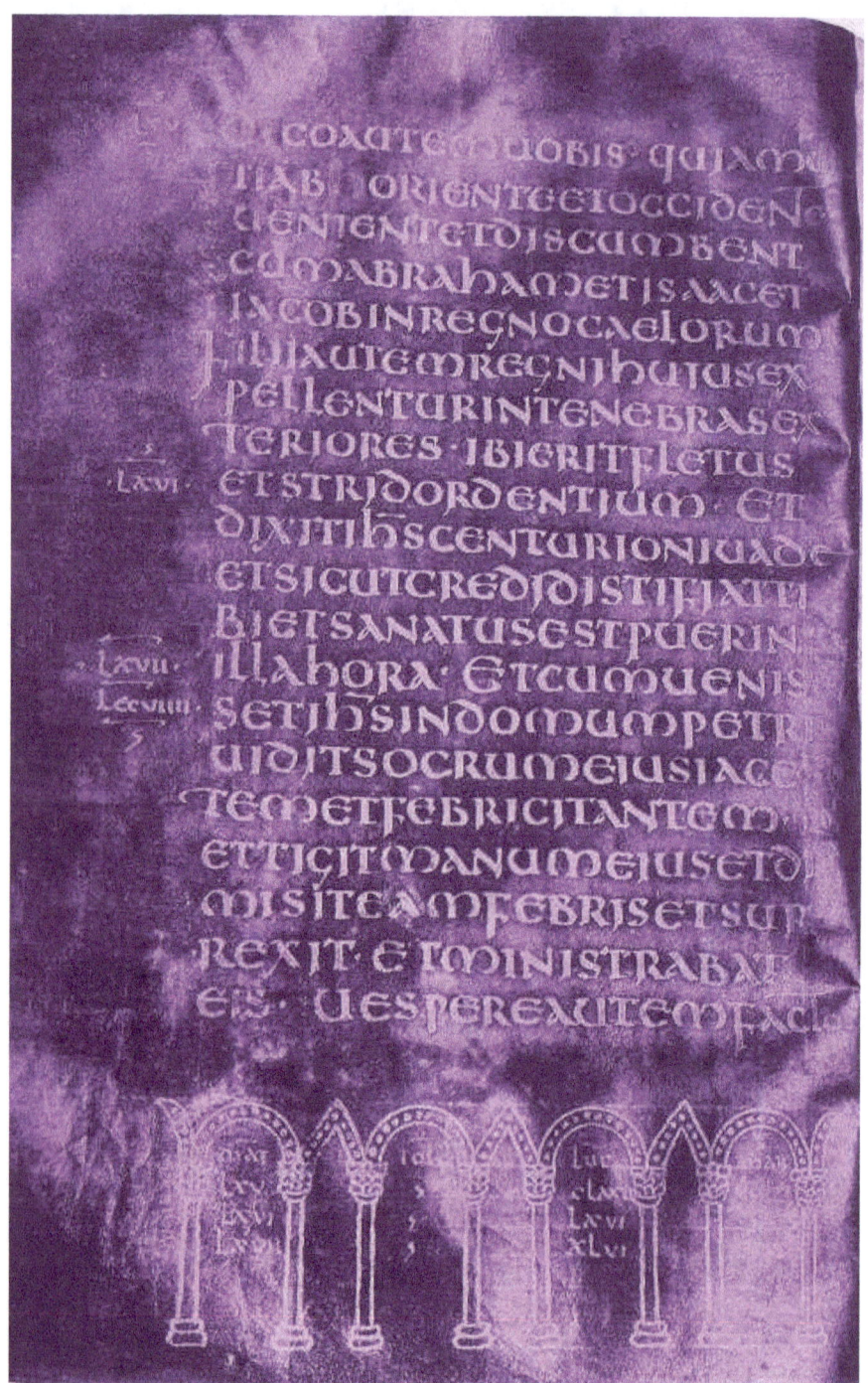

Codex Brixianus

The First Five Hundred Years

This pure **Itala** is represented by an extant Italian Latin manuscript now known as the **Brixianus** manuscript named after the Italian city Brescia, where it is now kept. The text was written on purple dyed vellum with silver ink, and its text is distinctly Byzantine. In the Roman and Byzantine Empires, purple parchment was reserved for imperial manuscripts. It was dyed purple so that the gold and silver writing would stand out more prominently.

This beautiful **Brixianus** illustrates the type of exemplar or model that set the quality stage for the **Vetus Italica** or **Itala Bible**. The **Itala** version (also sometimes just called the "**Old Latin**" or the "**Old Latin Vulgate**") was named "**Itala**" because it dominated the Italic district (the regions of northern Italy where the Vaudois later inhabited).

"Among the translations themselves, the Italic is to be preferred, because the most literal and perspicuous." (*Townley's Biblical Literature*, vol.1, p.85)

The word perspicuous simply means *"Clear to the understanding; that may be clearly understood; not obscure or ambiguous."* In other words, the **Itala** was clear to the understanding and not ambiguous.

The **Itala** manuscripts, as already pointed out, were translated directly from the original pure Greek manuscripts, and some scholars even believe that it was possibly done before the death of John the Revelator.

The **Itala** has been documented and known to have been in existence at least by the year **157**. It is represented by about 20 copies that survive today, not including fragments of copies. The renowned scholar Beza states that the Italic Church dates from **120**. The Italic Church handed down the scriptures in their apostolic purity. It is from this same source in apostolic times, that the pure Latin translation, used among the Spanish Christians in Spain through the first several centuries, may be found.

Another term for the **Itala** manuscripts is "Antehieronymian" which translated means *"before Jerome."*

In the first few centuries after the time of Christ, various heretics, schismatics, and half-converted pagans, began to change the Bible to fit their various desires. They not only introduced false doctrines, but they also produced counterfeit manuscripts as well as altering and changing some of the existing manuscripts.

"Mutilations of the Sacred Scriptures abounded. There were at least eighty heretical sects all striving for supremacy. Each took unwarranted license in removing or adding pages to Bible manuscripts." (*Truth Triumphant*, p.51)

Marcion of Sinope (**85–160**) taught that the world was created by the God of the Old Testament, but that this God was an impossibly strict God that condemned all humanity and that Jesus Christ came to release us all from His clutches. His followers, Marcionites, believed that the old admonitions about judgment and damnation could be replaced with a new message of love and salvation.

"Heretical professors of the gospel, Hebrew doctors, and cavillers of every description, from the half-converted to the declared infidel, were glad enough to exhibit copies of the Old or New Testament, with false readings, and passages rendered questionable either by omissions, or interpolation." (*Vigilantius and His Times*, p. 116)

Interpolation is simply, *"The act of foisting a word or passage into a manuscript or book; A spurious word or passage inserted in the genuine writings of an author."*

Irenaeus (**130–202**), a disciple of Polycarp, was sent as a missionary into Gaul and became the Bishop of Lyons. He was one of the first known missionaries to carry the Gospel into the Waldensian area of Northern Italy.

Irenaeus

"Irenaeus himself, therefore, a disciple of Polycarp, who was the hearer of St. John the Apostle, might have trodden the mountain paths of the Vaudois, in his journey to the metropolis of the world, and might have preached that apostolic faith, which abided pure in the wilderness, when it became corrupted in cities. There is a temptation to fix upon this Father, as a person not unlikely to have been, by himself or his clergy, the first herald of the Gospel to the natives of our subalpine valleys, which is quite irresistible. His diocese extended to, and perhaps comprised the chain of mountains, among which the forefathers of the Vaudois dwelt."
(*Waldensian Researches*, p.50)

Irenaeus spent much of his time fighting against the heresy of mixing Gnosticism with Christianity.

By **150**, there was a flourishing group of scholars known as Gnostics who worshiped knowledge. Gnosticism was originally founded by Simon Magus, the sorcerer referred to in Acts 8:9.

> *"The founder of Gnosticism was the sorcerer Simon Magus of Samaria…"*
> (*UFOs and the New World Order Connection*, p.222)

Gnosticism placed between the highest God and the 'world of matter' many "Eons" or beings, including not only the "Demiurge" and the "Logos" but also Christ and Jesus, who were regarded as two separate entities. They did not believe that Jesus Christ was a member of the Godhead, but that all humanity has a spark of divinity hidden in them and Jesus had just provided mankind with the knowledge to free it. This group was made up of those who were seeking to mix paganism with Christianity.

> *"Gnosticism was eating its way into those sections of the church which were compromising with paganism."* (*Truth Triumphant*, p.49)

These beliefs are known as Gnosticism or "the worship of knowledge" and this religion was in various areas, but appears to have been centered around Alexandria.

> *"Cardinal Newman praised Alexandria, the seat of Gnosticism, which powerful movement rejected the Old Testament and with it the Ten Commandments."*
> (*Truth Triumphant*, p.55)

> *"Egypt was the birthplace of speculative theology, which may be said to have begun with the Gnostics in the first half of the second century."*
> (*The Greek and Eastern Churches*, p.560)

During this time period, some Jewish writings appeared. They were known as the Talmud (oral traditions) and the Cabbala or Kabbalah (the writings of Jewish mysticism). The Kabbalah was derived from occultic Zoroastrianism around **70–100 AD**.

> *"There are two Talmuds, one called the Jerusalem Talmud, the other the Babylonish Talmud. The Jerusalem Talmud, compiled principally for the Jews of Palestine, was composed about A.D. 250. The principal, or Babylonish Talmud, was begun by Rabbi Asseh, and completed by his successors about A.D. 500. The Talmuds are divided into two parts, the Mishna and the Gemara. The Mishna is the oral Law, which the Jews say God delivered to Moses on Sinai, as explanatory of the written Law. These unwritten traditionary explanations were delivered, say they, by Moses to Joshua, by Joshua to the elders, and so on to the year of Christ 150, or, according to others, 190; when Rabbi Judah Hakkadosh, or the Holy, collected all the traditions, and committed them to writing that they might not be lost…The Gemara, or Completion, as it is called, contains the commentaries and additions of succeeding rabbins."* (*Townley's Biblical Literature*, vol.1, p.151)

> "Besides the Mishna, the Jews pretend to have received from the divine Author of the Law another and more mystical interpretation of it. This mystical exposition they term Cabbala, a word signifying tradition, or reception,...the Cabbala teaches the mysteries couched under those rites and ceremonies [of the Mishna], and hidden in the words and letters of the Scriptures."
>
> (*Townley's Biblical Literature*, vol.1, p.153)

Another heretical view of the incarnation that appeared was Docetism, the theory that Christ's human nature was not real but merely an appearance.

Yet another heretical sect that developed were the Ebionites, who taught, among other things, that Paul was an apostate from Jewish law and that Jesus Christ had become the Messiah by obedience to the Jewish law and they denied His pre-existence. They also venerated Jerusalem as the house of God. Their teachings were also connected with the Qumran sect where the **Dead Sea Scrolls** were later found.

Adoptionism asserted the false belief that Jesus was born a mere man and then became the Son of God through the indwelling of the Logos and the descent of the Holy Spirit upon Him at baptism.

Thomasines believed the Gnostic teachings that humanity all has a share in divinity and that Jesus just teaches them how to rediscover it. They rejected hierarchy and believed in greater freedom of personal expression. They also taught an openness in the role of women and a greatly decreased sense of guilt.

Justin Martyr (**110–165**) was a philosopher who converted to Christianity, but he believed in exalting tradition above the truth.

> "First, the original founders of the ecclesiastical college at Alexandria strove to exalt tradition. Justin Martyr, as early as 150, had stood for this."
>
> (*Truth Triumphant*, p.48)

Justin Martyr

Justin claimed to be Christian, but he continued to hold on to many of the philosophies that he had learned as a pagan. It is said that Justin was later killed for his faith by the Romans.

> "Justin, originally a pagan and of pagan parentage, afterward embraced Christianity and although he is said to have died at heathen hands for his religion, nevertheless, his teachings were of a heretical nature. Even as a Christian teacher, he continued to wear the robes of a pagan philosopher."
>
> (*Our Authorized Bible Vindicated*, p.16)

Justin was the spiritual 'father' and guide of Tatian (**120–180**) who embraced the Gnostic heresy. Tatian combined the four gospels into one work and changed them to fit what he believed to be accurate around **160–175**. This work is called the **Diatessaron**.

> *"The Gospels were so notoriously corrupted by his hand that in later years a bishop of Syria, because of the errors, was obliged to throw out of his churches no less than two hundred copies of this Diatessaron, since church members were mistaking it for the true Gospel."* (*Our Authorized Bible Vindicated*, p.16)

Later, Tatian also became the instructor of Clement of Alexandria.

Rome claims to have sent missionaries to the areas of France and the British Isles, however evidence shows that the ancient Britons of the British Isles and France actually received their Christianity from their brethren in Asia Minor and not from Rome.

The Galatians in Asia Minor were in constant contact with their relatives in Gaul. It was the Greeks from the East who traded with the Britons through land and sea commerce. The the form of Christianity among the Britons was the same as from the East and not the type from Rome.

In actuality, the "missionaries" from Rome did not come to Gaul until around **250 AD**. When they arrived in the area, they discovered groups of Christians who were already well established and keeping the 7th-day Sabbath of the Bible.

> *"Persecution from pagan emperors, which extended even to these far-off shores, was the only gift that the first churches of Britain received from Rome. Many of the Christians, fleeing from persecution in England, found refuge in Scotland; thence the truth was carried to Ireland, and in all these countries it was received with gladness. When the Saxons invaded Britain, heathenism gained control. The conquerors disdained to be instructed by their slaves, and the Christians were forced to retreat to the mountains and the wild moors. Yet the light, hidden for a time, continued to burn. In Scotland, a century later, it shone out with a brightness that extended to far-distant lands."* (*Great Controversy*, p.62)

The **Gallic Bible**, which is also from the pure stream, was possessed by the Christians of Vienne and Lyons in Gaul (which was Southern France) when the persecutions by the pagans broke out on them in **177**. Evidence suggests that they were a religious colony originating from Asia Minor, or Phrygia, and when they wrote about their sufferings and martyrdom, they did not send it to Rome, but to their brethren in Asia Minor. Many of them that escaped, migrated to Ireland and formed the Celtic church which Patrick found in existence when he arrived there almost two centuries later.

Sword Unsheathed

Tertullian, who lived in Carthage approximately from **155–240**, was a convert to Christianity and was believed to be the son of a Roman centurion. In his own writings he cites, about 2,500 times, various Latin quotations directly from the pure **Old Latin Vulgate** (**Itala**). He detested Greek philosophy and was very outspoken against Gnosticism. However, he held other types of mystic beliefs, and it was also in his writings that the term "Lord's Day" was first applied to Sunday instead of Saturday, the Biblical 7th-day Sabbath – so not all of Tertullian's theology was correct. He does provide evidence, however, of how far the true gospel had already been spread by the apostles and their associates by his day. He states:

"In whom other than in the Christ, who has already come, do all the nations believe? For in him have believed the most diverse peoples: Parthians, Medes, Elamites; those who inhabit Mesopotamia, Armenia, Phrygia, Cappadocia; the dwellers in Pontus, Asia, and Pamphylia; those occupying Egypt, and inhabiting the region of Africa beyond Cyrene, Romans and natives, even Jews dwelling in Jerusalem, and other nations; nay, the different tribes of the Getulians, and many territories of the Moors, all parts of Spain, the different peoples of Gaul, and parts of Britain not reached by the Romans but subjugated to Christ... In all these the name of the Christ, who has already come, reigns."

(*Ante-Nicene Fathers*, vol. 3, pp. 157, 158)

On the other hand, Tertullian had a contemporary, Titus Flavius Clemens, who later became known as Clement of Alexandria. Clement was born to pagan parents in Athens, Greece and lived around the same time, about **150–217**. He was a pagan philosopher who was fascinated with Greek philosophy, the teachings of Plato, and Gnosticism.

Clement

When he converted to Christianity and became a teacher in the Catechetical School of Alexandria, he mixed the teachings of Christianity with the teachings of pagan philosophy.

"First, the original founders of the ecclesiastical college at Alexandria strove to exalt tradition. Justin Martyr, as early as 150, had stood for this. He was the spiritual father of Tatian, who in turn was, in all probability, a teacher of Clement. Second, Clement, most famous of the Alexandrian college faculty and a teacher of Origen, boasted that he would not teach Christianity unless it were mixed with pagan philosophy." (*Truth Triumphant*, p.48)

Clement taught that Plato's work was inspired in the same sense as Scripture. He also didn't believe the Bible could be understood in a literal sense, so he spiritualized the scriptures away.

The First Five Hundred Years

While Alexandria was the capital of the amalgamated form of Christianity with paganism, Rome had been for centuries, the capital of paganism itself, and it was rapidly becoming the capital of 'paganism baptized.'

> "Victor 1, bishop of Rome, entered into a compact with Clement, about **190**, to carry on research around the Mediterranean basin to secure support to help make Sunday the prominent day of worship in the church." (Truth Triumphant, p.48)

This of course, would use the pagan's "Sun" day to displace over time the Biblical 7th-day Sabbath that had been established by God Himself and kept by all the true early Christians in the first centuries. Victor later excommunicated all the churches of the East that would not go along with his idea to make the pagan holiday of Easter always fall on a Sunday.

One of Clement's pupils was Adamantius Origen. Origen was born in Alexandria, Egypt and lived from **185–254**. He was a Greek philosopher, Gnostic, and a devout follower of Clement's Neo-Platonism (which was a strange combination of Aristotelian logic and Oriental cult teachings).

Origen

Woefully, Origen attempted to add and amalgamate "Christianity" to its views. Around the year **227**, Origen traveled extensively throughout Palestine, Greece and Asia Minor. He was a textual critic and everywhere he found Greek New Testament manuscripts, he had them changed and altered to fit his own doctrine. He did this by "translating" them. He also originated some popular false doctrines that are commonly taught today.

> "Even before the establishment of the papacy the teachings of heathen philosophers had received attention and exerted an influence in the church. Many who professed conversion still clung to the tenets of their pagan philosophy, and not only continued its study themselves, but urged it upon others as a means of extending their influence among the heathen. Serious errors were thus introduced into the Christian faith. Prominent among these was the belief in man's natural immortality and his consciousness in death. This doctrine laid the foundation upon which Rome established the invocation of saints and the adoration of the Virgin Mary. From this sprang also the heresy of eternal torment for the finally impenitent, which was early incorporated into the papal faith."
> (Great Controversy, p.58)

It was Origen who brought into the Christian Church the false doctrine of the "Immortality of the Soul," which he had borrowed from the Greek philosopher Pythagoras. Until Origen introduced this false doctrine into the Christian church, the Christians had all held the Biblically correct doctrine that when a person dies, they are unconsciously sleeping in the grave awaiting the resurrection.

In blatant defiance of the Bible's testimony that when a person dies, their existence ceases (Ecclesiastes 9:5-6, Psalm 146:4); and the Bible's testimony that God *"only hath immortality"* (1 Timothy 6:16), Origen began promoting the false idea that a person's soul is immortal and when they die, only their body goes into the grave but their "soul" goes to heaven. This was nothing but a subtle way of incorporating into the Christian Church the pagan philosophy, originating with the serpent in Eden, that humans can be god – *"ye shall be as gods"* (Genesis 3:5).

This false doctrine opened the way to introduce the next false doctrine of an imaginary place where these supposed "immortal" souls could be placed.

"Doctor Adam Clarke indicates Origen as the first teacher of purgatory"
(Our Authorized Bible Vindicated, p.46)

Contrary to the false doctrine of Origen, the pure-line Bibles teach that a person's "soul" is "created" – it didn't exist before! God created each person's *"soul"* by the combining of the body (dust) with God's *"breath of life"* (Genesis 2:7)

Body (Dust) + Breath (Spirit) = A Living Soul

This means that when a person dies, that mathematical equation is simply reversed. The *"breath"* returns to God, the body lies in the grave (returns to dust) and the soul then ceases to exist (Ecclesiastes 12:7, Ezekiel 18:20).

Body (Dust) - Breath (Spirit) = Dead Soul/No Soul

Origen's false doctrine of the "natural immortality of the soul" is actually based in the devil's first lie given to Eve in the Garden of Eden, *"Ye shall not surely die"* (Genesis 3:4).

The purpose of the "resurrection" which is to take place at the Second Coming of Jesus Christ, is for God to recreate the souls of the righteous, by recombining His "breath of life" with the dust (bodies) of His "saints." God can easily do this, because He was their Creator in the first place, so He has a correct memory of every characteristic that they had. This is also why Jesus refers to physical death as sort of like a form of unconscious "sleep" (John 11:11-14, Mark 5:39).

It is during this time (that of Origen, Clement, etc.), about **100-325**, that the testimony of Revelation 2:8-9 about those who claim to be God's people but are really of the *"synagogue of Satan,"* truly applied.

"And unto the angel of the church in Smyrna write; ...I know the blasphemy of them which say they are Jews, and are not, but are the synagogue of Satan."

On every hand, false professors of Christianity were working to undermine and destroy the Bible.

*"Christ speaks of the church over which Satan presides as **the synagogue of Satan**. Its members are the children of disobedience. They are those who choose to sin, who labor to make void the holy law of God. **It is Satan's work to mingle evil with good, and to remove the distinction between good and evil.**"*
(Review and Herald, December 4, 1900)

Origen worked to mystify the Bible and give it a secret meaning. He attempted to make it incomprehensible to the common man.

Origen himself stated:
"The Scriptures are of little use to those who understand them as they are written." (quoted in The Two Republics, p.220)

Yet, the warning counsel has been given:
"The truths most plainly revealed in the Bible have been involved <u>in doubt and darkness by learned men</u>, who, with a pretense of great wisdom, teach that the Scriptures have a mystical, a secret, spiritual meaning not apparent in the language employed. These men are false teachers. It was to such a class that Jesus declared, "Ye know not the Scriptures, neither the power of God." [Mark 12:24.] The language of the Bible should be explained according to its obvious meaning unless a symbol or figure is employed. Christ has given the promise, "If any man will do His will, he shall know of the doctrine." [John 7:17.] <u>If men would but take the Bible as it reads</u>, if there were no false teachers to mislead and confuse their minds, a work would be accomplished that would make angels glad, and that would bring into the fold of Christ thousands upon thousands who are now wandering in error."
(Spirit of Prophecy, vol.4, p.416)

Around **240**, Origen produced an edition of the scriptures blending Christian truths with Greek philosophy and paganism. It was known as the "**Hexapla**."

It contained six different translations of the Bible in parallel columns.

• In **column 1** were the Hebrew Scriptures.

• In **column 2** Origen transliterated the Hebrew words from the first column into the parallel letters of the Greek alphabet, which, of course, only showed how to pronounce the Hebrew words in Greek letters, but didn't actually give the Greek meaning of the words.

• In **column 3** was a Greek translation from the Hebrew made in **128** by a man named Aquila. Aquila had claimed conversion to Christianity after seeing miracles performed by disciples of the deceased apostles. He deliberately translated many sections of scripture pertaining to the Messiah so as to make it impossible to apply those texts to Jesus Christ. Aquila was later excommunicated from the church for refusing to give up astrology, magic, and the practice of necromancy.

• In **column 4** was a Greek translation from Hebrew made by Symmachus between **180–192**. Symmachus was born a Samaritan, but became a Jew and later professed the Christian faith, only to subsequently join himself to the Ebionites.

• In **column 6** was a Greek translation which had been from another Greek text by Theodotion between **161–181**. He had once professed faith in Christ but had also apostatized to become an Ebionite.

• The **5th column** was Origen's own translation of the Hebrew into the old Hellenistic Greek that he named the **Septuagint** or **LXX** after the legend found in the Letter of Aristeas. This translation would later have an important influence in the making of the **Codex Sinaiticus**, the **Codex Alexandrinus**, and the **Codex Vaticanus**.

Of this **Septuagint** it is stated, *"...as a whole the work of translation was doubtless carried out at Alexandria, where it was begun; and the Greek Bible of the Hellenistic Jews and the Catholic Church may rightly be styled the Alexandrian Greek version of the Old Testament."* (An Introduction to the Old Testament In Greek, p.27)

Perhaps God's counsel about Egypt should be taken into consideration by those consulting Alexandrian manuscripts: *"Woe to them that go down to Egypt for help; and stay on horses, and trust in chariots, because they are many; and in horsemen, because they are very strong; but they look not unto the Holy One of Israel, neither seek the LORD! ... Now the Egyptians are men, and not God; and their horses flesh, and not spirit. When the LORD shall stretch out his hand, both he that helpeth shall fall, and he that is holpen shall fall down, and they all shall fail together."* Isaiah 31:1-3

Here with Origen's **Hexapla** is the origin of the **LXX** that is commonly referred to today. Origen's original **Hexapla Bible** (the only complete one) was believed to have been lost years later in the destruction of the Library of Caesarea in **638**, and it also is no longer in existence.

Callistus I, bishop of Rome from **217–222**, was the first to use the emperor's title, *Pontifex Maximus*, in public reference to himself. This title was later shortened to just 'Pontiff.' Pontifex Maximus is Latin for "greatest priest" – in direct opposition to the Biblical declaration: *"And call no man your father upon the earth: for one is your Father, which is in heaven. Neither be ye called masters: for one is your Master, even Christ. But he that is greatest among you shall be your servant."* Matthew 23:9-11

Sabellius was a priest and theologian in Rome who lived in the early part of the 3rd century. He was excommunicated in **220 AD** for his erroneous teaching which became known as Sabellianism – which was that the Father, the Son, and the Holy Spirit are merely three ways in which God has revealed Himself – sort of like one being with three faces.

Monarchianism, another similar teaching that arose, represented God as one person appearing and working in the different "modes" as the Father, the Son, and the Holy Spirit.

The First Five Hundred Years

Pamphilus was a great admirer of Origen and his amalgamated theology. He established a library at Caesarea.

*"Pamphilus of Caesarea (died **309**) did not write much, but he founded a great theological library at Caesarea which included the works of Origen. He was a disciple of Origen."* (Introduction to Textual Criticism, p. 140)

Nonetheless, Pamphilus was also later killed by the pagans for his supposed "Christian" faith.

In **257**, Gregory the Illuminata was born. When he went to take the gospel to Armenia, he discovered Bible Christians all over the country, which had gotten their churches and faiths from the labors of the apostles Thaddeus and Bartholomew. The Armenians didn't have an alphabet in their own language at this point and so they used the original **Peshitta** until the 5th century when they finally received the Bible in their own tongue.

Arius (**256–336**) was a priest in Alexandria, Egypt that around **318 AD** began teaching another error. He taught that the Son of God had a beginning. He further erroneously instructed that before the foundation of the world, God the Father had created the Son out of nothing and that as a result Jesus Christ was subordinate to the Father, but that the Son is somehow also God. His teachings became known as Arianism. Arius was excommunicated and considered by some to be the "forerunner of Antichrist."

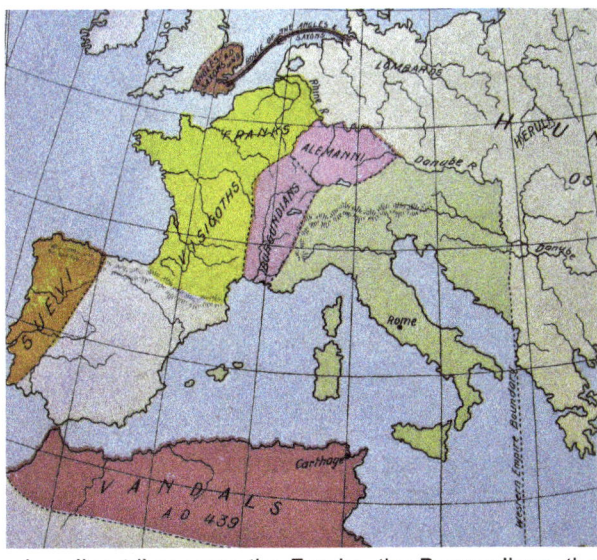

For more than two centuries, from about **250** to about **500 AD**, the Teutonic masses poured over the provinces of Western Europe invading Rome and establishing their kingdoms. These wars and invasions overthrew the pagan Roman Empire and formed the powerful nations of Western Europe that covered the land we know today as England, France, Germany, Switzerland, Austria, the Czech Republic, Spain, Portugal, Italy, and Hungary. The names of the invading tribes were the Franks, the Burgundians, the Huns, the Vandals, the Lombards, the Angles, the Saxons, the Alamanni, the Heruli, the Suevi, the Visigoths, and the Ostrogoths.

Gradually, some tribes were conquered or absorbed into the others, eventually leaving only 10. The Roman Catholic Church gradually converted many of these tribes to Catholicism.

About **250 AD**, a man by the name of Lucian was born at Antioch in Syria. He became a devout scholar and defender of the pure apostolic faith.

Lucian

Lucian gathered all the writings of the apostles together (at least the ones not already gathered by Polycarp and John) and produced the **Greek Vulgate** New Testament - which is known today as the **Received Text** (**Textus Receptus**). (Though the name "**Textus Receptus**" was not coined until **1633**)

Lucian of Antioch also translated the Old Testament from the original Hebrew into the Greek Vugate language in order to counteract the text by Origen and to fight against all the various "corruptions" that were being incorporated into the Word of God by all the various heretical sects that were in existence at that time. This translation of the Old Testament into Greek, is also called the "**Septuagint**" by some scholars today – but Lucian's Greek text is not like Origen's **Septuagint** – they are different. Lucian's text agrees with the original pure manuscripts, while Origen's text agrees with the corrupted Alexandrian texts.

It was **Lucian's Greek** text that was used across Asia Minor and in Constantinople. **Lucian's Greek text** was the **original Greek Orthodox Bible** until, in later years, it seems that they began to use Origen's corrupt **Septuagint**.

> "Not only did Lucian certify the genuine New Testament, but he spent years of arduous labor upon the Old Testament. As the Greek language was the prevalent tongue in which leading works were published throughout the civilized world, he translated the Hebrew Scriptures into Greek. He did this work so well that even Jerome, his bitter opponent, admitted that his Greek translation of the Old Testament held sway in the capital city of Constantinople and in most of the Near East." (Truth Triumphant, p.51)

Lucian's manuscripts became known to history as the **Lucianic Byzantine**, or Syrian, text and there are no originals extant. However, large fragments of it are extant in the writings of John Chrysostom.

Lucian fought against both Gnosticism and Manichaeism. (*Manichaeism rejected creation and denied a miracle-working God. It taught celibacy of its leaders, and commanded worshiping the sun as the supreme dwelling place of Deity. It also ridiculed the Sabbath of the fourth commandment and exalted Sunday worship.)*

Lucian founded a Christian college at Antioch to try to counteract the dangerous ecclesiastical alliance between Rome and Alexandria.

The bishops of Rome and Alexandria, embroiled in controversy over the teachings of Monarchianism and Adoptionism, appealed to the pagan emperor Aurelian in **270** to settle the matter, but he refused to make a decision and submitted the judgment of the matter to the bishops of Rome. This act led to the belief that Rome was the head of the whole Christian Church. This came across as recognition from the pagan state to Pope Felix which, in turn, led to their false concept and doctrine of the 'primacy of Peter.'

"About the time of Paul's second arrest, Peter also was apprehended and thrust into prison. He had made himself especially obnoxious to the authorities by his zeal and success in exposing the deceptions and defeating the plots of Simon Magus the sorcerer, who had followed him to Rome to oppose and hinder the work of the gospel. Nero was a believer in magic, and had patronized Simon. He was therefore greatly incensed against the apostle, and was thus prompted to order his arrest." (*Sketches from the Life of Paul*, p.328)

Lucian recognized Rome's "Primacy of Peter" doctrine as a form of "man worship" and he also realized that it was actually the sorcerer, Simon Magus, who was the real origin of the "Peter" that was considered as the "head of the church." Rome had even taken a statue of the pagan god Jupiter and renamed it as St. Peter.

Lucian was viciously opposed to such false doctrines and was very outspoken against it. He also opposed other false doctrines and teachings of Alexandria and Rome. *"...when Victor I, in lordly tones, pronounced excommunication on all the churches of the East who would not with him make Easter always come on Sunday, Alexandria supported this first exhibition of spiritual tyranny by the bishop of Rome. Lucian opposed Alexandria's policies and for this has been bitterly hated and his name kept in the background."* (*Truth Triumphant*, p.48)

Pagan Jupiter/St. Peter

Because of his opposition to their false doctrines and the fact that he had provided a pure translation of the Bible for the people, he was hated by Rome and martyred in **312 AD**. To this very day, Lucian of Antioch's name is secretly hated by the leaders of the Roman Church.

It was during this century that Hesychius, a bishop in Alexandria, Egypt produced his version of the "**Septuagint**," compiled from various Egyptian manuscripts. As could be expected, his **Septuagint** agrees with the corrupt Alexandrian texts.

"His revision of the Septuagint was received and adopted by the churches of Egypt; so that the three editions by Origen, Lucian, and Hesychius shared the world among them; and from one or other of them are derived all the manuscript copies of the Septuagint that are now extant, or at least known."
(*Townley's Biblical Literature*, vol.1, p.98)

To recap, the term "**Septuagint**" used today can sometimes refer to different Greek texts of the Old Testament. But the majority of the time, when the term "**Septuagint**" is used today, it is in reference to Origen's version. Both Origen's **Septuagint** and Hesychius' **Septuagint** are corrupt texts and agree with corrupt Alexandrian texts.

Only **Lucian's Greek** text (the **Lucianic OT** and the "**Received Text**" of the NT) comes from the pure line of manuscripts.

"Lucian…used different manuscripts from those used by Origen."
(*Truth Triumphant*, p.57)

The **Greek Orthodox Bible**, has been in use from apostolic times in the Greek Orthodox Church. As already mentioned, the original Greek text that they used was the **Received Text** of the NT, and that Greek translation of the OT that was done in the first centuries in the Byzantine area by Lucian. However, the authorized **1904** text of the Ecumenical Patriarchate of Constantinople does not follow the **Received Text** and some modern critical sources are also claiming that the Orthodox Church now use Origen's **Septuagint** (**LXX**), so, obviously there has been a "falling away" in standards that has taken place.

During all this time, the Church in Rome had been growing in power and they were joining with the Church in Alexandria in mixing paganism with Christianity. The Church of Rome had begun to take all the various aspects of Paganism, and absorb them into their own worship services, renaming the pagan practices and the pagan gods with supposedly Christian terms.

"And every where through Italy one sees their sacred Inscriptions speaking the pure Language of Paganism, and giving the same Powers, Characters and Attributes to their Saints, as had formerly been ascribed to the Heathen Gods."
(*A Letter from Rome*, p.42-43)

"For nothing, I found, …so much help'd my Imagination to fancy myself wandering about in Old Heathen Rome, as to observe and attend to their Religious Worship; all whose Ceremonies appeared plainly to have been copied from the

Rituals of Primitive Paganism, as if handed down by an uninterrupted Succession from the Priests of Old to the Priests of New Rome..." (*A Letter from Rome*, p.13)

Alexandria is where the practice of making the "sign of the cross" originated in the year **300 AD**. Also in **300** Rome adopted the heathen practice of saying prayers for the dead.

Rome also gradually exalted the bishop of the church until he was later made "*the Vicar of the Son of God.*" This blasphemous claim the Papacy declares in these words: *"...we define that the Roman Pontiff is the successor of the Blessed Peter, Prince of the Apostles, and the true Vicar of Christ, the Head of the whole Church, the Father and Doctor of all Christians, and we declare that to him, in the person of the Blessed Peter, was given, by Jesus Christ our Savior, full power to feed, rule and govern the universal Church."* (*The Faith of Our Fathers*, p.105)

The church in Spain remained relatively free of Roman Catholic influence for centuries. The council held at Elvira, Spain in **305** revealed three things: first, up until the time of that council, the Church of Spain had adopted no creed, and certainly not the creed later adopted at Nicaea; secondly, punishment of faulty members by the church did not go farther than dismissal, for there was no appeal to civil law; thirdly, up to the time of the Council of Elvira, movements toward a union of the church and the state had made no progress. At this time, the church in Spain also observed the Biblical Sabbath.

"*Canon 26 of the Council of Elvira reveals that the Church of Spain at that time kept Saturday, the seventh day.*" (*Truth Triumphant*, p.249)

Eusebius, bishop of Caesarea (**270–339**), was *"a pupil and protégé of Pamphilus." (Introduction to Textual Criticism, p. 140)*

He became a Roman historian and Bible critic who wrote many historical records but, just like his teacher, he also worshiped at the altar of Origen's teachings. He helped Pamphilus write a collection of six books called the *Defense of Origen*, and he collected eight hundred of Origen's letters, and restored and preserved Origen's library which was at Caesarea.

Eusebius was also a good friend and counselor of Emperor Constantine.

Eusebius

"Probably, however, his importance was due even more to his close relations with the great emperor, whose entire confidence he enjoyed. He occupied the first seat to the emperor's right...and delivered the opening address to Constantine when he took his seat in the council-chamber..." (*Dictionary of Christian Biography*, p.319)

Sword Unsheathed

Eusebius was also a friend of Arius and a follower of Arianism.

Eusebius was commissioned by Constantine in **331**, to produce an "ecumenical Bible" that would be more "politically correct" and not offend the pagans. Eusebius then produced 50 Bibles for Constantine which were based on the **fifth column** of Origen's corrupt **Hexapla Bible**. Many of these 50 Bibles were then spread around Asia Minor in order to try to counteract the influence of Lucian's text. However, Lucian's Bible was hard to overthrow, and Rome needed more help to overcome Lucian's pure text.

Gradually, over time, these Bibles ordered by Constantine were lost. Two of Constantine's lost **Hexapla LXX**-based Bibles would resurface years later to become known as the **Vaticanus** and the **Sinaiticus**.

The supposed "conversion" of the Roman emperor Constantine to the Christian faith in the year **312 AD** had opened the door for paganism to infiltrate throughout the church almost unobstructed.

Constantine was the one who first passed a Sunday law in **321 AD**, calling for people to cease from work on the first day of the week.

"*On March 7, 321, was issued the first national Sunday Law in history. This was the first 'blue law' to be issued by a civil government.*" (*The Fabulous First Centuries of Christianity, p.443*)

Though this Sunday worship concept had been subtly introduced by Victor I years before, it was in reality, Constantine's good friend, Eusebius, who first boldly promoted in the church, the concept that the Sabbath day of the Bible had been changed from Saturday, the Biblical 7th day of the week, to Sunday, the 1st day of the week. Speaking of Constantine's Sunday Law, it is stated: "*The royal mandate not proving a sufficient substitute for divine authority, Eusebius, a bishop who sought the favor of princes, and who was the special friend and flatterer of Constantine, advanced the claim that Christ had transferred the Sabbath to Sunday. Not a single testimony of the Scriptures was produced in proof of the new doctrine. Eusebius himself unwittingly*

LATIN TEXT
IMPERATOR CONSTANTINUS AUG. HELPIDIO: OMNES JUDICES, URBANÆQUE PLEBES ET CUNCTARUM ARTIUM OFFICIA VENERABILI DIE SOLIS QUIESCANT. RURI TAMEN POSITI AGRORUM CULTURÆ LIBERE LICENTERQUE INSERVIANT, QUONIAM FREQUENTER EVENIT, UT NON APTIUS ALIO DIE FRUMENTA SULCIS AUT VINEÆ SCROBIBUS MANDENTUR, NE OCCASIONE MOMENTI PEREAT COMMODITAS CŒLESTI PROVISIONE CONCESSA.

TRANSLATION
CONSTANTINE, EMPEROR AUGUSTUS, TO HELPIDIUS: ON THE VENERABLE DAY OF THE SUN LET THE MAGISTRATES AND PEOPLE RESIDING IN CITIES REST, AND LET ALL WORKSHOPS BE CLOSED. IN THE COUNTRY, HOWEVER, PERSONS ENGAGED IN AGRICULTURE MAY FREELY AND LAWFULLY CONTINUE THEIR PURSUITS; BECAUSE IT OFTEN HAPPENS THAT ANOTHER DAY IS NOT SO SUITABLE FOR GRAIN SOWING OR FOR VINE PLANTING; LEST BY NEGLECTING THE PROPER MOMENT FOR SUCH OPERATIONS, THE BOUNTY OF HEAVEN SHOULD BE LOST.

Constantine's Sunday Law

acknowledges its falsity and points to the real authors of the change. 'All things," he says, 'whatever that it was duty to do on the Sabbath, these we have transferred to the Lord's Day.' –Robert Cox, Sabbath Laws and Sabbath Duties, page 538. *But the Sunday argument, groundless as it was, served to embolden men in trampling upon the Sabbath of the Lord. All who desired to be honored by the world accepted the popular festival."* (Great Controversy, p.574)

In other words, neither the apostles nor the early Christian church knew anything about Sunday worship – they all kept the Biblical 7th-day Sabbath!

"The modern doctrine of the change of the Sabbath was therefore absolutely unknown in the first centuries of the Christian church." (History of the Sabbath, p.207)

The papacy refused to recognize the obligatory observance of the Sabbath of God's fourth commandment and as such, believed that they could change it at will. They therefore derogatorily called the Biblical Sabbath, the "Jewish Sabbath," and tried to incorporate the pagan's "Sun-day" as the new supposedly "Christian" Sabbath.

However, the Bible specifies that the 7th-day Sabbath was made by God Himself as a commemorative sign of His work as the Creator, over 2,000 years before the "Jews" even existed! *"Thus the heavens and the earth were finished, and all the host of them. And on the seventh day God ended his work which he had made; and he rested on the seventh day from all his work which he had made. And God blessed the seventh day, and sanctified it: because that in it he had rested from all his work which God created and made."* Genesis 2:1-3

But Sunday worship is not the only thing that Constantine brought into the church. It was also Constantine who blended the partying, gift-giving festivities of the pagan holiday of Saturnalia (December 17-23) with the feasting and the pagan commemoration of the birth of Mithras known as Dies Natalis Solis Invicti (the birthday of the unconquered sun – December 25–January 1).

In **336**, Constantine brought these two pagan festivals into the Christian church and renamed them as the "birthday of Christ." This is the very first year that the holiday commonly known as Christmas (Christ-Mass) was celebrated in the Christian Church. Then in **350**, carrying on Constantine's work of blending paganism with Christianity, Pope Julius I made December 25 the official Christmas date for the Christian church.

Historically, Paganism and Christianity were mixed during this time period.

"Such was the tendency of the times [the fourth century] *to adulterate Christianity with the spirit of paganism, partly to conciliate the prejudices of worldly converts, partly in the hope of securing its more rapid spread. There is solemnity in the truthful statement which Faustus makes to Augustine: 'You have substituted your agape for*

the sacrifices of the pagans; for their idols your martyrs, whom you serve with the very same honors. You appease the shades of the dead with wine and feasts; you celebrate the solemn festivals of the Gentiles, their calends and their solstices; and as to their manners, those you have retained without any alteration. Nothing distinguishes you from the pagans, except that you hold your assemblies apart from them.'" (History of the Intellectual Development of Europe, Vol. 1, p.309, 310)

For quite a while, the Roman Catholic Church had been sending its agents into Africa to establish churches and monasteries and to convert the nomadic Arabs who inhabited that land. Almost everywhere that there was a historic Christian settlement that had been established by the labors of the apostles and early disciples, Rome built her own monasteries to try to counteract the true Christian influence. Many Christian Arabs converted to Catholicism, but some stayed true to the real Christianity and refused Rome's advances.

The Church of Rome also wanted to capture Jerusalem for itself and get rid of the Jews and the true Christians. Rome saw in the Arab tribes a huge source of untapped manpower and intended to use them for that purpose, so they began plotting how to gain control of the Arab tribes.

During this time, many Christians were captured by the Goths in Asia Minor and carried back into Dacia (modern Romania). These Christians succeeded in eventually winning many of the Goths to the Christian faith. One of these captive Christians was Ulfilas.

"The Goths carried back these Christian captives (from Asia Minor) into Dacia, where they were settled, and where considerable numbers embraced Christianity through their instrumentality. Ulfilas was the child of one of these Christian captives, and was trained in Christian principles." (Truth Triumphant, p.137)

Ulfilas (Ulphilas), who lived from **311-383**, was born to a captive Christian family in Dacia. He was

Ulfilas

an expert in both the Greek and Latin languages and was also a 7th-day Sabbath keeper. He spent his life as a missionary to the Gothic people.

"It, therefore, became a proverb among the Goths, 'Whatever is done by Ulphilas, is well done.'" (Gothic & Anglo-Saxon Gospels, p.iii)

"Since the Goths had no written language, Ulfilas, was compelled to invent an alphabet. He reduced Gothic sounds to writing." (Truth Triumphant, p.139)

The Gothic alphabet and language of Ulfilas is the origin of the language that everyone knows today as "English" – this was the source root from which the English language grew. The Gothic alphabet, designed by Ulfilas, was originally formed by converting the Greek letters. These letters later developed into what is known today as the English alphabet.

It was then that Ulfilas began his important work of translating the Gothic Bible (**330–350**). He translated it from the **Greek Received Text** of Lucian and the **Brixianus** Latin manuscript.

"The Gothic version was made about A.D. 383, by Ulphilas. There is a copy of the original edition in Upsal, Sweden." (*The Parallel Bible* introduction)

Gothic Writing (Matthew 6:9)

Ulfilas translated the whole Bible except for the books of 1st & 2nd Kings because he thought that the accounts of the wars of the Jews would inflame the warlike passions of the Goths which he was trying to calm. This masterpiece of translation faithfully follows the Greek text but not so closely as to do violence to the Gothic idiom.

"The first great piece of literature which the people of these vast nations, lying north of the empire's frontiers, looked upon was the Bible. It became the bond of union amongst the Gothic peoples. It was the parent of Teutonic literature."
(*Truth Triumphant*, p.139)

"The literary fame of Ulfilas is connected with his Gothic translation of the Bible, the one great monument of that language now extant."
(*A Dictionary of Christian Biography*, p.994)

This Gothic translation of Ulfilas no longer exists in a complete state. The surviving manuscripts that are extant today are the **Codex Argenteus**, **Codex Carolinus**, and the **Milan fragments**.

There is no Arianism in the surviving remains of the Gothic translation, showing that, contrary to modern opinion, the Goths which learned about Christianity from Ulfilas were not Arian in their beliefs.

"We are certain of this, that so far as the translation of Ulphilas has been recovered, there is not a trace of Arianism to be found. On the contrary, in passages clearly unfavourable to the doctrine of Arius, Ulphilas has honestly and plainly given

Sword Unsheathed

the literal meaning of the Greek. The chief point in which we are now concerned, is this, that those who read the Gothic version of Ulphilas are not likely to be led into error, as it is a faithful representation of the Greek."
(The Gothic and Anglo-Saxon Gospels, p.iv)

Contrary to what the 'Catholic-influenced' history books teach today, the Goths that had been influenced by Ulfilas, in general, were not Arian, nor blood-thirsty pagan barbarians – many of them were Bible-believing Christians and followers of Jesus Christ.

"The Goths and the Vandals did not fight because of a bloodthirsty temperament, but because they were blocked by the Romans when driven westward by the wild masses from Scythia and Siberia." (Truth Triumphant, p.141)

"In the first place, it was a great thing for Europe that when the Goths poured over Italy and even captured Rome they came as a Christian people, reverencing and sparing the churches, and abstaining from those barbarities that accompanied the invasion of Britain by the heathen Saxons. But, in the second place, many of these simple Gothic Christians learned to their surprise that they were heretics, and that only when their efforts toward fraternizing with their fellow Christians in the orthodox Church were angrily resented."
(The Greek and Eastern Churches, p.306 {Quoted in Truth Triumphant, p.141})

It is Rome that has rewritten history in order to paint the Christian Goths as a barbaric and evil power!

The Council of Nicaea, convened in **325** by Emperor Constantine, was the first general Council of the whole church. It joined the powers of the church and state together, and sought to compel all Christians to accept their new mandated doctrines. Among other things, this council started the religious controversy which has never ceased to this day, on how to properly view the relationship of the Three Persons of the Godhead: Father, Son, and Holy Ghost.

The argument at this council mainly focused on the relationship between the Father and the Son, and it centered over the use of two words which were spelled almost identically:

HOMOOUSIAN

HOMOIOUSIAN

The council passed the ruling that the godhead was "homoousian" (English = "consubstantial") which means "of one substance" or "identical substance." This Greek term "homoousian" originated with and was first developed and used by the Gnostics years before the Council of Nicaea ever met. The council termed this "homoousian" doctrine with the term that it is more commonly called today "Trinitarianism" (the doctrine of the Trinity).

The problem is that this term "homoousian" (aka. Trinity) basically means that there is no division or separation involved. In other words, the Godhead is viewed sort of as one single person (substance) who can display himself as either the Father, Son, or Holy Ghost, depending on which aspect he wants to show at the moment – which is exactly how the followers of Monarchianism and Sabellianism used it.

Some claimed that "homoousian" could mean that the Father and the Son were two separate persons, but that they were made of the same "divine type" of substance. But because this term was so vague and could be easily understood to represent the false *"one being with three modes or faces"* concept, many of the true early Christians refused to use or accept that term for the Godhead.

"The Roman Catholic church has many other heathenish practices: such as sprinkling for baptism; and that man is immortal and goes directly to heaven or hell at death...<u>The doctrine called the trinity, claiming that God is without form or parts; that the Father, Son and Holy Ghost, the three are one person</u>, is another."
(Adventist Review and Sabbath Herald, July 10, 1856, p.87)

The other term in discussion at the council was "homoiousian" which means "similar substance." The council rejected this term. All those true Christians who held Biblical beliefs like that the Godhead is three similar yet individual beings, the Father, Son, and Holy Ghost – All part of the Godhead and united in one purpose – were accused of believing in the "homoiousian" type of doctrine and falsely labeled by Rome to be heretics and Arians.

"In English the word is "consubstantial," connoting that more than one person inhabit the same substance without division or separation. The original term in Greek is homoousios, from homos, meaning "identical," and ousia, the word for "being."

"However, a great trouble arose, since there are two terms in Greek of historical fame. The first, homos, meaning "identical," and the second, homoios, meaning "similar" or "like unto," had both of them a stormy history. The spelling of these words is much alike. The difference in meaning, when applied to the Godhead, is bewildering to simplehearted believers. Nevertheless, those who would think in terms of homoiousian, or "similar," instead of homoousian, or "identical," were promptly labeled as heretics and Arians by the clergy."   (Truth Triumphant, p.90)

This is important to understand for more than one reason.

First, because there were many opposed to Rome's false teachings that were falsely labeled as followers of Arianism (and are still claimed to be Arian in many history books of today). Many of these Christians did not ascribe to Arian beliefs at all, but to the true understanding of the Godhead and/or other true doctrines – yet Rome still classed them with the Arians!

Second, there are some Protestant religions today that believe in the correct "homoiousian" doctrine of the Godhead (three separate individuals united in one purpose) who erroneously refer to their belief as the "Trinity." This referral to their belief with the wrong term is the result of not having a correct understanding of the origin of the word "Trinity" and the doctrine of Trinitarianism. What they actually believe in, is a "heavenly trio" – three individual persons that make up the Godhead.

In **330**, Constantine built his imperial residence in Byzantium and renamed it "Constantinople" in his honor. From this point onward, Constantinople grew into a capital of the Eastern Church.

"When Constantine moved his capital to the 7-hilled city of Byzantium, he renamed the city after himself...Constantine called this city 'New Rome'..."
(*The Trail of the Serpent*, p. 15)

The second ecumenical Council was held in **381** at Constantinople to formulate an orthodox statement on the doctrine of the Trinity. It was during this time period that a "hierarchical structure" began to come into the church.

"One of the most obvious symptoms of spiritual sickness, the growing scission in the body of the church, caused the rift between the clergy and the laity. In the earliest stage the whole church was regarded as 'a chosen race, a royal priesthood, a holy nation.'...There was no dichotomy here between clergy and laity; the church was a representative democracy in which elders and deacons exercised no greater authority than that of 'shepherds of the flock.' But indifference of the laymen to their own spiritual privileges led to a gradual transfer of authority to the elected leadership...a measure of authority begets hunger for more authority. Authority unchecked tends to become absolute." (*The Biblical Meaning of History*, p.152)

This is the process by which the early Christian church fell away from its Biblical structure and became the hierarchy of the Papal Church.

Gregory Nazianzen began to promote Mariolatry (the worship of Mary) in **389**.

John Chrysostom (**349–407**) was a notable Christian bishop for the Eastern Christian Church at Antioch and wrote many works in which he quoted extensively from the Greek and Syrian manuscripts. He was a great preacher and greatly loved by the church at Antioch, but in **397**, he was kidnapped by agents sent by Aelia Eudoxia, the wife of the Byzantine Emperor Arcadius, and taken to Constantinople where he was made bishop to the Empress herself. His sermons against corruption in high places earned him powerful enemies.

> *"Worst of all, he won the hostility of the vigorous Empress Eudoxia, by reasons of denunciations of feminine extravagance in dress, which she thought aimed at herself. Chrysostom was certainly as tactless as he was fearless in denouncing offenses in high places."* (*A History of the Christian Church*, p.142)

Chrysostom was sent into exile where he later died in **407 AD**.

Due to the influence of the gospel work by Thomas, the early Armenians were 7th-day Sabbath keepers and kept Saturday as the Sabbath.

> *"The Armenians in Hindustan preserved the Bible in its purity, and their doctrines are, as far as the author knows, the doctrines of the Bible. Besides they maintain the solemn observance of Christian worship, throughout our empire, on the seventh day."*
> (*Christian Researches in Asia*, page 266 {quoted in *Truth Triumphant*, p.318})

The **Armenian Bible** was translated from Greek after **400**. Some claim that Chrysostom is the one who translated this Bible while he was in exile, though this is not certain. There are 1,244 copies of this version still in existence.

Helvidius (**350–420**) was of the church who strove to pass on the pure unadulterated faith of the apostles. He is famous for his exposure of Jerome for using corrupted Greek manuscripts in bringing out his version of the **Latin Vulgate**. Rome has tried to erase all record of Helvidius, and successfully destroyed most historical records of him. If it weren't for the writings of Jerome railing against him, little would be known about him. He was a student of Auxentius who was the bishop of Milan.

> *"Duchesne points out that Auxentius, for twenty years at the head of the diocese of Milan, was from Asia Minor and impressed on those regions the Syrian leadership in Christianity."* (*Truth Triumphant*, p.68)

Auxentius was succeeded as bishop in **374** by Ambrose – who was himself a 7th-day Sabbath keeper.

> *"Ambrose was born in Trier, now in western Germany...about 337-340...He died in **397**."* (*A History of the Christian Church*, p.140-141)

At the Council of Laodicea **365**, the Roman Catholics passed a decree stating that *"Christians must not Judaize by resting on the Sabbath, but must work on that day."*

Sword Unsheathed

While the emperors courted the help of the popes for political reasons, the popes sought the assistance of the emperors to destroy the Christians they claimed were 'Arians.'

Theodosius, the Emperor of the East, in **380**, issued an edict on the issue of the Catholic doctrine of the Trinity which said:

"We order those who follow this law to assume the name of Catholic Christians: we pronounce all others to be mad and foolish, and we order that they bear the ignominious name of heretics....These are to be visited... by the stroke of our own authority..." (Italy and her Invaders, Vol. I, p. 335)

In **381**, Theodosius arranged for a general council of the clergy at Constantinople, which finally established as rule this false Catholic doctrine.

During the 4th century, the Goths, Celts, and Franks had mostly forgotten their days of invasion and their religious quarrels, and were uniting in the bonds of community life. They prized their **Old Latin Bible** (the **Itala**) and it was read publicly in all the churches of Italy, France, Spain, Africa, and Germany, where Latin was understood.

However, because the **Itala Bible** condemned their pagan practices and hierarchical authority, Rome desperately wanted to overthrow it.

Eusebius Sophronius Hieronymus *[Latin]* was born in northeast Italy sometime around **331-345 AD**. He is known better by his English name, Jerome. *(Jerome=Geronimo [Spanish] =Girolamo [Italian])*

Jerome became secretary to Pope Damasus I in **382**. Rome needed some sort of Bible that would wean people off of Lucian's Bible and get them into the Eusebio-Origen Bibles, so the pope commissioned Jerome to "revise" the **Itala** or **Old Latin Bible** so that it would agree with the Alexandrian and Arian theology of Origen and Eusebius and support Rome's pagan corruptions.

In order to properly do his translation work, Jerome moved to Bethlehem where he would have easy access to Eusebius' library in Caesarea and all of manuscripts of Origen. In this library was a copy of the Greek Bible that was made by Eusebius for Constantine and Jerome was able to use it in his translation work.

He didn't follow Eusebius completely because then his work would not be able to compete with Lucian's Bible. He worked to make his **Latin Vulgate** agree as much with Lucian's Bible as he could and yet still keep Eusebius' Origenism.

> *"In preparing the Latin Bible, Jerome would gladly have gone all the way in transmitting to us the corruptions in the text of Eusebius, but he did not dare. Great scholars of the West were already exposing him and the corrupted Greek manuscripts."* (*Our Authorized Bible Vindicated*, p.48)

Jerome finished his Old Testament translation in late **404** or **405**.

> *"Jerome was a rapid and voluminous writer. The translation of Tobit was finished in one day; and the three books of Solomon he calls "the work of three days."* (*Townley's Biblical Literature*, vol. 1, p.135)

Jerome's **Latin Vulgate** was considered "highly acceptable" to Rome, but it was rejected by the Bible-believing Christians.

In **400**, the false doctrine of "eternal security" better known today as "once saved, always saved" was brought into the church, in direct opposition to Biblical texts such as Ezekiel 33:13; Luke 9:62; 2 Peter 3:17; Hebrews 10:38,39; 2 Peter 2:20,21; and Romans 11:17-21.

Jovinian (**330–390**) was another reformer, along with Helvidius, that protested against Rome and her false doctrines. Jovinian also protested against Jerome and his work of corrupting the Latin Bible.

Vigilantius Leo (**364–408**), the "Forerunner of the Reformation," was born in southern France near the Pyrenees Mountains. He was early exposed to both the pure gospel of the true Christians and the corrupt and idolatrous practices of the priests and monks. He not only witnessed the ecclesiastical riots and abominations promoted by the Church of Rome, but also the protests and demand of reform preached by Helvidius, Jovinian, and their associates.

Vigilantius, still trying to understand the difference between the Papal Church and true Christians, determined to pay a visit to Jerome who was at that time living in Palestine. In **396** he went to Palestine to visit Jerome, but was totally disgusted by the error, superstition, and idolatrous lifestyle and attitude of Jerome and the other monks. He returned to Italy and determined to follow the examples of Helvidius and Jovinian and raise his voice in protest against the idolatry of Rome.

> *"'I have seen,' says Jerome, 'that monster called Vigilantius. I tried by quoting passages of Scripture to enchain that infuriated one; but he is gone; he has escaped to that region where King Cottius reigned, between the Alps and the waves of the Adriatic. From thence he has cried out against me, and, ah, wickedness! there he has found bishops who share his crime.'*
> *"This region, where King Cottius reigned, once a part of Cisalpine Gaul, is the precise country of the Waldenses."* (*Short History of the Italian Waldenses*, p.9)

"In the Cottian Alps, in that region lying between the Alps and the Adriatic Sea, Vigilantius first began public efforts to stop the pagan ceremonies that were being baptized into the church. Why did he choose that region?

"Because there he found himself among people who adhered to the teachings of the Scriptures. They had removed to those valleys to escape the armies of Rome."
(*Truth Triumphant*, p.72)

In these mountain valleys, were many descendants from the first Christians in the area. Some of these Christians had fled to this area from Rome after Paul was martyred.

The Vaudois worship secluded in the Alps

"The Vaudois are, in fact, descended from those refugees from Italy who, after St. Paul had there preached the gospel, abandoned their beautiful country and fled, like the woman mentioned in the Apocalypse, to these wild mountains, where they have to this day handed down the gospel from father to son in the same purity and simplicity as it was preached by St. Paul." (*The Glorious Recovery by the Vaudois*, p.xiv)

These original Christians had received their doctrines directly from early apostolic missionaries and their followers like Irenaeus. Their roots extend back to the days of the Apostles. It could be referred to as the Pre-Waldensian Church, and this fact also ties the Waldensians in with the early Christians who populated the area around Milan, Brescia, and the Italic Church from the 1st & 2nd century.

These valley inhabitants were originally called the Vallenses (which literally means "Valley-inhabitants") and this name is the actual origin of the name "Waldenses." The alpine churches of these valleys had not accepted Rome's idolatry and they were fired with enthusiasm at Vigilantius' preaching. This is the recognized origin of the people that would later be referred to as the Waldenses or Vaudois. They also were called Leonists, named after Vigilantius Leo.

"The earliest leader of prominence among the noble Waldenses in northern Italy and southern France is Vigilantius." (*Truth Triumphant*, p.63)

"Long before the time of Peter the Waldo of Lyons, they bore the name of Leonists from one of their teachers, named Leo. But even he is not considered their founder, and some of the present Waldenses believe their origin is in a direct, unbroken line from the primitive Christians. This traditional Leo of the Waldenses is

no other than the famous Vigilantius Leo, or Vigilantius, the Leonist of Lyons..."
(*Short History of the Italian Waldenses*, p.9)

The Waldenses were the true "church in the wilderness" spoken of in Revelation 12:14. *[Vallenses/Waldenses/Vaudois are the names given to those true Christians who inhabited the valleys of the Italian Piedmont and Alps. The name Albigenses is the name given to those true Christians who first settled around Albi and the spread across south-eastern France on the French side of the Alps. There are also inhabitants of the Canton de Vaud in Switzerland who are even today called Vaudois but they were a separate group from the Italian Vaudois.]*

Unfortunately, Rome appears to have succeeded in destroying all the writings of Vigilantius, but because he was associated with Helvidius, Auxentius, Ambrose, and Jovinian, and taught the same doctrines, it is very probable that they were all 7th-day Sabbath keepers.

Evidently, others have also come to this conclusion. *"Since Helvidius and Vigilantius were practically contemporaneous and preachers of the same message, it is safe to conclude that Auxentius, Ambrose, Helvidius, and Vigilantius were Sabbathkeepers."* (*Truth Triumphant*, p.68)

Revelation 12:17 states, *"And the dragon was wroth with the woman, and went to make war with the remnant of her seed, which keep the commandments of God, and have the testimony of Jesus Christ."*

Likewise Rome, in an effort to discredit the Vaudois, has destroyed most of the records of the early beginnings of the Vaudois and their ties to the early Christian church.

"Every scrap of paper, and every book upon which the harpies of oppression could lay their hands, during the various persecutions of the Vaudois, were seized and sent to Turin, and nothing was permitted again to see the light, which did not please the court and the priesthood...Leger, the Vaudois historian of the seventeenth century, declared that there was no artifice, no exertion, no expence [sic] spared by the enemies of his church, both in quiet and troublesome times, to efface all records of the ancient Vaudois from the face of the earth"
(*Waldensian Researches*, p.78)

In the effort to portray herself as the church originating from the apostles, Rome has attempted to portray the Vaudois as a later developed sect in the 12th century (around **1170**). Yet, in spite of all of Rome's efforts to erase the early Vaudois history, there are still bits and pieces of their early history that survive in various places showing that the Vaudois, and not Rome, were the true successors of the apostolic church.

"Thus was the primitive church preserved in the Alps to the very period of the Reformation. The Vaudois are the chain which unites the reformed churches with the first disciples of our Saviour. It is in vain that Popery, renegade from evangelical verities, has a thousand times sought to break this chain; it resists all her efforts. Empires have crumbled – dynasties have fallen – but this chain of scriptural testimony has not been broken, because its strength is not from men, but from God." (*The Israel of the Alps*, Vol.1, p.29)

"The faith which for many centuries was held and taught by the Waldensian Christians was in marked contrast to the false doctrines put forth from Rome. Their religious belief was founded upon the written word of God, the true system of Christianity. But those humble peasants, in their obscure retreats, shut away from the world, and bound to daily toil among their flocks and their vineyards, had not themselves arrived at the truth in opposition to the dogmas and heresies of the apostate church. <u>Theirs was not a faith newly received</u>. Their religious belief was their inheritance from their fathers. <u>They contended for the faith of the apostolic church</u>,—'the faith which was once delivered to the saints.' 'The church in the wilderness,' and not the proud hierarchy enthroned in the world's great capital, was the true church of Christ, the guardian of the treasures of truth which God has committed to his people to be given to the world." (*Great Controversy*, p.64)

The Vaudois were also called *Insabbati*, *Sabati*, and *Inzabbatati Sabotiers* because they kept Saturday, the seventh-day Sabbath, instead of the papal "Sunday," (the first day of the week), with which Rome had "replaced" God's Biblical seventh-day Sabbath.

"For centuries evangelical bodies, especially the Waldenses, were called Insabbati or Ensavates, that is, Insabbatati, because of Sabbathkeeping."
(*Truth Triumphant*, p.228)

"...the term Insabbatati refers to the keeping of the seventh day as the Sabbath." (*Truth Triumphant*, p.252)

Some critics try to contradict this fact by claiming that the term "Insabbati" refers to the Waldensians wearing sandals *(they claim that the word for sandal in Latin is "Sabbatum")*. This is totally a fictitious tale that was produced by Rome's agents to try to hide the Waldensian links to the true Sabbath. The Latin word for sandal is "*sandalum.*" The Latin word for Sabbath is "*Sabbati*" – and even the Catholic **Latin Vulgate** calls the Sabbath "*Sabbati.*"

The Waldenses used the **Itala (Old Latin) Bible** and they made many manuscript copies of it to distribute throughout the land in their missionary efforts. They also used the **Itala** to translate the Bible into the 'Lingua Romana' or Romaunt tongue, which was their native language.

The First Five Hundred Years

One writer tells us that: *"The Waldenses were the first of all the peoples of Europe to obtain a translation of the Scriptures. Hundreds of years before the Reformation, they possessed the entire Bible in manuscript in their native tongue. They had the truth unadulterated, and this rendered them the special objects of hatred and persecution. They declared the Church of Rome to be the apostate Babylon of the Apocalypse, and at the peril of their lives they stood up to resist her corruptions. While, under the pressure of long-continued persecution, some compromised their faith, little by little yielding its distinctive principles, others held fast the truth. Through ages of darkness and apostasy, there were Waldenses who denied the supremacy of Rome, who rejected image worship as idolatry, and who kept the true Sabbath. Under the fiercest tempests of opposition they maintained their faith. Though gashed by the Savoyard spear, and scorched by the Romish fagot, they stood unflinchingly for God's word and his honor. They would not yield one iota of the truth."* (Spirit of Prophecy, vol.4, p.70)

During this time, which parallels the time the church was "in the wilderness," God's Word was "clothed in sackcloth." In Revelation, it was declared thus, *"And I will give power unto my two witnesses, and they shall prophesy a thousand two hundred and threescore days, clothed in sackcloth. These are the two olive trees, and the two candlesticks standing before the God of the earth."* Revelation 11:3,4

Rome extremely hates the unadulterated Bible because it undermines her authority. She has always sought, either directly or through her false theology, to destroy the Bible or, at least, to regulate access to the Word of God. She has done this by burning or destroying it in some way, or by either locking it away from the general public in restricted archives, or by purposely altering it by explaining it "her way" with annotations and commentaries.

False theology crucifies the Scriptures

"Books of the Sacred Scriptures cannot be published unless they have been approved either by the Apostolic See or by the conference of bishops; for their vernacular translations to be published it is required that they likewise be approved by the same authority and also annotated with necessary and sufficient explanations.' These are not the rules of the thirteenth century; they are the present Cannon Law of the Roman Church-State."
(Ecclesiastical Megalomania, p.182)

Jerome's **Latin Vulgate** was considered by the true Christians to be extremely corrupted and they rejected it for almost 1,000 years and continued to use the pure **Itala (Old Latin Vulgate)**.

Sword Unsheathed

> *"The old Latin versions were used longest by the western Christians who would not bow to the authority of Rome – e. g., the Donatists; the Irish in Ireland, Britain, and the Continent; the Albigenses, etc."*
> (Catholic & Protestant Bibles Compared, p. 200 quoted in Our Authorized Bible Vindicated, p.27)

In reality, Jerome's corrupt **Latin Vulgate** was not accepted by the true Christians until around **1280 AD** when Latin began dying out as a commonly understood language.

> *"The Old Latin Vulgate was used by the Christians in the churches of the Waldenses, Gauls, Celts, Albigenses, and other fundamental groups throughout Europe. This Latin version became so used and beloved by orthodox Christians and was in such common use by the common people that it assumed the term "Vulgate" as a name. Vulgate comes from "vulgar" which is the Latin word for "common." It was so esteemed for its faithfulness to the deity of Christ and its accurate reproductions of the originals, that these early Christians let Jerome's Roman Catholic translation "sit on the shelf." Jerome's translation was not used by the true Biblical Christians for almost a millennium after it was translated from corrupted manuscripts by Jerome in 380 A.D. Even then it only came into usage due to the death of Latin as a common language, and the violent, wicked persecutions waged against true believers by Pope Gregory IX during his reign from 1227 to 1242 A.D."*
> (Understandable History of the Bible, p.67-68)

In other words, from about **404** and onward through history, there are two **Latin Vulgate Bibles** – one that is from the pure stream of the **Brixianus** and **Itala**, and one that is from **Jerome's corrupt Vulgate**, the stream based in Alexandrian manuscripts. This is an important point to remember, because in many historical works, reference is sometimes just made to "the **Latin Vulgate**" Bible – so it is important to determine which one is mentioned. As a general rule however, the term "**Vulgate**" today is usually used as a reference to Jerome's corrupted version which later became the standard Bible for the Papal Church. Many people have almost totally forgotten about the pure **Latin (Itala) Bible**.

In **354**, Augustine of Hippo was born in Algeria, Africa. He became a devout Roman Catholic bishop. In his work titled *On Christian Doctrine*, he even admitted to the superiority of the **Itala Bible** of Northern Italy over the other Bible manuscripts.

Augustine

> *"Now among the translations themselves the Italian (Itala) is to be preferred to the others, for it keeps closer to the words without prejudice to clearness of expression."*
> (On Christian Doctrine, Bk. 2, Ch. 15)

However, Augustine of Hippo did not follow the teachings of the **Itala**, as he held to the Manichaeism doctrines and was a follower of neo-Platonism. It was actually Augustine himself who later laid the foundation for the Papal Inquisition.

"Augustine, from his episcopal throne in north Africa, gave to the papacy a deadly weapon; he invented the monstrous doctrine of "Compel them to come in!" Thus he laid the foundation for the Inquisition. Intoxicated with Greek philosophy, he cried out that its spirit filled his soul with incredible fire. He had wandered nine long years in Manichaeism, which taught the union of church and state and exalted the observance of the first day of the week. Augustine found many reasons why the doctrines and practices of the church should be enforced by the sword. The doctrine "Compel them to come in," sent millions to death for no greater crime than refusing to believe in the forms of ecclesiastical worship enforced by the state."
(Truth Triumphant, p.73)

It seems that it was sometime around Augustine's time, that the Papal Church endeavored to change the fourth Commandment of the Law of God, by removing the majority of the text, including the specification that the 7th day was the Sabbath. [see Note I]

Augustine's priests and monks were very efficient at searching out the genuine Bible manuscripts of the true Christians in northern Africa and destroying them. He, and those of his monasteries, also spent much of their time converting the Arabs to Catholicism.

"A striking illustration of Rome's policy toward those who disagree with her was given in the long and bloody persecution of the Waldenses, some of whom were observers of the Sabbath. Others suffered in a similar manner for their fidelity to the fourth commandment. The history of the churches of Ethiopia and Abyssinia is especially significant. Amid the gloom of the Dark Ages, the Christians of Central Africa were lost sight of and forgotten by the world, and for many centuries they enjoyed freedom in the exercise of their faith. But at last Rome learned of their existence, and the emperor of Abyssinia was soon beguiled into an acknowledgment of the pope as the vicar of Christ. Other concessions followed. An edict was issued forbidding the observance of the Sabbath under the severest penalties. But papal tyranny soon became a yoke so galling that the Abyssinians determined to break it from their necks. After a terrible struggle, the Romanists were banished from their dominions, and the ancient faith was restored. The churches rejoiced in their freedom, and they never forgot the lesson they had learned concerning the deception, the fanaticism, and the despotic power of Rome... Upon obtaining supreme power, Rome had trampled upon the Sabbath of God to exalt her own; but the churches of Africa, hidden for nearly a thousand years, did not share in this apostasy. When brought under the sway of Rome, they were forced to set aside the true and exalt the false Sabbath; but no sooner had they regained their independence than they returned to obedience to the fourth commandment."
(Great Controversy, p.578)

Sword Unsheathed

This repulsion of Catholicism from the Christian communities in Africa, began a subtle hatred in the heart of Rome for the Bible-believing Africans.

It is stated: *"...that the court of Rome never forgets or forgives an affront."*
(*History of the Inquisition*, p.150)

This hatred in the heart of Rome would later result in retaliation against the Bible Christians of Africa with the creation of the African Slave Trade in the year **1452 AD**.

During all these first centuries a gulf was growing between the Greek Churches of the East and the Latin Churches of Rome. *"...a deep hatred sprang up between Greek and Latin churches, and Greek and Latin ecclesiastics hurled bitter words at one another. These theological controversies arose because both churches had grown ambitious and had allied themselves with kings and emperors. At length, in 1054, the Greek and Latin churches separated. Long before this the Latin State church feared the effect of the accumulated stores of Greek literature. Latin was made the ecclesiastical language of Western Europe. The Greek language, with its literature, was condemned by Roman ecclesiasticism, its study forbidden, and its writings anathematised."* (*Truth Triumphant*, p.27)

However, down through the medieval centuries, the Celtic church of Ireland remained the center for learning in Greek even while it was banned by Rome and had virtually disappeared from Western Christendom. This division between the western Romish Church and the eastern more apostolic church also helps explain the animosity and war that separated Catholicism and Christian churches in Gaul and the British Isles.

Biblical Christianity and Roman Catholicism can never coexist in peace, for they represent two totally different religions. *"The denial of freedom of religion and liberty of conscience has been the policy of the Roman Church-State whenever it has had the opportunity to put its principles into practice. As we have seen, one of the bases for such a denial is unity."* (*Ecclesiastical Megalomania*, p.178)

Maewyn Succat

A man named Maewyn Succat was born around **360** in Strathclyde, Scotland, to Christian parents. He is better known today by the name of St. Patrick.

His father's name was Calpurnius and his mother was Conchessa. Their Christian faith, the Christian faith that first reached France and England, was from the same lines as the Apostle John who had labored among their brethren in Asia Minor and Galatia, so the Christian faith of that area was of a Greek type originating from Asia Minor rather than the Latin type coming from Rome.

Patrick was kidnapped and taken to Ireland and sold into slavery when he was a teenager. Years later, after gaining his freedom, he returned to Ireland as a missionary in **390**. He helped to organize the Celtic church among the Christians he found already there, as well as worked among the pagans to convert them to Christ. He also established Bible training centers which later grew into colleges and large universities.

Though England and Ireland held to the original faith passed on to them from the Greek church in the east, the language used was Latin, so Patrick and the Celtic church used the **Old Latin Vulgate Bible (Itala)**, which had actually originated from Antioch. In fact, *"For centuries scholars of the Celtic church quoted from the Itala."* (*Truth Triumphant*, p.27)

"'It is just such an account of himself as a missionary of that age, circumstanced like St. Patrick, might be expected to compose...It quotes the ante-Hieronymian Vulgate **[Itala]***, and contains nothing inconsistent with the century in which it professes to have been written.' So far concerning the Confession of St. Patrick."* (*Ireland and the Celtic Church*, p.27-28)

Patrick and his Celtic churches were also keepers of the 7th-day Sabbath. *"...the churches he established in Ireland, as well as the mother church in Scotland and England, followed the apostolic practice of keeping the seventh day Sabbath, and of working on Sunday..."* (*Facts of Faith*, p.137)

Pro-Catholic writers have concocted many fictitious legends and pictures of Patrick to try to make him into a tool of Rome. Rome knew that all "true" knowledge of the conversion of Ireland through Patrick's missionary work had to be suppressed and erased. So Rome concocted numerous fairy tales and legends of a fictitious person named St. Padraig and attributed these fictitious stories and miracles to Patrick.

Rome even sent a counterfeit missionary to the Celtic Church by the name of Palladius in **430** so that they could counterfeit the work of Patrick and ascribe the characteristics of Patrick to the Roman Catholic faith, but Palladius and his papal teachings were not welcomed by the followers of Patrick, and Palladius was forced to leave Ireland.

Fictitious Legends

"About two hundred years after Patrick, papal authors began to tell of a certain Palladius, who was sent in 430 by this same Pope Celestine as a bishop to the Irish. They all admit, however, that he stayed only a short time in Ireland and was compelled to withdraw because of the disrespect which was shown him." (*Truth Triumphant*, p.86)

The historical evidence shows that the "real" Patrick was not connected with the Roman Catholic Church at all, but rather was opposed to its false doctrines, rituals, and superstitions. Patrick was a firm follower and promoter of the true, pure Christianity that had come from Asia Minor and the Apostles – and that was the religion that he preached to the people of Ireland.

It was not until many years later, that the true Christians were driven out and slaughtered by the Papacy, and Catholicism was implanted in Ireland. With the arrival of the Catholic false doctrines and superstitions came the legends and stories about St. Patrick that society erroneously believes to be true today.

The barbaric tribe of the Huns, from about **356–453**, began sweeping west over Europe and invading the areas known today as Hungary, Germany, and northern Italy. This invasion of the Huns from the east, forced the other tribes to push westward conquering other territory for themselves as they were pushed out of their various homelands.

The Ostrogoths (eastern Goths) by **377-453** were established in Pannonia — what is now the modern area known to us as Austria, Slovenia, Croatia, and northeastern Italy.

The Visigoths (western Goths) by **378-403** were established in eastern Spain and the southwest part of Gaul (France).

During these *"dark"* centuries, the Roman Catholic Church had begun to incorporate more and more rites and doctrines from pagan religions into their own practice. They would adopt various pagan practices and simply rename them with supposedly "Christian" names and assign them supposedly "Christian" meanings.

The Mass, as a daily celebration, was incorporated into the Roman Catholic worship service in **394**. The "Mass" is a blasphemous ritual of re-crucifying Christ that is performed by the priests of Rome in contradiction to the testimony of the Word of God that specifically states: *"...the offering of the body of Jesus Christ once for all...he had offered one sacrifice for sins for ever..."* Hebrews 10:10-12

The First Five Hundred Years

The priests make the bold, blasphemous claim that they have the power to command God and force Him to come down and inhabit their little wafer. A former Roman Catholic priest tells us what the Papal Church teaches about the supposed power of her priests: *"Is not the priest the true representative of Christ on earth? In his ordination, is not the priest made the equal, and, in a sense, the superior of Christ? <u>for when he celebrates Mass he commands Christ, and that very Son of God is bound to obey!</u> It is not in the power of Christ to resist the orders of the priest. He must come down from heaven every time the priest orders Him. The priest shuts Him up in the holy tabernacles or takes him out of them, according to his own will."* (Fifty Years in the Church of Rome, p.134-135)

Wafer at Mass

The **Syriac Bible** that was made about **400** is a version of both the Old and New Testaments translated into the Syriac language. It was related to the **Peshitta** and appears to follow the same pure text, although the source language is in doubt, some insisting it was translated by Jews from the Hebrew, and others insisting it was translated by early Christians from the Greek.

The Franks by **407** were established in all of Gaul north and west of the Moselle (northern France, Belgium, southern Netherlands).

The Vandals by **407 AD** were established in the area of North Africa (Morocco, Algeria, Tunisia), with their capital at Carthage.

The Sueves and Alans by **407** were established in western Spain and Portugal.

The Burgundians by **407** were established in west Switzerland and the valleys of the Rhone and Saone in the southeast of Gaul (south-east France, corner of Italy).

With Rome under attack from the barbarian tribes, the emperor withdrew the Roman legions from Britain in **410** and sent them to Rome to help protect it. This left Britain unprotected from invaders and it was overrun by the pagan Anglo-Saxons. The Angles and Saxons, by **449–476**, were established in Britain.

Sword Unsheathed

Nestorius (**386–451**) was born in the city of Germanicia in what is now part of Turkey. He received his religious training in Antioch and lived in this area until he was later promoted and made the Archbishop of Constantinople (**428–431**).

Nestorius was much opposed to Arianism as well as the Roman Catholic referral to Mary as the "God-bearer" since he realized that "God" could not be "born."

In combating these heresies, Nestorius taught that Christ was a conjunction of two separate natures (a divine nature & a human nature) in one person. His teaching on the nature of Christ can be illustrated like this:

Nestorius' enemies, such as Cyril of Alexandria, accused him of teaching that Christ was two different and distinct persons who had merged to form one.

Nestorian Doctrine

"His dogmatic standpoint was essentially that of the school of Antioch; yet he would not admit that there were in Christ two persons – the doctrine with which he was charged. 'With the one name Christ we designate at the same time two natures... The essential characteristics in the nature of the divinity and in the humanity are from all eternity distinguished.'"

(*A History of the Christian Church*, p.145)

Because of Cyril's attacks, Nestorius was excommunicated by Rome and Alexandria and forced into exile for his teachings. His followers were known as Nestorians. The name "Nestorian" was also applied by the Papal Church to many other Christians who did not agree with Rome in other doctrines.

Cyril, the patriarch of Alexandria (**412–444**) and the one instrumental in getting Nestorius exiled, believed that Jesus was not a regular individual man, but rather a human that had obtained divinity. Indeed, *"Cyril, following the Alexandrian tradition, and in consonance with the Greek conception of salvation, saw in Christ the full making divine of the human."* (*A History of the Christian Church*, p.146)

Cyril began the teaching of miaphysitism which many people consider just a type of monophysitism. Miaphysitism (from the Greek mia meaning 'one' and physis meaning 'nature') teaches that both the divine nature and the human nature of Christ were blended into a single nature.

Monophysitism (from the Greek monos meaning 'one' and physis meaning 'nature') teaches that Christ has only one nature – Godlike – and that the "divine nature" and the "human nature" blended into this single divine nature.

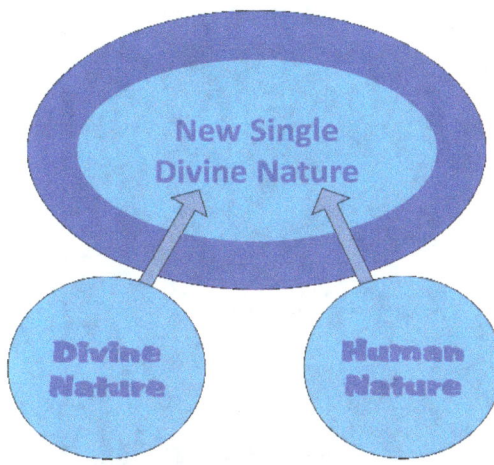

Miaphysite and Monophysite Doctrine

Monophysitism is opposed to the Nestorian position which holds the true doctrine that Christ has two separate and distinct natures, one divine nature and one human nature.

Followers of the inaccurate Monophysite doctrine had several branches – Abyssinians, Copts of Egypt, Jacobites, and Armenians. However, both parties (Monophysites and Nestorians) for some time, continued to observe the 7th-day Sabbath, just like the Church of Antioch did.

The beginning of the exaltation of Mary was in the 5th century. The term "Mother of God" was first applied to her by the third ecumenical Council of Ephesus in **431 AD**. Yet, even Christ himself did not exalt His mother in this way as evidenced by Luke 11:27,28 *"And it came to pass, as he spake these things, a certain woman of the company lifted up her voice, and said unto him, Blessed is the womb that bare thee, and the paps which thou hast sucked. But he said, Yea rather, blessed are they that hear the word of God, and keep it."* That Christ's "physical" family was not to be exalted above others is reiterated in Luke 8:19-21. *"Then came to him his mother and his brethren, and could not come at him for the press. And it was told him by certain which said, Thy mother and thy brethren stand without, desiring to see thee. And he answered and said unto them, My mother and my brethren are these which hear the word of God, and do it."*

Around **433**, the Armenians received the Bible in their own language and it was by this means that they gained their own alphabet.

Exaltation of Mary

As the Goths had moved westward and overtaken other tribes, those tribes had incorporated some of the Gothic language and portions of it were adopted by the Angles and the Saxons into their language which they called "Engle." These different tribes had all originated from the north-central European area, so the languages were very similar to each other. Here was established the cornerstone (so to speak) of the Old English language – the Gothic and Anglo-Saxon.

The Alexandrian manuscript, **Codex Alexandrinus (A)** is an early 5th-century (**400–440**) manuscript of the Greek Bible whose Old Testament is based on **Origen's Septuagint**.

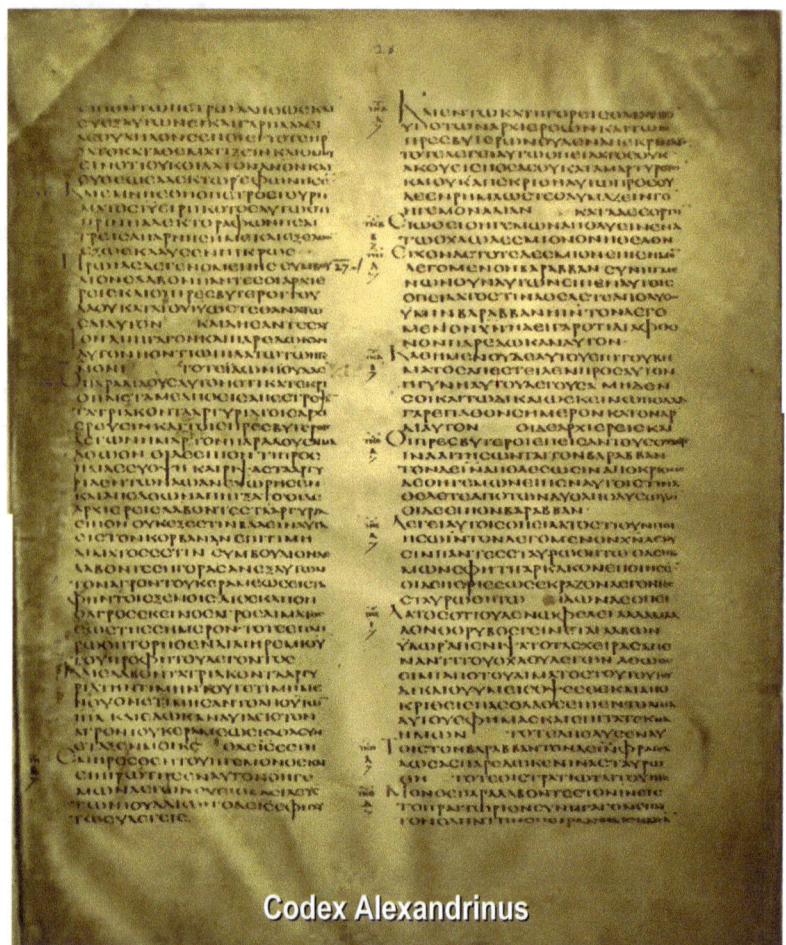

Codex Alexandrinus

While the four gospels of the manuscript do appear to have some Byzantine characteristics, the manuscript appears to be a mixture of good and evil. Because not only are there a number of Alexandrian features also present in the four gospels, but from the beginning of the book of Acts to the end of the manuscript it is all based on and in agreement with the corrupted critical Alexandrian text of the Vatican manuscript.

The **Alexandrinus** manuscript was presented to the patriarch of Alexandria in the 11th century, and kept in Alexandria until it was moved to Constantinople in **1621**. Then it was given to Charles I, King of England, as a gift in **1627**.

The First Five Hundred Years

"Codex Alexandrinus became a basis for criticizing the Textus Receptus."
(Wikipedia - Codex Alexandrinus)

Codex Ephraemi Rescriptus (Codex C) is a palimpsest which was originally written sometime in this period of time (5th century) and was later erased and reused in the 12th century to write treatises composed by Ephrem the Syrian, a prominent bishop of the mid-4th century. It contained parts of several Old Testament books and parts of most of the New Testament books when it was originally written. Some 209 leaves (pages) of the codex are extant today *(145 from the New Testament, 64 from the Old Testament)*. Its New Testament is primarily Alexandrian type text. It is considered sort of an intermediate text between the text of **Vaticanus** and the text of the **Alexandrinus**. In addition, before the discovery of the **Sinaiticus**, it was considered by critical scholars, second only to the **Vaticanus**.

In **451**, Attila the Hun crossed the Rhine and invaded Gaul. In the Battle of the Catalaunian Fields, Attila was defeated and retreated back across the Rhine. The Huns eventually returned east, and the ones that stayed behind in the Western Roman Empire were absorbed into the other tribes.

Also in this year (**451**) the fourth ecumenical council of the Christian church was held, known as the Council of Chalcedon. The council rejected the Monophysite doctrine and, as a result, the Ethiopian Church, the Coptic Church of Egypt, the Jacobite Church of Syria, and the Church of Armenia broke off all connection with Rome.

The Alemanni were established in North Switzerland, Swabia, Alsace, and Lorraine (modern south-western Germany) by **457 AD**.

The Lombards were established in the north of Germany by **453-483** and in Hungary by **526**.

The Heruli, by **476 AD**, were established in Italy. The leader of the Heruli, Flavius Odoacer became the first King of Italy and reigned from **476–493**. His reign marks the end of the Western Roman Empire (**490**).

In **493**, as the Ostrogoths moved into Italy; Odoacer was killed and replaced by Theodoric, the leader of the Ostrogoths, marking the end of the Heruli nation. The remains of the tribe were absorbed into the Ostrogoths.

Odoacer Captures Rome

Sword Unsheathed

Theodoric was known for his stand on what is called, today, religious freedom. He allowed his subjects to hold whatever religious views they desired – letting the Catholics remain Catholic and the Christian Goths to remain Christian.

> *"The whole career of Theodoric was marked with a spirit of tolerance and moderation. The old theory of the Roman law that every citizen might choose his own religion was adopted as best suited to the condition of the people…"*
> (Bible Sourcebook, p.445)

Of Theodoric it is said that, *"…he was favourable to the Orthodox Christians, and always studied to employ himself for the good of his subjects. He was an excellent Prince…"* (Royal Genealogies, p.347)

However, toward the end of his life, Theodoric began to realize that Justinian was trying to overthrow his throne and restore Catholicism as the only religion. This caused him to take a stand firmly against Catholicism.

The conversion of Clovis, king of France, to Catholic Christianity in **496**, basically brought most of the barbarian pagans of the realm into submission to the Christian faith. But when the prominent powers of Europe gave up their attachment to paganism, it was only so they could practice its abominations in the form of Christianized paganism, as it was exhibited in the Roman Catholic Church.

The Burgundians who, around the close of the 5th century, inhabited Switzerland and the south-eastern section of France, refused to bow to the dictates of the Roman Catholic Church. So Clovis was sent by the Papal power to conquer and destroy their power in **524 AD**.

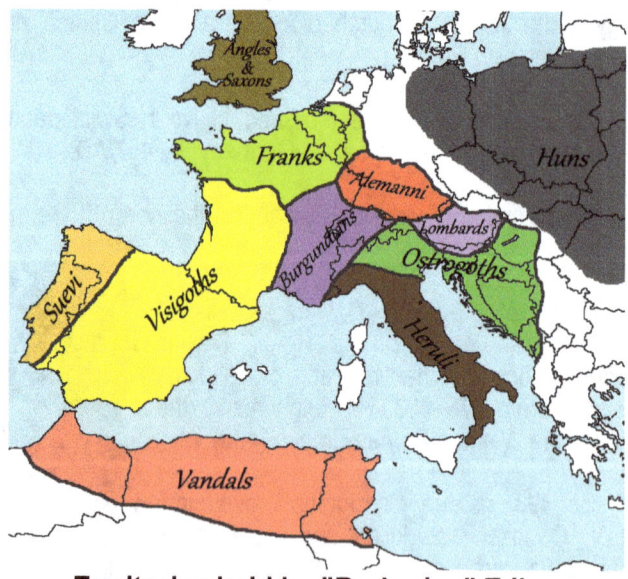

Territories held by "Barbarian" Tribes

From 500 AD to 1000 AD

By the year **508 AD**, paganism had so far declined and Catholicism had increased so much that, for the first time, the Catholic Church was powerful enough to be able to wage a successful war, not only against the pagan civil authority of the empire, but also, against the church of the East in which some had, to a certain degree, embraced the Monophysite doctrine. This war by the Catholic Church resulted in the extermination of 65,000 supposed "heretics" (Rome's definition) and more enslavement to her false doctrines.

In **507**, Clovis had attacked and defeated the Visigoths in the Battle of Vouillé, in which the Visigothic king Alaric was killed. The Visigoths retreated into Septimania which they continued to hold, while Clovis pushed farther into their territory. In **508**, they were completely defeated by Clovis and driven out. For his service, emperor Anastasius gave Clovis the titles and dignity of Roman Patricius and Consul.

This date of **508** marks the *"taking away"* of the *"daily"* (paganism) foretold in Daniel 12:11 in order that the "abomination that maketh desolate" (Papacy) could be set up. This is the beginning of both the 1290 & 1335 time prophecies of Daniel 12.

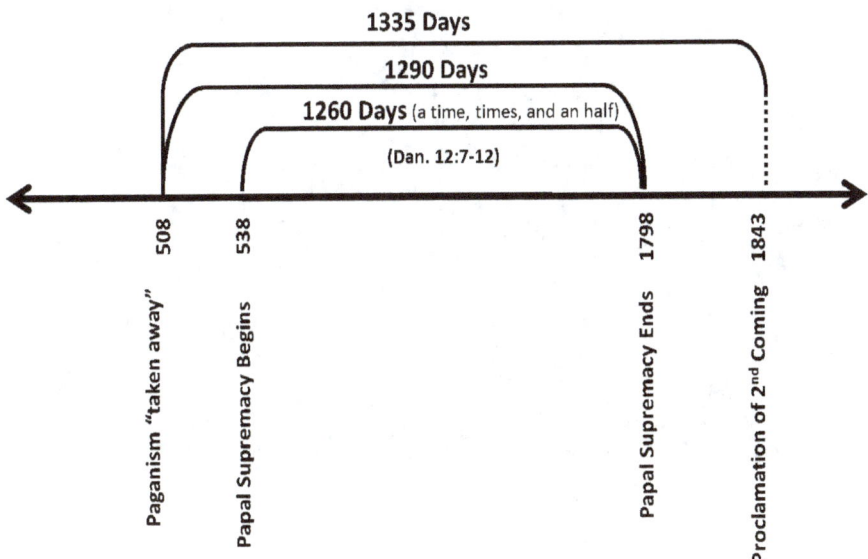

Jacob Baradai (**500-578**) was Bishop of Edessa and organized the Monophysite believers who were opposed to the state-dictated religion and formed the Jacobites.

Sword Unsheathed

The **Codex Argenteus** (Latin for "Silver Book") was written around **520** from the Gothic translation of the Bible that had been done by Ulphilas.

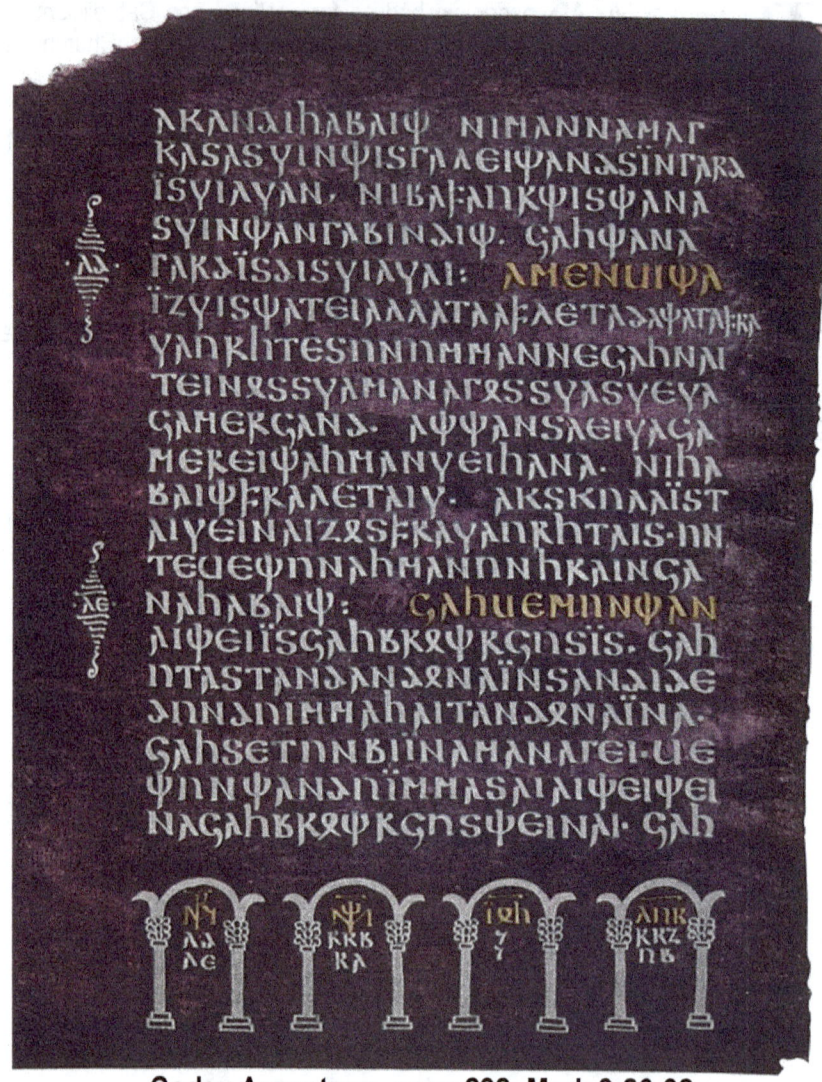

Codex Argenteus, page 292, Mark 3:26-32

The codex gets its name from its silver cover. The old original cover was replaced by a casing of beaten silver in **1668** by Magnus Gabriel De la Gardie, the chancellor of Sweden and Uppsala University.

"The 'Silver Bible' was probably written for the Ostrogothic King Theodoric the Great, either at his royal seat in Ravenna, or in the Po valley or at Brescia."

(Wikipedia - Codex Argenteus)

From 500 AD to 1000 AD

Today, the **Codex Argenteus** is the principle manuscript of the few surviving copies of the Gothic Gospels.

"Of this important version the principal remains are contained in the famous Codex Argenteus, or Silver Book, a MS. Preserved in the library of the University of Upsal, in Sweden. It is impressed, or written, on very fine, thin, smooth vellum, of a quarto form, and purple colour, though some sheets have a pale violet hue; and has received the name of Argenteus, from its silver letters; but the three first lines of the Gospels of St. Luke and St. Mark are impressed with golden foil, as those of St. Matthew and St. John would most probably be found to be, were they still in existence." (*Townley's Biblical Literature*, vol.1, p.118)

"The art of writing in letters of gold was called chrysographia."
(*Townley's Biblical Literature*, vol.1, p.146)

The text of the codex is so amazingly uniform, scholars originally thought that the manuscript had been printed with some sort of a stamp or printing instrument. But there are enough clues that have been discovered, that the scholars now recognize that the **Codex Argenteus** was actually hand written.

Columba, was born in Ireland in **521**. He was trained in one of Patrick's Bible training schools. He was well educated in both Latin and Greek languages, secular and ecclesiastical history, the principals of jurisprudence, the law of nations, the science of medicine, and the law of the mind. He founded a college on the island of Iona (**563**) which has been called "the light of the Western world." His followers held the island for six hundred forty-one years, until they were driven out of it in **1204** by Rome's Benedictine monks.

Columba

"From Ireland came the pious Columba and his colaborers, who, gathering about them the scattered believers on the lonely island of Iona, made this the center of their missionary labors. Among these evangelists was an observer of the Bible Sabbath, and thus this truth was introduced among the people. A school was established at Iona, from which missionaries went out, not only to Scotland and England, but to Germany, Switzerland, and even Italy." (Great Controversy, p.62)

Columba was a keeper of the 7th-day Sabbath and founded over 300 churches in Scotland and Ireland. He used the **Itala** version of the Bible and is credited with having personally produced 300 handwritten copies of the New Testament (to provide each of his churches with their own copy).

Columba taught his followers never to receive as religious truth any doctrine not sustained by proofs drawn from the Sacred Writings. The word "Culdee," meaning "man of God," was later used to designate the Columban churches who had developed from the teachings of Patrick and Columba.

Back on the mainland of Europe, Emperor Justinian passed a decree in **532** that reduced all true and sincere believers in Christ to the direst condition – by ordering that all true Christians embrace the authority of the Catholic Church within three months or be deprived of their homes, land, and possessions. Those who refused to follow Rome were forced to flee from their homes, stripped of their possessions and even their clothes, they were hunted and killed by the Catholic populace and the soldiers that guarded the routes of travel. This set the stage for the persecutions that would follow for the next 1260 years, which are described in Revelation 11.

Justinian

"'They shall prophesy a thousand two hundred and three-score days, clothed in sackcloth.' During the greater part of this period, God's witnesses remained in a state of obscurity. The papal power sought to hide from the people the word of truth, and set before them false witnesses to contradict its testimony. When the Bible was proscribed by religious and secular authority; when its testimony was perverted, and every effort made that men and demons could invent to turn the minds of the people from it; when those who dared proclaim its sacred truths were hunted, betrayed, tortured, buried in dungeon cells, martyred for their faith, or compelled to flee to mountain fastnesses, and to dens and caves of the earth – then the faithful witnesses prophesied in sackcloth." (Great Controversy, p.267)

The kingdom of the Vandals in Africa was conquered by Justinian in **533**. This war was, from beginning to end, avowedly a Catholic war, because the Vandals were opposed to the leadership of the Catholic Church.

With the Vandals subdued, Justinian, in **533**, decided to declare the Pope of Rome to be chief of the whole ecclesiastical body of the empire; thereby deciding the contest which had long existed between the sees of Rome and Constantinople as to which one should have the precedence, and exalting the Pope to the highest position on earth.

However, these provisions of the *Code of Justinian* could not be carried into effect at this time, because the Ostrogoths still held the power in Rome and Italy and they were opposed to the rulership of the pope.

From 500 AD to 1000 AD

Therefore, in order to overthrow the Goths, the Italian War was commenced in **534** by the same army which had conquered the Vandals, and by March of **538**, the Ostrogoths were overthrown and the Papacy was able to take full control.

This date of **538** marks the point when Roman Catholicism became the state religion and the beginning of the 1260 years of Papal supremacy spoken of in Daniel 12:7 & Revelation 11:2-3. [As seen on the chart on pg. 87] This time period of Papal Supremacy (**538–1798**) is what is today generally called the "Dark Ages."

After the *"plucking up"* (Daniel 7:8) of the Ostrogoths, the third and last of the three kingdoms that had been opposed to the Papal Church (Heruli, Vandals, Ostrogoths), the Lombards, led by their King Alboin, removed from their place in Noricum and northern Panmonia in **567–570**, and established their kingdom in Italy.

By **615** many of the Lombards had converted to Catholicism. In the middle ages, Lombardy *"was, indeed, for a time, the name for Italy itself."*
(*Encyclopedia Britannica*, "Lombards")

In **570**, Mohammed was born in Mecca, Saudi Arabia. *"Mahomet the Great Prophet of these Arabians, was born A.D. 570."* (*Royal Genealogies*, p.380)

When Mohammed went to the city of Medina in **622**, (this journey is known as the Hegira), he was accepted as a prophet and the Arabs saw in him the fulfillment of their prophecies.

Mohammed, through some dreams, mystical experiences, and various spiritual exercises, contrived

Mohammed

the idea of a god named "Allah" and the writings of the "Koran." He is considered the founder of Mohammedanism which is now called the religion of Islam.

"The Muslims were strongly influenced by earlier Arabic occultism and alchemy originally derived from Chaldean magic." (*Two Be One*, p.78)

Some of Islam's teachings are also tied with the Jewish Mysticism of the Kabbalah. One researcher expounds, *"Islam is a religion closely related to Judaism but yet so different."* (*Two Be One*, p.147)

Even today, one may find peculiar similarities between the two religions. For example, the most sacred site for the religion of Islam is Mecca, where the followers of Islam bow down, placing their forehead on the ground in ritualistic prayer to a large "black box" shrine known as the "Ka'ba" in their worship of their false god "Allah."

Sword Unsheathed

Likewise, the Jewish traditions also involve "black boxes" called Tefillin or phylacteries, that are worn on their foreheads while they go through ritualistic prayers.

Hence, one might find it quite striking that the Islamic names "Ka'ba" and "Allah" added together form the name of the "Kabbalah" of Jewish Mysticism. In addition, if the Hebrew letters for the name "Jehovah" are taken and rotated upside down and the letters are pressed together, it forms the Arabic word "Allah."

Shortly after his death, some of Muhammad's writings were compiled by his followers to form the *Koran*, the holy book of Islam.

As the Arabs grew in power, they began invading the Christian and Catholic countries of Europe, planning to conquer the whole world for their false god Allah.

Turkish Warrior

"Damascus fell in 635, Jerusalem and Antioch in 638, Alexandria in 641. In 651, the Persian kingdom was brought to an end. By 711, the Mohammedan flood crossed the Strait of Gibraltar into Spain, bringing the Visigothic monarchy to a close, and swept forward into France, where its progress was permanently checked by the Franks, under Charles Martel, in the great battle of 732, between Tours and Poitiers. In the East, Constantinople successfully resisted it, in 672-678, and again in 717-718. Syria, Egypt, and North Africa were permanently taken by the Mohammedans."

(*A History of the Christian Church*, p.160)

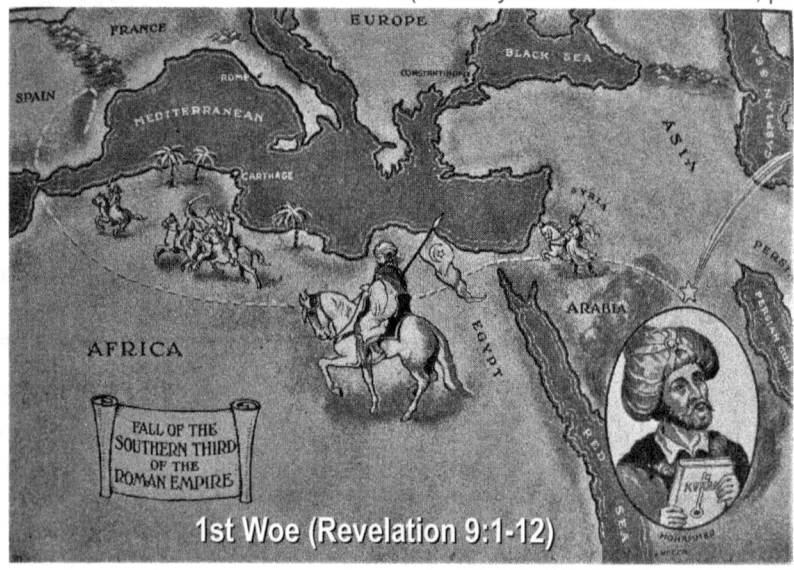

From 500 AD to 1000 AD

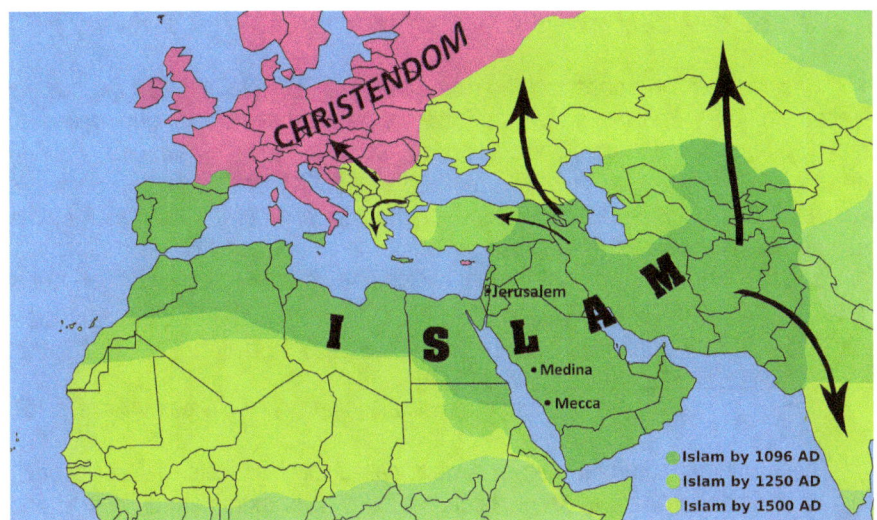

To battle the invading hordes of Mohammedans, the Vatican raised up armies from the Catholic countries of Europe, and sent them to go fight the Arabs in order to protect the papal possessions of Europe.

These wars were known in history as the "Crusades" and they lasted from **1096** to **1487**.

Though Islam has appeared, on the surface, to be an opposing force to Papal "Christianity" ever since its beginnings, yet, as will be shown later, Rome has used the invasions of the armies of Islam to act as a "diversion" in the political world, to draw the attention of the various nations away from what Rome herself was doing in the background.

Implements of the Crusades

Cassiodorus (**490–585**) was a Roman statesman and chief minister and literary adviser of Amalasuntha, Queen of the Ostrogoths. When Cassiodorus retired, he *"founded a monastery named Vivarium, to perpetuate the culture of Rome. Neither a great writer nor scholar, he collected manuscripts, enjoining his monks to copy pagan as well as Christian authors…"*   (Encyclopedia Britannica, "Cassiodorus")

Cassiodorus was instrumental in using **Jerome's Latin Vulgate** and **Origen's Septuagint** (which they erroneously call the "Greek original") to corrupt the **Old Latin (Italic) version**. History attests to forgeries, on this, and many other occasions.

> *"Forgery ran rampant all through the Middle Ages…all practitioners of forgery had the benefit of clergy…The great forgers were the monks."*
> (*The Roman Catholic Church and the Bible*, p.11)

Sword Unsheathed

We are told, *"Ancient writings were forged by monks."* (*Great Controversy*, p.56)

"Cassiodorus, who observed the dissimilarity still existing between the original Greek and Latin translation, which Pope Damasus had in vain undertaken to remedy by publishing a more correct version, took a more effectual mode of curing the evil. Calling in the aid of the Greek original [LXX], and taking St. Jerome's version as its best interpreter, he undertook the correction of the Old Italick by the Vulgate and Greek. And the method in which he performed this task effectually removed the dissimilarity between them, which had so obstinately continued to his times. <u>The monks who were employed in this work, were commanded to erase the words of the former translation, and to substitute those of the latter; taking due pains to make the new writing resemble the old.</u>"

(*Inquiry into the Integrity of the Greek Vulgate*, p.16)

These various corrupted versions were called the Pandects of Cassiodorus. This is an important fact to know, because today, it is extremely difficult to find manuscripts of the original **Italic (Old Latin) Bible** that the Waldensians used. Many of the ones that were located by the writer in the process of researching Bible history, were discovered, in some places, to be in agreement with Jerome's corrupt **Latin Vulgate**. The writer didn't understand why, until it was realized that they were not the originals, but rather some of the corrupted copies that Cassiodorus had made (even counterfeiting the ancient writing style of the old ones)!

In other words, the reader should understand that there are basically two types of **Vetus Italica** manuscripts in existence today – the originals which were from the pure stream, and the corrupted counterfeits from the stream of error!

Origen's invention of Purgatory, an intermediate step on the way to hell, was established as official Roman Catholic doctrine by Pope Gregory in the year **593 AD**.

Augustine (of Canterbury) [*some references just call him Austin*] was a Benedictine monk in Rome. In **595 AD**, Pope Gregory the Great chose him to take 40 monks and lead the 'Gregorian mission' to Britain to convert and *"Christianize"* King Ethelbert and his Kingdom of Kent from Anglo-Saxon paganism to Roman Catholicism. In this endeavor, Augustine was successful. This year marked the beginning of Catholicism in Britain.

However, Pope Gregory's real motive for this mission was to bring the Irish-Scotch (Celtic) church, which had been free from Rome, into subjection to the papal chair.

Augustine

From 500 AD to 1000 AD

To accomplish this, Augustine in **601**, with the help of Bertha, the new Catholic wife of King Ethelbert of Kent, immediately began war on the Celtic Church in Wales and Scotland. He demanded submission of the Celtic Church and addressed the leader of the Celts in these words:

"Acknowledge the authority of the Bishop of Rome."

The Celtic Church meekly replied, *"...he is not entitled to call himself the father of fathers, and the only submission we can render him is that which we owe to every Christian."* (History of the Reformation, p.684)

To this bold stand against the authority of Rome, Augustine hotly replied,

"If you will not have peace from your brethren, you shall have war from your enemies; if you will not preach life to the Saxons, you shall receive death at their hands." (Facts of Faith, p.139)

Augustine then instigated Ethelfrid, the pagan king of Northumbria, to send 50,000 warriors into the Celtic communities where they massacred in cold blood the 1,250 unarmed Celtic pastors and bishops, burned the halls, colleges, and churches and destroyed their libraries and manuscripts.

This 'master stroke' of Rome was a great blow to the native Christians. With their university, their colleges, their teaching pastors, and their ancient manuscripts gone, the Britons were greatly handicapped in their struggle against the aggression of Rome.

The title of "pope," or universal bishop, was given to Boniface III, by the emperor Phocas in **607**.

It was during this time (the 7th century) that the common Aramaic language of the Eastern Church merged into its sister language of Arabic as the Moslems overran the Middle Eastern countries.

Beda Venerabilis (**673–735**) commonly known as the Venerable Bede, was a Roman Catholic historian who wrote many well-known works. Though he was a devout Catholic, his writings are used by many authors today, including Protestants, to confirm events and dates of early Christian history.

Venerable Beade

In **742**, Charlemagne was born. He was to become the greatest Carolingian monarch of the Carolingian Dynasty (western Europe).

The second Council of Nicaea, held in the year **786**, instituted the Roman Catholic doctrines on the worship of the cross, the veneration of images, and the worship of relics. This was accomplished by totally removing the second Commandment from the Law of God, and then, to still preserve the number ten, they divided the tenth Commandment in half and made it both the ninth and tenth Commandments. [see Note 1]

These false doctrines were incorporated into the Roman Catholic faith from the teachings of paganism.

"The Church borrowed her symbols from paganism...Every article of dress, every ornament or accessory used by the Pope, either in his ecclesiastical functions or his duties as sovereign of his temporal possessions, has a special meaning...Cardinal Newman tells us the Church adopted 'the very instruments and appendages of demon worship.'" (Trail of the Serpent, p.135)

The *Donation of Constantine* is a 8th century forgery of a Roman decree supposedly by which emperor Constantine the Great in the 4th century, transferred all the authority over the Roman Empire to the Pope. This forgery was later used, especially in the 13th century, to support the papacy's claims of political authority.

On **December 25, 800**, pope Leo III crowned Charlemagne the Holy Roman Emperor. This act revealed that the Pope rejected the legitimacy of Empress Irene of Constantinople. This created even more tension between the church of the East and Rome in the west and eventually led to the crisis in **1054** when "medieval Christianity" split into two branches.

Charlemagne issued a series of legislative or administrative acts which are known as *Carolingian Capitularies*. In his ecclesiastical capitularies he attempted, among other things, to enforce Sunday worship with various Sunday regulations.

"The legislation of the Carolingian Capitularies is favorable to the clergy, to monasteries, to the cause of good morals and religion. The marriage tie is protected, even among slaves; the license of divorce restrained; divorced persons are forbidden to marry again during the life-time of the other party. The observance of Sunday is enjoined for the special benefit of the laboring classes. Ecclesiastical discipline is enforced by penal laws in cases of gross sins such as incest."
(History of the Christian Church, vol.4, p.392)

Charlemagne's *Capitularies* later gave influence to King Æthelstan's Sunday Laws in England.

"King Æthelstan appears to have been the first to attempt widening the scope of prohibited Sunday activities after the fashion of Carolingian Capitularies. Cap. 24.I of II Æthelstan, an ordinance assigned conventionally to the years 926-30, banned Sunday markets with a penalty of loss of goods and a fine of thirty shillings." (Old English Penitenials and Anglo-Saxon Law, p.106)

From 500 AD to 1000 AD

Claude, bishop of Turin, was a New Testament Christian that opposed the idolatry of Rome and in **820–839** set to work to destroy the image worship and idolatry from the churches in his area. The Vallenses of the Cottian Alps agreed with him, but Rome accused him of perpetuating the heresies of Vigilantius. This fact implies that he was also teaching many of the same Biblical truths that Vigilantius had also taught.

During the 1260 year period of the "Dark Ages," whenever the fourth commandment of God's Law was given its proper place, it was always because of the work of Sabbathkeepers, like the Vallenses (Waldenses) and Albigenses, of the Church in the Wilderness with their **Itala** Bible.

The Waldenses taught, *"that when a preacher advanced any doctrine which he did not prove from the Old and New Testaments, such preaching ought to be regarded as false;"* (*Townley's Biblical Literature*, vol.1, p.300)

About this same time, in the year **831**, a book was published called *"De Corpore et Sanguine Domini" (On the Body and Blood of Christ)*. It was written by Paschasius Radbertus, and in this book the blasphemous doctrine of Transubstantiation was first publicly promoted. Transubstantiation is the concept in the Romish theology, that the bread and wine in the Eucharist are converted into the actual real body and blood of Christ at the mass. Protestantism, in accordance with Scripture, rejects such theology and considers that the bread and grape juice are only symbolic representations.

"The principle on which transubstantiation was founded is unquestionably a Babylonian principle, but there is no evidence that that principle was applied in the way in which it has been by the Papacy. Certain it is, that we have evidence that no such wafer-god as the Papacy worships was ever worshipped in Pagan Rome. 'Was any man ever so mad,' says Cicero, who himself was a Roman augur and a priest 'was any man ever so mad as to take that which he feeds on for a god.' Cicero could not have said this if anything like wafer-worship had been established in Rome. But what was too absurd for Pagan Romans is no absurdity at all for the Pope. The host, or consecrated wafer, is the great god of the Romish Church. ...The Chaldean priests pretended, by their magic spells, in like manner, to bring down their divinities into their statues, so that their 'real presence' should be visibly manifested in them. This they called 'the making of gods;' and from this no doubt comes the blasphemous saying of the Popish priests, that they have power 'to create their Creator.' ...the doctrine of transubstantiation is clearly of the very essence of Magic..." (*The Two Babylons*, p.254-259)

In the year **864**, the king and nation of Bulgaria was converted to Christianity by Greek missionaries from the east, who had angered Rome by translating the Bible from the original Greek manuscripts instead of Rome's corrupted **Latin Vulgate**.

In other words, Bulgaria was originally converted to the Greek/Byzantine type of Christianity, not to Roman Catholic "Christianity."

Pope Nicholas I (**858–867**) was determined to gain control of Bulgaria, and bring the Bulgaria under the authority of the Papal Church. But instead, history records, *"Pope Nicholas I, in the ninth century, sent the ruling prince of Bulgaria a long document elucidating political, territorial, and ecclesiastical questions, and saying in it that one is to cease from work on Sunday, but not on the Sabbath. The head of the Greek Church, offended at the interference of the Papacy, declared the pope excommunicated."* (*Truth Triumphant*, p.223)

It is thought that sometime in the early part of the 10th century, the manuscript of the **Damascus Pentateuch** was written. It is an almost complete codex of the Pentateuch (the first five books of the OT). It is one of the oldest extant Bible codices, but it is a mixture, as its writer around 52% of the time follows the Ben Asher style of vowel marks, and around 46% of the time they follow the Ben Naphtali style of vowel marks.

Aaron Ben Moses Ben Asher (more commonly known as just Ben Asher) was a Rabbinic Jew who lived in Tiberias in the first half of the tenth century (died in **960**). He was a Masorete who supposedly wrote the Hebrew manuscript known as the **Codex Cairensis** in 895.

This codex is considered the oldest dated Hebrew Codex of the Bible in existence today. It contains the complete text of the books of Joshua, Judges, Samuel, Kings, Isaiah, Jeremiah, Ezekiel and the book of the twelve Minor Prophets. However, this manuscript has recently been proven to be, not from Ben Asher in the 9th or 10th century, but rather from some other source in the 11th century time period.

Codex Cairensis

In 916, the **Codex Babylonicus Petropolitanus (V^p)** was written. It is a Masoretic manuscript of Hebrew Bible books of Isaiah, Jeremiah, Ezekiel, and the Minor Prophets. Also known as the Petersburg Codex of the Prophets, it is kept in St. Petersburg, Russia, and it is considered one of the oldest Hebrew Bible manuscripts. The manuscript shows the Babylonian vowel pointing system and uses the Eastern signs, yet its consonantal text follows the Western tradition.

In **927**, the **Codex Complutensis I** manuscript was written. It is a Latin Bible, with much of the text following Jerome's **Latin Vulgate**, although some parts of the Old Testament appear to come from the **Old Latin** instead. It also contains Apocryphal books. It was used in **1517**, by Cardinal Ximenes, in editing the **Complutensian Polyglot**.

Around **930**, the **Aleppo Codex** was copied (produced) by the scribe named Shlomo ben Buya'a and verified, vocalized, and notated by Rabbi Aaron Ben Asher. It is considered the only known true representative of the Ben Asher text. The **Aleppo Codex** was stored in Aleppo, Syria from **1375** until **1947** when in the midst of riots, the synagogue that housed it was burned and the **Aleppo Codex** mysteriously disappeared. When it resurfaced 10 years later no more than 294 of the original 487 pages had survived. Many modern critical editions of the Bible are based on the **Aleppo Codex**.

During these earlier centuries, the "Old English" language was gradually changing into "Middle English." As it broadened and grew, it began incorporating Scandinavian, French, and Latin words into its vocabulary. By **987**, the frequent invasions of the Danes (Vikings) from Denmark and surrounding areas, had added 1,000 Scandinavian words to the English language.

Scandinavian Words

Awe
Trust
Dirt
Law
Call
Race
Skin
Aloft
Happy
Gift
Want

Cutting Edge Facts: Building Faith in God's Word

Many historical figures are identified in the pages of God's Word. Conservative lists include more than 100 biblical characters that can be conclusively identified within secular history.

Here are three (of many) Old Testament figures who are easily identified by secular historical sources:

Shishak, pharaoh of Egypt, is mentioned in 1 Kings 11:40 and 14:25. There are numerous inscriptions and historical records for this pharaoh. The record of his campaign against Palestine (dated as **924 or 925 BC**) is inscribed on the exterior south wall of the temple of Amun at Karnak in Thebes, and it conforms to the biblical account. There is no doubt about authenticity.

Hophra, another pharaoh of Egypt, is mentioned in Jeremiah 44:30. History confirms that he was indeed the pharaoh of Egypt during the time of the prophet Jeremiah and King Nebuchadnezzar of Babylon. Hophra's defeat by Nebuchadnezzar in **572 BC** and subsequent replacement by a general named Ahmes are confirmed in Babylonian records.

Cyrus, King of Persia, is mentioned in 2 Chronicles 26:22, 23; Multiple times in Ezra 1,3,4, 5, 6; Isaiah 44:28; 45:1, Daniel 1:21;6:28 and 10:1 History confirms the **Cyrus'** reign. There is even an artifact called the Cyrus Cylinder. History confirms that Cyrus conquered Babylon in just the way God said he would.

The New Testament has its own list of historical characters, such as: Luke 3:1,2 mentions **Tiberius Caesar**, **Pontius Pilate**, **Herod**, his brother **Philip**, **Annas** and **Caiaphas** in connection with the beginning of John the Baptist's preaching, which introduced Jesus Christ.

Tiberius is found on numerous Roman coins and lived from **42 BC to AD 37**. **Herod the tetrarch of Galilee** and his brother **Philip, the tetrarch of Iturea**, are mentioned by Josephus, the famous Jewish historian of the 1st century.

There is a stone inscription dedicated to **Pontius Pilate** that reads: "Pontius Pilate, prefect of Judea." In archaeology, it is called the Pilate Stone, and it is in the Israel Museum in Jerusalem.

Annas and **Caiaphas** are both mentioned by Josephus as being among the Jewish high priests of the 1st century.

From 1000 AD to 1600 AD

The **Leningrad Codex** (or **Codex Leningradensis [B19a] or [L]**) is dated about **1008–1009** according to its colophon and it is the oldest complete manuscript of the Hebrew Bible in Hebrew, using the Masoretic text and Tiberian vocalization, that is still in existence today. It originated in Cairo by copying from manuscripts of Ben Asher, but there are numerous alterations and erasures to the text, leading to the realization that it could not have been copied by a good Masorete. Scholars have used the **Aleppo Codex** to correct the **Leningrad Codex**.

Over the years, there were many forgeries being produced by Rome to promote Rome's authority. *"For seven centuries, the Greeks had called Rome the home of forgeries. Whenever they tried talking with Rome, the popes brought out forged documents, even papal additions to Council documents, which the Greeks, naturally, had never seen. Gregory went way beyond the Donation of Constantine. He had a whole school of forgers under his very nose, turning out document after document, with the papal seal of approval, to cater for his every need."*
(*Vicars of Christ, The Dark Side of the Papacy*, p.59)

In **1054**, the Greek patriarch, Michael Cerulanius, and another learned Greek monk, both attacked the Roman Catholic Church on a number of points, including fasting on the Sabbath. In retaliation, the Papal Church excommunicated the entire Eastern Greek Church. This split between the Eastern Orthodox Church and the Roman Catholic Church of Rome became known as the East-West Schism (or Great Schism) of **1054**.

With the Eastern Church problem finally removed for the time being, the pope turned his vengeance on the followers of Islam and the Waldensian Christians in Northern Italy.

In **1066**, the French Normans invaded Britain and over the next couple hundred years, some 10,000 French words were added to the English language.

The Papal Mass, begun in the 4th century and intimately connected with the falsehood of transubstantiation, developed gradually, changing from an overly excessive display of communion to a complete sacrifice itself.

"One searches the Holy Scriptures in vain to find mention of the liturgy of the mass. The objects which the Roman Catholic Church deems necessary in the performance of the mass are foreign to the word of God, for Christ made no such ostentatious display." (*The Wine of Roman Babylon*, p.60)

Attendance at mass was obligatory by the 11th century and in **1090**, Peter the

Sword Unsheathed

Hermit invented the Rosary, a mechanical praying with beads. Many other deceptions followed, as the Papal Church continued to "rewrite history" to portray herself as a legitimate power.

"This instant method of inventing history was marvellously successful, especially as the forgeries were at once inserted into canon law. By innumerable subtle changes, they made Catholicism seem changeless. They turned 'today' into 'always was and always will be', which even now, contrary to the findings of history, is the peculiar stamp of Catholicism."
(*Vicars of Christ, The Dark Side of the Papacy*, p.59)

With the Mohammedans invading Palestine, Pope Urban II summoned all kings, princes, bishops, and abbots to seize the sword and start for Palestine in **AD 1096**.

As previously mentioned, while Rome kept Europe's attention sidetracked (focused on the Crusades and conquering the Turkish invaders) - Rome persuaded mobs to attack the Albigenses in southern France. *"When pilgrims, returning from Jerusalem and the scenes of our Saviour's journeyings, told the pitiful stories of Moslem cruelties upon Christians, more fuel was added to the fire. The Vatican sent its agents up and down the land to inflame them to crush the Mohammedans and magnify the leadership of the Roman Catholic Church. In less than a century and a half there was the crushing defeat of four Crusades. In the midst of these, Rome aroused the mob and rabble under bloodthirsty swashbucklers to destroy the beautiful civilization of the Albigenses in southern France."* (*Truth Triumphant*, p.227)

In other words, Rome used the issue of "Islam" as a decoy (diversionary tactic) so that the nations of Europe would not realize what Rome was doing to the true Christians behind the scenes. [Because the Bible states that history repeats itself (Ecclesiastes 1:9), it is the writer's belief that Rome will again use the issue of "Islam" as a diversionary tactic while they set events in motion to destroy true Christians.]

Nicolaus von Amsdorf (**1483–1565**), the Lutheran theologian and personal friend of Luther, wrote: *"He (the Antichrist) will be revealed and come to naught before the last day, so that every man shall comprehend and recognize that the pope is the real, true Antichrist and not the vicar of Christ.....Therefore those who consider the pope and his bishops as Christian shepherds and bishops are deeply in error, but even more are those who believe that the Turk is the Antichrist. Because the Turk rules outside of the church and does not sit in the holy place, nor does he seek to bear the name of Christ but is an open antagonist of Christ and His church. This does not need to be revealed, but it is clear and evident because he persecutes Christians openly and not as the pope does, secretly under the form of godliness."* "Nicolaus von Amsdorf, Fürnemliche und gewisse Zeichen," sig. A2r.,v.
(*The Prophetic Faith of Our Fathers*, vol. 2, p.305)

From 1000 AD to 1600 AD

In **1104**, Peter de Bruys, a youth born in a Waldensian valley on the French side of the Alps, with the fire of the gospel in his heart, began his work of spreading true Christianity to southern France.

Peter de Bruys was finally apprehended by his Papal enemies and burned at the stake in **1124**. Peter's followers were labeled by Papal Rome as Petrobrusians and Rome falsely accused them of believing in the doctrines of Manichaeism. But according to the records that their enemies recorded of them, their doctrines were opposite of the doctrines of the Manichaeism religion.

Vaudois with the Bible

"The Vaudois churches, in their purity and simplicity, resembled the church of apostolic times. Rejecting the supremacy of the pope and prelate, they held the Bible as the only supreme, infallible authority."
(The Great Controversy, p.68)

"But the Petrobrusians, so far from denying that Christ had a material body, are actually said to have alleged, in their third point of doctrine, that it was the height of absurdity to adore the instrument on which the Lord was so horribly tortured and so cruelly put to death. Hence, assuredly, according to the testimony of their very enemies, Bruis and his disciples could, by no possibility, have been Manicheans."
(History of the Ancient Vallenses and Albigenses, p.177)

This was solely the false accusations of Rome, but some history books even today, continue to promote these false Papal claims. The Petrobrussians real beliefs were the same Biblical beliefs as the Waldenses.

"The leading tenets professed by his followers, the Petrobrussians, as we learn from the accusations of their enemies, were that baptism avails not without faith; that Christ is only spiritually present in the Sacrament; that prayers and alms profit not dead men; that purgatory is a mere invention; and that the Church is not made up of cemented stones, but of believing men. This identifies them, in their religious creed, with the Waldenses..." (History of Protestantism, vol.1, p.50)

Henry of Lausanne was a disciple of Peter de Bruys and carried on his work of carrying true Christianity to Europe. Henry's arch enemy was Bernard, the abbot of Clairvaux. Bernard was a devout Papist and a relentless persecutor.

In **1119**, Pope Calixtus assembled a council at Toulouse, France, and excommunicated the sect of heretics in those parts who were believers in

Sword Unsheathed

the teachings of Peter de Bruys and Henry of Lausanne. Pope Innocent II held a council at Pisa, Italy, in **1134**, to condemn as heresy all the doctrines taught by Henry.

During this time, Arnold of Brescia was openly denouncing the overgrown empire of ecclesiastical tyranny of Rome. Arnold had the makings of both an evangelist and a military general and his hometown of Brescia was a city with an independent spirit like Milan and Turin. It was from this city that the beautiful **Brixianus manuscript** comes.

Arnold did what the other reformers had failed to do – he attacked the union of Church and State. In **1139**, Arnold was forced to flee from Brescia to Switzerland. Later, he helped to temporarily expel the pope from the city of Rome and to establish a separate civil government instead of one controlled by the church. But when the pope and the emperor leagued together against Arnold, his friends and supporters deserted him and he was driven out of Rome and finally captured, killed, and burned.

Arnold is considered one of the 'spiritual fathers' of the Vaudois people and his teaching of the need for separation of Church and State powers was later taken up by the Protestant Reformation.

Arnold of Brescia

"Arnold had been burned to ashes, but the movement he had inaugurated was not extinguished by his martyrdom. The men of his times had condemned his cause; it was destined, nevertheless, seven centuries afterwards, to receive the favourable and all but unanimous verdict of Europe. Every succeeding Reformer and patriot took up his cry for a separation between the spiritual and the temporal..."
(*History of Protestantism*, vol.1, p.54)

Around **1070**, Malcolm III, king of Scotland, married Margaret of Wessex, a stanch Roman Catholic.

Margaret determined to conquer the Celtic 7th-day Sabbath-keeping church and destroy the faith that Columba had instilled in that country. She called an ecclesiastical congress and using her husband's position to her advantage, uniting Church and State – she demanded that the Celtic church submit to and acknowledge the Papal Church, and abandon their 7th-day Sabbath in favor of the Papal Sunday worship.

From 1000 AD to 1600 AD

"They worked on Sunday, but kept Saturday in a sabbatical manner....These things Margaret abolished." (*Facts of Faith*, p.141)

Through Margaret's influence on her son David, who became king of Scotland, the Christians lands were later confiscated and they were given the ultimatum that they conform to the rites of the Sunday-keeping monks or be expelled from Scotland. They chose to be expelled in **1130**.

In **1119**, the secret order of the Knights Templars was established to, supposedly, guard pilgrims traveling to the Holy Land.

"This was an establishment of armed monks, who made a vow of living, at the same time, both as anchorets and soldiers."
(*Townley's Biblical Literature*, vol.1, p.209)

In the year **1155**, Henry II, King of England, was commissioned by Pope Adrian IV to wage war on Ireland to bring the Irish into submission to the Church of Rome.

Around **1160–1170**, Peter Waldo, a wealthy merchant of Lyons, France, gave away all his goods and began to preach the genuine doctrines of the New Testament. Waldo declared the papacy to be the "man of sin," and the beast of the Apocalypse.

Peter Waldo devoted much of his time to the translation and distribution of the Bible.

Peter Waldo © Alexander Hoernigk (via Wikimedia Commons)

Peter Waldo is the individual commonly credited, in modern Catholic-influenced history books, with starting the Waldenses – although, as has been shown, Peter Waldo was only one in a long line of Vaudois leaders – the Vaudois existed long before Waldo's time.

"They were properly the descendants of the Cathari, or Puritans, who arose in the church some centuries earlier than the time of Peter Valdo, or Waldo, to whom, by a mistake originating in the similarity of names, the rise of this sect has usually been attributed." (*Townley's Biblical Literature*, vol.1, p.298)

"...it is absolutely false, that these Churches were ever founded by Peter Waldo...we must needs conclude it a pure forgery...that Waldo ought to be considered as the founder of them."
(*Ecclesiastical History of the Ancient Churches of the Piedmont*, p.192)

Sword Unsheathed

"In the close of the eleventh and beginning of the twelfth century, the Waldenses, called Albigenses in France, had several public and official writings, ... which contain such exhibitions of Bible truth, as will convince the intelligent reader that these were not then infant churches. In the Twelfth century, through the exertions of Bruys, Henry, Waldo, Arnold, and others, the Waldenses were not only much extended in France and Italy, but entered England, Germany and Bohemia."

(History of the Waldenses, Vol. 1, p.v)

"Roman Catholic writers try to evade the apostolic origin of the Waldenses, so as to make it appear that the Roman is the only apostolic church, and that all others are later novelties. And for this reason they try to make out that the Waldenses originated with Peter Waldo of the twelfth century." (Facts of Faith, p.119-120)

In **1179**, the third Lateran Council held in the Lateran Palace in Rome, refused to recognize the Waldensians as Christians. The council assured Papal "Christians" that if they would join the war against the heretics, if they were killed in the fight they would receive full forgiveness of their sins. This is where the bloody Inquisition "first raised its evil head!"

In **1180**, the **French Provencal (Romaunt)** version of the Bible was translated by Peter Waldo from the **Old Itala Bible.**

"He [Waldo] rendered an important service to the cause of reform, by procuring, at his own expense and under his supervision, a translation of the New Testament into the Romaunt tongue, then the vernacular of Southern France. This was the first complete translation of the Scriptures into any of the languages of medieval Europe, and was the only one available for popular use."

(1888 Great Controversy, Biographical Notes, p.693)

"<u>This Romaunt version was the first complete and literal translation of the New Testament of Holy Scripture</u>; it was made, as Dr. Gilly, by a chain of proofs, shows, most probably under the superintendence and at the expense of Peter Waldo of Lyons, not later than 1180, and so is older than any complete version in German, French, Italian, Spanish, or English. This version was widely spread in the south of France, and in the cities of Lombardy. It was in common use among the Waldenses of Piedmont, and it was no small part, doubtless, of the testimony borne to truth by these mountaineers to preserve and circulate it. Of the Romaunt New Testament six copies have come down to our day. A copy is preserved at each of the four following places: Lyons, Grenoble, Zurich, Dublin; and two copies at Paris. <u>These are small, plain, and portable volumes</u>, contrasting with those splendid and ponderous folios of the Latin Vulgate, penned in characters of gold and silver, richly illuminated, their bindings decorated with gems, inviting admiration rather than study, and unfitted by their size and splendour for the use of the people."

(History of Protestantism, vol.1, p.29)

From 1000 AD to 1600 AD

These **Itala**-based **Romaunt Bibles** are small, plain, and portable, revealing that they were designed for missionary work. Yet, the hand-copied manuscripts are beautifully and uniquely penned, showing the value the Waldensians placed on God's Word.

"Princes have persecuted me without a cause: but my heart standeth in awe of thy word." Psalm 119:161

Paris MS 7268

Grenoble MS 488

Even though the Papal persecutions managed to destroy most of these Waldensian Bibles, according to Baptist researcher Dr. David Cloud, there are actually seven copies of this Waldensian Bible that have survived up to today. One in the Cambridge University Library, one in the Old Library at Trinity College in Dublin, two copies in the Bibliotheque de Roi of Paris, one in Lyons, one in Grenoble, and one at Zurich.

Romaunt Bible Zurich MS

These **Romaunt Bibles** were used by the Waldensians to translate into the other languages (like Dutch, German, etc.) of the various people groups to which they were missionaries. In languages like Dutch, they not only translated the Bible, they even turned the scriptures into poetry (which would help the people to learn it better).

**Romaunt Bible
Paris MS 8086**

Paris MS 6833

"They turned the holy Scriptures, which the Clergy had taken from the people, and which Waldo had before translated into French, into Low-Dutch Rhimes, according to the custom of those Ages, and in imitation of those of the old Teutons, who were used to record their most memorable affairs in verse."

(*History of the Reformation in the Low Countries*, vol.1, p.14)

In contrast with the conscientious Waldensians who, at the peril of their lives, guarded and transmitted the Holy Scriptures, the Knights Templars were far more interested in learning the forbidden knowledge of the Sages and ancient Magi and using that secret knowledge to acquire wealth, than they were even in guarding pilgrims to the Holy Land.

"After the Moslems seized Jerusalem in 1187, a group of Templars returned to Europe and began to use their esoteric knowledge to amass a great deal of wealth. They soon became the central bankers of Europe, and both the Catholic Church and the monarchies began borrowing from them."

(*Brotherhood of Darkness*, p.125)

From 1000 AD to 1600 AD

This secret order of the Templars was, supposedly, later demolished in the 14th century, but in reality, they just changed their name and blended with other secret societies such as Freemasonry, Knights Hospitallers, and later, with the Jesuits.

"It must be remembered that Masonic Templary, then, is a revival of the old organization in which every Templar was a priest in the Church. Protestants do not realize that in going through the various grades of Masonry, they are being indoctrinated into Catholicism, they are being led on a parallel path." (*Trail of the Serpent*, p.89)

The Holy Office of the Inquisition was officially instituted by the Council of Verona in **1184**. It used intrigue, torture, and murder to attempt to stamp out the supposed "heresy" of people who believed differently than the Papal Church.

The Papal Church also began the practice of selling Indulgences (supposed forgiveness of sins) in **1190**.

In **1209**, King John of England was excommunicated by Pope Innocent III, for refusing to acknowledge the pope's choice for the position of Archbishop of Canterbury. In order to repent and again gain the support of the pope, King John signed a Charter in **1213**.

"...he signed a Charter, whereby he resigned to the Pope the Kingdom of England, and the Lordthip (sic) [Lordship] *of Ireland....From that moment he acknowledged himself a Vassal of the Holy See, and,...he agreed, that if himself, or any of his Successors, denied the submission due to the a Holy See, he should forfeit his right to the Crown."* (*The History of England*, Vol. 1, p.272)

This **1213** Charter surrendered England and Ireland to the pope and Rome. It also stipulated that the rulers of England would pay Rome a certain sum each year for the privilege of reigning on the throne; and that should anyone ever violate the terms of this Charter, ownership of the throne and the Crown of England would automatically revert back to the Vatican.

But then, in **1215**, King John himself violated the charter by signing the Magna Carta (Great Charter). The Magna Carta is one of the most important documents in history. Not only did it establish the principle that everyone is subject to the law, even the king, and guarantee the rights of individuals, the right to justice and the right to a fair trial – its signing also violated the previous Charter and by default, surrendered the Crown of England and Ireland to the Vatican. To demonstrate to England that the pope now held the ruling power of England, Innocent III annulled the Magna Carta.

"...he annulled and abrogated the Charter, declaring all its obligations and guarantees void." (*History of Protestantism*, Vol. 1, p.68)

Sword Unsheathed

The Papacy has, to this day, never given up this authority, and the Vatican is still the legal power ruling Great Britain. Apparently, the Royal Family are allowed as - figureheads to fool the general populace. When in **1982**, Pope John Paul II kissed the ground at the airport in England and then he and the Archbishop of Canterbury knelt at the spot of the murder of Archbishop Thomas Becket, it was a secret sign, recognized by the insiders, that the Papacy still rules Great Britain.

In **1215**, the Fourth Lateran Council, promoted anti-Semitism by commanding that all Jews had to wear a distinctive ensign and they were not allowed to hold any public office. This council also imposed on every member of the church the solemn discipline of confessing their sins at least once a year – showing that Rome believed that with the stroke of a pen, she could control the consciences of the people. It was also at this council that the doctrine of Transubstantiation was officially incorporated by Pope Innocent III.

Pope Innocent III also instituted the Franciscans for the purpose of restoring the reputation of the Papal Church.

"The order of Franciscans was instituted by Innocent III in the year 1215, and the Dominicans were sanctioned by his successor Honorius III a few years later (1218). The object of their institution was to recover by means of their humility, poverty, and apostolic zeal, the credit which had been lost to the Church through the pride, wealth, and indolence of the elder monks." (History of Protestantism, vol.1, p.78)

The city of Toulouse in southern France is a good example of how certain communities held fast to the doctrines of the apostles from the early days of Christianity until they aroused the fury of an exterminating crusade. Toulouse was blamed for being not only the breeding place of so-called heresy, but it also successfully housed rejecters of Rome throughout the centuries, first in the days of Gothic Christianity, and later in times of the Albigenses and Waldenses.

In the years **1208-1218**, Rome waged a bloody crusade against this Christian city and destroyed the beautiful Albigensian civilization. Then, at the Catholic Councils of Toulouse in **1229** and Tarragona in **1233**, the Bible was forbidden to laymen and common people, not just of France, but also of Spain and Northern Italy.

"The infamous council of Toulouse, held in the year 1229, by Romanus, cardinal of St. Angelo, and the pope's legate, formed the first courts of Inquisition, and published the first canon which forbade the Scriptures to the laity."
(Townley's Biblical Literature, vol.1, p.351)

"Almost 800 years ago at the Council of Toulouse in 1229, we find that the Catholic Church said: 'We prohibit also that the laity should be permitted to have the books of the Old or the New Testament....'" (Billy Graham and His Friends, p.418)

From 1000 AD to 1600 AD

Christians were demanded to hand over all their Bibles to authorities, which in the common man's language, was "to the ecclesiastical authorities." Most of the Bibles thus surrendered, were burned in the flames. Years later, the pure Bible was placed on the Papal Church's *Index of Forbidden Books*.

Through the centuries, from the time of Ulfilas and his Gothic Bible, the English language had spread and developed through the addition of Scandinavian and French to the Gothic and Anglo-Saxon Engle (English). During the 14th and 15th centuries, many Latin words were also added to the growing Middle English language making it a very "rich" language!

All through the "Dark Ages," the Waldenses were continually sending out missionaries from their valleys to all parts of Europe.

"Their missionaries were everywhere, proclaiming the simple truths of Christianity, and stirring the hearts of men to their very depths. In Hungary, in Bohemia, in France, in England, in Scotland, as well as in Italy, they were working with tremendous, though silent power." (*Cross and Crown*, p.32)

Around **1315**, a Waldensian pastor named Raynard Lollard (Sometimes called Lollardo), introduced the Bible teachings of the Waldenses into England.

"Lollardo, who was in great Reputation amongst the Evangelical Churches of Piemont, by reason of a Commentary that he made upon the Revelation: As also for having conveyed the knowledge of their Doctrine into England, where his Disciples were known by the name of Lollards."
(*History of the Evangelical Churches of the Valleys of the Piemont*, Book 1, p.184)

"Lollard, who paved the way for Wycliffe in England, was a missionary from these Valleys." (*Cross and Crown*, p.32)

John Wycliffe

John Wycliffe (**1320-1384**), was known as the "morning star of the Reformation." He gathered the different partial copies of the Old English Bibles which had previously been translated from the **Latin Vulgate** (Psalms, New Testaments, etc.) together along with the other English writings about the Bible, and using these and the **Latin Bible**, he translated the whole Bible into the Middle English of his day.

When at last Wycliffe's work was completed, it was the first complete English translation of the Bible ever made.

"The word of God was opened to England… He had placed in the hands of the English people a light which should never be extinguished. In giving the Bible to his countrymen, he had done more to break the fetters of ignorance and vice, more to liberate and elevate his country, than was ever achieved by the most brilliant victories on fields of battle." (The Great Controversy, p. 88)

The work indeed fulfilled Wycliffe's words to the papists, when previously, they had gathered around what they thought would be his death-bed waiting for a recantation – instead, he said with emphasis, *"I shall not die, but live; and again declare the evil deeds of the friars."* (History of the Reformation, Vol. 5, Bk. 17, Chptr. 7)

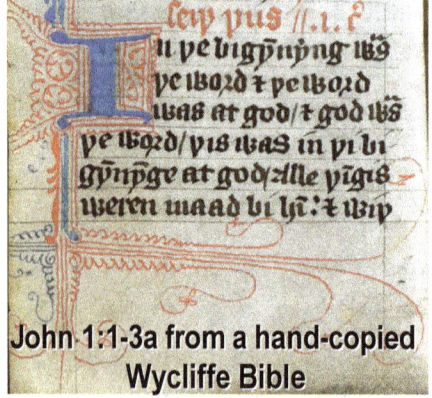

John 1:1-3a from a hand-copied Wycliffe Bible

The **Wycliffe Bible** went through two editions — the Early Edition in **1382** and the Later Edition, published after his death by his assistant, John Purvey, in **1395**.

Alas, though Wycliffe put his all into the translation project at hand, he could not read the Greek & Hebrew of the original manuscripts, and so the Bible manuscript that he had at hand to work with was **Jerome's corrupt Latin Vulgate.**

"Wycliffe's Bible had been translated from the Latin text, which contained many errors." (Great Controversy, p.245)

"Wickliffe was ignorant indeed of Greek and Hebrew; but was it nothing to shake off the dust which for ages had covered the Latin Bible, and to translate it into English? He was a good Latin scholar, of sound understanding, and great penetration; but above all he loved the Bible, he understood it, and desired to communicate this treasure to others." (History of the Reformation, vol.5 book 17, ch.8)

One such mistake transferred from the **Vulgate** is the use of the word "penance" in Matthew 3:1,2. *"In tho daies Joon Baptist cam, and prechide in the desert of Judee, and seide, Do ye penaunce, for the kyngdom of heuenes shal neiye."* (**KJV** - *"In those days came John the Baptist, preaching in the wilderness of Judaea, And saying, Repent ye: for the kingdom of heaven is at hand."* Matthew 3:1,2)

Though there were admittedly errors that were ignorantly incorporated into **Wycliffe's Bible** from **Jerome's Latin Vulgate**, Wycliffe was a Reformer ahead of his time. Surprisingly, there are not as many errors as one might expect under the circumstances, nor even as many differences as are found in some modern translations.

From 1000 AD to 1600 AD

Indeed, God blessed, and Rome cursed, Wycliffe's efforts to provide the Bible to the people in their own language. No longer could Rome keep the Bible "hidden" from the common man by disguising it in an unknown language. Because of this, Rome hated Wycliffe for translating the Bible into the Middle English of the people.

"No sooner had Wicliff completed his translation, and made it public, than he experienced the most violent opposition. The translation of the Scriptures into the vernacular tongue was accounted heresy, and regarded as a measure fraught with the direst ills." (*Townley's Biblical Literature*, vol.1, p.444)

To show their contempt for Wycliffe and what he had done, Rome had his bones dug up over 40 years after his death. They then burned them, and threw the ashes into a stream.

Wycliffe with Lollards

"The bitter feeling and hostility of the See of Rome did not end with Wycliffe's death, but by a decree of the Council of Constance his remains were disinterred in 1428, then burnt and the ashes cast into the Swift, a streamlet which runs by Lutterworth."
(*The Gothic and Anglo-Saxon Gospels*, p.xxi)

Because Wycliffe's teachings were, in essence, the exact same as those of Lollard before him, those who adhered to the teachings of Wycliffe were also labeled by Rome as Lollards.

"Wiclif's followers were called Lollards, from a German term, signifying to sing hymns to God; and increased so rapidly, that a contemporary writer affirms, "A man could not meet two people on the road, but one of them was a disciple of Wiclif." (*Townley's Biblical Literature*, vol.1, p.456)

Many of Wycliffe's followers were later burned at the stake or slaughtered by various other means. Yet, this time period marks the dawn of new beginnings that would spread and grow into the Protestant Reformation. It was a mighty movement, much like the departure of the children of Israel from the land of Egypt. It rejected the supremacy of the pope, and liberated practically all of northern Europe from the control of the papacy.

"The Reformation, with its rediscovery of the Bible and Christianity, which had been buried for a thousand years beneath the superstition, pageantry, preserved paganism, and corruption of the Roman Church-State, ended the rampant religious superstition of the Middle Ages and elevated the mores of societies and individuals far above those of the Middle Ages." (*Ecclesiastical Megalomania*, p.74)

Sword Unsheathed

John Huss

In **1365**, Jerome of Prague was born. He became a fellow Protestant reformer with John Huss, who was born about **1371**.

The **Tepl Bible** was translated in **1389**. It was named the **Tepl Bible** because it originated in, or was at least discovered in Tepl, Bohemia. It was a New Testament translation of the old Waldensian **Itala Bible** into an old German dialect which was spoken before the days of the Reformation.

"At Tepel, in Bohemia, has been found a Codex of the New Testament, in which the text in ancient German, too, but which is undoubtedly Waldensian in its marginal notes and comments. The size is very small (56:85 mm) as the Waldensian Missionary loved it, to be able to hide it easily."
(Assault on the Remnant, p.120)

The Tepl Bible was based on the **Itala** and **Brixianus** and its extremely small size shows it to be one of the Bibles translated by the Waldensians to carry with them in their travels. The Waldenses made it a habit not only to have the Bible in their possession, but also to hide it in their hearts. They often would sew portions of the Bible into their clothing where it would be hidden, but they also committed vast portions of the Bible to memory.

The Size of the Tepl New Testament

"Reinerius, who was a Roman Catholic writer, and an inquisitor, acknowledges that he saw and heard a peasant recite the book of Job by heart; and that there were others among them who could perfectly repeat the whole New Testament."
(Townley's Biblical Literature, vol.1, p.301)

In the middle of winter in **1400**, Borelli, a papal inquisitor, led an army into the Waldensian valley of Pragelas and slaughtered the inhabitants. Those who escaped had to flee over the mountain passes in the drifting snows and the majority of them died from the exposure.

"In Bohemia, Huss and Jerome were, in their labour, animated by the writings of Wycliffe, so that the light of truth, which the Papacy had quenched in the "Vallies" was flaring up in England and Bohemia." (Facts of Faith, p.147)

From 1000 AD to 1600 AD

In **1407**, an outspoken opponent of Wycliffe's teachings, Thomas Arundel, presided at a synod held at Oxford. This synod passed a number of constitutions to regulate preaching and Bible translation.

"The seventh Constitution began thus: 'Tis a dangerous undertaking, as St. Jerome assures us, to translate the Holy Scriptures. We therefore decree and ordain,' it continued, 'that from hence-forward no unauthorised person shall translate any part of Holy Scripture into English, or any other language, under any form of book or treatise. Neither shall any such book, treatise, or version, made either in Wicliffe's time or since, be read, either in whole or in part, publicly or privately, under the penalty of the greater excommunication, till the said translation shall be approved either by the bishop of the diocese or a provincial council, as occasion shall require.'" (History of Protestantism, vol.1, p.362)

In **1415**, Huss was burned at the stake for heresy. This act temporarily frightened his fellow Reformer, Jerome, who recanted his beliefs. But then, after struggling with a guilty conscience, and finding, like others that recanted, *"that the fires which remorse kindles in the soul are sharper than those which the persecutor kindles to consume the body,"* he withdrew his recantation and followed Huss to the stake.

"After Huss was burned, July 6, 1415, and Jerome, May 30, 1416, their work of reform was carried on by their followers." (Facts of Faith, p.148)

These followers of Huss and Jerome were from Bohemia and Moravia and they became known as the Hussites, the Moravian Brethren, and the Unity of the Brethren. Many of them were also 7th-day Sabbath keepers. *"Bishop A. Grimelund of Norway speaks of them as 'the anciently arisen, but later vanished sect of Sabbatarians in Bohemia, Moravia, and Hungary.'"* (Facts of Faith, p.149)

In **1438-1439**, the Council at Farrara and Florence declared the non-scriptural Papal doctrine of "Purgatory" as dogma.

In **1448**, Pope Nicholas V brought to the Vatican the ancient Bible manuscript now known as the **Vaticanus**. It was supposedly dated to around **362**, but had been lost for over 1000 years. It is said, *"Of the history of this MS. before the sixteenth century nothing is certainly known."* (An Introduction to the Old Testament in Greek, p.127) However, evidence suggests that the **Codex Vaticanus** is actually one of Constantine's 50 lost Eusebius/Origen Bibles.

For hundreds of years the Papal Church guarded the **Vaticanus** manuscript so closely that no Protestant scholar was allowed to examine it, and anyone who was allowed to look at it was searched to make sure that they didn't have any paper or ink in which they could copy any of it. If they were observed to be looking too long at any specific text, the manuscript was snatched away by papal attendants. It was not until **1866** that Tischendorf was allowed to copy it under very close supervision.

Sword Unsheathed

The **Vaticanus** manuscript is in exceptionally good condition for its age, and true to most Papal Bibles, the Vaticanus contains the Apocryphal books intermingled among the canonical books. Yet strangely enough, even though its pages are in such good condition, the manuscript is missing quite a lot of information!

The **Vaticanus** is missing the first 45 chapters of Genesis and most of the 46th chapter as well as Psalms 105:27-137:6b, 2 Kings 2:5-7, 10-13, Matthew 16:2-3; 1 & 2 Timothy, Titus, Philemon; Hebrews 9:14– 13:25; and the entire book of Revelation. Also when considering the four Gospels alone, it leaves out many words, clauses, and even whole sentences.

Printing Press

Johannes Gutenburg is credited with inventing the printing press in Mentz, Germany in **1450**, although this history is questioned. He shared his concepts with a goldsmith named Fust and persuaded him to advance him large sums of money to begin production. The first book to ever be printed on it was **Jerome's Latin Vulgate Bible**.

Printing Gains Popularity in Europe

"The expenses incurred by this publication were so considerable, that Fust instituted a suit against Gutenberg; who was obliged to pay interest, and also part of the capital advanced. In consequence of this suit the partnership was dissolved; and the whole of Gutenberg's printing apparatus fell into the hands of Fust. But Gutenberg was not to be discouraged from following his pursuits: he established a new press, and continued to exercise his art until 1465...After the separation between Gutenberg and Fust, which took place in 1455, Fust began to print on his own account..."
(*Townley's Biblical Literature*, vol.1, p.478)

When Mentz was sacked and plundered by the Archbishop Adolphus in **1462**, Fust's workmen became dispersed, and they carried the news of the invention of printing into nearly every country in Europe, and the art of printing quickly gained popularity and began to flood Europe with books.

True to Rome's habit of never forgetting what others had done to them, on **June 18, 1452**, in retaliation against the Biblical Sabbath-keeping Christians

From 1000 AD to 1600 AD

in Africa, pope Nicholas V issued his papal bull titled *Dum Diversas*, which gave the king of Portugal the command to subjugate the enemies of the Roman Catholic Church.

> *"...we grant to you full and free power, through the Apostolic authority by this edict, to invade, conquer, fight, subjugate the Saracens and pagans, and other infidels and other enemies of Christ...and to lead their persons in perpetual Servitude..."* (*Dum Diversas* [English Translation])

This papal bull began the Portuguese slave trade from West Africa.

> *"From the earliest times the Roman Church advocated human slavery. In the Middle Ages, when feudal slavery flourished, the church fattened on the exploitation of the serfs who were bought and sold with the land...In short, serfdom was the basis of the wealth of the papacy."* (*Assassination of Abraham Lincoln*, p.82)

> *"From its inception until the twentieth century, the Roman Catholic Church has endorsed slavery."* (*Ecclesiastical Megalomania*, p.136)

It is an important principle to remember:

> *"...Rome never slumbers nor sleeps. Rome never forgets. For successive years and even centuries she plans and secretly works out the accomplishment by any means in her power."* (*The Dignity of Man*, p.155)

In **1453**, the Muslim Turks captured Constantinople and many of the Greek scholars fled to the West, bringing with them their valuable manuscripts from the East where Christianity had originated. God used this invasion of Constantinople as a means to open to Western Europe the empire's libraries with their thousands of eastern manuscripts.

For nearly a thousand years the ecclesiastical power seated in Rome had outlawed and eliminated the study of Greek language and Greek literature, and held Western Europe in the darkness of ignorance, but with the fall of Constantinople and the newly discovered art of printing, the nations lying west of Constantinople awoke from the sleep of centuries of papal *Dark Ages*.

It was then that Greek and Hebrew learning revived in the West. With this influx from the East came also the **Syrian Bible** which was used by the early church at Antioch in Syria (Acts 11:26) and which had been translated directly from the original Hebrew and Greek manuscripts long before the **Massoretic text (OT)**, was even compiled.

Entry into Constantinople

Sword Unsheathed

Verily, *"The manuscripts of the Hebrew and Greek Scriptures have been preserved through the ages by a miracle of God."* (EGW Letter 32-February 14, 1899)

On **January 5, 1455** the pope issued to the king of Portugal another papal bull, *Romanus Pontifex*, which besides sanctifying the seizure of non-Catholic lands, also encouraged the enslavement of native, non-Catholic peoples in both Africa and the New World.

In **1466**, the German **Mentel Bible** was published in Strasbourg. This edition was a literal translation based on a fourteenth-century manuscript translation of the **Latin Vulgate** – which today, no longer exists.

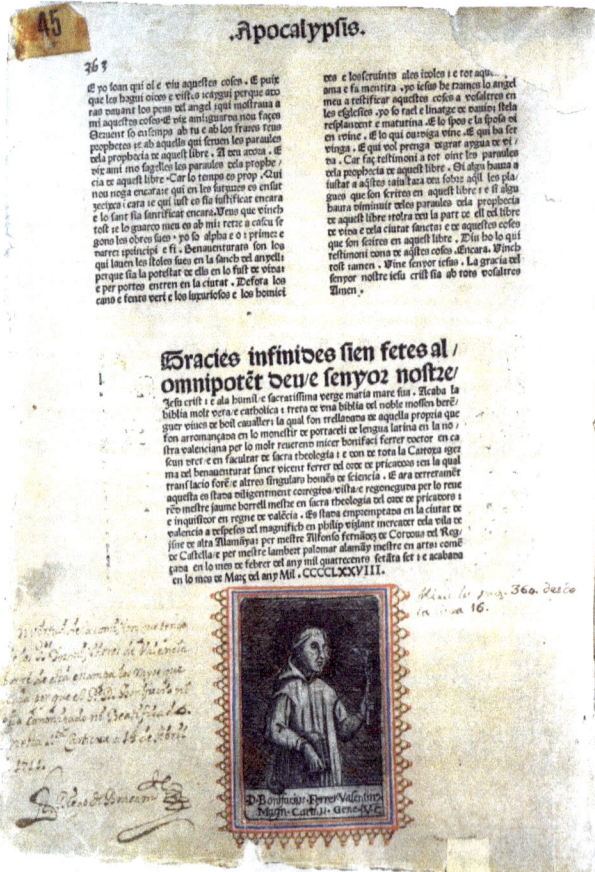

One of the only known existing pages of the Valencian Bible

In the year **1478**, the Spanish Inquisition was started. During this same year, Bonifacio Ferrera published the Spanish **Valencia Bible**. But since his Bible, like the **Wycliffe Bible** put the Bible into the language of the common people, it was proscribed by the papists. Almost all of the copies were burned, and thus there is very little evidence left of this Bible.

In the year **1483**, Martin Luther was born in Eisleben, Germany.

In **1487 AD** Pope Innocent VIII issued a papal bull for the extermination of the Vaudois people. This persecution continued on until **1532 AD**.

Indeed, it has been expressed, *"The papacy sanctions murder; the avowed defender and promoter of the papacy is necessarily involved in that sanction... No man defends the papacy who has not accommodated*

From 1000 AD to 1600 AD

his conscience to the idea of assassination."   (*Ecclesiastical Megalomania*, p.113)

Jacob ben Chayyim was born about **1470**. He was a Masoretic scholar and a Jewish Rabbi who converted to Christianity. He compiled textual notes on the Hebrew Bible, and compiled many ancient manuscripts of the Bible. He had a profound acquaintance with the Masora and rabbinical learning.

In **1488**, the first complete Hebrew Bible was printed on a printing press by a Jewish printer, Joshua Soncino and his nephews, Moses and Gershom Mose in Soncino, Lombardy (Italy).

In **1484**, a Portuguese nobleman of very high standing named Cristóbal Colón (commonly known today as Christopher Columbus) defected to Spain. However, some evidence shows that he was actually connected with the Knights Templar order and that his "defection" was simply a story to confuse the Spanish so that he could begin to work as a "double agent," getting the Spanish government to trust him as one of their own.

Whatever is the real version of Colón's history, the fact remains that he was to play an important role in bringing the western hemisphere into the knowledge of the eastern world.

In **1490**, Torquemada, the Inquisitor-General, burned more than 6,000 volumes and many Hebrew Bibles in an Auto-da-fe at Salamanca.

In **1491**, Inigo Lopez de Recalde was born in the castle of Loyola in the providence of Guipuzcoa, Spain. He later Romanized his name to Ignatius Loyola.

In **1492**, Colón sailed west and landed in the "New World" which would later become known as North and South America.

In **1494**, Gerson Mose of Soncino printed a second complete Hebrew Bible at Brescia.

Ignatius Loyola

"At the close of the fifteenth century there were in Bohemia and Moravia about two hundred churches of the 'Brethren,' who rejected all connection with the Roman church and had their own ministers and bishops..."   (*Facts of Faith*, p.148)

In **1501**, pope Alexander VI published his bull *Index Librorum Prohibitorum* censuring the printing of books unapproved by the Papacy.

Sword Unsheathed

"Having been informed that, by means of the said art, [of printing,] many books and treatises, containing various errors and pernicious doctrines, even hostile to the holy Christian religion, have been printed...and being desirous, without further delay, to put a stop to this detestable evil; – we...strictly forbid all printers, their servants, and those exercising the art of printing under them, in any manner whatsoever...under pain of excommunication, and a pecuniary fine,...to print hereafter any books, treatises, or writings, until they have consulted on this subject the arch bishops, vicars, or officials,...and obtained their special and express license, to be granted free of all expense; whose consciences we charge, that before they grant any license of this kind, they will carefully examine, or cause to be examined, by able and Catholic persons, the works to be printed; and that they will take the utmost care that nothing may be printed wicked and scandalous, or contrary to the orthodox faith." (*Townley's Biblical Literature*, vol.1, p.494)

At this point, a great movement to publish Bibles began to form. Within only 36 years (**1500-1536**) hundreds of Bibles in various languages would be rolling from the presses.

"...no fewer than five hundred and sixty-eight editions of the entire Scriptures, or portions of them, in different languages, printed in the space of thirty-six years; thus preparing the way for that most happy Reformation, and that increased circulation of the word of God, which so soon followed."
(*Townley's Biblical Literature*, vol.2, p.153)

Around this time, the Portuguese considered themselves to be the nation chosen by destiny to be the emissaries of the pope.

Vasco Da Gama

In **1502**, Vasco Da Gama led an expedition to India, with 20 armed ships and plenty of soldiers and Roman Catholic priests to enforce Catholicism on the conquered people. On the way, they ran into a ship filled with Muslim pilgrims returning from Mecca. Da Gama forced the pilgrims to pay a huge ransom to redeem their lives, but then he ordered their ship set on fire. The pilgrims managed to extinguish the fire, but Da Gama then returned and set the ship on fire again, killing all the men, women, and children aboard.

Da Gama then proceeded on to India, and massacred whole towns there. As they invaded India, they encountered many Christian communities which were established by the Apostle Thomas or his converts. These Christians were using the **Syriac Bible** from Antioch. These Christians would later be persecuted and brought under the control of Rome when the Jesuits arrived in the **1540**'s.

From 1000 AD to 1600 AD

Desiderius Erasmus was born in **1466** and died in **1536** at the age of seventy. Erasmus spent his life, from the time he was a child, studying the ancient manuscripts and, as some have said, "devouring libraries."

Erasmus

He came to Cambridge as professor of Greek in **1509**. His own manuscript collection was so large and valuable, it was coveted by scholars across Europe and was even temporarily seized by customs officials but then returned.

Erasmus' published his first Greek and Latin New Testament (later known as the **Textus Receptus**) in 1516, which sold out in three years – but because he was rushed to meet the deadline of the printer, the work was hastily done and he was not quite satisfied with its quality. No future translation was ever based on this text nor did any future translator ever use this first text of Erasmus.

Erasmus worked extensively to correct any possible flaws, and using a manuscript which had been loaned to him by the King of Hungary, two manuscripts from the Austin Priory of Corsidonk, and a Greek manuscript borrowed from the Monastery at Mt. Saint Agnes, he published his second edition in **1519**. This second edition had about 400 changes from first edition, but because of the primitive state of printing technology of the day, it still suffered from many typos. This second edition of **Erasmus' Greek and Latin New Testament** was used, in part, by Martin Luther for his **German Bible** translation.

"The Revival of Learning produced that giant intellect and scholar, Erasmus. It is a common proverb that 'Erasmus laid the egg and Luther hatched it.' The streams of Grecian learning were again flowing into the European plains, and a man of caliber was needed to draw from them their best and throw it upon the needy nations of the West."   (Our Authorized Bible Vindicated, p.53)

Around **1514-1517**, under the patronage of Cardinal Ximenes, the **Complutensian Polyglot** Bible was published by Jacobus Stunica. The **Complutensian Polyglot** contained columns of the **LXX**, **Jerome's Latin Vulgate**, the **Aramaic Targum of the Pentateuch**, the Hebrew text of the Old Testament (which was made from seven manuscripts), and the **Traditional Greek "Received Text"** of the New Testament.

Erasmus published his third edition of the **Textus Receptus** in 1522. Tyndale used this third edition in translating his Bible.

Although Erasmus had not included the text of 1 John 5:7 in his first two editions of the New Testament, he did include this verse in his third edition. This was because it was Erasmus' desire to provide the best translation that he could. In addition, of the Greek manuscripts that he had, none of them contained this text, so he accordingly, he left it out.

> *"If he had had a Greek manuscnpt with the Comma Johanncum then he would have included the Comma but he had not found a single such manuscnpt and consequently he omitted the Comma Johanneum."*
> (Erasmus and the Comma Johanneum, H.J. DE JONGE)

The commonly told story promoted by the critics of the Erasmus text is that Erasmus haphazardly made the rash promise that if anyone could produce a Greek manuscript with that text, that he would then add it to his New Testament, whereupon someone forged a Greek manuscript with this text and Erasmus, not wanting to break his promise, then added the text to his work even though he knew the manuscript was false.

But though this is the commonly circulated story, it is a fictitious story which was concocted in the attempt to discredit Erasmus. There is absolutely no evidence to support this story, and none of the historians of that time period say anything about it. Evidence shows that this false story first originated with the higher critics that began attempting to change the Bible in the middle of the 19th century, and has been promoted by various higher critics ever since. Promoters of this fictitious story have included Tregelles, Westcott, Hort, Nestle, Scrivener, Kenyon, and Bruce Metzger.

Consider this reference quoting Bruce Manning Metzger, a textual critic and longtime professor at Princeton Theological Seminary – Metzger was a Bible editor who served on the board of the American Bible Society and United Bible Societies.

> *"'Erasmus promised that he would insert the Comma Johanneum, as it is called, in future editions if a single Greek manuscript could be found that contained the passage. At length such a copy was found—or made to order.'* (Bruce Metzger)

"However, on pg 291 (n2) of the (new) 3rd edition of The Text of the New Testament Bruce Metzger writes:
*'What is said on p. 101 above about Erasmus' promise to include the Comma Johanneum if one Greek manuscript were found that contained it, and his subsequent suspicion that MS. 61 was written expressly to force him to do so, needs to be corrected in the light of the research of H.J. de Jonge, a specialist in Erasmian studies who finds no explicit evidence that supports this frequently made assertion; see his "Erasmus and the Comma Johanneum", Ephemerides Theologicae Lovanienses, lvi (1980), pp 381-9.'"

(https://www.theopedia.com/johannine-comma)

From 1000 AD to 1600 AD

The facts show that, rather than this text coming about from some rash promise, Erasmus included 1 John 5:7 in his third edition because he was constantly trying to improve his New Testament to remove any flaws. By the time that his third edition came out, not only were there other Greek manuscripts containing the Johannine Comma that had been discovered, but Erasmus had also become concerned that the omitting of 1 John 5:7 would lead many to go into the error of Arianism. [see Note C for this and more information on the Johannine Comma]

When Erasmus published his fourth edition in **1527**, it was in the format of three Columns – his own Greek **Textus Receptus**, **Jerome's Latin Vulgate**, and Erasmus' own revised Latin – in which he corrected the many errors of the Catholic **Latin Vulgate** to match the accurate Waldensian **Itala**.

He used, in the preparation of this fourth edition, seven different manuscripts, including the **Textus Receptus** readings in the **Complutensian Polyglot**.

In **1535** Erasmus published his fifth edition in which he completely omitted **Jerome's Latin Vulgate**.

**Erasmus' 5th Edition of the Greek-Latin Textus Receptus
1539 printing,   Matthew 1:1-6**

This is the edition of Erasmus that Robert Stephens used for his third and fourth editions of the **Greek New Testament**.

This fifth edition of Erasmus is also the edition from which, through Stephens' editions, the textual basis of the **King James Bible** can be traced.

Sword Unsheathed

Erasmus' fifth edition went through a total of 69 printings before Erasmus died.

Erasmus (Mirrored)

"When Erasmus published this work, at the dawn, so to say, of modern times, he did not see all its scope. Had he foreseen it, he would perhaps have recoiled in alarm. He saw indeed that there was a great work to be done, but he believed that all good men would unite to do it with common accord. "A spiritual temple must be raised in desolated Christendom," said he. "The mighty of this world will contribute towards it their marble, their ivory, and their gold; I who am poor and humble offer the foundation stone," and he laid down before the world his edition of the Greek Testament. Then glancing disdainfully at the traditions of men, he said: "It is not from human reservoirs, fetid with stagnant waters, that we should draw the doctrine of salvation; but from the pure and abundant streams that flow from the heart of God." And when some of his suspicious friends spoke to him of the difficulties of the times, he replied: "If the ship of the church is to be saved from being swallowed up by the tempest, there is only one anchor that can save it: it is the heavenly word, which, issuing from the bosom of the Father, lives, speaks, and works still in the gospel." These noble sentiments served as an introduction to those blessed pages which were to reform England. Erasmus like Caiaphas, prophesied without being aware of it."   (History of the Reformation, p.729)

"It is customary even to-day with those who are bitter against the pure teachings of the Received Text, to sneer at Erasmus. No perversion of facts is too great to belittle his work. Yet while he lived, Europe was at his feet. Several times the King of England offered him any position in the kingdom, at his own price; the Emperor of Germany did the same. The Pope offered to make him a cardinal. This he steadfastly refused, as he would not compromise his conscience. In fact, had he been so minded, he perhaps could have made himself Pope. France and Spain sought him to become a dweller in their realm, while Holland prepared to claim her most distinguished citizen."   (Our Authorized Bible Vindicated, p.53)

Modern critics try to claim that Erasmus' text was full of errors and that he didn't have access to the most ancient manuscripts – but this is an erroneous claim put forth by Rome. In reality, the "errors" claim is not new, nor is it valid at all.

"Writing to Peter Baberius August 13, 1521, Erasmus says: 'I did my best with the New Testament, but it provoked endless quarrels. Edward Lee pretended to have discovered 300 errors. They appointed a commission, which professed to have found bushels of them. Every dinner-table rang with the blunders of Erasmus. I required particulars, and could not have them.'
There were hundreds of manuscripts for Erasmus to examine, and he did; but he used only a few."   (Our Authorized Bible Vindicated, p.54)

From 1000 AD to 1600 AD

In other words, the modern critics are just promoting the same groundless accusations that the critics were leveling at Erasmus in his day. Erasmus had access to hundreds of manuscripts (all the same manuscripts available today – with the exception of ones like the **Sinaiticus** which had not been discovered yet). He had collated many Greek MSS of the New Testament, and was surrounded by all the commentaries and translations, by the writings of Origen, Cyprian, Ambrose, Basil, Chrysostom, Cyril, Jerome, and Augustine.

He had investigated the texts and compared all the manuscripts and separated them into two classes – those that followed **Lucian's Textus Receptus** and those that agreed with Rome's Vatican manuscripts. He eventually only used a few manuscripts for the basis of his work, because he recognized, by extensive research, that the few he had chosen were in agreement with the vast majority of the manuscripts – the **Majority Text**!

Erasmus purposely rejected the **Vulgate translation of Jerome** for its many errors. He corrected the amphibologies, obscurities, Hebraisms, and barbarisms, of **Jerome's Vulgate**; and caused a list to be printed of the errors in that version and he translated his own fresh rendering of the Greek New Testament text that he had collated from six or seven partial Lucian-based New Testament manuscripts into a complete Greek New Testament. Indeed, *"Erasmus rejected the manuscripts of Origen, as did Lucian."* (Truth Triumphant, p.57)

Erasmus' work of producing his Greek and Latin translation, beginning in **1516** and progressing through the final edition in **1535**, in essence, restored **Lucian's pure Textus Receptus**.

"In 1516, a year before the appearance of Luther's theses, Erasmus had published his Greek and Latin version of the New Testament. Now for the first time the word of God was printed in the original tongue. <u>In this work many errors of former versions were corrected, and the sense was more clearly rendered.</u> It led many among the educated classes to a better knowledge of the truth, and gave a new impetus to the work of reform." (Great Controversy, p.245)

All the English Bibles of the 16th and 17th century were based on Erasmus' text. Remarkably, though he was well-educated, Erasmus felt that all Christians had a right to study the Bible. He said,
"Only a few can be learned, but all can be Christian, all can be devout and – I shall boldly add – all can be theologians." (Erasmus)

Jacobus Faber Stapulensis was born about **1455** and by **1493**, as a doctor of divinity, he was also a professor in the University of Paris. He is commonly known by his Latin name Jacques Lefevre.
"This great man, who is usually called Jacobus Faber Stapulensis, [or] latinizing his name... Jacques le Fevre of Estaples..." (Townley's Biblical Literature, vol.1, p.573)

Sword Unsheathed

Lefevre was a devout Roman Catholic, but about the year **1512**, he had a conversion experience and rejected the Papal superstitions and practices and began to teach his students the truths of the Bible.

One of his students who accepted these new teachings was a man named William Farel. Farel had been born about **1489** in Dauphiny and was also a devout Roman Catholic.

Jacques Lefevre

"While Lefevre continued to spread the light among his students, Farel, as zealous in the cause of Christ as he had been in that of the pope, went forth to declare the truth in public." (Great Controversy, p.214)

The papal forces began persecuting the teachers of these Bible doctrines and Lefevre and Farel were later forced to flee to other parts of the country.

"During the persecution of Meaux, the teachers of the reformed faith were deprived of their license to preach, and they departed to other fields. Lefevre after a time made his way to Germany. Farel returned to his native town in eastern France, to spread the light in the home of his childhood." (Great Controversy, p.219)

"...Theodore Beza, speaking of Lefevre, hails him as the man "who boldly began the revival of the pure religion of Jesus Christ;" ...The Reformation was not, therefore, in France a foreign importation. It was born on French soil; it germinated in Paris; it put forth its first shoots in the university itself, that second authority in Romish Christendom. God planted the seeds of this work in the simple hearts of a Picard and a Dauphinese, before they had begun to bud forth in any other country upon earth. The Swiss Reformation, as we have seen, was independent of the German Reformation; and in its turn the Reformation in France was independent of that of Switzerland and of Germany. The work commenced at the same time in different countries, without any communication one with the other...The time had come, the nations were prepared, and God was everywhere beginning the revival of his Church at the same time. Such facts demonstrate that the great revolution of the sixteenth century was a work of God."
(History of the Reformation, p.441)

William Farel

William Farel helped to establish the Protestant Reformation in France and he later worked with John Calvin to spread the Reformation in Switzerland as well.

"Farel entered upon his work in Switzerland in the humble guise of a schoolmaster. Repairing to a secluded parish, he devoted himself to the instruction of children.

From 1000 AD to 1600 AD

Besides the usual branches of learning, he cautiously introduced the truths of the Bible, hoping through the children to reach the parents." (Great Controversy, p.231)

Back in **1516**, a printer in Venice named Daniel Bomberg had published a text of the Old Testament under the name "**First Rabbinic Bible**." It had been edited by Felix Pratensis who was a former Jewish member of the order of Hermits of St. Augustine.

This text was followed in **1525** by Bomberg's second and more complete edition (the **Second Great Rabbinic Bible** – also called **Bombergiana**) printed at Venice and compiled by Jacob Ben Chayyim, from original ancient Hebrew manuscripts.

Daniel Bomberg's Second Great Rabbinic Bible – The Ben Chayyim Text

"Another and improved edition, in four volumes folio, was published by Bomberg in 1525, 1526, who employed R. Jacob ben Chaim, a learned Jew of Tunis, as editor." (*Townley's Biblical Literature*, vol.2, p.151)

This **Second Great Rabbinic Bible** is greatly valued on account of its superior accuracy. It was published in four volumes - Volume 1 contained the books of Genesis, Exodus, Leviticus, Numbers, and Deuteronomy; Volume 2 contained the books of Joshua, Judges, 1 & 2 Samuel, and 1 & 2 Kings; Volume 3 contained the books of Isaiah, Jeremiah, Ezekiel, Hosea, Joel, Amos, Obadiah, Jonah, Micah, Nahum, Habakkuk, Zephaniah, Haggai, Zechariah, Malachi; Volume 4 contained the books of Psalms, Proverbs, Job, Song of Solomon, Ruth, Lamentations, Ecclesiastes, Esther, Daniel, Ezra, Nehemiah, and 1 & 2 Chronicles.

These four volumes are commonly known today as the **Ben Chayyim Masoretic Text**, and it became the standard Masoretic text used for the next 400 years. It was the "**Textus Receptus**" of the Hebrew Old Testament. Nobody translated the Old Testament except by using Ben Chayyim's text. This text is the one that was used by the translators 100 years later, to translate the Old Testament portion of the **1611 King James Bible**.

On **October 31, 1517**, Martin Luther, a dauntless monk and university professor, nailed his *"95 Theses"* to the Wittenberg Castle Church door.

The key Bible doctrine that Luther had discovered and that he promoted was *"The just shall live by faith."* (Romans 1:17) and that enabled him to stand against and counter the penances and indulgences of the Papal Church. His followers became known as Lutherans and this was the beginning of the Lutheran Church.

Luther's Protest against Indulgences

In **1520** Luther wrote, *"I feel myself now more at liberty, being assured that the popedom is antichristian and the seat of Satan."* (Romanism and the Reformation, p.103)

Luther believed that all men should have access to the Bible. *"This book, Luther argued from the Bible itself, was addressed to all men; and therefore all men had the right to read it and to interpret it. The Church had no monopoly on Scripture, either its reading or its interpretation. Every man was a priest charged with the duty of reading and rightly understanding the revelation that God had*

From 1000 AD to 1600 AD

graciously given to men. The Bible itself was addressed to men of all classes and callings. It was not addressed only to popes – they are not even mentioned in Scripture – nor only to bishops or deacons, but to all men without distinction. Each man would answer directly to God at the last Judgment – no priest or pope would be there to intercede for him; each man was responsible for the salvation or perdition of his own soul; each man would be required to give an account of the deeds he had done on Earth; and therefore each man had the right to read the Bible for himself."

(*Ecclesiastical Megalomania*, p.18)

Martin Luther

In **1521**, Luther translated the New Testament into German from Erasmus' Greek/Latin New Testament, otherwise known as the **Textus Receptus**. He also used the **Tepl Bible** and published his German New Testament in September of **1522**. Fifty-eight editions of the **Luther Bible** were printed between the years **1522** and **1533**: seventeen editions were printed at Wittenberg, thirteen at Augsburg, twelve at Basel, one at Erfurt, one at Grimma, one at Leipzig, and thirteen at Strasburg.

After his return to Wittenberg from Wartburg Castle, Luther proceeded to the translation of the Old Testament. He spared no pains to make sure that his translation was accurate. Luther (with the assistance of Melancthon) even requested a collection of gemstones to be loaned to them so that they could accurately describe the gemstones of the New Jerusalem in Revelation.

"We wish the book to be distinguished for the simplicity of its style. To accomplish this, in one difficult passage, we beg you will furnish us with the names, colours, and, if possible, a sight, of the precious stones mentioned in Revelation xxi."

This request had reference to the elector's collection of gems. Spalatin complied with the wish of his friends, and transmitted to them the precious stones in question, which, after due examination, they sent back."

(*Townley's Biblical Literature*, vol.2, p.9)

Luther Bible

129

Sword Unsheathed

"By the friendly aid of Spalatin, he obtained much information respecting different species of insects and reptiles, as well as of wild beasts and rapacious birds. He also employed butchers to dissect different animals, at his own house, that by examining their different parts, he might accurately express the sacrificial terms." (*Townley's Biblical Literature*, vol.2, p.10)

Luther's Old Testament was first printed in four parts during the years **1523** to **1533**, and finally the entire Bible was published in a single volume in **1534**.

Colorized version of a Revelation 17 illustration from the 1534 Luther Bible

"The Pentateuch, or five books of Moses, appeared in 1523; the book of Joshua, and the rest of the historical books, except Job, in 1524; and later in the same year, Job, the Psalms, Proverbs, Ecclesiastes, and Solomon's Song. In 1526 were printed the Prophecies of Jonah and Habakkuk; in 1528 Zechariah, and afterward Isaiah. In 1529 the Book of Wisdom was published; in 1530 the Prophecy of Daniel, and during the same year the remainder of the Apocryphal books. In 1531 Luther published a new and more liberal translation of the Psalms: and in 1531 and 1532 completed the rest of the Prophets. In 1534 the Bible was first published complete: the Psalms in this edition were those of the translation of 1531." (*Townley's Biblical Literature*, vol.2, p.11)

Lefevre translated the New Testament into French in **1522** and it was printed at Meaux by Simon de Colines.

"Lefevre desired to enable the Christians of France to read the Holy Scriptures. On the 30th October 1522, he published a French translation of the four Gospels; on the 6th November, the remaining books of the New Testament; on the 12th October 1524, all these books together, at the house of Collin in Meaux; and in 1525, a French version of the Psalms." (*History of the Reformation*, p.453)

Although **Lefevre's** first **French edition** was based on **Jerome's Latin Vulgate**, he did succeed in doing the same thing that Wycliffe had done – getting the Bible into the common man's language and into the hands of the people.

By the time Lefevre published his last editions of the Bible, he was including footnotes for the corrected pure-line readings of the Bible.

From 1000 AD to 1600 AD

"Lefevre undertook the translation of the New Testament, and at the very time when Luther's German Bible was issuing from the press in Wittenberg, the French New Testament was published at Meaux. The bishop spared no labor or expense to circulate it among his parishes, and soon the peasants of Meaux were in possession of the Holy Scriptures." (Great Controversy, p.214)

Ulrich Zwingli

Ulrich Zwingli (**1484-1531**) was born to a shepherd family in the Swiss Alps only seven weeks after Luther's birth. While Luther's main discovery in true Bible doctrine was "Righteousness by Faith," Zwingli's main discovery in true Bible doctrine was the the Bible itself!

"Zwingli's dominating principle was the sole authority of the Word of God, by which he dethroned reason from the supremacy which the schoolmen had assigned her, and brought back the understanding and conscience to Divine revelation." (History of Protestantism, Vol. 1, pg. 431)

Zwingli began promoting reforms in the church. Zwingli was more inclined to reform slowly and orderly, but some of his associates didn't want to merely reform the church; they wanted to wholly restore it to its initial purity and simplicity. They wanted to do away with usury and military service. Some of these individuals wanted a totally self-governing church, free of government interference. Though some of their stated views, such as *"Infant baptism is a horrible abomination, a flagrant impiety, invented by the evil spirit and Pope Nicholas of Rome."* (History of Protestantism, vol.2, p.61) were correct, thus gleaning in honest believers, other factions were more excessive. Some became fanatical and promoted antinomianism which teaches the unbiblical doctrine that God's grace did away with any obligation to keep the Moral Law (this false doctrine also joined forces with Gnosticism's false "once saved, always saved" doctrine). Some went so far as to throw out the authority of the Bible, burning it and stating, *"The letter kills."* (p.61) One of the leaders of this fanatical group was Thomas Müntzer. Other leaders included Conrad Grebel, Hans Hut, Pilgram Marpeck, Melchior Hoffmann, Jacob Hutter, and Balthasar Hubmaier.

In **1521**, Muntzer, the leader of one of the groups of antinomians, published his Prague Manifesto which justified violence in the elect. This left in its wake violent excesses and murders. And so Zwingli, in **1525**, realizing Muntzer and his party's errors, parted ways with them and cut his ties to their false theology. However, the "Anabaptists," as they were called for not believing in infant baptism, went on to begin their own separate Protestant movement which became known as the Anabaptist faith. Though it had started in Switzerland, it quickly spread to Moravia and throughout Germany.

In general, the Anabaptists correctly rejected the papal doctrine of infant baptism and believed in Biblical baptism by immersion. They also believed in separation of church and state, congregationalism, and many of them in non-violence. In many ways, they were ahead of the other Protestant reformers in their rediscovery of Biblical truths.

Sword Unsheathed

Tragically though, not all the Anabaptists groups held those same views. As with most reformatory movements, the devil always gets some fanatics to join up so that he can use them to slow or stop the reform. Anabaptists were no different. Because of their false "antinomian view" of the Moral Law, some of their groups became disorderly and radical and some even began to practice polygamy.

A few of the groups under the leadership of Muntzer didn't hold to the non-violence belief and began promoting revolutionary ideas about overthrowing the feudal systems and church-controlled governments. This eventually led to the "Peasant's War" which turned violent and resulted in many deaths.

The Catholics then used this event as an excuse to condemn all Protestant principles, and the Protestants in turn, realizing the error of antinomianism, condemned the whole group of Anabaptists – even though very few Anabaptists were actually involved in the war. As is usually the case, many Anabaptists suffered because of the few fanatics that had caused the trouble. Protestants and Catholics increased their persecution of Anabaptists throughout Europe without discriminating between the belligerent minority and the pacifist majority. In the end, Muntzer and many of his fanatical followers were executed by burning, beheading, or drowning. Other groups of Anabaptists continued to spread throughout Germany.

Thomas Müntzer

During this time, the **Zurich Bible**, a Swiss-German (Swiss-tinted German) version, was translated by the Protestant reformers Ulrich Zwingli & Leo Judd. They began with the NT, which they published between **1524-1529**, and the whole Bible was published in **1530/31**. Zwingli and Judd used, as the basis of their translation, the original Hebrew and Greek, as well as the various parts of **Luther's German Bible** that were already completed, actually finishing the entire translation four years before Luther finished his. This made making Zwingli's **1531** edition the first complete German Protestant Bible ever published. **Zwingli's Zurich Bible** was the standard Bible in Switzerland for many years, and was printed by Christoph Froschauer, the first book printer in Zurich, which is why it is sometimes called the **Froschau Bible** or the **Froschauer Bible**.

2 Timothy 3:16 in Zwingli's Zurich Bible

William Tyndale (**1484-1536**) *"as became an accomplished Greek scholar... was resolved to translate the New Testament from the original language, and not as Wycliffe had done, from the Latin Vulgate* [Jerome's]*; and the only edition of the Greek text which had yet appeared, the only one at least likely to be in Tyndale's possession, was that issued by Erasmus at Basle."* (*Our Authorized Bible Vindicated, p.50*)

Tyndale was fluent in eight different languages – Hebrew, Greek, Latin, Italian, Spanish, English, French, and German (and had partial knowledge of others, including Welsh). It was correctly stated by a friend of Erasmus that William Tyndale was so skilled in the use of these languages that *"whichever he spoke you would suppose it his native tongue."* (*Our Authorized Bible Vindicated*, p.56)

The priests tried to condemn Tyndale's view of the Bible. *"'The vulgar cannot understand the Word of God,' said the priests; 'it is the Church that gave the Bible to men, and it is only her priests that can interpret it.' 'Do you know who taught the eagles to find their prey?' asked Tyndale; 'that same God teaches his children to find their Father in his Word. Far from having given us the Scriptures, it is you who have hidden them from us.'"* (*History of Protestantism*, vol. 3, p.362)

William Tyndale

Once Tyndale was in a discussion with a papist theologian who was putting the Pope's laws above God's Law. Recorded for us is Tyndale's bold response. *"I defy the Pope, and all his laws; and if God spare my life, ere many years, I will cause a boy that driveth the plough, to know more of the Scripture than you do!"* (*The Annals of the English Bible*, vol.1, p.36)

Tyndale started translating the Bible while he was a tutor in England, but because of the opposition against him and against anyone suspected of reading Protestant writings, he had to take his manuscript and flee to Europe. He went to Hamburg, Germany, and resumed his translation work, with the help of William Roye. Tyndale based his Bible on the Greek text of **Erasmus' Third edition**.

"Tyndale was to complete the work of Wycliffe in giving the Bible to his countrymen. A diligent student and an earnest seeker for truth, he had received the gospel from the Greek Testament of Erasmus." (*Great Controversy*, p.245)

Tyndale began to publish his English New Testament, but just as the 10th page was in the press, he received notice that word of his work had been leaked out, and the authorities were on their way to seize his translation. He quickly packed up his translation and the printed sheets, and taking his assistant Roye, fled to Worms – just minutes before the authorities arrived at the publishing house. Safely at Worms, Tyndale finished publishing his newly translated edition of the New Testament in **1525/26**, and he *"...was the first to publish an English New Testament in print."* (*Handbook for Bible Students*, p.51)

Tyndale's New Testament was printed in octavo and this small size greatly facilitated its circulation. He had 1,500 copies shipped to England. This alarmed the authorities in England. Opposition in England was so strong that for over a year, all ships coming to England from European cities that were printing Tyndale's Bible were forbidden entry into English ports.

Sword Unsheathed

But God intervened, and in the spring of **1527** massive rainstorms prevented England from planting their crops. By the fall, England was suffering from food shortage and they began to allow ships with food in from Europe. Hidden among the cargo of "physical food" were many copies of Tyndale's Bible, bringing "spiritual food" to famished England.

The **Liesveldt Bible** was the translation of the Bible into the Low Dutch, or Belgic language by learned Protestant scholars. They used **Martin Luther's German Bible** as the basis of their translation. The first edition was published in **1526** by Jacob á Liesveldt, a famous printer of Antwerp, from whom the Bible received it's name. Several other editions followed, with the sixth and last edition coming out in **1542**.

The **Liesveldt Bible** was the first Dutch Protestant Bible made for the Netherlands, and it was this Bible that was cherished by the Protestant champions of the Reformation and helped to fuel the Protestant Reformation in the Low Countries. The publication of this Protestant Bible was immediately condemned by the Catholic Church and those involved with it were persecuted.

In fact, *"One of the first printers of this translation, Jacob á Liesveldt, was condemned, and beheaded at Antwerp, because in the annotations of one of his Bibles he had said, that the salvation of mankind proceeds from Christ alone!!"*
(*Townley's Illustrations of Biblical Literature*, vol.2, p.65)

On **October 12, 1532**, the Synod of Chamforan convened in Angrogna Valley. This gathering of the representatives of the Protestant churches in Switzerland, Bohemia, France, and Germany, with the representatives of all the Vaudois churches and the Albigensian churches, marked the point where the Waldensians joined in union with the Protestant Reformation. It was determined by the Vaudois to provide a French Protestant Bible to their fellow brethren in the faith.

In **1533**, King Henry of England, having divorced his wife Catherine, married Anne Boleyn. Anne had a keen interest in Tyndale's writings and she loved his New Testament. Queen Anne became a devout and firm protector of the Protestants and their Biblical cause.

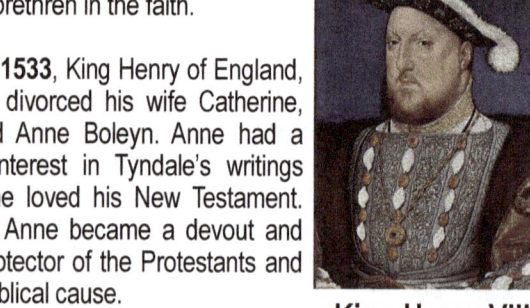

Queen Anne   **King Henry VIII**

Pierre Robert Olivetan, one of the most illustrious pastors of the Waldensian Valleys who had also joined the reformers, was one of the first Protestant Reformers to spread the new religious doctrines in the Catholic City of Geneva, in **1533**. At one point, upon hearing a preacher denounce Luther in the pulpit, Olivetan interrupted the speaker, and undertook to refute him, thus creating a disturbance which nearly cost him his life and led to his being banished from the territory of Geneva. As a result, he went to Neufchatel, where he began his work of translating the Bible into French, as was called for by the Waldensian Synod.

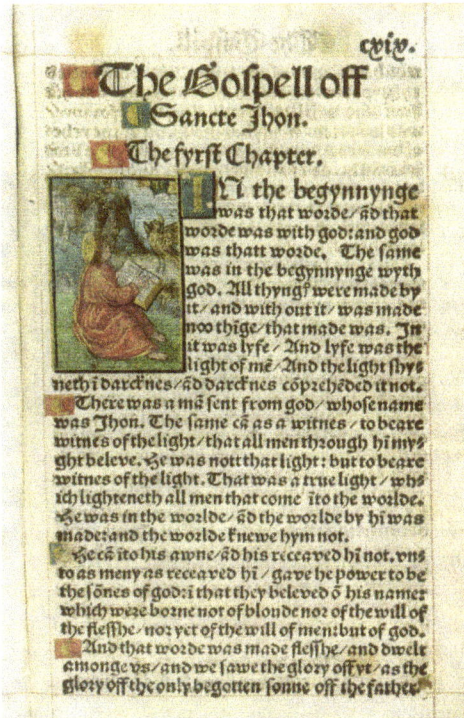

Entry to Gospel of John, Tyndale Bible

In **1534**, Tyndale published his new edition of the New Testament with the corrections he had made. **Tyndale's Bible** was the first English Bible to be printed by printing press. Tyndale was also working on translating the Old Testament from the original Hebrew. And he had already completed the books of Genesis through 2 Chronicles and the book of Jonah, before he was imprisoned for his "crime" of publishing the Bible in English.

"Even his enemies have admitted that his work was excellent. Its language is pure, appropriate and clear to the understanding. Evidences of great learning and research give it a pre-eminent position among the enduring monuments of human intelligence and skill." (*The Parallel Bible* introduction)

"... the best that the Wyclif translators could do with the Latin Fiat lux et lux erat was 'Be made light, and made was light', or 'Light be made, and light was made'. It was Tyndale, from the Hebrew, who gave us, for ever after, 'Let there be light, and there was light'." (Introduction to *Tyndale 1526 New Testament Facsimile Edition*)

Because the English language did not always have a word that would correctly represent the original Hebrew and Greek terms, Tyndale found it necessary to coin some new words for his English translation. Tyndale originated compound words like "Passover" and "scapegoat" to portray the original text in English.

On **August 16, 1534**, Ignatius Loyola and his few followers made their vow in the Church of Saint Peter of Montmartre in Paris. This vow was the beginning of the Society of Jesus – the Jesuit Order. The *Church of Saint Peter of Montmartre* sits today on the site of and in the shadow of the famous 19th century Basilica of the Sacred Heart in Paris. This is the not so commonly known connection between the "Sacred Heart" and the Jesuit order.

Sword Unsheathed

Symbols containing the "Sacred Heart" or "Flaming Heart" are symbols secretly used to reveal to insiders the institutions that are run and controlled by the Jesuit order.

"Faber circulated amongst his parishioners a History of the Sacred Heart, in which he advocated the adoration of the material heart of our Lord – a modern custom invented by the Jesuits." (*The Secret History of the Oxford Movement*, p.34)

When Jesuit Pope Francis addressed the Evangelicals in **2014**, and stated that he was going to speak in the "*language of the heart*" – his address was given in "code language" to be understood by his fellow Jesuits. It is said of the Jesuits:

"It was a marvellous [sic] *instrument that Ignatius constructed, combining the individualism of the Renaissance – each man assigned to and trained for his peculiar work – with the sacrifice of will and complete obedience to the spirit and aims of the whole. It stands as the very antithesis of Protestantism."* (*A History of the Christian Church*, p.426)

Ignatius Loyola

The Jesuits became the militia for the pope and began the Counter-Reformation to crush the Protestants and bring them back to Rome.

"Ignatius Loyola came forward and must have said in substance to the Pope: Let the Augustinians continue to provide monasteries of retreat for contemplative minds; let the Benedictines give themselves up to the field of literary endeavor; let the Dominicans retain their responsibility for maintaining the Inquisition; but we, the Jesuits, will capture the colleges and the universities. We will gain control of instruction in law, medicine, science, education, and so weed out from all books of instruction, anything injurious to Roman Catholicism. We will mould the thoughts and ideas of the youth. We will enroll ourselves as Protestant preachers and college professors in the different Protestant faiths. Sooner or later, we will undermine the authority of the Greek New Testament of Erasmus, and also of those Old Testament productions which have dared to raise their heads against the Old Testament of the Vulgate and against tradition. And thus will we undermine the Protestant Reformation."
(*Our Authorized Bible Vindicated*, p.60)

"At this time, the order of the Jesuits was created, the most cruel, unscrupulous, and powerful of all the champions of popery. Cut off from every earthly tie and human interest, dead to the claims of natural affection, reason and conscience wholly silenced, they knew no rule, no tie, but that of their order, and no duty but to extend its power...There was no crime too great for them to commit, no deception too base for them to practice, no disguise too difficult for them to

assume. Vowed to perpetual poverty and humility, it was their studied aim to secure wealth and power, to be devoted to the overthrow of Protestantism, and the re-establishment of the papal supremacy. When appearing as members of their order, they wore a garb of sanctity, visiting prisons and hospitals, ministering to the sick and the poor, professing to have renounced the world, and bearing the sacred name of Jesus, who went about doing good. But under this blameless exterior the most criminal and deadly purposes were concealed."   (Great Controversy, p.234, 235)

John Calvin

Olivetan was a cousin of John Calvin (**1509–1564**), and the two cousins had often met, and discussed together the matters that were disturbing Christendom. Olivetan tried to share the Protestant faith with Calvin, but for a while, Calvin would have nothing to do with it.

"'There are but two religions in the world,' said Olivetan, the Protestant. 'The one class of religions are those which men have invented, in all of which man saves himself by ceremonies and good works; the other is that one religion which is revealed in the Bible, and which teaches men to look for salvation solely to the free grace of God.' 'I will have none of your new doctrines,' exclaimed Calvin; 'think you that I have lived in error all my days?'

"But thoughts had been awakened in his mind which he could not banish at will. Alone in his chamber he pondered upon his cousin's words. Conviction of sin fastened upon him; he saw himself, without an intercessor, in the presence of a holy and just Judge."   (Great Controversy, p. 220)

The seed that Olivetan had planted in Calvin's mind began to grow, and in **1534** Calvin broke away from Roman Catholicism and began working in earnest to promote the Reformation. Calvin later became one of the leading Protestant reformers and was instrumental in promoting and establishing Protestantism throughout Europe. In **1536**, Calvin began working in Geneva to promote the Reformation, and he was instrumental in turning Geneva from Catholicism to Protestantism. Calvin's followers were also known as Calvinists.

"From Geneva, publications and teachers went out to spread the reformed doctrines. To this point the persecuted of all lands looked for instruction, counsel, and encouragement. The city of Calvin became a refuge for the hunted reformers of all Western Europe. Fleeing from the awful tempests that continued for centuries, the fugitives came to the gates of Geneva."   (Great Controversy, 1888, p.236)

In **1535**, Pierre Robert Olivetan, published his French translation of the Bible at Neuchatel. It was called the **Olivetan Bible** and was printed in folio size. The New Testament of the **Olivetan Bible** is based on a NT in Waldensian vernacular and on Erasmus' **Textus Receptus**. The cost of its publication was defrayed by the churches in Waldensia who collected the sum of 1,500 gold crowns for this purpose.

The **Olivetan Bible** was a gift of the Waldenses to the Protestant Reformation showing to the Protestants that the Waldenses considered the Protestants brethren in the truth.

"Leger, when he calls the Olivetan's French Bible of 1537 'entire and pure' says: 'I say"'pure" because all the ancient exemplars, which formerly were found among the Papists, were full of falsification...one must confess it was by means of the Vaudois of the Valleys that France today has the Bible in her own language. This godly man, Olivetan, in the preface of his Bible, recognizes with thanks to God, that since the time of the apostles, or their immediate successors, the torch of the gospel has been lit among the Vaudois...and has never since been extinguished.'" (Our Authorized Bible Vindicated, pg. 32 quoting from Leger, *General Hist. of the Vaudois Churches*, p. 165)

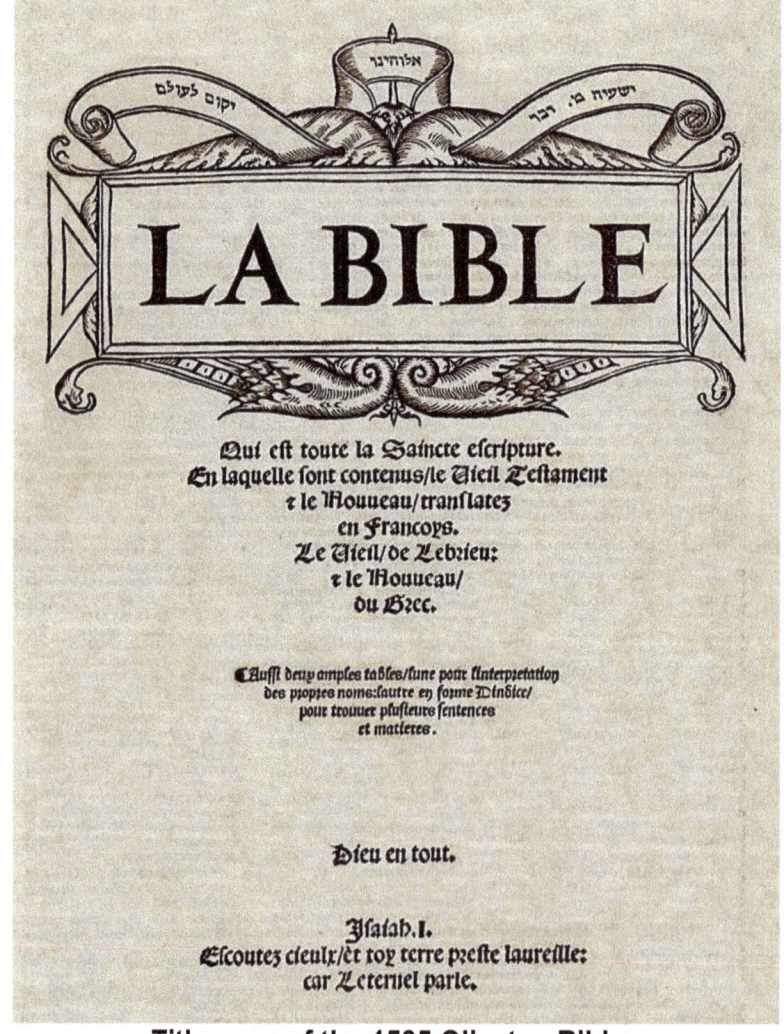

Title page of the 1535 Olivetan Bible

From 1000 AD to 1600 AD

On the last page of the **Olivetan Bible** was written a poem titled **Au Lecteur de la Bible** [To the Bible Reader]. It reads:

"Lecteur entends, si Verite addresse,
Viens donc ouyr instament sa promesse
Et vif parler: lequel en excellence
Veult assurer nostre grelle esperance.
Lesprit Jesus qui visite, et ordonne
Nos tendres meurs, icy sans cry estonne
Tout hault raillart escumant son ordure.
Remercions eternelle nature:
Prenons vouloir bienfaire librement;
Jesus querons veoir eternellement."

It is very difficult to translate this poem into English because it is not only very "Old French" which is very different from the modern French of today, but it also contains "poetic license" which does not transfer over into modern English either. However, even with these difficulties, one can at least get an idea of what it said even though, because of the poetic license some of it doesn't make normal sense in English.

In English, this poem would roughly read something like:
*Reader listen, if truth is speaking.
Come therefore hear urgently its promise
And living word: which with excellence
Aims to assure our frail hope.
The Spirit of Jesus which visits and orders
Our tender morals, here without crying out storming
All high jeering foaming its garbage.
Let's Thank eternal nature:
Let's take to want to do well freely;
Jesus, let's hope to see eternally.*

The real importance of this poem though, is not to be found in the English, but in the original French. When this poem is decoded, a hidden message is revealed. The Vaudois were accustomed to carefully hiding their information where the Papal authorities would not think to look.

When the first letter of each "French" word of this poem is taken and put together, it is found to be an "acrostic" spelling this important declaration:
*"Les Vaudois, Peuple Evangelique,
Ont mis ce Thresor en publique."*
This acrostic translated into English says,
*"The Vaudois, that evangelical people,
have given this treasure to the public."*

Sword Unsheathed

The Papal Church hated Olivetan for translating the Bible into the common French language and sought to destroy it. After translating the **Olivetan Bible**, Olivetan was obliged to leave Switzerland and he went into Italy, quite possibly as a missionary. He was poisoned by his enemies while on a short stay in Rome and died in **1538**. *"Olivetan died at Rome in 1538, not without strong suspicion of being poisoned."* (Townley's Biblical Literature, vol.2, p.127)

Later, Calvin edited a second edition of the **Olivetan Bible**. Amongst other changes, the Gothic font of the original was replaced with an easier to read Roman font. This Bible became known as the **Sword Bible**.

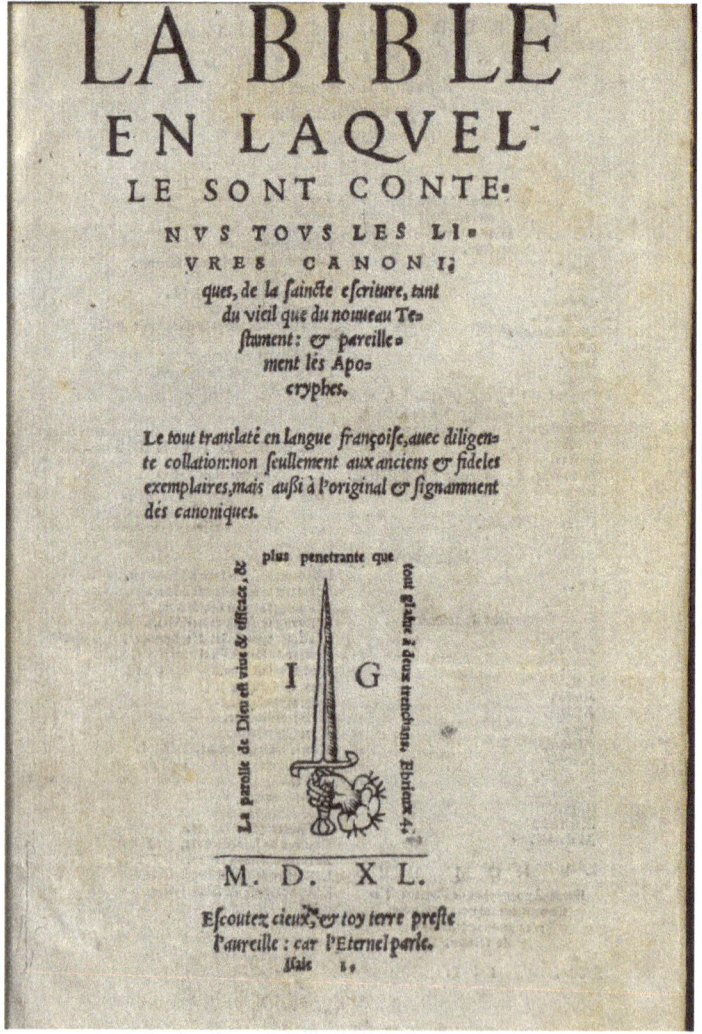

Title page of the 1540 Sword Bible

From 1000 AD to 1600 AD

"A second edition of the Olivetan version was printed at Geneva, in 1540, in small quarto. De Bure attributes the revision of it to Calvin...De Bure further remarks, that the representation of a sword, on the title-page, has occasioned this edition to be known in the republic of letters by the name of the "Sword Bible..."
(*Townley's Biblical Literature*, vol.2, p.126)

Miles Coverdale

A friend of Thomas Cromwell, the Earl of Essex, was Miles Coverdale (**1488–1568**) who had helped Tyndale with his translation work in Europe. Coverdale knew German and Latin well and had some knowledge of Greek, Hebrew, and French. It was his desire to translate the whole Bible into the English language.

"But Scripture ought to exist in Latin only," objected the priest. *– "No,"* replied Coverdale again, *"the Holy Ghost is as much the author of it in the Hebrew, Greek, French, Dutch, and English, as in Latin... The word of God is of like authority, in what language soever the Holy Ghost speaketh it."* (*History of the Reformation*, vol.5, book 20, ch.2)

On **October 4th, 1535**, Miles Coverdale and John Rogers, another of Tyndale's assistants, published the first complete English Bible known as the **Coverdale Bible**. They had finished **Tyndale's Old Testament**, but translated from the Latin and German instead of the Hebrew. Coverdale used **Tyndale's New Testament**, and Tyndale's Pentateuch and Jonah. He also used the **Textus Receptus** of Erasmus as reference. For the books of Joshua through Esther and Psalms, Coverdale used **Luther's German Bible**, and for the books of Job and Malachi he used the **Zwingli's German/Swiss Bible**.

> Thou shalt be called the maker vp of hedges, and ẏ buylder agayne of ẏ waye of the Sabbath.

1535 Coverdale Bible, Isaiah 58:12b

In **1535**, a Catholic priest named Menno Simons, threw off his connection with the Catholic Church and joined the Anabaptist faith of the Swiss Brethren. Around **1537**, he went to the Netherlands and rallied the pacifist Anabaptists in the Netherlands and northern Germany. These Anabaptist followers of Menno Simons later became known as Mennonites.

In **1535**, William Tyndale was arrested for his "crime" of providing the Bible in the common man's tongue. *"Those who opposed the reading of the Scriptures in the language of the people were enraged when they saw the increased supply of the English version; and, availing themselves of the imperial decree, they employed*

Sword Unsheathed

secret influence and agency for the capture of Tyndale. Henry Philips was sent to Antwerp, who, under the guise of friendship, inveigled him from the house of Poyntz in August 1535, and then delivered him into the hands of the officers, sent to apprehend him as a denounced heretic."

(The Gothic and Anglo-Saxon Gospels, p.xxvii)

Queen Anne herself played a direct role in Henry VIII's proclamation in **1535** that the Bible should be printed and deposited in every church, in a place where the people might read them. This proclamation was not carried into effect however, because not long after this, in January of **1536**, Anne's son died shortly after childbirth.

Because Henry was infatuated with Jane Seymoure and he resented Anne's support for the Protestants, he had Anne falsely charged with adultery and beheaded on **May 19, 1536**. Henry married Jane the day after Anne's execution.

King Henry VIII

In England, it was still illegal to translate or possess the Bible in English. On **October 6, 1536**, Tyndale was first strangled and then burned at the stake for the heresy of translating and publishing the Bible. As Tyndale was about to be killed, he cried out, "Lord, open the King of England's eyes."

"The prayer of the dying martyr was heard; for, before the close of 1536, the first volume of the Holy Scriptures in English ever printed in this country, the folio edition of the New Testament issued from the press of the king's own printer, with the name of William Tyndale on the title." (The Gothic and Anglo-Saxon Gospels, p.xxviii)

Then, in **1537**, only one year later, **Tyndale's translation** in connection with **Miles Coverdale's translation** was published by Tyndale's friend, John Rogers, who, operating under the assumed name "Thomas Matthew," produced the "**Matthew-Tyndale Bible**" or "**Matthews Bible**." The name "**Thomas Matthew's Bible**" was used as a pseudonym because Tyndale's name was still held in ill-favor by King Henry VIII.

This translation was given to Archbishop of Canterbury, Thomas Cranmer, who pronounced it better than any other translation that had been made. It has been stated that, *"Cramer [sic] could repeat the entire New Testament from memory..."*
(Encyclopedia of 7700 Illustrations, p.187)

Cranmer forwarded the **Matthews Bible** on to Cromwell who recommended it to the king. The king sanctioned it and authorized it *"to be bought and read within this realm"* – thereby unknowingly sanctioning the work of Tyndale whom he had so ruthlessly persecuted and killed.

The clergy did not appreciate the prologue and notes in the **Matthew's Bible**, so they wanted another version without the notes.

Cranmer, by request of the King, hired Miles Coverdale to prepare a revision of the Matthew's Bible to be overseen by Cromwell. Coverdale began working on this revision with the printer Grafton in Paris.

"Some of the Prologues and notes of Tyndale had been introduced into Matthew's Bible, and given offence and raised opposition. To remove these objections Archbishop Cranmer, with the king's sanction, proposed the publication of the whole Bible without note or comment. He had the translation of Tyndale copied, and sent in portions to the Bishops for their correction, and then to be returned to him for his final revision." (*The Gothic and Anglo-Saxon Gospels*, p.xxviii)

On **September 5, 1538**, Cromwell issued a royal decree in the name of Henry VIII that stated that the clergy should provide a copy of the Bible in every church, and should encourage the common people to read it. The common people became so overjoyed at the freedom to read the Bible for themselves, that they were disrupting church services by reading the Bible aloud so that everyone else could hear. This prompted the King to later issue a proclamation in **April of 1539**, forbidding people to read the Bible aloud during church services.

In **December of 1538**, the Inquisitor-General in Paris called an ecclesiastical tribunal and forbade the Englishmen printers to finish their translation work or to take away the sheets that they had already finished. The printers fled Paris, leaving behind the unfinished sheets, and these were immediately seized by the inquisitors and doomed to the flames. But the lieutenant-general, whose desire for gain outweighed his hatred of heresy, decided to sell much of the sheets for waste paper. He sold them to a merchant to wrap his merchandise in – who in turn, resold them to Grafton, which enabled the printers to finish the Bible revision.

In **1539**, the new revision was published. It was called the **Great Bible** and was done by Miles Coverdale and published by Edward Wilchurch.

"When the King saw it he said, 'In God's name, let it go forth among our people!' Thus Tyndale's dying prayer was, at least, in part answered. This, therefore, was the first really Authorized Version of the Bible, 'and appointed to be used' in public worship. It is known as the 'Great Bible' owing to its size. It is also called the 'Chained Bible,' because it used to be chained to the desks of the churches for safe keeping. And it has been called the 'Treacle Bible,' because Jer. 5:22 was rendered, 'Is there no treacle in Gilead?'" (*All About the Bible*, p.36)

Sword Unsheathed

The first edition of the **Great Bible** was also called by some, the **Wilchurch edition**. By the decree of the King, a reader was to be provided so that the illiterate could hear the Word of God in their own language.

The second edition of the **Great Bible** in 1540 AD is sometimes called the **Cranmer Bible** due to the fact that Thomas Cranmer was the one who had proposed and supported the work and he wrote the Prologue for it.

1540 Cranmer Great Bible (Title Page Center)

Also in **1539** another Bible was published by Richard Taverner. It was known as the **Taverner Bible**, and it was based on the **Matthew's Bible**.

September 27, 1540, the Pope issued the papal bull *Regimini Militantis Ecclesiae* which officially recognized Loyola's organization known as the Society of Jesus, the Jesuit Order. They became the official militia of the Papal Church, put in place to destroy the Protestant Reformation and bring everyone back under the control of Rome.

> *"France"*, wrote Mr. Boehmer, *"is the cradle of the Society of Jesus, but in Italy it received its programme and constitution. Therefore in Italy it first took root and from there it spread abroad."* (*The Secret History of the Jesuits*, p.31)

The mark or seal symbol for the Jesuit order is the abbreviation "IHS" inside a circle or sun symbol. IHS is "In Hoc Signum" or "in this sign."

> *"...wherever this Seal is openly displayed the Jesuit Order is in Control..."* [Excepting where it is being used for exposure and educational purposes – like in this book.]
> (*Vatican Assassins*, p.81)

The **Swedish Gustav Vasa Bible** (Uppsala) was published in **1541** by Laurentius and was based from **Erasmus' Textus Receptus** and **Luther's German Bible**.

From 1000 AD to 1600 AD

Also in **1545**, a friend of Loyola, Jesuit Francis Xavier, exploring the church problems of the Orient, called for the King of Portugal to establish the cruel and bloody Inquisition to put a check on what he called "the Jewish wickedness" of 7th-day Sabbath keeping that was spreading through his Eastern dominions. With the support of the Portuguese guns, Xavier traveled to India and in **1560**, set up the Inquisition at Goa, to bring the apostolic Christians into allegiance with Rome.

War against the Sabbath is precisely what the Jesuits made in Abyssinia, which for centuries kept the 7th day of the week as the Sabbath.

"When the Jesuit, Francis Xavier, and his colaborers, were sent to India, they displayed the true spirit of Romanism. 'The Inquisition was set up at Goa, in the Indies, at the instance of Francis Xaverius, who signified by letter to Pope [King] John III, Nov. 10, 1545, "that the Jewish wickedness spread every day more and more in the parts of the East Indies, subject to the kingdom of Portugal, and therefore he earnestly besought the said king, that to cure so great an evil, he would take care to send the office of the Inquisition into those countries..." 'The Jewish wickedness" of which Xavier complained was evidently the Sabbathkeeping among those native Christians..."   (Facts of Faith, p.156)

Those who refused to ally with Rome were tortured and destroyed. Their **Syriac Bibles** were burned at the stake with them and those that were not destroyed were altered to match **Jerome's Latin Vulgate**.

"The Portuguese, finding the people still resolute in defending their ancient faith, began to try more conciliatory measures. In 1599, Don Aleixo de Menezes, who had been appointed to the archbishopric of Goa, convened a synod at Diamper, near Cochin, at which he presided. At this compulsory synod one hundred and fifty of the Syrian clergy were present, who were called upon to abjure certain practices and opinions, or to suffer suspension from all church benefices. <u>In the third session of this synod it was ordained, by Decree II., that all the apocryphal and other books, and passages which were wanting in the Syriac copies of the Bible, should be supplied from the Vulgate Latin, 'which the synod commandeth to be translated, and the passages that are wanting to be restored to their purity, according to the Chaldee (or Syriac) copies which are amended, and the vulgar Latin edition, made use of by holy mother church, that so this church may have the Holy Scriptures entire, and may use it with all its parts, as it was written and as it is to be used in the universal church</u>; to which end the synod desireth the reverend father Francisco Roz, of the society of Jesus, and professor of the Syriac tongue in the college of Vaipicotta, in this bishopric, that he would be pleased to take the trouble thereof upon him, for which he is so well qualified by reason of his great skill both in the Syriac language and the Scripture.'"

(Townley's Biblical Literature, vol.2, p.219)

Sword Unsheathed

The **Indian Syriac Bible** was known to have survived the Goa Inquisition. A copy of it was later given to a Dr. Buchanan who placed it in the Cambridge University Library for safe-keeping.

"These measures produced, however, only a temporary submission in the Christians of St. Thomas, as they are usually called, for the greater part of them proclaimed eternal war against the inquisition, hid their books, fled to the mountains, and sought the protection of the native princes, who had always been proud of their alliance. In 1806 and 1807 the Rev. Dr. Claudius Buchanan visited these churches, and found many thousands of these Christians not subject to the papal jurisdiction. "Acting," says he, "as our librarians, they have preserved the Holy Scriptures, during the dark ages, incorrupt in the sacred Syriac languages; (and) they have presented an ancient and valuable manuscript copy of the Old and New Testaments to the English Church." This, with many other valuable MSS., was presented by Dr. Buchanan to the public library at Cambridge."

(*Townley's Biblical Literature*, vol.2, p.221)

John Knox

In **1545**, the Scotsman John Knox (**1505-1572**) became a convert to Protestantism. He became a bold defender of the Protestant faith and is known as "the Luther of Scotland." He had to flee to Europe when Bloody Mary took the throne in **1553** and spent some years at Geneva. While there, he also helped with the translation of the **Geneva Bible**.

Knox returned to Scotland under the reign of Queen Elizabeth and was instrumental in firmly establishing the Protestant Reformation in Scotland.

Immanuel Tremellius (**1510–1580**) was an Italian Jew who converted to Protestantism in **1541**. He was professor of Hebrew at the University of Strasbourg in **1542**, but during the European wars, he fled to England and served as king's reader in Hebrew at the University of Cambridge until the persecutions under Mary Tudor, when he again returned to Germany. He was known as a leading Hebraist and Bible translator, and his most well known work was a Latin translation of the Bible from Hebrew and Syriac and his Aramaic and Syriac grammar both published in Geneva in **1569**.

The Papal Church hates the true Bible and they did not want the common people to have access to it. The papal clergy were so ignorant of the Bible themselves that they would promote the most ridiculous lies about it. One deceived monk even told his congregation:

"A new language is discovered, called Greek, and is the parent of all heresy. A

book written in that language is everywhere got into the hands of persons, and is called the New Testament. It is a book full of daggers and poison. Another Language has also sprung up, called the Hebrew, and those who learn it become Jews." (*Townley's Biblical Literature*, vol.1, p.591)

During the Council of Trent, which opened in **1545**, the Papal Church declared 'Tradition' as an equal authority with the Bible – in spite of the Bible's warnings, such as Matthew 15:3-6, Mark 7:9-13, and Colossians 2:8.

"The very first propositions to be discussed at length and with intense interest, were those relating to the Scriptures. This shows how fundamental to all reform, as well as to the great Reformation, is the determining power over Christian order and faith, of the disputed readings and the disputed books of the Bible."
(*Our Authorized Bible Vindicated*, p.60)

"...when the eighteenth day was come...Gasparo del Fosso, Archbishop of Rheggio, made the Sermon. His subject was the authority of the Church, Primacy of the Pope, and the power of Councils. He said that the Church had as much authority as the Word of God; that the Church hath changed the Sabbath, ordained by God, into Sunday, and taken away Circumcision, formerly commanded by his Divine Majesty, and that these Precepts are changed, not by the preaching of Christ, but by the authority of the Church." (*History of the Council of Trent*, p.439)

The French king, Francis I, in zeal for the Papal Church, issued the "Arrêt de Mérindol" on **January 1, 1545**.

The soldiers took the villages of Mérindol and Cabrieres and also devastated and destroyed about 26 other neighboring Waldensian villages, killing thousands of innocent Waldenses.

The Jesuit Order became a political power in **1546** when the pope chose two Jesuits, Lainez and Salmeron, to represent him at the Council of Trent as "Pontifical Theologians." This marks the commonly recognized beginning of the Jesuits' "Counter-Reformation" – their plan of destroying the Protestant Reformation and bringing the world back under the control of the Papacy.

"As the object of the society was the propagation and strengthening of the Catholic faith everywhere, the Jesuits naturally endeavored to counteract the spread of Protestantism. They became the main instruments of the counter-Reformation; the reconquest of southern and western Germany and Austria for the church, and the preservation of the Catholic faith in France and other countries were due chiefly to their exertions."
(*The Catholic Encyclopedia*, Vol. 14, art. "Society of Jesus" p. 81)

Sword Unsheathed

On **April 8, 1946**, Rome's Council of Trent decreed **Jerome's corrupt Latin Vulgate** as the standard Catholic Bible.

Council of Trent

"The second decree [of the council of Trent] declares the Vulgate to be the sole authentic and standard Latin version, and gives it such authority as to supersede the original texts..."
(Rome's Challenge, p. 22-23)

Rome also added the Apocryphal books in **1546**, declaring that they were equal with the inspired Word of God as well.

However, by this point, there were so many different versions of **Jerome's Latin Vugate**, Pope Sixtus V had to issue a papal bull defining which one was correct – which he did based, not on any scholarly training, but rather on his gift of "infallibility." This supposedly "perfectly correct" edition was printed at Rome in **1590**, accompanied by a Papal bull forbidding the least alteration in this "infallible" text.

"Scarcely, however, had the Sixtine edition made its appearance before it was discovered to abound with errors..." (Townley's Biblical Literature, vol.2, p.170)

This caused Sixtus's successors to immediately set about to change that bull and all available copies of the Bible of Pope Sixtus were called in and burnt, though they did not manage to retrieve them all. Pope Clement VIII, in **1592**, ordered a better edition to be made, accompanying it with a similar papal bull, totally contradicting papal policy as declared in their own documents.
"...every pope confirms and improves upon the devices of his predecessor..."
(Ecclesiastical Megalomania, p.135)

Jesuit Robert Bellarmine suggested to the pope Clement VIII how he could engage in a cover-up of the corrupted text without appearing to contradict his predecessor.

"This result could be achieved by removing inadvisable changes as quickly as possible, and then issuing the volume with Sixtus' name upon it, and a preface stating that owing to haste some errors had crept into the first edition through the fault of printers and other persons...The deceit did not stop there...With the new text should go a preface saying Sixtus had published a Bible revised according to his orders but, on examining it, he had discovered that many errors had crept into it owing to unseemly haste. This was not so unusual in first editions. Sixtus, therefore, decided that the work must be done all over again. At his death, his successors were keen to carry out his wishes. Hence the new edition."
(Vicars of Christ, The Dark Side of the Papacy, p.218-219)

From 1000 AD to 1600 AD

Pope Clement VIII issued a Papal Bull forbidding printers or booksellers to print or sell any Bible that was not conformed to his purportedly perfect and correct **Latin Vulgate**, which was published in **1592**. Then in **1593**, a second edition of the Clement VIII **Latin Vulgate** was published that made many corrections to the supposedly already "correct" text.

"One copy [of Sixtus' edition] found its way into the Bodleian Library in Oxford. Its first librarian, Dr Thomas James...wrote a book contrasting the two Bibles of Sixtus and Sixtus-Clement. He found 'that the two popes did notoriously differ amongst themselves, not only in the number of the verses...but in the body of the text and in the Prefaces and Bulls themselves'. James claimed to see a remarkable thing: two popes warring in open contradiction of each other...We have here one Pope against another, Sixtus against Clement, Clement against Sixtus, disputing, writing and fighting about the Jerome Bible.'"

(*Vicars of Christ, The Dark Side of the Papacy*, p.220)

"The difference between the papal editions is considerable, and strikes a fatal blow at the infallibility of the popes." (*Townley's Biblical Literature*, vol.2, p.170)

It is interesting to note that because the Papal Church has officially recognized the Arian **Latin Vulgate of Jerome's** as the true Bible, it lends to the realization that though Rome claims to the public to be anti-Arian, in reality, their "Anti-Arian" stance is only for the exoteric people (regular lay people) and that in the esoteric circles (the elite insiders), Rome is itself – Arian in belief!

The Council of Trent also gave the pope the responsibility to develop and publish the Papal Index of Prohibited Books.

"Ever since the first 'Index of Prohibited Books' was issued by Pope Paul IV, in 1599, the Bible has had a prominent place in these lists of forbidden books."

(*Facts of Faith*, p.11)

Because the Bible's truth revealed the need of a lot of reforms, the common people started pushing for reform in the Church of England. Due to the demand for reform and Rome's influence to halt the free access to the Bible, in **1543**, parliament banned the **Tyndale Bible**, and ordered that no common man should read the Bible on pain of imprisonment. Only the highly educated were allowed to read it.

Robert I Estienne, also called by the name Robert Stephens (**1503–1559**), a publisher in Paris, published four editions of the Greek New Testament.

Robert Stephens

Stephens first edition, published in Paris in **1546**, was based on the third edition of **Erasmus' Textus Receptus**. He published another edition in **1549**, and then one in **1550**. The fourth and last edition of **Stephens New Testament** was published in Geneva in **1551**, and was based on the fifth edition of **Erasmus' Textus Receptus**. This fourth edition of **Stephens Greek Bible** is where the dividing the New Testament into numbered verses was first established.

King Christian III

When the Danish king, Christian III, broke away from the Roman Catholic Church, he determined that he wanted to give the Danish people the opportunity to read the Bible for themselves in their own language. Parts of the Bible had been published in the Danish language before, but never the whole Bible.

"Detached portions of it had already been published at different times, but no edition of the whole had yet appeared."
(*Townley's Biblical Literature*, vol.2, p.52)

King Christian III had been greatly influenced by Luther, and he set about to have produced the first complete Bible written in Danish. He engaged a famous and very fine linguist, Christian Pedersen, to make a translation into fine, plain, understandable Danish, a language meant for the common man. He also used **Erasmus' Textus Receptus**.

King Christian hired the same printer, Lodowich Dietz, from Germany who had printed **Luther's Bible** and paid to import both his personnel and equipment from Germany to do the printing. He also stipulated that the **Danish Bible** should be printed and produced in exactly the same way and with the same material as the Luther Bible.

"In 1546 the paper destined for the work arrived, (most probably from Holland,) at Elsinore... It was not, however, till 1550 that the Bible was completed."
(*Townley's Biblical Literature*, vol.2, p.53)

The **Danish Bible, Biblia, det er den gantske**, was published in **1550** and was also called the **King Christian III Bible**.

In **1546**, King Henry VIII himself ordered that nobody was to have possession of **Tyndale's** or **Coverdale's New Testament**, and hundreds of those Bibles were confiscated and publicly burned. This order appears to have sealed the king's fate, because shortly thereafter, he became sick and died. When King Henry died in **1547**, his nine year old son, Edward, became king and immediately revoked the King's restrictions on the Bible.

From 1000 AD to 1600 AD

When Edward was crowned, he was given three swords, symbolizing the three countries that he ruled. Yet, his youthful strength of character was demonstrated when he asked where the fourth sword was, stating that the Bible, *"is the sword of the Spirit, and to be preferred before these swords."*
(*The Translators Revived*, p.43)

Once again, the churches were commanded to provide Bibles for all to read and Protestantism flourished.

King Edward

But King Edward only reigned six years and then he died of poisoning on **July 6, 1553**, at the age of 15. On his death bed, in order to secure the Protestant religion, he declared his Protestant cousin, Lady Jane Grey, as his successor and she was proclaimed Queen of England.

Lady Jane Grey's love of the Protestant Bible can be seen in her statement about reading it:
"The highest earthly enjoyments are but a shadow of the joy I find in reading God's word." (*The New Dictionary of Thoughts*, p.48)

Sadly, Lady Jane would not survive to rule England.

On **July 12, 1553** Mary Tudor, Edward's Roman Catholic half-sister, *"...defeated the Party of Lady Jane Grey, whom she beheaded..."*
(*Royal Genealogies*, p.748)

Mary also beheaded Lady Jane's husband and her father-in-law. Mary then reigned five years. She was known in history as "Bloody Mary" and under her evil reign the Bibles were confiscated and burned.

She married King Philip of Spain on **June 25, 1554**, and before the year was over, she had banished every preacher, printer, and bookseller and returned

Bloody Mary

Protestant England to the Papal Church. She also had her Protestant sister Elizabeth imprisoned in the Tower of London.

In **1555**, she had John Rogers ("Thomas Matthew") and Thomas Cranmer both burned at the stake. The Queen went on to kill over 288 Protestants by means of burning at the stake, as well as innumerable others who died at her command through imprisonment, torture, sickness, and starvation.

Sword Unsheathed

Mary Tudor died **November 17, 1558** and her Protestant sister Elizabeth took the throne.

In **1553**, some Jews who had fled the Spanish Inquisition, and found protection under the Duke of Ferrara in Italy, published a Spanish Old Testament translation of the Hebrew Bible. It was written in Ladino (JudeoSpanish), which is a Romance language derived from Old Spanish. This Bible is called the **Ferrara Bible**, and came in two editions, one designed for Jews and one designed for Christians. The edition for Jews was dedicated to Donna Gracia Naic, a Jewish Portuguese Dutchess and translated by Abraham Usque. The edition for Christians was dedicated to Don Hercules d'Este II., the Duke of Ferrara, and was translated by Duarte Pinel (Abraham Usque's "Christian" name) – and this edition is sometimes called the **Pinel Bible**.

In **1556**, Juan Perez de Pineda, who had fled from the dreaded Spanish Inquisition to Geneva, published his Spanish translation of the New Testament. Fearing the deadly Inquisition, Juan could not put his name on his work nor give the correct location of its publishing. He chose to mask his identity by publishing his Bible under the pseudonym "John Philadelpho" and naming the location as "Venice."

The 1556 **Pineda New Testament** was written in Castilian Spanish (the original pure Spanish) and it was translated from the original Greek text.

It's title page shows a large "Y" with one wide arm and one narrow arm illustrating the two paths that a sinner can take – the broad way to eternal destruction or the narrow way to everlasting life.

1556 Pineda Spanish New Testament Title page

By **1556**, the Jesuit Order was well established and at work throughout Europe and in India, China, Japan, and the New World. It was at work to undermine the Protestant Reformation and bring the whole world back under the control of Rome.

"The Jesuits rapidly spread themselves over Europe, and wherever they went, there followed a revival of popery." (The Great Controversy, p.235)

Theodore Beza

Theodore Beza (**1519–1605**), was a Protestant champion and friend of Calvin. As a professor of theology and a teacher of Greek, he was well versed in the Scriptures and spent much of his life translating the Bible and committing parts of it to memory. It is said that *"Beza could repeat all Paul's epistles in Greek at the age of 80."*
(*Encyclopedia of 7700 Illustrations*, p.187)

In **1556**, Beza published his Latin translation of the New Testament in France. **Beza's Latin** was based on the pure **Itala Bible** of the Waldenses. It was reprinted more than 100 times.

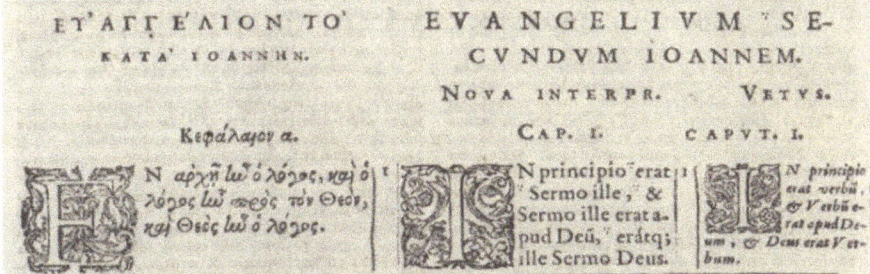

Beza's 1598 Greek- Latin New Testament (John 1:1)
L-Greek, Center- Beza's Latin from Ancient Manuscripts, R- Jerome's Vulgate

In **1557-1560**, reformers who had fled to Geneva, Switzerland under Mary Tudor's reign, under the supervision of John Calvin and William Whittingham, prepared a revision of the **Great Bible** called the **Geneva Bible**.

The New Testament was published in **1557** and the whole Bible in **1560**. It was circulated in England and ran through 160 editions – it became known as "the people's Book" and was the Bible of choice for 100 years. This Protestant Bible was also based largely on **Tyndale's Bible** and the **Olivetan Bible**.

Others who helped in the making of the **Geneva Bible** were Miles Coverdale, Christopher Goodman, Anthony Gilbey, Thomas Sampson, William Cole, William Kette, John Baron, John Pullain, and John Bodley. John Knox also helped with the work, as he was a pastor in Geneva at this time.

Sword Unsheathed

THE BIBLE
AND
HOLY SCRIPTVRES
CONTEYNED IN
THE OLDE AND NEWE
Testament.

TRANSLATED ACCOR-
ding to the Ebrue and Greke, and conferred With
the best translations in diuers langages.

WITH MOSTE PROFITABLE ANNOTA-
tions vpon all the Lord places, and other things of great
importance as may appeare in the Epistle to the Reader.

AT GENEVA.
PRINTED BY ROVLAND HALL
M.D.LX.

**1560 Geneva Bible Title Page
Featuring the Crossing at the Red Sea and Psalm 34:19**

From 1000 AD to 1600 AD

The **Geneva Bible** was the first Bible in English to make use of numbered verses. It was also the very first English Bible to contain the whole Old Testament translated directly from the original Hebrew. Also, *"This was the first Bible in which italics were used to indicate words which are not in the original."*

(*All About the Bible*, p.39)

Due to the word "Breeches" being used, some people referred to the **Geneva Bible** as the **Breeches Bible**. This was because in the passage in Genesis which describes the fig leaf clothing of Adam and Eve, which they fashioned for themselves after their fall, the word was translated as "Breeches" (an antiquated form of "Britches" or trousers).

The **Geneva Bible** was among the first Bibles taken to America, and the Bible most often used by the Puritans and the Pilgrims.

It is important to note, that due to the relative novelty of publishing Bibles in English, as well as to the sheer number of printings of the **Geneva Bible**, its many and varied editions often varied in content and presentation style as well, differing from others in various places in the wording as well as in doctrine.

Just to give one example, the original **1560 edition**, printed in Geneva, translated the correct Biblical doctrine of hell in 2 Peter 2:9 *"...to reserve the unjust unto the day of judgment to be punished:"* (future tense)

> 9 The Lord knoweth to deliuer the godlie out of tentation, and to reserue the vniust vnto the day of iudgement to be punished:

2 Peter 2:9 in the Geneva Bible, 1560 Edition

The **1599** and **1595** edition, printed by Christopher Barker in London, (as well as the **1587** edition on E-sword) has altered 2 Peter 2:9 to the incorrect and false doctrine of an ever-burning hell: *"...to reserve the unjust unto the day of judgment under punishment:"* (present tense)

Another fact to be aware of, is that there are many facsimile reprints of the "**Geneva Bible**" today – and some of them have had modern "introductions" and "prefaces" added to them which were not in the original. Some of these additions are very derogatory of other pure-line Bibles. In other words, just because it says that it is a facsimile "**Geneva Bible**," doesn't necessarily mean that it is really a faithful representation of the true **Geneva Bible** that was printed at Geneva. Careful discernment is necessary for the Bible researcher to sift through all the disinformation and false details that have been incorrectly attached to some modern **Geneva Bible** facsimiles.

Sword Unsheathed

Princess Elizabeth I

In **1558**, after Bloody Mary died, Princess Elizabeth I became queen and took the throne. Bibles were once again provided for the people.

In **1558** a Dutch version was published by Steven Mierdmans and Jan Geylliaert.

Then in **1560**, Nicolaes Biestkens published another Dutch Bible, known as the **Biestkens Bible** based on their **1558** edition. This edition was a Mennonite Bible and the first complete Dutch translation with numbered verses. Both of these Dutch Bibles are based on Erasmus' **Textus Receptus**.

The Council of Trent ended in **1563**.

In **1565**, Theodore Beza began publishing editions of the **Beza Greek New Testament** – two in **1565**, and one in **1567, 1580, 1582, 1588, 1590, 1598,** and **1604**. (Although some evidence also shows editions from **1559** and **1560** as well).

Beza also had collected quite a few manuscripts for his own collection. One of these manuscripts was the **Codex Bezae (D)**. The **Codex Bezae** manuscript had supposedly been stolen from the monastic library at Lyons, when it was ransacked in **1562**, and been given to Beza. Believing it might be a corrupted manuscript, Beza expressed his doubts about its accuracy when presenting it to the University of Cambridge in **1581** – so it is viewed by scholars with suspicion. Another one was **Codex Claromontanus (D2)** which he had obtained from the monastery of Clermont in Northern France.

But in spite of his collection of exotic manuscripts, Beza chose to base his own **Greek New Testament** on the fourth edition of **Stephanus Greek New Testament** which was, in turn, based on Erasmus' fifth edition of the Greek/Latin **Textus Receptus**.

Mary Queen of Scots gave birth to a son and in **1567**, James VI (**1566–1625**), though still an infant, was crowned king of Scotland. John Knox preached his coronation sermon. He ruled Scotland for 36 years and was a Bible Christian.

Amazingly, while his mother was a Roman Catholic, James was raised from childhood with the Protestant **Geneva Bible** and could quote whole chapters of the Bible from memory. As he got older, he leaned more and more toward Protestantism.

Having come from the translation work of exiled and persecuted Protestants,

From 1000 AD to 1600 AD

the marginal notes of the **Geneva Bible** were vehemently against the institutional Church of the day and that did not rest well with many in authority. Another version, one with a less inflammatory tone was desired, so in **1568**, the bishops prepared a new translation without the marginal notes to present to Queen Elizabeth. It was called the **Bishop's Bible**.

Commentary from Geneva Bible Margins
1 Kings 14:16, Exodus 1:13-22, Daniel 3:19-29

In spite of 19 different printings between 1568 and **1606**, the **Bishop's Bible** never gained popularity among the people. The **Geneva version** was simply too trusted to compete with.

Casiodoro de Reina

Casiodoro de Reina (1520-1594) was the first to translate the entire Bible into Spanish. Born in Seville, Reina was raised Roman Catholic and became a monk at the San Isidro Monastery in Seville.

The Superior of the monastery was Dr. Blanco Garcia Arias, who had been influenced by the **Old Latin Bible** of the Waldenses and their preaching which had infiltrated the iron hand of Rome in Spain. Arias became a Believer and began reading to his students the writings of the Reformers.

Reina listened intently to the teachings of the Reformers and by reading **Pineda's New Testament** was converted to the Reformed Faith. He began to publicly proclaim the Reformation theme of "justification by faith." This brought persecution from Rome and it's Inquisition and Reina had to flee his homeland in **1557**.

Reina began his work on a translation of the Spanish Bible and in **1569**, he published the entire Bible in Spanish.

Reina's Spanish edition is commonly referred to as **"La Biblia del Oso"** or the "**Bear Bible**" because it used as its symbol a bear retrieving honey from a tree. The symbolism in the picture tells us a story. It is said that the hammer and the honey both represent the Word of God, and that the bees represent those faithful men who worked diligently to translate it into the common man's language. The bear (beast) represents the Roman Catholic Church which was trying to seek out and destroy God's Word, and the birds in the picture were used to symbolize the Inquisitor agents who were trying to catch and consume the translators before they could finish their work.

LA BIBLIA,
QVE ES, LOS SA-
CROS LIBROS DEL
VIEIO Y NVEVO TE-
STAMENTO.

Trasladada en Eſpañol.

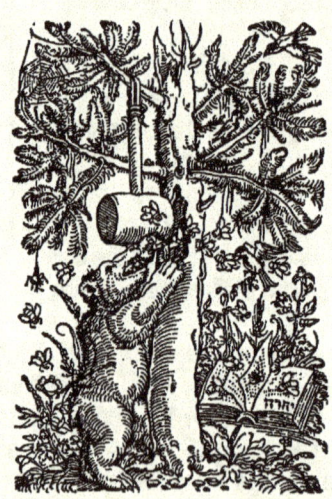

דבר אלהינו יקום לעולם

La Palabra del Dios nueſtro permanece para ſiempre. Iſa. 40.

M. D. LXIX.

1569 Spanish Bear Bible

From 1000 AD to 1600 AD

Reina used the **Masoretic Hebrew** text for the Old Testament, as well as the **Old Latin** text and **Ferrara's Spanish Old Testament**. For the New Testament he used the **Greek Textus Receptus** and compared it with the **Old Latin** and **Old Syraic manuscripts** known to him. Like many early Protestant Bibles, it does include the Apocrypha from the **Latin Vulgate**. However, in this case, the Apocrypha is scattered throughout the Old Testament in the same order set forth in the **Latin Vulgate** instead of segregated from the rest of the Bible as in many other Protestant Bibles.

In the Preface of the **Bear Bible**, Reina pointed out that he had not followed the **Latin Vulgate** completely because of *"the many errors"* that it had. It is evident that he recognized its many inaccuracies. He also expressed the desire for Christendom to get together a larger body of scholarly men, instead of having just a single translator, to produce a good translation that would match the original text.

Indeed, it is wise to realize that *"a translation should never be considered as complete as long as it has passed through the hands of one person only."*
(*Manuscript Releases*, Vol. 8, pg. 327)

However, God was using Reina as a step in the process of giving the pure Spanish Bible to the people.

Cipriano de Valera was born in **1531**, and his life mirrored that of Reina's. He, too, was a monk at the San Isidro Monastery in Seville and studied under the teaching of Dr. Arias. He was also influenced by **Pineda's New Testament**.

Valera was one of the ten who fled Spain with Casiodoro de Reina in **1557**.

Cipriano de Valera

Because Reina and Valera were out of the reach of the Inquisition and it could not destroy Reina and Valera themselves, on **April 26, 1562**, the Inquisition vented its anger by burning statues of Reina and Valera.

"...Reina and Valera, were condemned as Lutherans, and statues representing them were burned." (*Spanish Reformers of Two Centuries*, p.150)

In 1572 AD, the **Spanish Polyglot** or **Antwerp Polyglot Bible** was published. It was also called the **Plantin Polyglot** or the **Biblia Regia**.

The work of putting this Bible together was paid for by Philip II of Spain and was supervised by the Spanish scholar Benedictus Arias Montanus and printed in Antwerp by a well-known printer, Christopher Plantin. It was approved by Cardinal

Sword Unsheathed

Spinosa, the general of the inquisition, and received the approbation of the Pope. It contained the **Latin Vulgate**, the **Greek Septuagint**, and the **original Hebrew text**, along with the **Aramaic Targum** and the **Syriac Peshitta**.

On **August 24, 1572**, Jesuit and papal conspirators began forcing open doors and murdering Protestants throughout the city of Paris and continuing on to other towns in France. This rampage is known as the St. Bartholomew Day Massacre and results in an estimated 100,000 innocent and unsuspecting persons being murdered in cold blood, simply because they were Protestants.

"Over all Paris did the work of massacre by this time extend. Furious bands, armed with guns, pistols, swords, pikes, knives, and all kinds of cruel weapons, rushed through the streets, murdering all they met. They began to thunder at the doors of Protestants, and the terrified inmates, stunned by the uproar, came forth in their night-clothes, and were murdered on their own thresholds. Those who were too affrighted to come abroad, were slaughtered in their bed-rooms and closets, the assassins bursting open all places of concealment, and massacring all who opposed their entrance, and throwing their mangled bodies into the street."
(*History of Protestantism*, Vol.2, bk 17, p.603)

This butchery of innocent Protestants aroused the horror and indignation of the Protestant nations of Europe, but Rome celebrated this massacre and the Pope even had a coin minted in commemoration of this event.

The Jesuits were expelled from Protestant England in **1579**.

In **1582-1609**, the Jesuits translated the English **Douay-Rheims Bible** in France (using Jerome's corrupt **Latin Vulgate** for the source text), with the expressed purpose of sending their Bible into England to infiltrate that Protestant country from the inside and undermine the Protestant faith.

The **Douay/Rheims** was designed to counterfeit the **Geneva Bible**. The Jesuits' idea, since the Protestant principle "Sola Scriptura" didn't allow for Rome's corrupt theology, was that by adding corrupt English versions of the Bible to the market like the **Douay/Rheims**, it would cause confusion in place of the simple gospel. This is in accordance with, *"...the Jesuit motto, 'Where we cannot convince, we will confuse.'"* (*Truth Triumphant*, p.224)

When mankind rebelled against God and built the Tower of Babel, God "confounded" the rebel's language. So in retaliation, the devil and his agents, seek to "confuse" God's Word, by altering, changing, and counterfeiting it.

From 1000 AD to 1600 AD

The New Testament was translated at the Catholic College in the city of Rheims in **1582** and the Old Testament was translated in **1609** at the College in the city of Doway (also spelled Douay and Douai). Thus, the combined product is commonly referred to as the **"Douay/Rheims" Version**.

The Preface –*"To the English Reader"* of the **1582 Douay/Rheims** openly attacks at the root of all Protestant Bibles, saying *"that both the Hebrew and Greke editions are fouly corrupted by Jews and Heretikes."* For example, the **Douay/Rheims**, not suprisingly, classes as heretics both Wycliffe and the Waldensians. The preface goes on to praise **Jerome's Latin Vulgate** and to *"challenge English Protestants for corrupting the text"* purposely *"for the mainteyning of their peculiar opinions against the Catholliques."*

It is interesting to consider the title page after reading the preface. While it is obvious in the preface that only **Jerome's Latin Vulgate** is considered *"authentical"* as it is described on the title page; after the preface has called the Greek and Hebrew *"fouly corrupted"*, the title page claims to have *"diligently conferred with the Hebrew, Greeke, and other Editions in divers languages."* It is indeed evident that, historically, Catholics and Protestants maintained distinctly different (yet similar) Bibles.

A good example of how the **Douay/Rheims** changes the Word of God to agree with Papal theology while appearing to be within the scope of translation would be in James 5:16. The Protestant pure-line Bibles all use the word *"faults"* - such as this reading in the **Geneva Bible**, *"Acknowledge your faultes one to another, and pray one for another, that ye may be healed…"*

But the Papal versions like the **Douay/Rheims** say, *"Confess therefore your sins one to another: and pray one for another, that you may be saved…"* Admitting *"faults"* to one another and apologizing where the individual has trespassed, is totally different from confessing *"sins"* to one another. The Protestants understood this because God's Word specified it. Individuals are only to confess their sins to God, and Him alone! But Papalism claims God's prerogative and teaches mankind to confess their sins to a priest. Therefore, in many Papal-influenced Bibles, the word *"faults"* is changed to the word *"sins."*

But this change was only one of many ploys. Indeed, *"the Jesuits were operating all over Europe, inflaming the minds of kings and statesmen against the Reformation, and forming them into armed combinations to put it down."*

(History of Protestantism, vol.3 book 23, p.446)

Because copies of **Reina's Spanish Bear Bible** were extremely limited and it was very difficult to find copies of it, and also because it had some accidental mistakes and places that the translation could be improved in it, in **1582**, Valera began the work of revising Reina's **Bear Bible**.

Sword Unsheathed

In **1586** an English traitor named John Ballard who had received training from the Jesuits in Rheims contrived what became known in history as "the Babington Plot."

The Jesuits plan was to assassinate the Protestant Queen Elizabeth and call the Roman Catholics to arms. Then, while the flames of insurrection were raging in England, a Spanish army would land on its shores and besiege and sack any city that opposed them. They would then place Elizabeth's Roman Catholic cousin, Mary Queen of Scots, on the throne and return England to the Papal Church. However, all did not go as they had planned!

Mary Queen of Scots

Francis Walsingham

In the providence of God, Sir Frances Walsingham, who was not only an excellent statesman but also a loyal party to Queen Elizabeth, discovered the plot.

He kept quiet about what he had discovered until he had been able to find out all the names of the group of conspirators and then he disclosed the information to the authorities.

The conspirators were captured and executed and Mary Queen of Scots was found to be guilty of plotting with the Jesuits to assassinate her cousin. Mary was executed in **1587**.

In retaliation, the Jesuits arranged for King Philip II of Spain (former husband of "Bloody" Mary Tudor) to send his naval fleet in May of **1588**, to attack England and destroy both Elizabeth and Protestantism.

This navy was called the Spanish Armada and was considered one of the largest and most powerful navies that had ever existed. It consisted of 136 heavily armed ships, some of them with 50 cannons apiece, some 30,000 men and 180 Catholic priests.

England at this time did not have a military navy and could only gather about 30 regular ships with a few cannons, so from a human perspective, they did not stand a chance of winning any naval battle. But, after a little fighting, God again intervened and the Spanish Armada was hit with violent storms and wrecked on the rocks off the coast of England thereby suffering defeat in **1588**. Only 51 ships and about 10,000 survivors managed to limp back to Spain, while England lost no ships and only 60 men.

From 1000 AD to 1600 AD

Queen Elizabeth

With this victory over Spain, Queen Elizabeth and her kingdom of England became the champion and defender of Protestantism and the "ruler of the seas."

England became the impassable wall of defense which confined Catholicism to Europe, and by means of her territorial possessions, England committed the continent of North America to a Protestant future.

"Its [the Order of Jesuits] services to Roman Catholicism have been incalculable. The Jesuits alone rolled back the tide of Protestant advance when that half of Europe which had not already shaken off its allegiance to the Papacy, was threatening to do so, and the whole horrors of the counter-reformation are theirs singly."
(Encyclopedia Britannica, 9th Ed., art., Jesuits, par. 11)

Francisco Ribera

Between **1580** and **1590**, a Jesuit priest named Francisco Ribera, published his commentary on Revelation to promote the teaching of Futurism, which takes the Bible prophecies revealing that the Roman Catholic Church is the Antichrist system and applies them to some future time at the end of the Christian dispensation.

By misapplying the Bible prophecies in this way, his false doctrine points the finger in another direction and *"takes the heat off"* of the Catholic Church.

William Morgan

Also in **1588**, William Morgan published the first complete **Welsh Bible** from the Greek and Hebrew manuscripts. He also used the **Bishop's Bible** and the **Geneva Bible** as references in his translation work. Some of the orthography was changed/corrected in **1620** and this Bible formed the foundation stone on which modern Welsh literature has been based.

In **1599**, the **Nuremberg Polyglot Bible** was published by Elias Hutter (**1554–1602**) at Nuremberg. He was a Protestant professor of Hebrew in Leipzig and an unsurpassed linguist who had founded a "school of languages" which was without precedent in any school or university. He developed the ingenious plan to print the Hebrew Bible and have the radical letters in solid black and the servile letters in hollow white, while the quiescents were printed in smaller characters and placed above the line. This enabled the reader at a glance to be able to tell the root or elementary principle of each word. Hutter's success in this undertaking led him to produce the **Nuremberg Polyglot**.

"Hutter had meditated a Polyglot edition of the Old and New Testament, in twelve languages: of the Old Testament, the above, which extends only to Ruth, is all that ever appeared. The New Testament is in two volumes…" (*Introduction to the Knowledge of Rare and Valuable Editions of the Greek and Latin Classics*, p.16)

The **Nuremberg Polyglot** contained the entire New Testament in twelve languages laid out with exceptionally fine type-setting in Syriac, Hebrew, Greek, Latin, German, Bohemian, Italian, Spanish, Gallic, English, Danish, and Polish. Except for the Latin, the **Nuremberg Polyglot** was developed from Protestant Bibles.

The Syriac was taken from **Tremellius's 1569 second edition**, with certain additions by Hutter himself. The Hebrew was Hutter's own 1587 translation. The Greek was the **Textus Receptus**. The Latin he included for contrast was from **Jerome's Latin Vulgate** although he added Protestant "corrections" to some of the texts. The German he took from **Luther's German Bible**. The Bohemian, which is the old Czech dialect, he copied from a 1593 edition of the **Kralice Bible**.

Hutter Polyglot Title Page

The Italian he took from the Genevan version of **1562**. The Spanish he got from the **1562 Bear Bible** of Reina's. The French he copied from the Genevan revision of **1588**. The English he took from the **1562 Great Bible**.

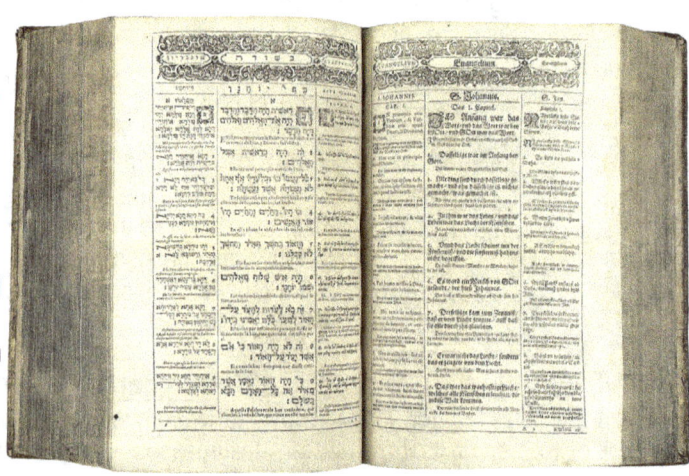

Hutter's Polyglot – 12 languages

The Danish was from the **King Christian III Bible**. The Polish was from the **1596** edition that had been translated from **Luther's German Bible**. The **Nuremberg Polyglot** was recognized by scholars as the New Testament study Bible and it is also commonly called the **Hutter Polyglot**.

From 1000 AD to 1600 AD

"The Polyglot Bible of Elias Hutterus...ranks among the scarcest books in bibliography." (*An Introduction to the Knowledge of Rare and Valuable Editions of the Greek and Latin Classics*, p.17)

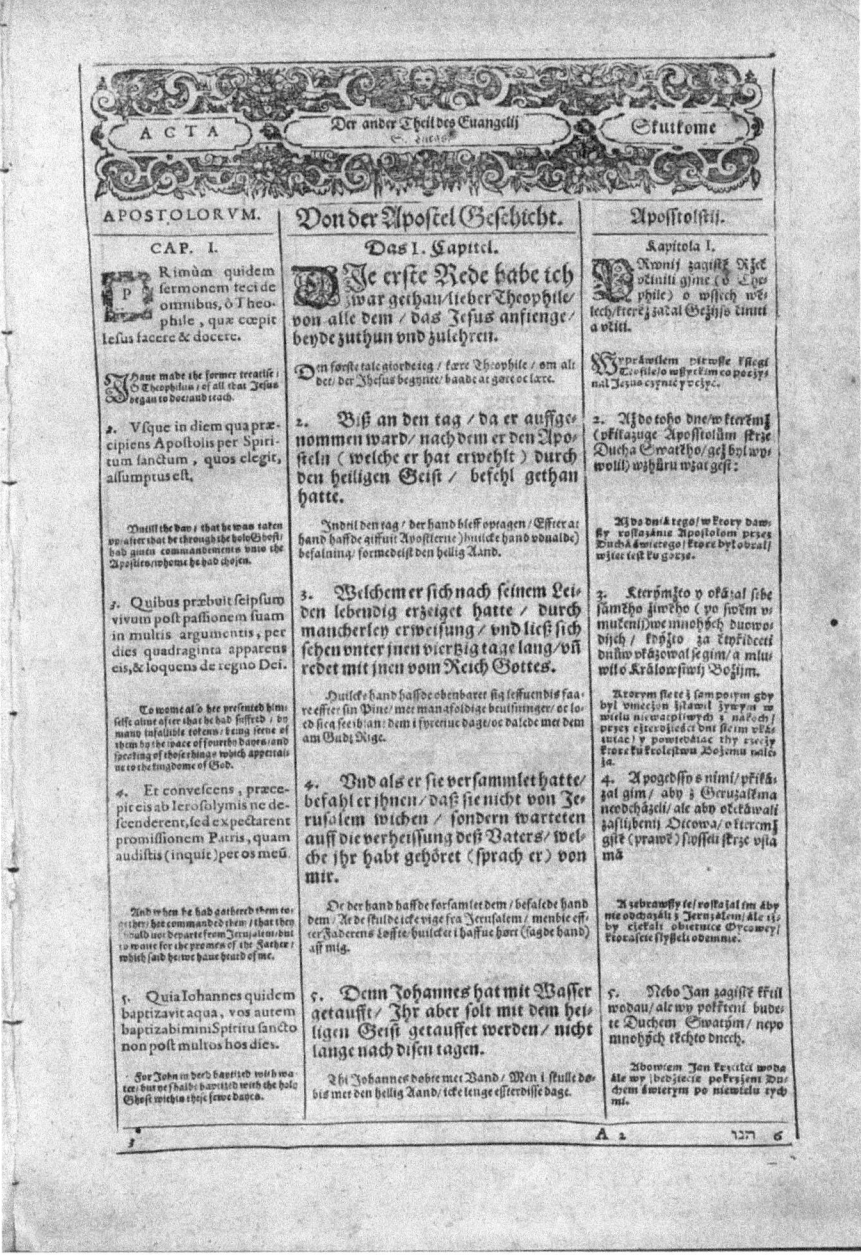

Nuremberg Polyglot – Page from Acts, Chapter 1

In **1601**, Pope Clement VIII caused an edict to be issued giving the Waldenses 60 days to attend mass and submit to the Roman Catholic Church or forfeit their lands to Rome. The Waldenses had to leave their homes and flee for refuge. Some went to the higher mountain valleys to resist the advancing armies, most of them fled to Geneva, and Switzerland opened her doors to welcome the poor refugees.

In **1602**, Cyril Lucar was elected Patriarch of Alexandria, Egypt. (This is a different Cyril from the one in the 5th century.) Cyril was friends with Beza and Calvin and was himself a fellow reformer and opponent of Rome.

"Cyril Lucar (1568-1638) born in the east, early embraced the principles of the Reformation, and for it, was pursued all his life by the Jesuits."
(Our Authorized Bible Vindicated, p.79)

During the years of his service in Alexandria, Cyril kept up active correspondence with the Protestant leaders in Europe.

"The fate of the Patriarch Cyril Lucar is well known; from his firm resistance to papal domination he was for many years unremittingly persecuted by the agents of Rome, who at last accomplished his murder in 1638."
(Eighteen Centuries of the Orthodox Greek Church, p.11)

After 20 years of labor, Valera finished his revision of Reina's **Bear Bible** in **1602**, and published what has become known as the **Reina-Valera Version**. Both Reina and Valera used **Pineda's New Testament** in their translation work. Changes that Valera made with Reina's **Bear Bible**, included placing back in the text some of the words and phrases evidently accidentally left out in Reina's **Bear Bible**. For example, Valera returned to its place the rightful Hebrews 12:29 *"Porque nuestro Dios es fuego confumidor"* as well as adding the missing *"by faith"* phrase in Romans 3:28. The Apocrypha was removed from the Old Testament and placed between the two Testaments to agree with most Protestant Bibles of that day. Valera also added a note, as the **Geneva Bible** did, stating the historical importance of the Apocrypha and yet denying its inspiration.

The title page of the Reina-Valera Version shows two men planting and watering a tree. It is believed that Valera was illustrating his belief that the planter of the seed was Reina, while he viewed himself as simply the one who watered Reina's version through revision.

Picture on the Title Page of the Reina-Valera Bible

From 1000 AD to 1600 AD

The **Czech Kralice Bible** was translated by leading Protestant scholars of Huss' Unity of the Brethren and printed in their print shop in Kralice in Southern Moravia. Jan Blahoslav translated the New Testament from the original Greek in **1564** and from **1579** to **1593**, five additional volumes of the Old Testament was published by Zacharias Solin. In **1596**, a single volume edition was printed, followed in **1602** by the second revision and then by a third revision printed in **1613**.

It was this **1613** edition that became the standard text for the Czech Bible for centuries to come. This Bible was for Bohemia, Moravia, and Slovakia what the **KJV** was for England. However, it was illegal to own a copy of this translation. Because of this, it had to be read in secret. Many **Kralice Bibles** were destroyed and their owners were prosecuted by Rome when they were found.

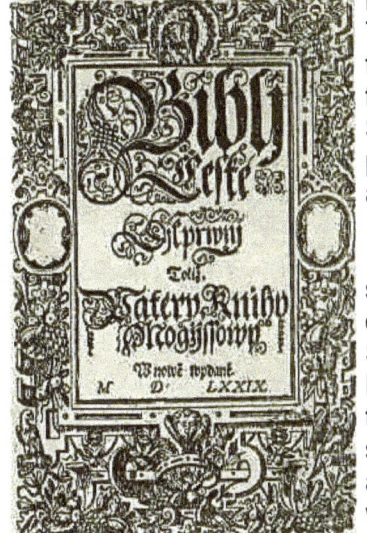

Czech Kralice Bible Title Pg.

Queen Elizabeth I died **March 24, 1603** and in **April 1603**, James VI, King of Scotland, traveled south from Scotland to London to take the throne and become King James I of England.

In **1604**, King James I ordered the work begun to create the **King James Bible**. (See the next chapter for more details)

In **1605**, 13 Jesuit terrorists plotted to kill King James and the entire Anti-Papal Parliament. They smuggled 6,000 pounds (36 barrels) of gunpowder through secret tunnels and hid them under the Parliament building with the plan to detonate it while Parliament was in session with the King in attendance. They left Guy Fawkes alongside the gunpowder with orders to ignite it at a certain time.

God intervened again and on **November 5, 1605**, just hours before the powder was to be detonated, the scheme was discovered and the plot was foiled. The conspirators were caught and executed. This was known in history as the Gunpowder Plot.

Later, the people of the United Kingdom began celebrating the failure of this Jesuit plot on November 5 with bonfires. It is called "Guy Fawkes Night" and is still celebrated today, though many people seem to be ignorant of the real story behind the celebration. Many people even wear a Jesuit Guy Fawkes mask when staging events incognito.

Fawkes Mask

Sword Unsheathed

Giovanni Diodati, who succeeded Beza in the chair of Theology at Geneva, translated **Erasmus' Received Text** into Italian in **1606** and published it in **1607**. This **Italian Bible of Diodati** was also adopted by the Waldenses.

Giovanni Diodati

"During their severe persecutions the Waldenses came into contact with the Reformers at Geneva, and thus their Bible, which had been preserved in its apostolic purity, was brought to the Reformers." (Facts of Faith, p.18)

The Waldensian historian and pastor, Leger, revealed details in his own **Diodati Bible**.

"...preserved in one of the pages of an old Italian Bible, now in the possession of the Dean of Winchester. It was Leger's own Bible, and in it he traced these melancholy lines with his own hands.

"'Questa S. Biblia e' l'unico tesoro che di tutti miei beni ho potuto riscampare dagl' orribile massacri è incomparabile incendie che la corte di Torino ha fatti eseguir nelle valli di Piemonte del 1655, ce per questo (oltre che vi sono piu nottule di mia mano) raccommando et commando a miei figli di conservarla come una preciosissima reliqua, e di transmetterla di mano in mano alla loro posterita. GIOVANNI LEGERO, Pastore.'

"'This holy Bible is the only treasure which, of all my goods, I was able to rescue from the horrible massacres, and unparalleled destructions which the court of Turin put in execution, in the valleys of Piemont, in 1655, and for this reason (besides that there are in it many small remarks in my own hand-writing) I recommend and command my children to preserve it as a most valuable relic, and to transmit it, from hand to hand, to their posterity. John LEGER, Pastor.'

From 1000 AD to 1600 AD

"The title-page of this Bible runs thus:
'La Sacra Biblia, tradotta in Lingua Italiana, e commentata da Giovanni Diodati, di Nazione Lucchese, Seconda Editione migliorata ed accresciuta con l'aggiunta di Sacri Salmi messi in rime per lo medesimo. Per Pietro Chovet, MDCXLI.'
"By the kindness of the Dean of Winchester I have been enabled to present my readers with a fac simile of this curious memorandum."

(Waldensian Researches During a Second Visit to the Vaudois of Piemont, Section III, pg. 79,80)

1641 Diodati Bible Title Page

Indeed, the **Diodati Bible** preserved the treasure of the holy scriptures and the gospel that so many Waldensians gave their lives to protect, and so the Reformation continued.

Facsimile of John 3:16 from the 1607 Italian Diodati Bible

In **1609**, John Smyth, an English separatist exiled in Amsterdam, started his own church, which later grew into the Baptist church. The name Baptist was so called after a main tenent of "believer's baptism" which follows the biblical Mennonite and Anabaptist belief of baptism by immersion. And thus the succession of truth continues.

Whether considering English Bibles or foreign Bibles, with their multiudes of reformers, martyrs, scribes, and translators, J.A. Wylie's words state well, *"We owe the Bible – that is, the transmission of it – to those persecuted communities which we have so rapidly passed in review. They received it from the primitive Church, and carried it down to us. They translated it into the mother tongues of the nations. They colported it over Christendom, singing it in their lays as troubadours, preaching it in their sermons as missionaries, and living it out as Christians. They fought the battle of the Word of God against tradition, which sought to bury it. They sealed their testimony for it at the stake. But for them, so far as human agency is concerned, the Bible would, ere this day, have disappeared from the world."* (History of Protestantism, vol.1, book 1, p.56)

Waldensian Bible Translators

The King James Bible (KJV)

The Hampton Court Conference was held **January 14-16, 1604**. It was here that the Puritans presented their requests for reform in the Church of England to the king. Even though King James, who, as the King of England, was also the head of the Church of England, had grown up with the **Geneva Bible**, he did not approve of all the marginal notes in the **Geneva Bible** because they were very much opposed to hierarchical church government.

King James

After much discussion and argument, and at the suggestion of the Puritan leader, Dr. John Reynolds, it was decided, *"That a translation be made of the whole Bible, as consonant as can be to the original Hebrew and Greek; and this is to be set out and printed, without any marginal notes, and only to be used in all Churches of England in time of divine service."* This decision was the conception of the **King James Bible**.

By **June 30, 1604**, the names of 54 men who would work on the translation project had been chosen. A few of these names are not found in the records today, but those which are have been listed below along with a sample of some of their qualifications.

The men were divided into six companies and assigned certain portions of the Bible. Each company had a leader or **director*** who was in charge of the group. The members of the different companies are as follows:

I. The Old Testament Translators at Westminster
Translated Genesis through the Second Book of Kings.

Lancelot Andrews

- ***Dr. Lancelot Andrews D.D.**, Dean of Westminster; was called the "star of preachers" and one of the "rarest linguists in Christendom." This was because Andrews could speak 15 current languages fluently and he could easily read and understand at least six other ancient languages – including Latin, Greek, Hebrew, Chaldee, Syriac, and Arabic.
- **Dr. John Overall D.D.**, Dean of St. Paul's Cathedral; knew several languages and was a fluent speaker of Latin.
- **Dr. Hadrian Saravia D.D.**, Prebendary of Westminster; knew several languages including Spanish, Hebrew, French, and Dutch
- **Dr. Richard Clarke D.D.**, Vicar of Minster and Monkton in Thanet
- **Dr. John Laifield D.D.**, Rector of the Church of St. Clement's, Dane's, in London; skilled in architecture

- **Dr. Robert Tighe D.D.**, Archdeacon of Middlesex; Vicar of the Church of All Hallows, Barking, London; excellent textuary and profound linguist
- **Francis Burleigh D.D.**, Vicar of Bishop's Stortford
- **Geoffry King**, Regius Professor of Hebrew at King's College, Cambridge;
- **Richard Thompson**, Fellow of Clare Hall, Cambridge; Philologist [one versed in history and the construction of language], known all over England, Italy, France, and Germany
- **Dr. William Bedwell**, Vicar of Tottenliam High Cross, near London; expert in Mathematics and conversant in eastern languages especially Arabic, he wrote a seven volume Lexicon called Lexicon Heptaglotten which contained Hebrew, Syriac, Chaldee, and Arabic.

II. The New Testament Translators at Westminster
Translated the books of Romans through Jude

- ***Dr. William Barlow D.D.**, Prebendary of Westminster; Dean of Chester
- **Dr. John Spencer D.D.**, Vicar of St. Sepulchre's beyond Newgate, London; Greek lecturer for Corpus Christi College, Oxford
- **Dr. Roger Fenton D.D.**, Rector of St. Bennet's, Sherehog; Vicar of Chigwell, in Essex
- **Dr. Ralph Hutchinson D.D.**, President of St. John's College
- **William Dakins**, Professor of Divinity at Gresham College, London; Dean of Trinity College; skilled in the original languages; (died in **1606** before translation work was completed)
- **Michael Rabbet**, Rector of the Church of St. Vedast, Foster Lane, London; Bachelor in Divinity
- **[Thomas(?)] Sanderson D.D.**, Archdeacon of Rochester; (not known if he was on the committee)

III. The Old Testament Translators at Cambridge University
Translated First Chronicles through Ecclesiastes.

- ***Edward Lively**, King's Professor of Hebrew (died May, **1605**, before translation work was done); was considered "one of the best linguists in the world", Hebraist & Orientalist
- **Dr. John Richardson D.D.**, Master of Peterhouse & King's Professor of Divinity; considered a "most excellent linguist"
- **Dr. Lawrence Chaderton D.D.**, Master of Emanuel College; conversant in Spanish, French, Latin, Greek, Italian, and Hebrew, as well as familiar with the Rabbinical writings
- **Francis Dillingham**, Fellow of Christ's College, Cambridge; noted as an excellent linguist
- **Dr. Roger Andrews D.D.**, Master of Jesus College, Cambridge; a famous linguist; brother of Lancelot
- **Thomas Harrison**, Vice-Master of Trinity College, Cambridge; exquisite skill in the Hebrew and Greek idioms

The King James Bible (KJV)

- **Dr. Robert Spaulding D.D.**, succeeded Edward Lively as Regius Professor of Hebrew
- **Dr. Andrew Bing D.D.**, Subdean of York; later became Regius Professor of Hebrew

    IV. The Apocrypha Translators at Cambridge
         Translated the apocryphal books.

- *****Dr. John Duport D.D.**, Precentor of St. Paul's, London
- **Dr. William Brainthwaite D.D.**, Master of Gonvil and Caius College
- **Dr. Jeremiah Radcliffe D.D.**, Vice-Master of Trinity College, Cambridge
- **Dr. Samuel Ward D.D.**, Master of Sidney Sussex College
- **Dr. Andrew Downes D.D.**, Regius Professor of Greek at St. John's College, Cambridge
- **John Bois**, Greek lecturer at St. John's College, Cambridge; he was an expert in both Hebrew and Greek [had read the whole Bible in Hebrew by age five, could write fair and elegant Hebrew by age six – spent eight hours/day in study and was considered "second to none" in the Greek tongue]; wrote a voluminous commentary on the Gospels in the Latin language; (After his work on the Apocrypha with his company was finished, he was asked to help the Old Testament committee at Cambridge after the death of their president Edward Lively.)
- **Dr. John Ward D.D.**, Prebendary of Chichester; Rector of Bishop's Waltham in Hampshire.
- **Dr. John Aglionby D.D.**, Rector of Islip; Principal of St. Edmund's Hall, University of Oxford; excellent linguist and very knowledgeable in the writings of the fathers and the schoolmen; (Died in **1609**)
- **Dr. Leonard Hutten D.D.**, Vicar of Flower in Northamptonshire; expert in Greek, elegant scholar, and well versed in history of England, the fathers, the schoolmen, and the learned languages.
- **Dr. Thomas Bilson D.D., Bishop of Worcester; well skilled in languages**
- **Dr. Richard Bancroft D.D.**, Archbishop of Canterbury; the one to oversee the business part of the translation of the **KJV** and make sure the rules were followed.

    V. The Old Testament Translators at Oxford
        Translated Isaiah through Malachi.

- *****Dr. John Harding D.D.**, President of Magdalen College; Royal Professor of Hebrew
- **Dr. John Reynolds D.D.**, President of Corpus Christi College; had a photographic memory and had studied the Scriptures in all the original tongues, and read all the Greek and Latin fathers, and all the ancient records of the Church – could at any time turn to any sentence he had ever read in any work – was known as "a living library"
- **Dr. Thomas Holland D.D.**, Rector of Exeter College; familiar with several languages and science

John Reynolds

- **Dr. Richard Kilby D.D.**, Rector of Lincoln College; Prebendary of the Cathedral church of Lincoln; excellent critic in the Hebrew and Greek languages
- **Dr. Miles Smith D.D.**, Canon-residentiary of the Cathedral church of Hereford; expert in Chaldee, Syriac, and Arabic languages, and well acquainted with history, the Greek and Latin fathers, and the Rabbinical writings
- **Dr. Richard Brett D.D.**, Rector of Quainton in Buckinghamshire; expert in Latin, Greek, Hebrew, Chaldee, Arabic, and Ethiopic languages
- **Daniel Fairclough (Featley) D.D.**, Fellow of Corpus Christi College; chaplain to Sir Thomas Edwards

VI. The New Testament Translators at Oxford

Translated the four Gospels, the book of Acts, and the book of Revelation.
- ***Dr. Thomas Ravis D.D.**, Bishop of Gloucester
- **Dr. George Abbot D.D.**, Vice-Chancellor of Winchester University
- **Dr. Richard Eedes D.D.**, Dean of Worcester; chaplain to Queen Elizabeth and King James; (He died on Nov. 19th, **1604**, soon after his appointment to be one of the translators and was replaced by Dr. Leonard Hutten)
- **Dr. Giles Tomson D.D.**, Dean of Windsor; chaplain to Queen Elizabeth
- **Sir Henry Saville**, Warden of Merton College; Provost of Eton College; expert in Greek and mathematics as well as tutor to Queen Elizabeth; highly knowledgeable in learning and world history, translated into English and Latin languages many renowned works
  - **Dr. John Peryn D.D.**, Vicar of Wafting in Sussex; King's Professor of Greek at St. John's College, Oxford
  - **Dr. Ralph Ravens D.D.**, Vicar of Eyston Magna, (appointed to translation committee, but did not participate for some reason and was replaced by Dr. John Aglionby)
  - **Dr. John Harmar D.D.**, King's Professor of Greek; adept in the art of translating into Latin, French, and English

Henry Saville

The translators were given the following specific set of 15 rules to control the translation project.

"1. The ordinary Bible read in the Church, commonly called the Bishops Bible, to be followed, and as little altered as the Truth of the original will permit.
2. The names of the Prophets, and the Holy Writers, with the other Names of the Text, to be retained, as nigh as may be, accordingly as they were vulgarly used.
3. The Old Ecclesiastical Words to be kept, viz. the Word Church not to be translated Congregation &c.
4. When a Word hath divers Significations, that to be kept which hath been most commonly used by the most of the Ancient Fathers, being agreeable to the Propriety of the Place, and the Analogy of the Faith.
5. The Division of the Chapters to be altered, either not at all, or as little as may be, if Necessity so require.

The King James Bible (KJV)

6. No Marginal Notes at all to be affixed, but only for the explanation of the Hebrew or Greek Words, which cannot without some circumlocution, so briefly and fitly be expressed in the Text.
7. Such Quotations of Places to be marginally set down, as shall serve for the fit Reference of one Scripture to another.
8. Every particular Man of each Company, to take the same Chapter or Chapters, and having translated or amended them severally by himself, where he thinketh good, all to meet together, confer what they have done, and agree for their Parts what shall stand.
9. As any one Company hath dispatched any one Book in this Manner they shall send it to the rest, to be considered of seriously and judiciously, for His Majesty is very careful in this Point.
10. If any Company, upon the Review of the Book so sent, doubt or differ upon any Place, to send them Word thereof; note the Place, and withal send the Reasons, to which if they consent not, the Difference to be compounded at the general Meeting, which is to be of the chief Persons of each Company, at the end of the Work.
11. When any Place of special Obscurity is doubted of, Letters to be directed by Authority, to send to any Learned Man in the Land, for his Judgement of such a Place.
12. Letters to be sent from every Bishop to the rest of his Clergy, admonishing them of this Translation in hand; and to move and charge as many skillful in the Tongues; and having taken pains in that kind, to send his particular Observations to the Company, either at Westminster, Cambridge, or Oxford.
13. The Directors in each Company, to be the Deans of Westminster, and Chester for that Place; and the King's Professors in the Hebrew or Greek in either University.
14. These translations to be used when they agree better with the Text than the Bishops Bible, viz.: Tyndoll's [Tyndale's], Matthew's, Coverdale's, Whitchurch's [Great Bible], Geneva.
15. Besides the said Directors before mentioned, three or four of the most Ancient and Grave Divines, in either of the Universities, not employed in Translating, to be assigned by the vice-Chancellor, upon Conference with the rest of the Heads, to be Overseers of the Translations as well Hebrew as Greek, for the better observation of the 4th Rule above specified."

(*The History of the English Bible*, p.330-331)

From **1604** to **1606**, each man worked privately on the chapters that had been assigned to him, carefully weighing each word and digging deeper to understand the true meaning of each word, before he wrote it down.

When he finished his chapters, they were then given to each other man in his company who then translated them himself in the same way. In this way, each chapter was checked by each man in the company.

Then when a book was completed it was then sent to each of the other companies, who would then carefully go through it and double-check it and make suggestions. The suggestions were then resolved by the directors of each of the companies.

The meetings of the six different companies took another three years, from **1607–1609**. *"By this judicious plan, each part must have been closely scrutinized at least fourteen times."* *(The Translators Revived, p.69)*

It was understood that if there was any special difficulty or obscurity discovered, that all the learned men of the land could be called upon by letter for their judgment in the matter. Each bishop also kept the clergy of his diocese notified concerning the progress of the work, and if any one felt impressed to send in any particular observations or recommendations, he was allowed to do so at any time.

In other words, all the religious leaders of England had a voice in the translation work of the **King James Bible**. This also helped to ensure that no one man or even a small group of men would have any undue influence on any part of the scripture.

The **King James Bible** is the only translation that has ever been done that was screened by, not just the translators, but by the whole church body – before it was published. It could well be described as a translation "by the people" and "for the people."

"A translation should never be considered as complete as long as it has passed through the hands of one person only. For the translation of the Holy Scriptures, in many lands, a large number of men were chosen who labored together, closely examining and mutually criticizing their work."
(Manuscript Releases, vol.8, p.327)

The Bibles and Bible Manuscripts that were referenced, used, and compared by the translators in their translation work included (but were not limited to):

Ben Chayyim Masoretic Text
Bishop's Bible
Diodati Bible
Tyndale's Bible
Matthew's Bible
Luther's Bible
Coverdale Bible
Olivetan Bible
Great Bible
Geneva Bible
Tepl Bible

Beza's 1598 edition
Hutter's 1599 Nuremberg Polyglot
1588 Pastor's Bible
Spanish Valencia 1478 Bible
Pinel 1553 Bible
Reina's 1569 Bible
1572 Antwerp Polyglot
Valera 1602 Bible
Stephanus 1550/1551 editions
Erasmus' 5th Textus Receptus

The King James Bible (KJV)

The translators looked at all the original manuscripts in Greek, Hebrew, and vernacular (native language) as well as comparing to the other foreign language Bibles and manuscripts.

It is also important to realize that with the extensive knowledge of the many languages that the translators had, they could easily read and understand every word in every translation and manuscript available. ALL the translators spoke English and were fluent in Hebrew, Greek, and Latin and they could easily read **Beza's Latin text** which preserved the old original Latin (**Itala**) and was helpful in identifying the most ancient readings.

The **KJV** translators also collected all the chief manuscripts of Chrysostom whose manuscripts contain numerous scripture citations from the pure manuscripts that circulated around Antioch. These scripture citations from Chrysostom are of equal antiquity and better authority than the corrupt MSS of **B** and **Aleph**.

Henry Saville himself paid scholars beyond the seas, what would amount to about $1,116,900.00 in today's American money, just so he could obtain the best manuscripts of Chrysostom for the translators to use in reference. He later compiled these manuscripts into an eight volume collection and had them published in **1613** under the title *S. Johannis Chrysostomi Opera, Graece.*

Finally, after all the Bible books had been translated and circulated among all the companies, three complete copies were sent to London – one copy from the groups at Oxford, one copy from the groups at Cambridge, and one copy from the groups at Westminster.

Then two of the ablest members of each of the six companies who were thoroughly conversant in the work from the beginning were chosen to go to London to prepare a single copy from these three copies. These 12 well-qualified men formed the general committee who then assembled daily at Stationer's Hall to carefully consider the completed work of the six companies.

Each man was given the part of the Bible that he was considered to be the most proficient in. Then he would read it aloud while the other 11 men followed along in another Bible from another language such as Greek, Hebrew, Latin, French, Italian, Spanish, etc. If they discovered any problem at all, they would interrupt and state the problem and revise the phraseology. If not, they remained silent while he continued to read.

It is said of the **KJV** translators that *"They wrote with a sense of rhythm, as if the words were meant to be sung."*

In the **1500's** and early **1600's**, the Apocrypha books were accepted reading

Sword Unsheathed

based only on its "historical value." For this reason, they were many times included in historical works, and in various Bibles.

King James

Protestants did not accept them as scripture and, in fact, they were not accepted as Scripture by anyone outside of the Catholic Church.

King James himself said, *"...as to the Apocrypha books, I omit them, because I am no Papist, as I said before; and indeed some of them are no ways like the dictation of the Spirit of God."*

The **KJV** translators knew that the Apocryphal books were not part of the "inspired Word of God" and this is why they chose to simply place them in a separate section by themselves, but between the Old and New Testaments for use as a "historical reference." They did not integrate the Apocryphal books into the Old Testament text as the corrupt Alexandrian manuscripts do.

The reasons which they gave for not incorporating it into the text of the **KJV** are:

1. *None of the Apocryphal books are in the Hebrew language, which was what was used by the writers of the Old Testament.*
2. *None of the writers lay any claim to inspiration.*
3. *These books were never acknowledged as sacred Scriptures by the Jewish Church, nor sanctioned Christ.*
4. *They were not allowed among the sacred books during the 1st four centuries of the Christian Church.*
5. *They contain fictitious statements, and statements which contradict not only the canonical Scriptures, but the writings themselves; such as when, in the two Books of Maccabees, Antiochus Epiphanes is made to die three different deaths in three different places.*
6. *They teach doctrines at variance with the Bible, such as prayers for the dead and sinless perfection.*
7. *They teach immoral practices, such as lying, suicide, assassination and magical incantation.*

Whenever the translators found it necessary, for the sake of clarity in English, to insert a word that was not in the original, they put it in italics, so that the reader would be immediately alerted to the fact and recognize that it was a supplied word and not in the original manuscript.

When the final translation was done, it was delivered to the printer, which then took nine months to print the Bible. The first two original printings of the **King James Version Bible** were then made available to the public in **1611**.

The King James Bible (KJV)

Due to the primitive technology of printing in **1611**, there were various printing errors associated with these printings as was to be expected in any printing. Type had to be set by hand, letter by letter, and it was usually done indoors by the light of a candle or by lamp light. This caused there to be numerous "spelling" errors and misprints.

In **1612-1613**, they begin to change the typography from the Gothic type to the Roman type in the **KJV**.

The **1611** edition had been printed in the Gothic style font which was meant to simulate the handwriting of the Middle Ages. This font was difficult to read and in order to make the Bible easier for the common people to read, the Gothic font was changed to the Roman style which is what is commonly used today.

Gothic Font

Roman font

"Change in the type font from Gothic (originating in Germany) to Roman type font style. Originally the printers chose the Gothic style for its beauty. In 1612 the first King James Bible was printed in Roman type font style. For example,
  a) a Gothic lower case "s" at the beginning or middle of a word looks like our "f", so that "also" was written as "alfo", and "set" was written as "fet".
  b) Gothic "v" was written as "u", and Gothic "u" was written as "v", so that "love" was written as "loue", "us" was written as "vs", and "ever" was written as "euer".
  c) Gothic "j" was written as our "i", so that "Jesus" was written as "Iefus", and "joy" as "ioy".
Key: These are type style changes, not spelling changes. These changes account for most of the so called "thousands" of changes in the KJV, yet do no harm to the text." (Serious Omissions in the NIV Bible, p.110)

In **1629**, another edition of the **King James Version** was printed at Cambridge that corrected about 72% of the 400 printing errors of the former editions. They also updated some of the orthography (capitalization and spelling).

In **1638**, only 27 years after the original printing, another edition was printed to correct the rest of the printing errors and orthography.

These two editions (**1629** & **1638**) were assisted by *"Dr. Samuel Ward and Mr. [John] Bois, two of the original Translators"* (Translators Revived, p.222) who had access to the original notes of the translators and could easily double check the spelling.

An example of these corrections would be the **1611** reference to Matthew 26:34 where, *"Jesus said unto him, Verily I say unto thee, That this might, before the cock crow, thou shalt deny me thrice."* As the reader can discern, the early printers accidentally put an "M" into the type instead of the letter "N." This was corrected, and by the **1638** edition it reads, *'Jesus said unto him, Verily I say unto thee, That this night, before the cock crow, thou shalt deny me thrice.'*

These two editions were not new revisions, but were two stages of one process: the purification of the orthography and early printing errors.

It took the **KJV** a few years to become as popular with the common people as the **Geneva Bible** had been but it eventually became the Bible for the English people.

In **1647**, the Archbishop of Canterbury, in the *Westminster Confession of Faith*, "officially" repudiated the Apocrypha from the canon of the English Bible. At this point, some Bible printings ceased to include the Apocryphal books altogether.

"The Books commonly called Apocrypha, not being of Divine inspiration, are no part of the Canon of the Scripture and therefore are of no authority in the Church of God, nor to be any other wise approved, or made use of, then other humane Writings." (Westminster Confession of Faith, p.3)

In **1762**, another edition of the **KJV** Bible was made at Cambridge by Dr. Thomas Paris, as the first of a two stage process to standardize the spelling into more modern English and also to fix punctuation marks. The next edition produced at Oxford by Dr. Benjamin Blayney in **1769** finished this process.

An example of these language standardizing changes would be changing the spelling in Matthew 1:17 from the **1611** reading, *"So all the generations from Abraham to David, are fourteene generations: ..."* to the **1769** reading of, *"So all the generations from Abraham to David are fourteen generations; ..."* The reader can easily see that all they did was change the spelling of the word "fourteen" to the modern spelling of that word, remove a comma, and change the colon to a semi-colon.

This **1769** edition completed the standardization of the spelling of the **KJV**. It is from this edition (except for a few changes in punctuation), that many of the non-copyrighted authorized **KJV** Bibles of today are made.

The King James Bible (KJV)

Title Page of 1611 King James Version

Sword Unsheathed

The Translators had made it clear that their united goal in translating the **King James Bible** was to do such a thorough job and produce such a perfect translation, that it would never need to be retranslated.

The Board of Managers of the American Bible Society in **1852**, 240+ years after it was first produced, had this to say about the **King James Version**:

"The English Bible as left by the translators has come down to us unaltered in respect to its text…With the exception of topographical errors and changes required by the process of orthography in the English language, the text of our present Bibles remains unchanged, and without variations from the original copy as left by the translators."

The **KJV** became the most printed book in the history of the world. For around 250 years, the **King James Version** reigned without a rival. It stands as the "best-selling book of all time" and the "most glorious document in the history of the English language."

"…during the reign of our late good Queen Victoria, who in her natural and characteristic manner told, and told truly, the inquiring prince from the far-off land that the Bible was 'the secret of England's greatness,' the unparalleled prosperity of the country, the enormous growth of its population, and the increase of its power, must at once appeal to the minds of all." (All About the Bible, p.43)

The deposit of many words from many other languages into the English word bank has led to its highly distinctive feature of having different words to express the same thing. A person can **"rise"** up in the Anglo-Saxon language (Matthew 20:19), **"mount"** up in the French (Isaiah 40:31), or **"ascend"** up in the Latin (John 20:17).

This rich English vocabulary gives the **King James Bible** a vast storehouse from which to draw in order to create its alliteration, rhythm, and rhyme. It also gives the **King James Bible** an international vocabulary which can, with a little effort, be recognized by many nationalities which share the Latin alphabet, even if they don't understand English. If the reader compares a text from the various time periods, he can decipher some of the words and meaning, even though he may not be able to wholly read the old text.

Matthew 7:13 from the **Gothic Scriptures** of 360 AD reads:
"Ïnngaggaiþ þairh aggwu daur; unte braid daur, yah rums wigs sa brigganda ïn fralustai, yal managai sind þai ïnngaleiþandans þairh þata."

Matthew 7:13 from the **Anglo-Saxon Scriptures** in 995 AD reads:
"Gangaþ inn þurh ðæt nearwe geat; forðon ðe ðæt geat is swýðe wid, and se weg is swiðe rúm ðe to forspillednesse gelǽt, and swýðe manega synt ðe þurh ðone weg faraþ."

The King James Bible (KJV)

Matthew 7:13 from **Tyndale's** 1526 Bible reads:
"Enter in at the strayte gate; ffor wyde is the gate, and broade ys the waye thatt leadeth to destruccion, and many there be which goo yn there att."

Matthew 7:13 in the **1611 King James Bible** reads:
"Enter ye in at the strait gate, for wide is the gate, and broad is the way that leadeth to destruction, and many there be which goe in thereat:"

One point of interest is that the translators used the word "LORD" (all in capital letters) in most of the verses where the Greek and Hebrew manuscripts used the word "Jehovah." One of the reasons for this, is because they were translating the Bible into the English language, and the word "Jehovah" is the Hebrew word. Since the translators (and the Protestant Reformation) were all about having the Bible in the language of the people, they were trying to use an English equivalent to the Hebrew word – hence their use of "all caps." However, there are four texts (Ex. 6:3; Ps. 83:18; Is. 12:2; Is. 26:4) where they found it necessary to use the specific Hebrew name "Jehovah."

Note: Capitals make a difference. The word "LORD" (all caps) in the **KJV** is "Jehovah" which is the personal name of God (Ex. 15:3). The word "lord" (lower case) in the **KJV** is the word "adon" which means "master" "owner" or "controller" and it can be used in reference to a man (Gen. 18:12). The word "Lord" (with only L in caps) in the **KJV** is "Adoni" or "Adonay" which is the emphatic form of "adon" and it is used as a proper name or title of God only (Ps. 68:20).

Contrary to popular opinion, the English language that is used in the **King James Bible** was not the common English used in the 17th century. In fact, the English found in the **1568 Bishops Bible** is more like our common simpler English today than some of the English found in the **King James Bible**. The truth of the matter is, that the English that is found throughout the **King James Bible** was not the common English that was spoken anywhere or at any time in history. The English that is found in the **King James Bible** is so unique and distinct, that it can accurately be labeled as "Biblical English." It was the English that resulted from the translators giving a faithful and accurate translation of the original Greek and Hebrew into the English language.

One author wrote of the language of the **KJV**: *"Each word was broad, simple, and generic. That is to say, words were capable of containing in themselves not only their central thoughts, but also all the different shades of meaning which were attached to that central thought. Since then, words have lost that living, pliable breadth. Vast additions have been made to the English vocabulary during the past 300 years, so that several words are now necessary to convey the same meaning which formerly was conveyed by one. It will be readily seen that while the English vocabulary has increased in quantity, nevertheless, single words have lost their many shades, combinations of words have become fixed, capable of only one* *meaning, and therefore less adaptable to receiving into English the thoughts of the Hebrew which likewise is a simple, broad, generic language. New Testament Greek is, in this respect, like the Hebrew."* (Our Authorized Bible Vindicated, p.74)

Let's take a look at some of the wording used in the **King James Version**.

For example: Critics ignorantly like to claim that the use of words such as "thee" and "thou" are old and archaic English that are not commonly used anymore and should be replaced with more modern words like "you" and "your."

What they fail to realize is that "thee" and "thou" was not common English when the **KJV** was translated, the words "you" and "your" were what was commonly used in everyday speech. This can easily be shown by reading the **1611** *"Dedication to King James"* and the translator's *"To The Reader Preface"* – neither of which use the words "thee" or "thou" in its text.

The translators chose to use words like "thee" and "thou" in the translation of the scriptures because they carry a very different meaning than "you" or "your." The "Thee" and the "Thou" are both "singular" while "You" and "Your" are both "plural." The original Hebrew and Greek manuscripts differentiated between singular and plural, and the **KJV** translators, in order to stay faithful to the original, used "Thee" and "Thou" in the text of the **King James Bible** to make these singular and plural distinctions clear. All the newer Bible translations that change the singular wording to the plural "You" and "Your" lose this accurate distinction.

Also, if the critics arguments were true, then one should not see the "Thee" and "Thou" used together with "You" and "Your" in the **KJV** – the text should all be "old and archaic" language.

But that is not what is found! There are hundreds of places in the **KJV Bible** that use both the singular and plural forms in the same verse – proving that the "archaic language" argument is not true. And when one rightly understands the difference between these singular and plural terms, there is much more meaning added to the verse.

Here is just one example where the singular and plural pronouns make a distinction that is lost in the modern versions. John 14:9:
*"Jesus saith unto him, Have I been so long time with **you** [all the disciples], and yet hast **thou** [Philip] not known me, Philip? he that hath seen me hath seen the Father; and how sayest **thou** [Philip] then, Shew us the Father?"*

An easy way to remember the singular and plural difference is that those words which begin with "T" (one line on top) are "singular" and those that begin with "Y" (two lines on top) are "plural."

The King James Bible (KJV)

T = Singular	**Y = Plural**
Thee *(Objective Case)*	**You** *(Objective Case)*
Thou *(Nominative Case)*	**Ye** *(Nominative Case)*
Thy	**Your**
Thine	**Yours**

In other words, any English Bible that changes the "thees" and "thous" to the word "you," is a less accurate version and does not match the distinctions found in the original manuscripts!

The original Hebrew and Greek are known as "synthetic" languages, which means that a single word blends its meaning with an inflected ending.

For example: The single word "love" can be identified as "lovest" which indicates it is a verb and identifies the verb's subject.
  1st Person – "I love"
  2nd Person – "thou love**st**" ("**s**" = second person)
  3rd Person – "he love**th**" ("**t**" = third person)

English began as a synthetic language. The **KJV** is written in this synthetic style, which is why there are many words in the **KJV** that end with "est", "eth" or other inflected endings. Single words contain the information in themselves, to clarify the sentence. Synthetic languages use inflection (many different forms of a single word in different situations).

But, as modern English has degraded, it dropped its beautiful synthetic language characteristics and moved to an "analytical" language which now requires added words and specific word order to clarify a single meaning. The reader now has to "analyze" the sentence to try to figure out what part of speech the word is. The modern (newer) Bibles follow this "analytical" language concept and lose the "synthetic" distinction – thereby actually **losing information** that was contained in the original manuscripts.

The **King James Bible** also contains its own built-in dictionary, which will define to the reader what the meaning is, for the more difficult words.
For example: Genesis 49:17 *"Dan shall be a **serpent** by the way, an **adder** in the path, that biteth the horse heels, so that his rider shall fall backward."*

Notice that even though the word "adder" is a more difficult word, that some people may not know the meaning of, the verse itself defined the word. An "adder" is a "serpent."

Here is another example of how the **KJV** defines its own difficult words.

Proverbs 26:23-26 says,*"Burning lips and a wicked heart are like a potsherd covered with silver dross. He that hateth dissembleth with his lips, and layeth up deceit within him; When he speaketh fair, believe him not: for there are seven abominations in his heart. Whose hatred is covered by deceit, his wickedness shall be shewed before the whole congregation."*

If one looks at the surrounding texts, the context defines what the word "dissembleth" means. The dictionary definition of "dissemble" means, "to conceal under a false appearance; actor, hypocrite;" The **KJV** built-in dictionary shows that "dissembleth" means to "cover by deceit" – to cover and hide something with deceit.

These are just a couple examples of how the **KJV** supplies its own built-in dictionary. Sadly, many of the modern corrupted versions also lose this built-in dictionary feature!

As man has sunk lower and lower in sin, God sought to lift him up to a higher standard. Instead of God lowering the quality of His Word to match man's degraded condition, He chose to exalt the standard of His Word and call man "up" to match His exalted standard.

God designed the language of **King James Bible** simple enough for a common man to understand, but exalted enough to lift his mind up to a more refined and polished condition. Indeed, *"The words of the LORD are pure words: as silver tried in a furnace of earth, purified seven times."* Psalm 12:6-7

It has been demonstrated more than once among people who could barely read, that those who began to try to read through the **King James Bible** from Genesis to Revelation, when they finished, their reading level had increased to a college reading level. As Psalm 119:99 predicted, *"I have more understanding than all my teachers: for thy testimonies are my meditation."*

The following quotations also reveal that historically, in those countries where Protestantism has flourished because of the **King James Bible** (and its fellow pure-line Bibles), society has grown and advanced in arts, sciences, knowledge, and technology. In stark contrast, in those countries that are predominately Catholic or heathen, and therefore did not give the **KJV** (and its fellow pure-line Bibles) prominence, society has not advanced correspondingly.

President Abraham Lincoln stated: *"The history of these last thousand years tells us that wherever the Church of Rome is not a dagger to pierce the bosom of a free nation, she is a stone to her neck, and a ball to her feet, to paralyze her and prevent her advance in the ways of civilization, science, intelligence, happiness and liberty."* (Fifty Years in the Church of Rome, p.697)

The King James Bible (KJV)

"Sir George Smith, addressing a great meeting in the Albert Hall, London on March 7th, 1904, drew attention to this remarkable fact in the following words: 'History showed that the periods of reform and revival synchronized with the increase of attention to the Word of God.' Moreover, the state of the world to-day furnishes a similar testimony. In every country where the Bible is freely circulated and read there is knowledge, intelligence, prosperity, and power; while in those countries from which the Bible is largely excluded (whether due to heathen or Roman influences) the exact reverse is the case. The present condition of South America and Spain speak eloquently on this point. In Spain, that priest-ridden land, out of a population of about seventeen million, twelve million can neither read nor write; while in South America there are, generally speaking, no settled governments, no inventions, no men of letters — indeed, there is scarcely anything indicating progress or enlightenment which ever originates there."
(All About the Bible, p.44)

"The Reformation, with its rediscovery of the Bible and Christianity, which had been buried for a thousand years beneath the superstition, pageantry, preserved paganism, and corruption of the Roman Church-State, ended the rampant religious superstition of the Middle Ages and elevated the mores of societies and individuals far above those of the Middle Ages." (Ecclesiastical Megalomania, p.74-75)

"As Protestants, as Christians, as free men, as philanthropists, as those who are acquainted with the teachings of history, we deplore the existing state of things; we regard all these changes as a retrograde movement of the most dangerous character, and we feel constrained to renew the grand old PROTEST to which the world owes its modern acquisitions of liberty, knowledge, peace, and prosperity. We recognize it as a patent and undeniable fact, that the future of our race lies not with Papists, but with Protestants. Its leading nations this day are not Papal Italy, Spain, and Portugal, but Protestant Germany, England, and America. What has made the difference? The nations that embraced the Reformation movement of the sixteenth century have never since ceased to advance in political power, social prosperity, philanthropic enterprise, and general enlightenment; while the nations that refused it and held fast to the corruptions of Rome have as steadily retrograded in all these respects." (Romanism & the Reformation, p.2)

Cutting Edge Facts – Building Faith in God's Word

Many historical PLACES identified in the pages of God's Word have been unearthed by archaeologists.

The theater at Ephesus
"And the whole city [Ephesus—vs.35] was filled with confusion: and having caught Gaius and Aristarchus, men of Macedonia, Paul's companions in travel, they rushed with one accord into the theatre." Acts 19:29

Excavations have uncovered the theater, which is set into a steep hillside at Ephesus. Massive in scale, the semicircular Roman theater held 25,000 seats and was one of the largest in the ancient world.

The Hittites Ruins- *"The Amalekites dwell in the land of the south: and the Hittites, and the Jebusites, and the Amorites, dwell in the mountains: and the Canaanites dwell by the sea, and by the coast of Jordan." Numbers 13:29*

Although mentioned several times in the Biblical texts, the actual existence of the Hittites was largely forgotten and denied until the late 19th century. With the discovery of Hattusa in **1834**, the city that was for many years the capital of the Hittite Empire, the Hittites were finally recognized as one of the great superpowers of the ancient Middle East.

From the KJV to 1870

Luis De Alcazar **(1554-1613)**, a Jesuit priest, published his commentary in **1614** to promote the concept of Preterism – which takes all the prophecies revealing that the Roman Catholic Church is the Antichrist system and applies them to some distant time in the past at the beginning of the Christian dispensation. By so doing, Alcazar's doctrine takes the "heat" off the Roman Catholic system.

In **1620**, the first English Puritans, who today are called "Pilgrims," sailed from Plymouth, England to the New World on board a ship called the Mayflower. They were seeking a land where they would have religious freedom and be free from the religious persecution from the Church of England and the Papal Church. Both the **Geneva Bible** and the **King James Bible** was on board the Mayflower. Governor William Bradford's Bible was a **Geneva Bible**. Assistant Governor John Alden's Bible was a **King James Bible**. (Both of these Bibles are in the collection of the Pilgrim Hall Museum in Plymouth, Massachusetts.)

By the **1620**'s, Austria, Bohemia, Hungary and other nations of Europe, were in major turmoil. *"The Jesuits were multiplying their hives, and beginning to swarm like wasps."* (*History of Protestantism*, vol.3, book 20, p.232)

"Stop the fountains, and the streams will dry up of themselves. Acting on this maxim, it was resolved to banish the pastors, to shut up the churches, and to burn the books of the Protestants... The churches of the banished ministers were given to the Jesuits." (*History of Protestantism*, vol.3, book 19, p.213-214)

Among the tactics that the Jesuits used to undermine the truth and the Protestant faith was introducing "religious drama" into the church services. As might be expected, this method amused and diverted the people, gradually replacing a relish for close Bible study, accurate facts, and the faithful Word, with a desire for mere entertainment.

"One of the popular employments and entertainments of the ecclesiastics in the middle ages, and one of the modes adopted by them for the instruction of the people, in the place of the Bible, was writing and exhibiting religious dramas..." (*Townley's Biblical Literature*, Vol.1, p.324)

Sword Unsheathed

"The reformers had nevertheless to repel the most virulent attacks of the adherents of the Church of Rome, who strove to pour contempt on the purer worship of the reformed; they also found it necessary to check the baneful influence of dramatic representations, and superstitious spectacles and shows."
(Townley's Biblical Literature, Vol.2, p.337)

The Elzevir brothers published three editions of the Greek New Testament in **1624**, **1633** and **1641**. They followed closely the work of Beza, who in turn had followed the standard set by Erasmus. In the preface to their edition of **1633** they coined the phrase "**Textus Receptus**" which became so popular that it was retrofitted to the texts which preceded it by many years. They stated in Latin *"textum ergo babes, nunc ab omnibus receptum..."* which in English is *"According to the text now held from the volume received..."* Here is the birth of the title "**Textus Receptus**" or "**Received Text**."

In January of **1655**, in the dead of winter, the Duke of Savoy, in obedience to Papal demands, issued an edict that gave the Waldenses a three day notice to either convert to Catholicism or to vacate all their homes and mountain valleys. Thousands of families were forced to flee through the winter snows in order to try to survive, but pursued by Rome's armies, many did not make it. The duke's armies captured and slaughtered thousands of them indiscriminately – men, women, and children were butchered by methods too barbarous and horrid to be described. In several cases, the Papal soldiers even boiled, fried, and ate their victims. This bloody massacre became known as the Piedmont Easter and it excited the horror and indignation of all of Protestant Europe, who opened their countries to welcome the fleeing refugees.

In **1666**, another Protestant Reformation Bible, the **Armenian Bible**, as it was commonly called, was translated from the 4th century works of Chrysostom.

In **1686**, the Papal barbarity of the **1655** massacre was repeated. The remaining 18,000 Vaudois who had managed to survive, were again butchered and massacred by Papal soldiers in ways too horrible to be described. The 14,000 who survived were thrown into dungeons and there another 11,000 either starved to death or succumbed to illness from the poor conditions they were allowed to live in. When the winter arrived, the 3,000 survivors, emaciated skeletons as they were, were released from prison and forced to march over the snow covered Alps in the blizzards of December, to reach the Protestant haven of Geneva. In this death march, many more died. The few survivors were welcomed into Geneva with open arms.

Vaudois December Exile

From the KJV to 1870

In **1693**, Jakob Ammann, a Mennonite Anabaptist in Switzerland, tried to reform the Mennonite church in his area. He believed that they should follow stricter "shunning" rules for those who didn't abide by the established beliefs.

Hans Reist was the senior leader in the region and he didn't believe in "shunning."

There was a split in the church and those who agreed with Reist continued to be called Mennonites. Those who agreed with and followed Ammann formed a new church system which became known as the Amish faith.

Jakob Ammann

Richard Simon (**1638–1712**), a French Jesuit/Roman Catholic priest, called the *"Father of Higher Criticism"* and *"the forerunner of modern Biblical criticism,"* wrote *"A Critical History of the Old Testament"* in **1678**, laying down what he considered the rules for a more exact translation.

"It entitles him to be called the father of Biblical criticism."
"Simon's declared purpose was to show that the Protestants had no assured principle for their religion." (*Facts of Faith*, p.29)

In other words, the modern Biblical criticism and its various methods of Bible interpretation was founded by Rome for the expressed purpose of undermining Protestant foundations.

Between **1689** and **1695**, Simon continued to attack the Word of God by publishing a series of commentaries on the New Testament and continually criticizing the **Received Text** while promoting the underlying text of the **Douay-Rheims Jesuit Bible**.

It has already been shown that Higher Criticism (and all its various branches) had its root in Alexandria and Greek philosophy around 2,000 years ago – but Richard Simon and his associates were the ones who resurrected that philosophy and made it main-stream in the last 330+ years.

In fact, in addition to Catholic Jesuit Richard Simons, one finds that all the principal modern founders of the "Textual Criticism" movement have been Roman Catholic. It should be pointed out again, that all forms of "Higher Criticism" are Papal in nature – they all place some other source, whether the ideas of pope, priest, pastor, scholars' writings, theologian's arguments, or committee decisions as the interpreter of the Word of God. True Protestant doctrine is that the Bible is the only infallible authority and that the Word of God is only to be interpreted by the Holy Spirit Himself.

The great Protestant leader, Zwingli *"presented the word of God as the only infallible authority."* (*The Great Controversy*, p.177)

Sword Unsheathed

If the Bible is the "ONLY INFALLIBLE AUTHORITY" – then by default, there is not any other "authority" on planet earth that is "infallible."

Since only an "infallible source" can interpret an "infallible source" – the Protestant view that only the Bible itself (in connection with it's Author, the Holy Spirit) can interpret itself, is the correct view. It is utter foolishness to use a fallible source such as a set of writings from some theologian or a papal bull to interpret what the infallible Bible says! But this is the very mistake that many people fall for today, which in turn, leads to dozens of opposing doctrines in Christianity - simply because people are using man's words to interpret the Bible instead of allowing it to interpret itself.

These doubts, conjectures, and criticism of the Bible by Richard Simon and others would later bear poisonous fruit in the 19th century in the hearts of Westcott and Hort.

Nikolaus Zinzendorf (**1700–1760**) opened his estate to the followers of Huss and helped to form the Moravian Church.

> *"Scattered and torn by persecution, the old sect of Moravian Brethren wandered about till about the year 1720 Count Zinzendorf invited them to his estate, later called Herrnhut. He began to keep the Sabbath, and became the leader of these Brethren and the head of a great missionary movement."*
>
> (Facts of Faith, p.149)

In **1739 AD**, John Wesley began preaching reforms to the Church of England. The movement that he started formed the Methodist church in **1784**.

During the years of **1749–1752**, Catholic Bishop Challoner made a series of revisions to the **Jesuit Douay-Rheims Bible**. He removed some of the more vicious anti-Protestant marginal notes and attempted to make the **Douay-Rheims Bible** more closely align with the **KJV** in order to be more successful in luring Protestants back to Rome.

> *"The changes introduced by him were so considerable that, according to Cardinal Newman, they 'almost amounted to a new translation.' So also, Cardinal Wiseman wrote, 'To call it any longer the Douay or Rhemish Version is an abuse of terms. It has been altered and modified until scarcely any verse remains as it was originally published. In nearly every case, Challoner's changes took the form approximating to the Authorized Version."*
>
> (Our Authorized Bible Vindicated, p.69)

From the KJV to 1870

Due, in part, to all the doubt and criticism of the Bible, there was a general loss of faith in Christianity.

It is important for the reader to understand, that there are actually two types of individuals who go by the name of "Christians." There are the True Christians, who follow the Bible and the Bible only, and promote the Christian faith that was given by Jesus Christ Himself. Then there are others, who hold tradition, rituals, ceremonies, and man's ideas above the Bible. It is this latter class into which the Papal system and the Jesuit order fall. It is important to understand the difference, because many times, history books will just refer to "Christians" but won't define "which Christians" – this can confuse inattentive or careless readers.

The catastrophic Lisbon Earthquake of **November 1, 1755**, which killed around 100,000 people, and was felt some 2,000 miles away, was regarded by Christians as a fulfillment of Matthew 24:29.

In France there was a savage backlash against all those who organized the "flood of Christianity." To the French, this included all Christians, both Catholic and Protestant. One of the ultimate results of all this backlash was that on **July 21, 1773**, Pope Clement XIV abolished the Jesuit Order. *"The Pope's action was in response to pressure from France, Spain, and Portugal, which independently had come to the conclusion that the Jesuits were meddling in the affairs of the state and were therefore enemies of the government."* (The Unseen Hand, p.79)

For this act against the Jesuit Order, Pope Clement would pay with his life. The Jesuits poisoned him with a special delayed poison, a compound of arsenic and other poisons, known as Aqua Tofana, and on **September 22, 1774**, Pope Clement died.

"Nothing but the most tremendous necessity could have made Clement XIV issue this bull... On laying down his pen, after having put his name to the bull, he said to those around him that he had subscribed his death-warrant. The Pope was at that time in robust health, and his vigorous constitution and temperate habits promised a long life. But now dark rumors began to be whispered in Italy that the Pontiff would die soon. In April of the following year he began to decline without any apparent cause: his illness increased: no medicine was of any avail: and after lingering in torture for months, he died, September 22nd, 1774. "Several days before his death," says Caraccioli, "his bones were exfoliated and withered like a tree which, attacked at its roots, withers away and throws off its bark. The scientific men who were called in to embalm his body found the features livid, the lips black, the abdomen inflated, the limbs emaciated, and covered with violet spots. The size of the head was diminished, and all the muscles were shrunk up, and the spine was decomposed. They filled the body with perfumed and aromatic substances, but nothing could dispel the mephitic effluvia." (History of Protestantism, Vol. 2, Book 15, p. 419,420)

Sword Unsheathed

On **May 1, 1776**, an (ex)Jesuit priest by the name of Adam Weishaupt founded the Order of the Illuminati for the purpose of destroying all governments and religions.

"There is reason to believe that Weishaupt's contempt of religion started on July 21, 1773, when Pope Clement XIV 'forever annulled and extinguished the Jesuit order.'" (The Unseen Hand, p.79)

This secret society portrayed itself as atheistic and against all religion, but in reality, they worshiped Lucifer. They wanted to use atheism to overthrow not only the Papal Church but also all other Christian religions.

"...the links between revolutionary Freemasonry and the Jesuits re-appear with surprising and alarming regularity as we go into the 20th century..."
(The Hidden Agenda, p.122)

"Other Masonic and Rosicrucian authors speak of the 'pretended animosity' between their twin organizations and the church of Rome. Though this animosity is at times unquestionably real, the fact remains that the doctrines, symbols, and rituals of Masonry-Rosicrucianism and Catholicism are essentially the same."
(Breaking the Code of the Secret Societies, p.28)

"...Adam Weishaupt connected with the Masonic Lodge in 1777. He posed at first among the Freemasons as a reformer in religion and a liberal in politics. Because Freemasonry was also anti-papal, Weishaupt's anti-papacy policies in Germany became popular immediately." (Illuminati 666, p.183)

The Illuminati first infiltrated and began gaining control of another secret society known as Freemasonry in **1777**, to use that as a means of infiltrating high government positions which were already filled by Freemasons. Then Weishaupt's order gradually began spreading and gaining world control through its members who had taken control of key government positions.

 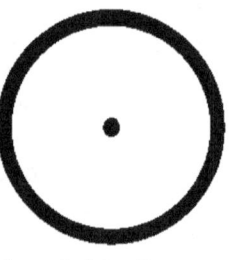

"Because the true purposes of Illuminism were so shocking, Weishaupt constantly encouraged the secretive nature of the order. No member was ever allowed himself to be identified as an Illuminati. The words Illuminism or Illuminati were never to be used in correspondence, but were to be replaced by the astrological symbol for the sun, a circle with a dot in the middle."
(Masonic & Occult Symbols Illustrated, p.29)

Note: These symbols, when used in context (ex. as a target for bowmen, or a letter in certain languages, etc.), may not necessarily implicate the user as being a member of the Illuminati.

From the KJV to 1870

The atheistic and/or pagan secret societies such as the Rosicrucians, the Illuminati, the Knights Templars, the Knights of Malta, the Freemasons, the Skull and Bones, as well as all the other various secret societies along with the Jesuits and the New Age Movement with its various fractions of communism, socialism, and fascism – all are portrayed in the Bible by the symbol of the <u>seven-headed beast from the bottomless pit that would make war on God's Word</u> and is shown to be rising about this time. (Revelation 11:7;17:7,8).

"The Apostle John was given a vision from our Lord, Jesus of Nazareth, that symbolized this New Age Movement as the Beast that ascendeth out of the Bottomless Pit." (*The Illuminati 666*, p.79)

"While both religious and humanist Utopians are preaching that Plato's lost paradise is to be regained, the gurus of the New Age Movement teach their students that this Golden Age will not come without first a series of violent, proletarian revolutions. This was also the thinking of Mr. Marx, the atheistic Utopian, and his most despicable disciples like Lenin, Stalin, Mao, and Castro...there are religious Utopians and there are atheistic Utopians...Some, who have studied deeply into the prophecies of Daniel and the Revelation...have most likely seen that this Utopian Dream of Spiritualism and atheism is symbolized in the book of Revelation as that red Beast which ascendeth out of the Bottomless Pit."
(*The Dragon, the Beast, and the False Prophet*, p.61)

The mysterious "Dark Day" which took place on **May 19, 1780**, when a strange and unexplainable darkness began to darken the land around 9:00 AM and by noon, left the countryside as dark as night, was regarded by Christians as a fulfillment of Matthew 24:29.

In **February 1787**, the controller general of finances in the nation of France proposed an increase in taxes on the privileged classes and this sparked the Aristocratic revolt which led to the formation of the Aristocratic terrorist order *"...known as the Society of the Friends of the Constitution..."* (*Illuminati 666*, p.186)

They met at the Jacobin Dominican Convent to develop their secret plan to overthrow the king and this is where their more common name, the Jacobin Club, was derived from.

"The Jacobin Club was the name these conspirators were using in France because their headquarters were located in an empty Roman Catholic Convent on Jacobin Street in Paris. Their German brethren were the Illuminati."
(*UFO's & the New World Order*, p.78)

This 500,000 member "club" of French Illuminists was the moving force behind the French Revolution which began in **1789**.

Sword Unsheathed

Because the Papal Church had taught unbiblical doctrines of God and Christ and had suppressed the Bible and had worked to destroy Protestantism and turn the population against the Bible (especially the **Olivetan Bible** and other Protestant Bibles), an army of atheists and revolutionaries was able to take over the government of France and plunge France into the dreadful horrors of the three and a half year "Reign of Terror."

The French Revolution declared open avowed war on the Bible, and this revolution of atheism against the Old and New Testament "witnesses" of the pure-line Bible was a fulfillment of the prophecy of Revelation 11:7-12.

> "And when they shall have finished their testimony, the beast that ascendeth out of the bottomless pit shall make war against them, and shall overcome them, and kill them. And their dead bodies shall lie in the street of the great city, which spiritually is called Sodom and Egypt, where also our Lord was crucified.

> "And they of the people and kindreds and tongues and nations shall see their dead bodies three days and an half, and shall not suffer their dead bodies to be put in graves. And they that dwell upon the earth shall rejoice over them, and make merry, and shall send gifts one to another; because these two prophets tormented them that dwelt on the earth. And after three days and an half the Spirit of life from God entered into them, and they stood upon their feet; and great fear fell upon them which saw them. And they heard a great voice from heaven saying unto them, Come up hither. And they ascended up to heaven in a cloud; and their enemies beheld them."

> "'When they shall have finished [are finishing] their testimony.' The period when the two witnesses were to prophesy clothed in sackcloth, ended in 1798. As they were approaching the termination of their work in obscurity, war was to be made upon them by the power represented as 'the beast that ascendeth out of the bottomless pit.' In many of the nations of Europe the powers that ruled in church and state had for centuries been controlled by Satan through the medium of the papacy. But here is brought to view a new manifestation of satanic power.

> "It had been Rome's policy, under a profession of reverence for the Bible, to keep it locked up in an unknown tongue and hidden away from the people. Under her rule the witnesses prophesied 'clothed in sackcloth.' But <u>another power</u> – the beast from the bottomless pit – <u>was to arise to make open, avowed war upon the word of God.</u>" (The Great Controversy, p.268-269)

> "...the Reign of Terror began in 1793. The worship of God was abolished by the French National Assembly. Bibles were collected and publicly burned. All religious worship was prohibited, and all Bible Institutions were closed and abolished."
> (The Antichrist 666, p.215)

From the KJV to 1870

Back on the American continent, in **1782**, the **Robert Aitken Bible** was printed. It was the first Bible printed in the English language in America and was called "The Bible of the Revolution." It was small enough to fit into the coat pocket of the Revolutionary War soldiers and was the only Bible printing ever called for by an act of the United States Congress. The **Aitken Bible** was a **King James Version** and helped to meet the need for scriptures while England was refusing to allow their Bibles to be imported by the "rebellious colonists," during the embargo of the Revolutionary War.

On **September 17, 1787**, the Constitution of the United States was signed and over the next 18 months it was ratified.

On **March 4, 1789**, the first Congress under the Constitution met and the first amendment to the constitution was introduced: *"Congress shall make no law respecting an establishment of religion, nor prohibiting the free exercise thereof."* This was followed by other amendments and in September of the same year, the ten amendments, known as the Bill of Rights, were adopted. The purpose of this First Amendment, was to guarantee that the U.S. would never experience the religious persecution that the founders of this country had experienced in Europe and England!

In **1780**, work was begun on a Spanish translation of the **Catholic Latin Vulgate**. This translation was done by Felipe Scío de San Miguel, a Roman Catholic priest from the order known as Piarists, which were sort of counterparts to the Jesuit Order.

From **1790** to **1793**, this Spanish **Latin Vulgate** known as the **Scio Bible** (**Biblia de Scio**) was published in several volumes. This was the first Spanish Bible published in Spain, because the other Spanish Bibles had been published outside the country by exiled Protestants, and then smuggled into Spain.

On the **10th** of **February** in **1798**, the French army under their General Louis-Alexandre Berthier, entered Rome and took the Pope and the cardinal prisoners. Within a week Pius VI, was deposed and carried captive to France where he later died in exile.

*"In **1798** Rome was made a republic by French arms, and Pope Pius VI (**1775–1799**) carried a prisoner to France, where he died."*
(A History of the Christian Church, p.558)

General Berthier Captures Pope

Sword Unsheathed

The papal church-state independence was abolished by France, and the son of Napoleon was declared king of Rome. This action fulfilled the prophecy of the "Deadly Wound" that would be inflicted on the beast in Revelation 13:3 – thereby ending the prophetic 1260 years of Papal supremacy as well as the 1290 time prophecy.

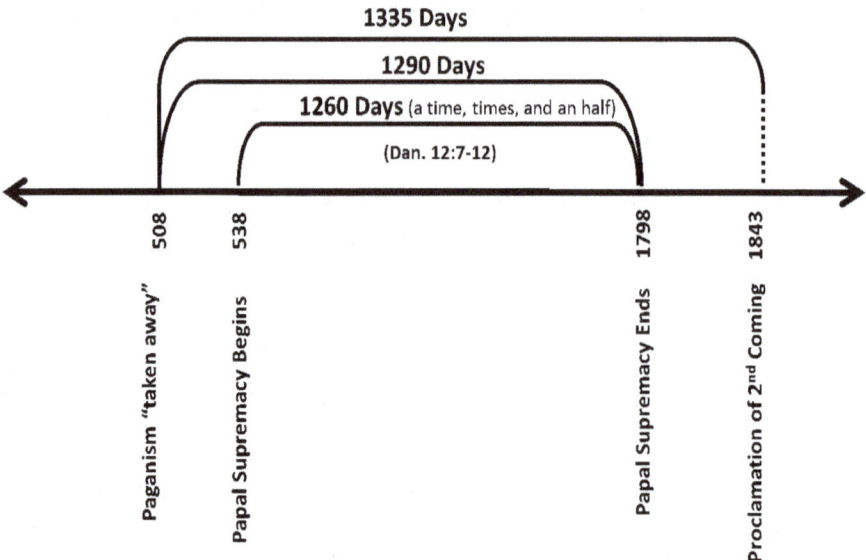

"Concerning the two witnesses the prophet declares further: 'And they heard a great voice from heaven saying unto them, come up hither. And they ascended up to heaven in a cloud; and their enemies beheld them.' Revelation 11:12. Since France made war upon God's two witnesses, they have been honored as never before. In 1804 the British and Foreign Bible Society was organized. This was followed by similar organizations, with numerous branches, upon the continent of Europe. In 1816, the American Bible Society was founded. When the British Society was formed, the Bible had been printed and circulated in fifty tongues. It has since been translated into more than two hundred languages and dialects. By the efforts of Bible societies, since 1804, more than 187,000,000 copies of the Bible have been circulated." (*The Great Controversy*, 1888 ed., p.287)

One might also well consider from this prophecy in Revelation that the pure Bibles completed at this time like the **Olivetan**, the **King James Version**, and the **Diodati** were a full and sufficient rule of faith, that God considered worthy to be exalted "to heaven." They were not Bibles requiring multitudinous "further improvements" as modern scholars would have us believe.

From the KJV to 1870

In **1804**, 36 Protestants met and formed the British and Foreign Bible Society for the purpose of printing and circulating the **King James Bible** (without the Apocrypha).

In **1808**, an American, Charles Thomson, published the first English translation of the **Septuagint** in Philadelphia.

In **1809**, the New York Bible Society was formed for the same purpose as the British and Foreign Bible Society had been formed.

Three years later, the War of **1812** began between England/Canada and the US. In **1814**, the Battle of Plattsburg decided the outcome of the War of **1812**. This battle was also the turning point in the religious experience of a captain of the forces in Fort Scott by the name of William Miller. This captain/farmer would later begin a religious revival throughout the New England states.

Also on **July 31, 1814**, Pope Pius VII reversed the order of Pope Clement XIV and universally restored the Jesuit Order.

"Pope Clement's action was short-lived, though, as Pope Pius VII in August, 1814 reinstated the Jesuits to all of their former rights and privileges."
(The Unseen Hand, p.79)

This restored the Jesuits back to England and they began infiltrating as many of the Protestant institutions as they could.

"Wherever the so-called Counter Reformation, started by the Jesuits, gained hold of the people, the vernacular was suppressed and the Bible kept from the laity. So eager were the Jesuits to destroy the authority of the Bible – the paper pope of the Protestants, as they contemptuously called it – that they even did not refrain from criticizing it genuineness and historical value." (The Influence of the Bible, p.136)

During the latter years of the 18th century and these early years of the 19th century, Georg W. F. Hegel was developing his philosophy that would later come to be known as the Hegelian Dialectic (otherwise known as Diaprax).

This system of philosophy can be illustrated simply like this -
problem → reaction → solution (**T**hesis + **A**ntithesis = **S**ynthesis).

In other words, if it is desired to get people to accept some idea that they would normally never accept (**S**), first one creates a "crisis" (**T**). Then he waits for the people to react (or overreact) to the crisis he produced (**A**). At this point, he can now provide the people with his desired solution (**S**). In this way, people can be tricked into accepting ideas, principles, laws, or other results that they never would have otherwise.

"In Hegel's world of thought, reason is God; therefore truth lies in reason and not in God's Word." (Assault on the Remnant, p.253)

Sword Unsheathed

The Hegelian Dialectic is the method that not only all the various tyrants and dictators have used to take control of the people, but that is also being used to steer the world's population into accepting the New World Order (Revelation 17:12-13). It is used to put nations into wars, which are then used to steer the populace into accepting things they would never have accepted before.

Hitler used this method to bring himself into power in Germany. His agents caused civil unrest and then placed the blame on the opposing party, swaying the nation to gladly accept Hitler and his promised "change for the better."

Most recently (currently), this exact same method was used with the COVID-19 coronavirus propaganda to convince the world (especially Americans) to freely give up their inalienable rights and constitutionally protected freedoms as a trade for the government's promised protection. This loss of freedom, which caused stress and higher tension in society, created an explosive situation, which was then ignited by acts of injustice perpetrated by "agents" that were used to then escalate society into riots and bring the nation to the brink of war. Time will reveal what the "Synthesis" is that these evil agents are pushing society toward.

In the realm of Bible study:
"Hegelian dialectics is higher criticism on steroids. It displaces faith in the Word of God with human reason and often in such a subtle manner that many do not know that they are being affected by it."   (Assault on the Remnant, p.253)

On **May 11, 1816**, the American Bible Society was founded in New York City.

In **1821**, Robert Haldane, a Scottish patron of the British and Foreign Bible Society, discovered that secret plans by infiltrators had been laid for the society to distribute Bibles which contained the Apocrypha, in predominately Catholic nations. This was in direct violation of why the society had been formed in the first place, and this discovery began an internal battle within the society.

In **1827**, because they disagreed with the resolutions of the British and Foreign Bible Society, all the Scottish bodies withdrew from membership with the Society, to follow their own independent course.

In **1830**, Sidney Rigdon, working through fellow Freemason Joseph Smith, founded the Mormon Church, which, although unbeknownst to most lower level Mormons, is actually based in Illuminism, Freemasonry, and Witchcraft.

A former Wiccan high priest, William Schnoebelen, tells that:
"...the head of the Druidic witches in North America told him that the highest form of witchcraft was practiced in Mormon temples."
              (Mysticism, Hollywood, and the Music Industry, p.53)

From the KJV to 1870

In **1831**, the British and Foreign Bible Society ran into more opposition from some of its members who wanted to begin the Society's meetings with prayer in the name of Jesus Christ, but it was felt by others that such a move would offend the few Unitarians that were members. Those who believed in the doctrine of the Trinity finally separated and formed a break-away society called the Trinitarian Bible Society.

Among the original members of the Trinitarian Bible Society were several men who were followers of the worldwide Advent movement that was beginning to sweep around the globe. They studied the prophecies, especially the books of Daniel and Revelation, and came to the conclusion that Jesus was coming back in the **1840**'s. During the **1830**'s there were over 700 ministers of the Church of England who had joined this Advent movement and were preaching this message.

> *"Three years after Miller was convinced of the near coming of Christ, that is, in 1821, Joseph Wolff, known as the "missionary to Asia," began to give the same message. He visited Egypt, Abyssinia, Palestine, Syria, Persia, Bokhara, and India,- everywhere proclaiming the soon coming of the Messiah."*
> (Story of the Seer of Patmos, p.77)

When Joseph Wolff visited Abyssinia (modern northern Ethiopia) he found that there were still many observers of the Bible Sabbath in that country. He stated, *"The Sabbath of the Jews, i. e., Saturday, is kept strictly among the Abyssinians in the province of Hamazien."* (Wolff's Journal, p.340)

In **1833**, Noah Webster produced his "revision" of the **KJV**, which is known as **Webster's Bible**. Even though he was not only the authority on contemporary English, but also knowledgeable of both Hebrew and Greek, it is of significance that he actually did not "revise" much, as he realized that the **KJV** translators had done an accurate job. Most of the changes he made were simply to update some areas of grammar that had become unused over time, or to modernize spelling so the Bible could be used as a textbook. (Examples – Genesis 1:29 *"meat"* meaning all types of food, updated to *"food"*; Exodus 20:12 *"honour"* becomes *"honor"*)

Webster also changed a few terms that had become more "offensive" since the time the **KJV** had been translated. According to Webster's introduction, he changed *"passages which cannot be repeated without a blush"* so as to make the Bible more usable for reading aloud in children's schools.

For example, perhaps his most drastic change, is 2 Kings 9:8:
KJV – *"...I will cut off from Ahab him that pisseth against the wall..."*
Webster's – *"...I will cut off from Ahab the males..."*

Again, the number of "changes" made by Webster are very limited, and one may read for many verses before discovering any difference from the **KJV**.

Sword Unsheathed

The center of the Church of England was Oxford University. In **1833** a movement was started to bring the Church of England back to Rome; it had several different names. Since it was mostly centered around Oxford it therefore became known as the Oxford Movement.

John Newman

The leader in this movement was John Henry Newman who was at first, a priest in the Church of England, but then later converted to Catholicism and then became a Catholic Cardinal in **1878**.

Newman stated to a friend, *"I expect to be called a Papist when my opinions are known. But (please God) I shall lead persons on a little way, while they fancy they are only taking the mean, and denounce me as the extreme."*
(*Secret History of the Oxford Movement*, p.6)
Here Newman demonstrates a truly Jesuitical spirit.

Newman had gone to Rome in **1833** with his friend Herrell Froude and asked the Pope what the Church of England needed to do in order to be restored to fellowship with Rome. He was told that the Church of England would have to accept the Council of Trent.

Newman and Froude believed that Protestantism was the anti-christ and worked to gain followers to help return England to Rome. They first began to instill in the Church of England different rituals that were very similar to Catholicism, yet different enough that nobody would notice. This led to the movement being called Ritualism. They worked secretly to bring people around to the Catholic mindset.

One of their key leaders, Dr. Edward Pusey stated, *"I know not that the Popish controversy may not just be the very best way of handling Ultra-Protestantism, i.e., neglecting it, not advancing against, but setting Catholic views against Roman Catholicism and so disposing of Ultra-Protestantism by a side wind, and <u>teaching people Catholicism, without their suspecting, while they are only bent on demolishing Romanism</u>. I suspect we might thus have people with us, instead of against us, and that they might find themselves Catholics before they were aware."*
(*Secret History of the Oxford Movement*, p.10)

In order to destroy faith in the Protestant Bible, promote Rome's corrupted text through the art of textual criticism, and to criticize Protestantism in general, from **1833** to **1841**, the Oxford Movement published 90 Tracts for the Times which were edited by Newman. This led to another name for the Oxford Movement – Tractarianism. Newman and the Jesuits, working through their secret society known as the Societas Sanctae Crucis (SSC) [Society of the Holy Cross], used several tactics to draw the Protestants away from their Bibles and into Romanism.

From the KJV to 1870

> "The English clergy were formerly too much attached to their Articles of Faith to be shaken from them. You might have employed in vain all the machines set in motion by Bossuet and the Jansenists of France to reunite them to the Romish Church; and so the Jesuits of England tried another plan. This was to demonstrate from history and ecclesiastical antiquity the legitimacy of the usages of the English Church, whence, through the exertions of the Jesuits concealed among its clergy, might arise a studious attention to Christian antiquity. This was designed to occupy the clergy in long, laborious, and abstruse investigation, and to alienate them from their Bibles." (*The Secret History of the Oxford Movement*, p.33)

The famous Leonid meteor shower of **November 13, 1833**, produced between 10,000-70,000 meteors per hour and it lasted from around 2:00 AM until the rising sun hid the meteors from view. This spectacular display was regarded by Christians as a fulfillment of Christ's statement about the falling of the stars in Matthew 24:29.

In April of **1837**, some of the members of the American Bible Society that desired to revise the **KJV**, left the Society and formed their own society, known as the American and Foreign Bible Society.

Newman was given the suggestion to revise the Protestant **King James Bible** in 1847 by the Superior of the Franciscans, Father Benigno, who suggested that they "correct" the **King James Version** by **Jerome's Latin Vulgate** and have a Dr. Whitty of St. Edmunds as one of the ones to help correct it. (It is no surprise to discover that Dr. Whitty was a Jesuit.)

This concept of *"correcting the* **King James Bible***"* by the **Latin Vulgate** began to grow in power; meanwhile a force of men to do the job would be being groomed by the Jesuits and England would being "conditioned" for just such a change. This concept would finally culminate in success in **1870-1901**.

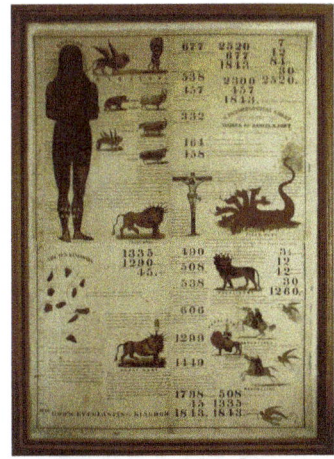

Millerite 1843 Chart

The Protestant historian D'Aubigne, warning England against the Oxford movement and the growing idea of correcting the **KJV** said, *"The moment that England abandons the faith of the Bible, the crown will fall from her head."* (*A Discourse Against Modern Oxford Theology*, p.57)

In **1840–1844**, a religious revival, sparked by the preaching of a farmer named William Miller, swept across the U.S. This religious revival was called the "Millerite Movement" or the "Advent Movement" and it opened up to people's minds the correct understanding of the "time prophecies" of the Bible and the hope of Jesus' Second Coming or Advent. (See Timeline Charts on page 369, 370)

Sword Unsheathed

William Miller

"We hold that the great movement upon the second advent question, which commenced with the writings and public lectures of William Miller, has been, in its leading features, in fulfillment of prophecy."
(*Sketches of Christian Life of William Miller*, p.6)

William Miller had originally held deistic beliefs while he had served as a captain in the army during the War of **1812**. But evidence of a a higher power overruling in the Battle of Plattsburg began a change in him.

After the war, in **1816**, Miller began studying his Bible without using commentaries and other "ideas of man." He rejected the "higher criticism" methods of Bible study and, with the aid of a concordance, simply followed the Proof-text method, allowing the Bible itself to be its own interpreter. [see Note G]

By **1818**, he had come to the realization that the Bible was true, and that the prophecies of the Bible foretold that Jesus was coming soon. God impressed him that he should tell others what he had learned, but he was reluctant to do public speaking. He finally began publicly sharing what Bible prophecy foretold in the early **1830**s, and his message began a religious revival which culminated in the **1840**s. The Bible that William Miller used and the one that drove this reform movement was the **King James Version**.

This same "Advent" revival was also simultaneously taking place in England and across Europe – led by various reformers, all preaching on Bible prophecy and of the soon coming of Jesus Christ. *"The advent movement of 1840-44 was a glorious manifestation of the power of God…"* (*Great Controversy*, p.611)

In **1842**, two years prior to Tischendorf's discovery, James Townley stated that, *"The two most noted MSS. of the Septuagint version are the Codex Alexandrinus and the Codex Vaticanus."* (*Townley's Biblical Literature*, vol.1, p.60)

This would change in **1844** with the additional "find" of the **Sinaiticus**.

On **October 27, 1842**, a Catholic priest in Carbeau, New York, angered that Protestant Bible Societies were distributing copies of the Bible to his parishioners, made a public burning of several Protestant Bibles. This incident caused a national firestorm of Protestant indignation and anti-Popery sentiment.

In **1843**, a comet appeared in the sky, almost like a herald of the soon coming of Christ. It is known as the Great Comet of **1843**.

"The comet of 1843 is regarded as, perhaps, the most marvelous of the

present age, having been observed in the day-time even before it was visible at night, – passing very near the sun, – exhibiting an enormous length of tail... streaming from the region of the sun, below the constellation of Orion."
(*Great Events of our Past Century,* p.301)

On **October 22, 1844**, the Millerites experienced severe disappointment when Jesus did not return as they expected. This event became known as the "Great Disappointment."

"When the great day arrived they went to their tabernacles and meetinghouses to sing hymns and await the Lord's coming. Nothing happened!... The newspapers had a field day. They told stories of Millerites climbing to the tops of trees and trying to fly to heaven to meet Christ – the result was, of course, disaster. They told of faithful followers, wearing white ascension robes, awaiting the end. Stories and rumors of suicides and murders by demented Millerites were passed about. <u>But none of this was true. The movement did cause a good deal of stir and excitement, but it produced no such extremes.</u>" (*The History of Protestantism in America,* p.162)

The Millerites had calculated the time prophecies correctly, but, due to a misunderstanding, they had misapplied the event that was to mark the end of those time periods. The Millerites/Adventists studied and learned from the **King James Bible** the teachings of the typical and anti-typical sanctuary service, and discovered that instead of **1844** marking the coming of Christ to earth as they had thought, **1844** was marking the transition of Christ in the heavenly sanctuary, when He moved from the Holy Place into the Most Holy Place, to begin the judgment process of humanity.

"The Millerites...insisted that according to the prophecy of Daniel [8:14], on October 22, 1844, Christ did cleanse the invisible heavenly temple. They were right to the time of the cleansing but wrong to the where and how. Thus the movement was consolidated and took its place in American Protestantism."
(*The History of Protestantism in America,* p.162,163)

This Millerite/Adventist movement then learned about the Bible Sabbath. The first group of Adventists that began keeping the 7th-day Sabbath was in Washington NH, in **December of 1844**.

"Washington, New Hampshire...In This Village Was Established the First Seventh-day Adventist Church, in 1844." (*Heavenly Visions,* p.104)

In **1844**, Philip Schaff from Germany became the Professor of Church History and Biblical Literature in the German Reformed Theological Seminary of Mercersburg, Pennsylvania. He promoted the same critical and Romanist concepts as Newman at Oxford University, and his teachings grew into a movement called Mercersburg Theology.

Sword Unsheathed

Also in **1844**, a German critic named Constantine Tischendorf, while visiting St. Catherine's Monastery at Mount Sinai, discovered many leaves of an ancient manuscript in a waste paper basket that was waiting to be burned. He was able to obtain about 45 of the leaves, but because he expressed such enthusiasm about the manuscript, the monks confiscated the rest of the pages.

Tischendorf informs us:

Constantine Tischendorf

"In visiting the library of the monastery, in the month of May, 1844, I perceived in the middle of the great hall a large and wide basket full of old parchments; and the librarian, who was a man of information, told me that two heaps of papers like this, mouldered by time, had been already committed to the flames. What was my surprise to find amid this heap of papers a considerable number of sheets of a copy of the Old Testament in Greek, which seemed to me to be one of the most ancient that I had ever seen. The authorities of the convent allowed me to possess myself of a third of these parchments, or about forty-five sheets, all the more readily as they were destined for the fire." (*When Were Our Gospels Written*, p.28)

The manuscript Tischendorf claimed to have found in the trash can, was a "rescript" and had been erased and corrected several dozen times. The monks had thrown it away considering that it was so erased and changed that it was worthless and could not possibly be accurate any more. But they became suspicious when Tischendorf excitedly wanted to take the manuscript. At least that was his story.

One problem with his "story" is that this manuscript is written on animal skin (vellum) – and anyone who has ever tried to "burn" animal skin knows that it doesn't burn well, it just smokes and smolders. The idea that the monks were using the pages for burning, seems absurd.

Another problem, which has never been solved, is that there was a famous forger named Constantine Simonides, who made the claim that the Sinaitic manuscript was his own forged work that he had produced as a gift for the Russian Czar.

"...the most amazing was his claim to have written when at Mount Athos in 1840 the Sinaitic Codex (Codex A), which Tischendorf discovered at Mount Sinai under highly singular circumstances...That Simonides was a good enough calligrapher, even at an early age, to have written the Codex, is hardly open to doubt..." (*Literary Forgeries*, p.59)

Some claim that Simonides was lying, others claim his story was true. But so far, there has not been conclusive evidence either way.

From the KJV to 1870

This Sinaitic manuscript became known as **Codex Sinaiticus (Codex Aleph)**.

There is also good reason to believe that this is quite possibly one of Constantine's lost Origen-based Bibles and another representation of **Origen's Septuagint**, and many scholars now believe this to be the true origin of this manuscript. Indeed, *"It is generally considered by scholars to have been written in the second half of the 4th century."* (King James Version Defended, p.116)

Though some scholars believe the **Sinaiticus** to be an accurate copy of the original Bible, those who have looked into the issue reject it on several bases. Among which is the fact that the **Sinaiticus** is so sloppily done that it contains many "corrections" on nearly every page of the manuscript by at least 10 different people at different times down through history.

Biblical scholar John Burgon stated about the **Sinaiticus**:
"On many occasions 10, 20, 30, 40 words are dropped through very carelessness. Letters, words, or even whole sentences are frequently written twice over, or begun and immediately canceled; while that gross blunder, whereby a clause is omitted because it happens to end in the same words as the clause preceding, occurs no less than 115 times in the New Testament."
(Last 12 Verses of Mark, p.75-76)

Sample of Rescripting

The full edition of the **Manuscript of Ephraem (Codex C)** was published by Tischendorf in **1845**. **Codex C** was a "rescript" or "palimpsest" that has two layers of writing – in other words, it was erased and re-written – the text of the bottom layer was from the 5th century and had been erased to make room for the top layer which was a treatise for St. Ephriam of Syria in the 12th century and the underlying Biblical text can be deciphered only with great difficulty. **Codex C** has many text similarities with the Vaticanus and Sinaiticus, and has been described as being sort of an intermediate between the text of the **Vaticanus** and the **Alexandrinus**.

Codex Vaticanus, **Codex Sinaiticus**, **Codex Alexandrinus**, and **Codex Ephraemi** are sometimes called the "Great Uncials."

In **1848**, the Fox sisters in New York began to communicate with a supernatural force that was knocking on the walls in their house. This began the modern movement of spiritualism – communicating with demons.

"It was the Fox sisters who started what became known as 'Spirit rapping,' which rapidly became a craze in the United States. The names of these young mediums were Leah, Margaret (Margaretta), and Kate."
(The Dragon, the Beast, and the False Prophet, p.76)

In **1850**, some of the officers of the American and Foreign Bible Society produced a revision of the **KJV** New Testament. This revision was not approved by the board, so those who agreed with the revision separated from the Society and formed their own society known as the American Bible Union, to promote their **American Bible Union Version**.

In **1851**, fellow spiritualists Brooke Foss Westcott and Fenton John Anthony Hort helped to found the spiritualist club called the Ghostly Guild in London – *"for the investigation of all supernatural appearances and effects."*
(Life and Letters of Brooke Foss Westcott, Vol.1, p. 117)

HORT wrote to John Ellerton, **December 29, 1851**:
"Westcott,... etc., and I have started a society for the investigation of ghosts and all supernatural appearances and effects, being all disposed to believe that such things really exist, and ought to be discriminated from hoaxes and mere subjective disillusions; we shall be happy to obtain any good accounts well authenticated with names. ... our own temporary name is the 'Ghostly Guild.'"
(Life and Letters of Fenton John Anthony Hort, Vol.1, p. 211)

WESTCOTT wrote:
"'We are learning with the help of many teachers the extent and the authority of the dominion which the dead have over us.' (Wescott, the Historic Faith, p. 249)."
(Men, Motives... Mutilations behind the Modern Bible Versions, pg. 21)

The reader should note, that the whole concept of a ghostly guild and communicating with the dead is unbiblical and one of the abominations forbidden by God in Deuteronomy 18:10-12 *"There shall not be found among ... an enchanter, or a witch, or a charmer, or a consulter with familiar spirits, or a wizard, or a necromancer.* ["*that asketh counsayle of the dead*" – Bishops Bible]. *For all that do these things are an abomination unto the LORD..."* (See also Job 7:9,10; Eccl. 9:5,6,10; Psalm 115:17).

Hermann Von Soden, was born in **1852** in Cincinnati, Ohio. He was a German Biblical scholar, and textual critic and his work would later give rise to a spurious **Majority Text**.

In **1859**, through the influence of the Russian Czar, Tischendorf was finally able to obtain the remaining pages of the **Sinaiticus** manuscript from the monks at St. Catherine's monastery.

From the KJV to 1870

Also in **1859**, Charles Darwin published his book on the evolutionary theory called *The Origin of Species*. This theory of evolution originated from the devil and it totally destroys faith in the Word of God.

During the early **1800**'s, Jesuit priests had been infiltrating the southern states and starting schools and training the American population with Catholic doctrines and theology, and trying to undermine the Protestant faith. Rome was seeking to find a way to undermine the United States, which was the "foothold" of Protestantism.

Rome found her opportunity in the early 60's. The southern states had been indoctrinated with the Roman Catholic concept of "slavery" and had been one of the largest buyers of the West African slave trade. Rome decided to use this issue as a "divide and conquer" technique to turn the Northern States (the Union) against the Southern States (the Confederacy) and by pitting brother against brother, to destroy the Protestant U.S. from the inside.

Abraham Lincoln

In **1861**, Abraham Lincoln, became President of the United States. He took his oath of office with his hand on a **1853** Oxford University Press edition of the **King James Bible**. This Bible would later come to be called the **Lincoln Bible**.

From **1861** to **1865**, the U.S. was embroiled in a Civil War. The Vatican was secretly sending funds and war aid to Jefferson Davis, in support of the cause of the South.

"The fact is, that the immense majority of the Roman Catholic bishops, priests and laymen, are rebels in heart, when they cannot be in fact; with very few exceptions, they are publicly in favor of slavery."   (*Fifty Years in the Church of Rome*, p.697)

President Lincoln ordered a naval blockade of all southern ports to try to block the support flowing to the south. But England and France, who were operating from central banks controlled indirectly by the Vatican, were building ships and smuggling supplies and support through the Union blockades to the southern states.

President Lincoln understood that it was not against the Protestant South that he was fighting, but against Rome. He stated: *"The common people hear and see the big noisy wheels of the southern confederacy cars, and they call him Jeff Davis, Lee, Thompson, Beauregard, Semmes, or others. They honestly think that they are the motive power, the first cause of our troubles, but it is a mistake, the true motive power is secreted behind the thick walls of the Vatican – the colleges and schools of the Jesuits; the convents of the nuns, the confessional boxes of Rome."*
     (*Assassination of Abraham Lincoln*, p.80)

"But there is a thing which is very certain; it is, that if the American people could learn what I know of the fierce hatred of the generality of the priests of Rome against our institutions, our schools, our most sacred rights, and our so dearly bought liberties, they would drive them away, tomorrow, from among us, or they would shoot them as traitors." (*Fifty Years in the Church of Rome*, p.697)

Yet, while the Americans were struggling to overthrow the papal supported slavery and Jesuit-influenced rebellion of the southern states, on **September 25, 1862**, F.J.A. Hort wrote concerning his feelings about the American Civil War and giving an insight into his view of the issue:

"While the war lasts, therefore, I fully sympathize with the South. ...I care more for England and for Europe than for America, how much more than for all the n___ [blacks*] in the world! and I contend that the highest morality requires me to do so. ...Surely, if ever Babylon or Rome were rightly cursed, it cannot be wrong to desire and pray from the bottom of one's heart that the American Union may be shivered to pieces." (*Life and Letters of Fenton John Anthony Hort*, Vol.1, p. 459)

*compiler altered Hort's original racist term

On **April 14, 1865**, President Lincoln was assassinated by the Jesuits. The assassination was shown in Thomas Harris' "Rome's Responsibility for the Assassination of Abraham Lincoln" to be a Roman Catholic Jesuit plot, as a Jesuit priest in St. Joseph, Minnesota (almost 1,000 miles away) told a Protestant that Abraham Lincoln had just been assassinated – **four hours before** the assassination actually happened.

"Brigadier General Thomas Harris, a member of the Military Commission that tried and condemned the conspirators found guilty of the crime, was convinced of the complicity of the Roman Catholic hierarchy in the assassination, and its responsibility for it. He wrote that there was 'positive evidence that the Jesuit fathers engaged in preparing young men for the priesthood away out in the village of St Joseph, in far off Minnesota, were in correspondence with their brethren in Washington City, and had been informed that the plan to assassinate the President had been matured, the agents for its accomplishment had been found, the time for its execution had been set, and so sure were they of its accomplishment, that they could announce it as already done, three or four hours before it had been consummated.'" (*All Roads Lead to Rome*, p.132-133)

The State Department later confirmed that John Wilkes Booth, David Harold, John Surratt, Mary Surratt, Dr. Mudd, and all the other conspirators involved in the assassination plot of Abraham Lincoln were all Roman Catholics with connections to the Jesuit order. A former Roman Catholic priest by the name of Charles Chiniquy says: *"I come fearlessly, to-day, before the American people, to say and prove that the President, Abraham Lincoln, was assassinated by the priests and the Jesuits of Rome."* (*Fifty Years in the Church of Rome*, p.718)

From the KJV to 1870

Conspirator John Surratt was actually tracked and pursued by the State Department, all the way to the Vatican itself, where they discovered him, in hiding, serving in the Pope's infantry of Papal Zouaves.

While all this American Civil War and Jesuit intrigue was taking place in the USA, the devil had other events unfolding in England and Europe.

Samuel Prideaux Tregelles (**1813-1875**) was a scholar and textual critic who also believed the erroneous "older is always better" theory and determined to go back to what he considered the most ancient manuscripts.

Samuel Tregelles

In **1845**, he had spent five months in Rome, with the hope of collating **Codex B** in the library of the Vatican. It was said to consist of 700 leaves of the finest vellum, and two priests were stationed to watch him. They would try to distract his attention if he seemed too intent upon a passage, and if he studied any part of it too long they would snatch away the book.

In **1862**, he visited Tischendorf at Leipzig to examine the **Codex Sinaiticus**.
He generally ignored the **Received Text** and the evidence of the great majority of cursive manuscripts, and favored the Alexandrian manuscripts instead.

"Though Tregelles added far less than Tischendorf to our store of critical material, he did more to establish correct principles of criticism..."
(*Encyclopedia of Religious Knowledge*, vol.2, p.282)

In **1862**, Tischendorf published the completed **Sinaiticus manuscript (Aleph)**.

At the end of the book of Esther in the **Sinaiticus** is a colophon written by the third corrector that states that from the book of Kings to the book of Esther was compared to a copy that had been *"corrected by the hand of the holy martyr Pamphilus."* This means that the Old Testament of the **Sinaiticus** is in essence, the **Hexapla LXX of Origen**. This also lends itself to the probability that the **Sinaiticus** is one of Eusebius' 50 Bibles for Constantine.

"...the colophon at the end of Sinaiticus {Aleph} stated that it was 'the Hexapla' of Origen. Hort concedes in his Introduction to the New Testament in the Original Greek that the LXX Aleph and B are "the same manuscript Bibles."
(*New Age Bible Versions*, p.537)

Westcott and Hort's introduction states as fact:
"...that the translations of the Old Testament which form the LXX were made at Alexandria, while the chief uncials of the New Testament agree in some prominent points of orthography and grammatical form (by no means in all) with the chief uncials of the LXX, the four oldest being moreover parts of the same manuscript Bibles..." (*The New Testament in the Original Greek*, p.264)

Another reference states:
"It (Sinaitic MS.) seems to have been at one time at Caesarea; one of the correctors (probably of the seventh century) adds this note at the end of Esdras, (Ezra): 'This Codex was compared with a very ancient exemplar which had been corrected by the hand of the holy martyr Pamphilus (d. 309); which exemplar contained at the end, the subscription in his own hand: "Taken and corrected according to the Hexapla of Origen: Antonius compared it: I, Pamphilus, corrected it"'... The text of Aleph (#) bears a very close resemblance to that of B."
(*Catholic Encyclopedia*, quoted in *Our Authorized Bible Vindicated*, p.21)

By **1864**, the Oxford Movement was flooding the Church of England with rituals that were so close to the Catholic rituals that moving the Church over to Catholicism was becoming almost effortless. Newman was also encouraging the idea of bringing the Protestant **King James Bible** into agreement with the **Roman Catholic Latin Vulgate**.

Newman was a believer and follower of Origen and is quoted as saying,
"I love...the name Origen. I will not listen to the notion that so great a soul was lost." (*Dr. Newman, Apologia pro vita sus*, Chapter VII, p. 282)

In **1865**, the American Bible Society (ABS) published a Spanish Bible that was translated from a mixture of the **King James Bible**, the old **Valera Bible** of **1602**, the **Latin Vulgate**, and the new "critical texts" from Tischendorf. Because of this, the **1865 Spanish Bible** was not accepted by the majority of the Spanish speaking world.

In **1867**, Tischendorf published his copy of the **Codex Vaticanus (Codex B)** from the Vatican library. The Vatican manuscript, dated from about **362**, but it had been secreted in the Vatican library with access restricted since the 15th century. The original was finally made available to public examination when a facsimile was published in **1890**.

The **Codex Vaticanus (B)** and its sister **Codex Sinaiticus (Aleph)** became the major representatives of the Western/Alexandrian corrupted stream in opposition to the major representative of the Eastern pure stream, the **Textus Receptus**.

From the KJV to 1870

"Had B (Vaticanus) and ALEPH (Sinaiticus) been copies of average purity, they must long since have shared the inevitable fate of books which are freely used and highly prized; namely, they would have fallen into decadence and disappeared from sight. Thus the fact that B and ALEPH are so old is a point against them, not something in their favour. It shows that the Church rejected them and did not read them. Otherwise they would have worn out and disappeared through much reading." (Bible Versions, p.24)

When the **Codex Vaticanus** was compared with the **Textus Receptus**, it was found that there were 7,578 verbal divergences in just the four Gospels alone – these consisted in 2,877 words being omitted, 536 words being added, 935 words being substituted, 2,098 words being transposed, and 1,132 words being modified.

The **Vaticanus** also omits the entire book of Revelation – which stands to reason, since evidence shows that Eusebius doubted the authenticity of Revelation and viewed it more in the same category as the spurious books "The Shepherd" and the "Revelation of Peter."

"Given Rome's long career of fraud and forgery, it would not be wise to put much trust in any document that has ever been in its possession. This would include the celebrated Vaticanus and Sinaiticus manuscripts."
(Assault on the Remnant, p.457)

Tischendorf also worked on publishing his **Editio Octava Critica Maior** which is a critical edition of the Greek New Testament based on his findings and opinions.

In **1867**, a revision of the **KJV** called the **Inspired Version (IV)** was published. It had been written by Mormon prophet Joseph Smith, prior to his murder in **1844**, and the manuscripts for it had been kept by his widow. This version is commonly known as the **Joseph Smith Translation** of the Bible and has never been accepted outside of Mormon circles.

Smith had also added his own significant changes to his revision of the Bible – totally altering the Word of God to say things that it never said, and adding much of Smith's own words.

For example, in the **KJV**, Genesis 1:1 reads: *"In the beginning God created the heaven and the earth."*

But in Smith's translation, one has to read down to verse three in order to find this line.

Joseph Smith, Jr.

"1. And it came to pass, that the Lord spake unto Moses, saying, Behold, I reveal unto you concerning this heaven and this earth; write the words which I speak.

2. I am the Beginning and the End; the Almighty God. By mine Only Begotten I created these things.
3. Yea, in the beginning I created the heaven, and the earth upon which thou standest."

Obviously, Joseph Smith totally disregarded God's warning in Revelation 22:18. *"For I testify unto every man that heareth the words of the prophecy of this book, If any man shall add unto these things, God shall add unto him the plagues that are written in this book:"*

In **1869**, Vatican Council I convened and on **July 18, 1870**, though it had been claimed by popes for some 800 years, the Papal doctrine of "Infallibility" was finally officially defined – declaring the Pope "infallible in matters of faith and morals as well as undisputed primate."

This declaration did not include the personal or private acts of the pope, but only those promulgated from the chair on faith and morals – in other words, the official statements and actions.

"What is known today as papal infallibility was not even hinted at in the early church, and any suggestion that a Bishop of Rome was himself infallible would have aroused at times a degree of mirth…A pope who stepped out of line in matters of faith was condemned as a heretic…Not merely the idea of infallibility but even the germ of the idea was lacking in patristic times."
(*Vicars of Christ, The Dark Side of the Papacy*, p.205)

In **1870**, Philip Schaff became a professor at Union Theological Seminary in New York City, where he continued to promote higher criticism of the Bible.

In **1875**, a Russian witch named Helena Petrovna Blavatsky founded the occult Theosophical Society in New York City.

She later wrote *The Secret Doctrine* and *Isis Unveiled* which reveal some of the inner workings and basis for the occult and secret societies. She also started the "Lucifer Publishing Company" which was later incorporated and renamed "Lucis Trust."

Philip Schaff

"The Trust has always been Lucis right from its incorporation in 1923. The publishing company, however was called at first the Lucifer Publishing Company as authored by H.P. Blavatsky earlier." (*The New World Order*, p.80)

In **1876**, Roman Catholic Bishop James Gibbons published his well-known book

The Faith of our Fathers. In this book, he reveals how much Rome still hates Protestantism and its Bible and doesn't want the Bible to be in the hands of the common people. He wrote:

James Gibbons

> "The Bible became in their hands a complete Babel. The sons of Noe attempted in their pride to ascend to heaven by building the tower of Babel, and their scheme ended in the confusion and multiplication of tongues. The children of the the Reformation endeavored in their conceit to lead men to heaven by the private interpretation of the Bible, and their efforts led to the confusion and the multiplication of religions." (*The Faith of our Fathers*, p.70)

The very next year, he was promoted to the position of Archbishop of Baltimore, and in **1886** he became Cardinal.

James Cardinal Gibbons advocated the creation of The Catholic University of America in **1887**.

The **Sinaitic Syriac manuscript** was discovered in **1892**, again at St. Catherine's Monastery. It was also a rescript of the Gospels with at least one-fourth of the manuscript not being decipherable at all.

Cutting Edge Facts – Building Faith in God's Word

Historians of the times corroborate the truth of many of the Stories of the Bible, including the Story of Jesus

Here is Jewish historian Flavius Josephus' testimony of Jesus Christ:

"Now there was about this time Jesus, a wise man, if it be lawful to call him a man; for he was a doer of wonderful works, a teacher of such men as receive the truth with pleasure. He drew over to him both many of the Jews and many of the Gentiles. He was [the] Christ. And when Pilate, at the suggestion of the principal men amongst us, had condemned him to the cross, those that loved him at the first did not forsake him; for he appeared to them alive again the third day; as the divine prophets had foretold these and ten thousand other wonderful things concerning him. And the tribe of Christians, so named from him, are not extinct at this day."

(*Antiquities of the Jews*, Book 18, Chapter 3, #3)

Publius Cornelius Tacitus was a prominent Roman senator who was born in **AD 56**. His most famous historical work, *Annals*, was published in **115/116**. Tacitus confirms the connection between Christ and Pilate and agrees with the biblical record that this took place during the reign of Tiberius.

Here is a quote from Tacitus (as it was translated from Latin by A.J. Church in **1876**) taken from *Annals* 15.44:

"Consequently, to get rid of the report, Nero fastened the guilt and inflicted the most exquisite tortures on a class hated for their abominations, called Christians by the populace. Christus, from whom the name had its origin, suffered the extreme penalty during the reign of Tiberius at the hands of one of our procurators, Pontius Pilatus, and a most mischievous superstition, thus checked for the moment, again broke out not only in Judæa, the first source of the evil, but even in Rome, where all things hideous and shameful from every part of the world find their centre and become popular."

Tacitus was no fan of Christ or Christianity, but notice that he confirms the existence of Jesus Christ as the founder of the Christian movement. He confirms that Pontius Pilate was the governor (or procurator) who convicted Christ and condemned Him to crucifixion (Matthew 27:2-22). In addition, he also confirms that all this happened during the reign of Tiberius Caesar (Luke 3:1). All the characters and dates line up with the Bible testimony.

The Revision of the KJV (RV)

By **1870**, the influence of the Oxford Movement, with its theological bias in favor of Rome, had become so powerful that it was affecting many men in high authority. The scholars in England decided to "revise" the **KJV** Bible. The Jesuits realized that in order to undermine Protestantism, they would have to change the Bible that it was founded on. Their feelings about the **KJV** Bible were expressed quite plainly in this quote:

"Then the Bible [the Authorized King James Version of 1611], that serpent which with head erect and eyes flashing threatens us with its venom while it trails along the ground, shall be changed into a rod as soon as we are able to seize it..."
(Vatican Assassins, p.267)

But in order to make the change look innocent enough, they could not do it themselves, they would have to use "critically minded" Protestant scholars to do the job. They formed two committees, one for the Old Testament and one for the New Testament.

John Newman was actually requested to sit on the committees, but he declined. It would "look bad" because he had already publicly shown his contempt for Protestantism and his sympathies with Rome, so he preferred instead to wield his influence for the new Bible translation secretly from behind the scenes.

When originally formed, the New Testament committee had 25 members and the Old Testament committee had 27 members, though these numbers fluctuated from time to time.

A few of these scholars were Brooke Foss Westcott, Fenton John Anthony Hort, J. B. Lightfoot, R. C. Trench, and A. B. Davidson. These men were all connected with Rome in various degrees.

Westcott & Hort, the two most prominent and influential committee members, were both Cambridge professors who not only denied Biblical inerrancy but also were theistic evolutionists.

Hort wrote to Westcott **3-10-1860**: *"Have you read Darwin? [Origin of Species] How I should like a talk with you about it! In spite of difficulties, I am inclined to think it unanswerable. In any case it is a treat to read such a book."*
(Life and Letters of Fenton John Anthony Hort, Vol.1, p.414)

John Hort   **Brooke Westcott**

As already pointed out, Hort was a papal and slavery sympathizer who supported the idea of the America Union being destroyed, and both Hort and Westcott were spiritualists, who had founded the Ghostly Guild organization. J. B. Lightfoot was also a member of the Ghostly Guild. These men were all fascinated with occult themes and promoted Spiritism.

What do the scriptures have to say about the Bible being transmitted by spiritualists? Isaiah 8:19-20 answers, *"And when they shall say unto you, Seek unto them that have familiar spirits, and unto wizards that peep, and that mutter: should not a people seek unto their God? for the living to the dead? To the law and to the testimony: if they speak not according to this word, it is because there is no light in them."*

Both Westcott and Hort were promoters of Greek philosophy and were strongly opposed to Protestantism in general. Both had a prejudiced animosity for the **Textus Receptus** upon which the **KJV** had been based (even referring to it as "Vile" and "Villainous") and they promoted the Alexandrian text of the **Vaticanus** and **Sinaiticus** as the more accurate manuscripts.

Hort wrote, *"I had no idea till the last few weeks of the importance of texts, having read so little Greek Testament, and dragged on with the villainous Textus Receptus...Think of that vile Textus Receptus leaning entirely on late MSS.; it is a blessing there are such early ones...."*
(*Life and Letters of Fenton John Anthony Hort*, Vol.1, p.211)

Westcott and Hort developed a theory on how various Bible manuscripts were developed by bringing two different texts together and combining them to produce a new text (part of manuscript A + part of manuscript B = conflated manuscript C). This theory is called the "Conflate Theory."

"This theory, of course, demands that the manuscripts from which the conflated text is derived are older and the conflated text itself is younger. In reality, the conflate theory is nothing but the musings of higher critics in an effort to displace the Received Text with the Aleph and B. Specifically it is form criticism. Basic to form criticism is an assumed growth pattern from a short text to a longer text."
(*Assault on the Remnant*, p.154-155)

In other words, where one sees this "conflate theory" promoted, they can know it is just form criticism trying to undermine the inspired Word of God. Indeed, Wescott and Hort did not even believe the basics of the Word of God. Westcott wrote on **March 4, 1890**: *"No one now, I suppose, holds that the first three chapters of Genesis, for example, give a literal history – I could never understand how anyone reading them with open eyes could think they did..."*
(*Life and Letters of Brooke Foss Westcott*, Vol. 2, p.69)

The Revision of the KJV (RV)

Consider Jesus commentary on the Genesis account written by Moses:
"For had ye believed Moses, ye would have believed me: for he wrote of me. But if ye believe not his writings, how shall ye believe my words?" John 5:46,47

Hort's rebellious mentality not only showed his disdain of liberty (as shown by his anti-American, pro-slavery comments) but he also promoted Greek philosophy and followed the writings of Plato. He did not believe that God created the world in six literal days, and he also believed that worshiping the virgin Mary was no different than worshiping Jesus Christ.

"I have been persuaded for many years that Mary-worship and Jesus-worship have very much in common in their causes and their results."
(Life and Letters of Fenton John Anthony Hort, Vol.2, p.50)

F.H.A. Scrivener

Another member of the revision committee was Frederick Henry Ambrose Scrivener, probably the foremost textual critic of the day in the manuscripts of the Greek New Testament and the history of the Text. He also collated the **Sinaiticus** with the **Textus Receptus**.

Scrivener was one of the only supporters of the **Textus Receptus** on the committee. It is said that if Scrivener had not been on the Revision Committee, then there might have been nobody vocal, who would stand up for the Traditional Text.

He was asked to produce a Greek text by "reverse engineering" (translating from the English **KJV** back into Greek).

He selected readings from various **Greek "Majority Text"** manuscripts that best matched the resulting English **KJV** and as a result, his **Greek Textus Receptus** is said to therefore be in close agreement with the **KJV**.

However, he was still a critical scholar and wanted to change places in the **Received Text** to more closely match what he thought was truth. His Greek text therefore contains many critical footnotes that undermine the text. He claimed that the **Textus Receptus** was different than the **Byzantine Text** and a brief reading of some of his writings bring to light comments and concepts that show that he had begun to doubt the **Textus Receptus** text.

Another leader in this revision committee was Dr. W. F. Moulton. A feel for his mindset on the Bible may be obtained by reading some of his statements, such as the following statement that he made in reference to **Jerome's Latin Vulgate**:

"The Latin translation, being derived from manuscripts more ancient than any we now possess, is frequently a witness of the highest value in regard to the Greek text which current in the earliest times and... its testimony is in many cases confirmed by Greek manuscripts which have been discovered or examined since the 16th century." (The English Bible, p.184)

It is stated that, *"Professor W. F. Moulton, a Revisionist, also wrote a book on the "History of the Bible." In this book he glorifies the* Jesuit Bible of 1582 *as agreeing "with the best critical editions of the present day." "Hence," he says, "we may expect to find that the* Rhemish New Testament *(Jesuit Bible of 1582) frequently anticipates the judgment of later scholars as to the presence or absence of certain words, clauses, or even verses." And again, "On the whole, the influence of the use of the Vulgate would, in the New Testament, be more frequently for good than for harm in respect of text."* (Our Authorized Bible Vindicated, p.112)

Another reviser who also took part in this revision of the **KJV** was Dr. F. Vance Smith, who held Unitarian beliefs and also denied the divinity of Christ.

What do the scriptures have to say of those with the mindset that Jesus is not divine? 2 John 1:9-11 answers *"Whosoever transgresseth, and abideth not in the doctrine of Christ, hath not God. He that abideth in the doctrine of Christ, he hath both the Father and the Son. If there come any unto you, and bring not this doctrine, receive him not into your house, neither bid him God speed: For he that biddeth him God speed is partaker of his evil deeds."*

Unlike the **KJV**, the revision committees met behind closed doors and the public was basically kept in ignorance of what was taking place.

The revision committees were always divided with many arguments and disagreements. The minority voice in the committees was represented principally by Dr. Scrivener. According to Chairman Ellicott, the countless divisions in the Committee over the Greek Text, *"was often a kind of critical duel between Dr. Hort and Dr. Scrivener."* However, Dr. Scrivener was continuously and systematically outvoted.

The New Testament revision committee met on 407 days over the period of 11 years and issued their new version in **1881**. The Old Testament revision committee met on 792 days over the period of 15 years and issued their new version in **1885**.

These new versions of the Old & New Testaments were combined and are called the **English Revised Version** or simply the **Revised Version (RV)**.

With the production of the **Revised Version**, Catholics rejoiced and declared that its use would be the "death knell" for Protestantism.

The Revision of the KJV (RV)

> "On the 17th of May the English speaking world awoke to find that its Revised Bible had banished the Heavenly Witnesses and put the Devil in the Lord's Prayer. Protests loud and deep went forth against the insertion; against the omission, none. It is well, then, that the Heavenly Witnesses should depart whence their testimony is no longer received. The Jews have a legend that shortly before the destruction of their Temple, the Shechinah departed from the Holy of Holies, and the Sacred Voices were heard saying, 'Let us go hence.' So perhaps it is to be with <u>the English Bible, the Temple of Protestantism</u>. The going forth of the Heavenly Witnesses is the sign of the beginning of the end. Lord Panmure's prediction may yet prove true — <u>the New Version will be the death knell of Protestantism</u>." (Dublin Review (Catholic), July 1881)

Many changes to the Word of God were made to make the **RV** agree with Catholic theology. For example, Acts 8:37 (which teaches that a person must make a knowledgeable decision for Christ in order to qualify for baptism) was totally dropped out of the text of the **RV** so that the reading would match the Catholic doctrine of infant baptism.

The Catholic doctrine of beating oneself was also endorsed by changing the **KJV** reading of 1 Corinthians 9:27 *"But I keep under my body, and bring it into subjection:..."* to the **RV** reading of *"but I buffet my body, and bring it into bondage:..."* To "keep under" is the correct Protestant rendering showing the subduing of the passions of the natural heart. But the Papal rendering of "buffet" changes the text drastically. To "buffet" something is to "beat it" or "strike it" (like many Catholics still do to this day, in order to make themselves "more holy").

When the **Revised Version** is compared to the **King James Version**, it is revealed that some 36,000 changes in English, and some 6,000 changes in the Greek text were made.

An example of these changes in the Old Testament can be seen by looking at Daniel 2:25. The **KJV** specifies that the fourth man in the furnace was the Son of God. *"He answered and said, Lo, I see four men loose, walking in the midst of the fire, and they have no hurt; and the form of the fourth is like <u>the Son of God</u>."*

But the **RV** destroys this meaning by changing it to: *"He answered and said, Lo, I see four men loose, walking in the midst of the fire, and they have no hurt; and the aspect of the fourth is like <u>a son of the gods</u>."*

In the New Testament, one can see examples of these changes, such as Matthew 6:13. In the **KJV** it reads: *"And lead us not into temptation, but deliver us from evil: <u>For thine is the kingdom, and the power, and the glory, for ever. Amen.</u>"*

But the **RV** removes half the verse, and totally leaves it out: *"And bring us not into temptation, but deliver us from the evil one."*

Shortly before the **RV** was published, in **1881**, Westcott and Hort published their own **Vaticanus**-based critical text of the Greek New Testament. They had quietly been working on this Greek NT since **1853**.

Only after it was published was it discovered that Westcott & Hort, under a pledge of secrecy, had circulated among the revision Committee copies of their own critical edition of the Greek New Testament to sway the translators into accepting Alexandrian-based text.

Consider that 2 Corinthians 4:2 condemns underhanded dealings like this: *"But have renounced the hidden things of dishonesty, not walking in craftiness, nor handling the word of God deceitfully; but by manifestation of the truth commending ourselves to every man's conscience in the sight of God."*

The New Testament of the **English Revised Version** is largely based on **Westcott and Hort's Greek translation.** The other three uncials that were occasionally consulted were, the **Codex Beza (D)**, **Codex Ephraemi (C)** and **Codex Alexandrinus (A)**.

When comparing the **Textus Receptus** to the **Wescott & Hort Greek Translation** one can discover around 5,604 changes that Westcott and Hort made. Of these, 5,604 alterations, there are 1,952 omissions (35%), 467 additions (8%), and 3,185 changes (57%). In these 5,604 places that were involved in these alterations, there were 4,366 more words included, making a total of 9,970 Greek words that were involved.

Wescott and Hort also promoted the false idea that "older is better" and they had to come up with an explanation of why the majority of manuscripts supported the Byzantine readings of the **Textus Receptus** while very few supported the Alexandrian readings of the Critical Text (the **Vaticanus** and **Sinaiticus**). To accomplish this, they made up the fictitious story that during the 4th century an official ecclesiastical command had been given to adopt a standard form of Greek Text, and that is why so many of the manuscripts that they considered corrupt all agreed with each other. This theory of theirs became known as the "Syrian Recension." However, within a short time, scholars proved this theory of Syrian Recension as an error because there was absolutely no evidence of any such ecclesiastical command. With the fall of their Syrian Recension theory, Westcott and Hort's scholarly treatise and translations were left without a foundation.

Dean Burgon

John W. Burgon, Dean of Chichester, was a contemporary with Westcott and Hort. However, he was a strong advocate of the **Textus Receptus** and was the nemesis, or archenemy, of Westcott and Hort's feeble arguments against it.

The Revision of the KJV (RV)

Burgon says on page v in the dedication of his book The *Revision Revised*,

"...the mischievous attempt which was made in 1881 to thrust upon this Church and Realm a Revision of the Sacred Text, which — recommended though it be by eminent names — I am thoroughly convinced, and am able to prove, is untrustworthy from beginning to end. The reason is plain. It has been constructed throughout on an utterly erroneous hypothesis...The English (as well as the Greek) of the newly "Revised Version" is hopelessly at fault. It is to me simply unintelligible how a company of Scholars can have spent ten years in elaborating such a very unsatisfactory production. Their uncouth phraseology and their jerky sentences, their pedantic obscurity and their unidiomatic English, contrast painfully with "the happy turns of expression, the music of the cadences, the felicities of the rhythm" of our Authorized Version. The transition from one to the other, as the Bishop of Lincoln remarks, is like exchanging a well-built carriage for a vehicle without springs, in which you get jolted to death on a newly-mended and rarely-traversed road. But the "Revised Version" is inaccurate as well; exhibits defective scholarship, I mean, in countless places. <u>It is, however, the systematic depravation of the underlying Greek which does so grievously offend me: for this is nothing else but a poisoning of the River of Life at its sacred source. Our Revisers, (with the best and purest intentions, no doubt,) stand convicted of having deliberately rejected the words of Inspiration in every page, and of having substituted for them fabricated Readings which the Church has long since refused to acknowledge, or else has rejected with abhorrence; and which only survive at this time in a little handful of documents of the most depraved type."</u>

The occult world, just like the Papal Church, despises the pure Word of God and was very pleased with the **RV**. Speaking of the original **King James Version**, the witch Helena Petrovna Blavatsky derogatorily stated:

"And King James's translators have made such a jumble of it that no one but a kabalist can restore the Bible to its original form." (*Isis Unveiled*, Vol.2, p.362)

Yet, when the revision came out in **1885**, Blavatsky rejoiced that the **Revised Version** had disassociated Lucifer's name from the fallen angel of Isaiah 14:12.

H. P. Blavatsky

The Revisers also made other changes from the **Authorized Version**, which were added to their new **Revised Version**. Quite a few of these changes confused the scriptures with error.

"In the use of italics the Revisers departed from the custom of the Authorized Version and adopted as their rule the following resolution of their company: 'That all such words now printed in italics, as are plainly implied in the Hebrew and necessary in English, be printed in common type.'"

(*The Revisers' Preface to the English Revised Version*)

The English Revision committee also translated the Apocrypha and published it in **1894**.

Hort himself also tells us that the writings of the Catholic textual critic Richard Simon played a large part in the movement to discredit the **Textus Receptus** class of MSS and Bibles.

Yet even while the critics fight against the **Textus Receptus** and try to discredit it, they can't help but admit that it is true and correct! For example, one critical scholar who has a whole chapter of his book dedicated to explain why the **Textus Receptus** cannot be used by scholars today, admits in the middle of his chapter:

"*It should be stated at once that the* Textus Receptus *is not a bad text. It is not a heretical text. It is substantially correct. Hort has put the matter well: 'With regard to the great bulk of the words of the New Testament, as of most other ancient writings, there is no variation or other ground of doubt, and therefore no room for textual criticism'...It is clear, therefore, that the Textus Receptus has preserved for us a substantially accurate text in spite of the long centuries preceding the age of printing when copying by hand was the only method of reproducing the New Testament.*" (*Introduction to Textual Criticism*, p. 21)

The **RV** set the stage for the desire for newer translations and therefore, the **English Revised Version (RV)** is regarded as the forerunner of the flood of modern Bible translations.

"*Many individual efforts produced different Greek New Testaments. Likewise furious attacks were made upon the Old Testament in Hebrew, from which the King James and other Bibles had been translated. None of these assaults, however, met with any marked success until the Revision Committee was appointed by the southern half of the Church of England under the Archbishop of Canterbury, — although the same church in the northern half of England under the Archbishop of York, refused to be a party to the project. This Revision Committee, besides the changes in the Old Testament, made over 5000 changes in the Received Text of the New Testament and so produced a new Greek New Testament. This permitted all the forces hostile to the Bible to gather themselves together and pour through the breach. Since then, the flood gates have been opened and we are now deluged with many different kinds of Greek New Testaments and with English Bibles translated from them, changed and mutilated in bewildering confusion.*"

(*Our Authorized Bible Vindicated*, p.2)

During the years that the Revision Committee was revising the **KJV** and the **Textus Receptus** in England (**1870-1885**), the Americans had also joined in the project. "*The corresponding American revision committee... was headed by another liberal evolutionist, Philip Schaff.*" (Defending the Faith, p.33)

The Revision of the KJV (RV)

Dr. Philip Schaff of the Union Theological Seminary in New York City, worked to form two committees with the Old Testament Company having 14 members, and the New Testament, 13. These men were chosen upon the basis that they should live near New York City in order that meetings of the committee might be convenient. Dr. Schaff was to America what John Newman was to England. His Mercersburg Theology was to America, what the Oxford Movement was to England.

Schaff was the president of both the OT and NT committees, but he died before the **American Standard Version (ASV)**, also known as the **Authorized Revised Version (ARV)**, was published.

The American Committee had no deciding vote on points of revision with the English committees. As soon as portions of the Bible were revised by the English committees, they were sent to the American committees for confirmation or amendment. If the suggestions returned by the American committees were acceptable to their English coworkers, they were adopted; otherwise they had no independent claim for insertion. In other words, the American committees were simply reviewing bodies.

The English agreed to publish the American preferences in an added appendix as long as the Americans would not issue their proposed Revision until 14 years after the English Revision had been published. This is why the Americans didn't publish their revision called the **American Standard Version**, until 1901.

The 1901 **American Standard Version (ASV)** differs very little from the 1885 **English Revised Version (RV)**. One of the main places where it differs, is that the **ASV** uses the name "Jehovah" in verses where the **RV** uses the word "LORD."

In **1901**, the British and Foreign Bible Society caved in to pressure and agreed to print and promote the **Revised Version of the KJV**.

The Trinitarian Bible Society on the other hand, knew that Unitarians had been on the revision committee and they therefore suspected that the "revision" was corrupt. In **1902**, the Trinitarian Bible Society officially rejected the **Revised Version**.

Nevertheless, in the **RV** and the flood of modern Bibles can be seen the fulfilling of this statement.

"Men act as though they had been given special liberty to cancel the decisions of God. The higher critics put themselves in the place of God, and review the Word of God, revising or endorsing it. In this way, all nations are induced to drink the wine of the fornication of Babylon. These higher critics have fixed things to suit the popular heresies of these last days..."

(*The Upward Look*, pg. 35 quoted from Lt48-1897)

Cutting Edge Facts – Building Faith in God's Word

The Bible is Established – "Because it Works"

Once upon a time a man who didn't love and believe the Word of God was talking with a Christian doctor who did love and believe it.

"I'm surprised that you put any faith in the Bible," said the unbeliever. "An educated man like you; why you can't even tell for sure who wrote many of the books in it! And how could anyone with any brains at all believe all those miracles?"

"Wouldn't you put faith in anything if you didn't know who wrote it?" asked the doctor.

"Certainly not, my good man!" replied the unbeliever.

"Do you know who wrote the multiplication table?" asked the doctor.

"Well—er—no!"

"Yet you believe it and use it all the time, don't you?"

"Well—er—yes" replied the unbeliever, beginning to feel uncomfortable. Then a gleam of hope came to him. "Well, you see, doctor, the multiplication table works so well that no one needs to know who wrote it."

Then the doctor replied, "The same is true of the Bible. It works well too! Did you ever hear a man say, 'I was a thief, a murderer, a drunkard, disgrace to my family; then I began to study mathematics, geology, or astronomy, and it made a new man out of me'?"

"Well—er—no!" replied the unbeliever.

"Well, answered the doctor, "I can show you not one or two or hundreds, but thousands of men and women who have become new creatures because they have loved and believed the Word of God."

This fact is exactly what the Bible teaches about itself.
*"When ye received the word of God... ye received it not as the word of men, but as it is in truth, the word of God, which **effectually worketh** also in you that believe."* 1 Thessalonians 2:13b

"Wherewithal shall a young man cleanse his way? by taking heed thereto according to thy word." Psalm 119:9

From the RV to 1979

In **1886**, Richard Francis Weymouth published his critical **Resultant Greek Testament** which most modern critical scholars agree with.

In **1898**, a German Biblical scholar, evolutionist, textual critic, and skeptic named Eberhard Nestle published an influential handbook of textual criticism and also his first edition of the Greek New Testament known as **Novum Testamentum Graece**. Nestle's New Testament was the **Wescott and Hort Text** collated with **Weymouth's edition** and **Tischendorf's Editio Octava Critica Maior**.

Eberhard Nestle

In **1901** three small fragments of a papyrus of the gospel of Matthew were discovered in Luxor, Egypt and sent to the Magdalen College library in Oxford. They were classified as **Papyrus 64**. Later it was discovered that **Papyrus 64** was actually part of the same manuscript as **Papyrus 67**, a fragment of Matthew housed in Barcelona, and **Papyrus 4**, a near complete page from the gospel of Luke housed in Paris. The **Magdalene Papyrus** is judged by some to be the oldest extant Greek manuscript, dating to around 200, but many scholars cannot agree on a date – some date it to the 4th century. It's uncial text type appears to be Alexandrian in nature.

Around **1902**, Hermann Von Soden published his writings of the New Testament which he had collated in their supposed oldest text form.

He introduced a new notation of MSS, and a new theory of textual history. He claimed that there were only three recensions of texts in the 4th century which he termed, H, I, and K. From these recensions, he reconstructed a hypothetical text which he called I-H-K. He claimed that all the 2nd and 3rd century writers had used this hypothetical text. However, even though Von Soden had compared several manuscripts, he had only compared less than 8% of the over 5,000 Greek manuscripts, and the writings of the 2nd and 3rd century writers did not match his theory.

H. Von Soden

"We find that Soden is in another class as an investigator and a student, and that his vision is circumscribed and Alexandrian. His text is a real mixture and quite unscientific." (Codex B and its Allies, p.460-461)

"As to the presentment of the combined critical material, after making every allowance for the division of work among forty people, it can only be said that the apparatus is positively honeycombed with errors, and many documents which should have been recollated have not been touched, others only partially, and others again have been incorrectly handled." (Von Soden's Text of the NT, JTS, 15-1914, p 307)

Sword Unsheathed

Speaking of all the errors in Von Soden's text, Professor Frederik Wisse states: *"Once the extent of error is seen, the word "inaccuracy" becomes a euphemism."* (*The Profile Method for the Classification and Evaluation of Manuscript Evidence*, p. 16)

Von Soden's inaccurate text will be seen again in future Bible translations such as the **New King James Bible** in 1979.

In **1902**, Dr. Walter Llewellyn Nash purchased the **Nash Papyrus** from an Egyptian dealer in antiquities. The fragment was said to have come from an area in middle Egypt known as Fayyum. It is dated around **100BC–100AD** and it contains the Hebrew Decalogue and Deuteronomy 6:4. In **1903** he presented it to the Cambridge University Library.

In **1903**, the **Weymouth New Testament**, otherwise known as **The New Testament in Modern Speech** was published. It was based on the text of **The Resultant Greek Testament** produced by Dr. Richard Francis Weymouth, an English schoolmaster and Baptist layman who devoted himself to textual criticism. He describes *"translation under a needless restriction to literality"* as *"intellectual handcuffs and fetters."* (*The Modern Speech New Testament*, Preface, pg. x)

Weymouth's Greek was what resulted from his compilation of readings from, Lachmann, Tregelles, Tischendorf, Lightfoot, Ellicott, Alford, Stephens (**1550**), Weiss, the Bâle edition (**1880**), Westcott and Hort, and the Revision Committee of London. Where these editions differed, Weymouth selected the reading favoured by the majority of editors.

An example of the differences in the **Weymouth** version is seen in Matthew 4:4. One might note that, in the **KJV**, the focus is on the Word, while Weymouth's wording unnecessarily leaves one open to "signs and wonders" or "appointed" popedoms.
   KJV–*"But he answered and said, It is written, Man shall not live by bread alone, but by every word that proceedeth out of the mouth of God."*
   Weymouth– *"Jesus answered, 'It is written, "IT IS NOT ON BREAD ALONE THAT MAN SHALL LIVE, BUT ON WHATSOEVER GOD SHALL APPOINT"' (Deut. viii.3)."*

In **1904**, the British and Foreign Bible Society adopted the fourth edition of **Nestle's New Testament** to replace the **Textus Receptus**.

In **1906**, Rudolf Kittel published the first edition of the Hebrew Bible called the **Biblia Hebraica (BHK)** and the second edition in **1912**. In these first two editions, he had used the good **Ben Chayyim text** although he deviated from this later. Indeed, Kittel was a German rationalist skeptic/higher critic. He rejected the idea of Biblical inerrancy and was firmly devoted to evolutionism.

Rudolf Kittel

After the death of Eberhard Nestle in **1913**, his son Erwin Nestle (**1883–1972**) took over the publication and contributed substantially to the constant "improvements" of the various editions of the **Novum Testamentum Graece**.

From the RV to 1979

In **1908**, 32 different religious denominations, including several wings of the Episcopal Church, Presbyterian Church, and Methodist Church, as well as numerous others, came together to form the Federal Council of Churches. The Federal Council of Churches promoted equal rights for all and the reduction of poverty. It became a communist front-group, to promote the communist concept of the equal distribution of wealth. They stated: *"We insist that the stewardship of property carries with it the obligation to supervise and moralize all property, and to consecrate its use to the public welfare."* (Federal Council of Churches Quadrennial Report, p.64)

In **1909**, the American Bible Society and the British and Foreign Bible Society decide to produced a Spanish translation to "correct the errors" of the **1865** edition. This **1909** Bible version became known as "**La Version Antigua**" ("**The Old Version**"). This revision made changes to the **1865** edition to make it agree more closely with the **Greek Textus Receptus**, and as a result, the 1909 **Version Antigua** was the closest to the **King James Bible** since the 1602 **Reina-Valera**. Though they did use the **Textus Receptus** in this translation, the finished product still contained influence from the critical texts.

In the early 20th century, the beginnings of the movement to bring all the world back to Rome began to take shape. This process is known as the "ecumenical movement." *"The World Missionary Conference at Edinburgh in 1910 brought the beginnings of the Faith and Order movement, which became the modern ecumenical movement."* (All Roads Lead to Rome, p.21)

In 1921-1922 the **Shorter Bible** (**SBK**) shortened the Bible down to a "conveniently readable" size. The Old Testament ritual and sacrificial system pointing to the death of Christ are gone. As a result, the New Testament references to Christ as the fulfillment of the Old Testament sacrifices are omitted. Whole books of the Old Testament are gone. Some portions of the books of the prophets are missing. From the New Testament 4,000 verses are totally removed while other verses are cut in two with only a fragment left. The great commission recorded in Matthew; the epistles of Titus, Jude, First and Second John, are entirely omitted, and only twenty-five verses of the second epistle of Timothy remain. Part of the third chapter of Romans is omitted with only one verse remaining from the fourth chapter. The twenty-fourth chapter of Matthew is missing and all the passages which teach the atonement through the death of Christ are gone.

In **1925** a meta-physical Bible was produced that was called **People's New Covenant** (**PNC**) or **People's New Testament** (**PNT**).

In **1929**, the International Council of Religious Education decided to "revise" the **American Standard Version** to match the new and improved standards of literary scholarship and textual criticism. However they had trouble raising the funds for the new translation, so work on it was postponed until **1936**.

Sword Unsheathed

In **1931**, the **Chester Beatty Papyri**, a group of twelve Greek MSS on papyrus, were obtained by Chester Beatty from a dealer in Egypt. It is said that they were found near Memphis, on the banks of the Nile. These MSS agree with the **Septuagint** and **Codex Sinaiticus**.

In the **1930**'s, the Nazi movement was growing into power and was itself being supported by the papal nuncio, Eugenio Pacelli. *"On July 20, 1933, the Roman Church-State signed a treaty with Hitler guaranteeing the loyalty of German Roman Catholics to the Hitler regime."* (*Ecclesiastical Megalomania*, p.165)

The Reich Concordat ensured that Nazism could rise into power unopposed by the Papal Church. *"In 1933 Pacelli found a successful negotiating partner for his Reich Concordat in the person of Adolf Hitler."* (*Hitler's* Pope, p.6)

Pacelli was then elected as Pope Pius XII in **1939** and held that office until the year **1958** – he has been called by some, "Hitler's Pope."

Hitler promoted the anti-Semitic theology of the fourth Lateran Council by commanding that all Jews had to wear a distinctive ensign and they were not allowed to hold any public office.

Pope Pius XII

"'I learned much from the Order of the Jesuits', said Hitler... 'Until now, there has never been anything more grandiose, on the earth, than the hierarchical organisation of the Catholic Church. I transferred much of this organisation into my own party...'" (*Secret History of the Jesuits*, p.164)

Rudolph Kittel's son, Gerhard Kittel, became attracted to the philosophies of Arianism and anti-Semitic hatred of the Nazi movement, and in **1933** he joined the Nazi party and helped to promote Hitler's agenda through his lectures and publications. Hitler knew that Germany was a professing Christian country and he needed some form of scriptural support for his planned extermination of the Jews. Gerhard Kittel was happy to oblige and began working on producing a dictionary of theology that would support the Nazi agenda.

"A close working relationship had developed between Grundmann and Hugo Odeberg, professor in Lund, and an expert on rabbinic Judaism who had worked with Kittel in producing critical editions of rabbinic texts."
(*The Theological Faculty of the University of Jena during the Third Reich*, p.9)

"Kittel's notorious Dictionary was published between 1932 and 42. Its notoriety is derived from its particularly denigrating descriptions of early Judaism..."

From the RV to 1979

In **1933**, George Lamsa published the **Lamsa Bible**. The **Lamsa Bible** claims to be from "ancient eastern manuscripts" and states that it is translated "from the **Peshitta**." However, much of it more closely resembles the corrupted **LXX** and Alexandrian readings, than the original **Peshitta** readings. The Preface states that Lamsa used the **Codex Ambrosianus** for the basis of the OT, and the so-called **"Mortimer-McCawley" manuscript** for the NT.

The **Codex Ambrosianus**, collectively called **Codices Ambrosiani A-E**, is the name for five different manuscripts written by different authors and with different alphabets. These manuscripts are dated between **550-1100** and represent a late form of the Aramaic text, not from the original **Peshitta**.

The so-called **Mortimer-McCawley manuscript** appears to have no existence outside of **Lamsa's Bible**. It seems that either it is a totally fictitious manuscript, or it is no longer known by that name. The writer/compiler could not find any evidence of it in any book or anywhere on the internet, other than a few blogs where other researchers were asking if anyone knew what that manuscript was.

An example of the corrupt changes made by Lamsa would be Isaiah 28:10-13 where the Word of God reveals how to study the Bible (precept upon precept). The **KJV** tells us: *"For precept must be upon precept, precept upon precept; line upon line, line upon line; here a little, and there a little: ...But the word of the LORD was unto them precept upon precept, precept upon precept; line upon line, line upon line; here a little, and there a little; that they might go, and fall backward, and be broken, and snared, and taken."*

But the **Lamsa Bible** destroys this meaning. It says: *"For filth is upon filth, filth upon filth; vomit upon vomit, vomit upon vomit; a little here, a little there; ...So the word of the Lord was to them filth upon filth, filth upon filth, vomit upon vomit, vomit upon vomit; a little here, a little there; that they might return and fall backward and be broken and snared and taken."*

In **1936**, work began on the "revision" of the **American Standard Version** which of course, was itself a revision of the **KJV**.

Spain was trying to throw off the control of the Vatican and become a free Republic. In the early **1930**'s, many baby skeletons were discovered in convents and other Roman Catholic buildings, revealing the abuse of the nuns by the priests and the abortions that were performed to keep the facts quiet. This caused massive outrage among the Catholic laity and escalated the move to separate from the Vatican. The people of Spain rebelled against Rome.

Beginning in **1936** and lasting until **1939**, the Spanish Civil War was fought by Rome to destroy the Republican Nationalists and bring Spain back into the control of the Vatican. The Jesuits were prime movers in this war.

Sword Unsheathed

"In 1936 the new Spanish inquisition exploded. It was called 'The Spanish Civil War,' secretly orchestrated in the Vatican...General Franco eventually became the Roman Catholic dictator of Spain. Franco's government was recognized Aug. 3, 1937, by the Vatican, just 20 months before the civil war ended."
(Vatican Assassins, p.474)

"<u>Fifth Column</u> is a term that refers to undercover agents <u>operating within the ranks of an enemy</u> to undermine its cause. These agents pave the way for military or political invasion. They may work within an army, a political party, or an industry. <u>Their activities include spying, sabotage, propaganda, agitation, infiltration, and sometimes, terror and revolt</u>.

"The term <u>fifth column was first used during the Spanish Civil War</u> (1936-1939) to describe the work of General Franco's followers in Loyalist Madrid. General Emilio Mola, a leader under General Franco, said, "I have four columns moving against Madrid, and a fifth will rise up inside the city itself."
(Worldbook Encyclopedia, Volume F-7, p.98)

"A cardinal technique of the <u>fifth column</u> is the infiltration of sympathizers into the entire fabric of the nation under attack and, particularly, into positions of policy decision and national defense. From such key posts, <u>fifth-column activists exploit the fears of a people by spreading rumours and misinformation</u>, as well as by employing the more standard techniques of espionage and sabotage."
(Encyclopedia Britannica, p.770, 15th ed., 1994, Vol. 4 Macropedia, "Fifth Column")

In other words, the term "Fifth Column" originated as a description of Jesuit tactics of infiltration, sabotage, and propaganda/misinformation – to destroy a country, institution, or entity from the inside! The reader will notice this same set of tactics being used in the realm of Bible translations.

In **1937**, Rudolph Kittel, using the peculiar logic that was gaining ground in Germany and elsewhere, which believed that "older must always be better," changed his Hebrew text from the **Ben Chayyim** to the **Ben Asher** text which was taken from the **Leningrad Codex (B19a)**.

The Jewish/Aristotelian philosopher Maimonides gives a clue to Asher's text by stating: *"The copy whereon we depend is the well-known copy in Egypt, which contains the twenty-four books, and which was many years at Jerusalem for the purpose of correcting copies from it; and upon it all of them depend; for Ben Asher revised it, and minutely corrected it; and revised it many times over: and upon the same I rely in the copy of the Law, which I have written according to his rule."*
(Townley's Biblical Literature, vol. 1, p.55)

In other words, the **Ben Asher text** was "revised" "many times over!"

From the RV to 1979

This Ben Asher-based third edition of the **Biblia Hebraica (BHK)** had about 20,000 changes from the first two editions that had been based on the **Ben Chayyim** text.

Both the **Ben Chayyim** and the **Ben Asher** texts are referred to as "Masoretic," so care must be taken as to which text is being referred to. Apparently Kittel didn't care that the **Ben Asher version** was based on a small few minor corrupt manuscripts like the **Leningrad Codex (B19a)**, while the **Ben Chayyim text** followed the vast majority of the pure Hebrew manuscripts available.

Also in **1937**, Rudolph's son, Gerhard, also published his first volume of his *Theological Dictionary of the Greek New Testament*. His other volumes were not finished yet when the war ended with the defeat of the Nazis. Gerhard was arrested, tried, convicted, and punished for his war crimes in the Jewish genocide. Matthew 7:20 says *"Wherefore by their fruits ye shall know them."*

Later, others finished Kittel's Theological Dictionary and published it. It is one of the sources used in the production of many modern Bible versions today.

By **1943**, the nine member **ASV** New Testament revision committee had finished their work, after meeting a total of 145 days and doing the rest by correspondence. However, because of wartime restrictions, the first edition of the **Revised Standard Version** New Testament did not appear until **February 11, 1946**. The Old Testament committee did not finish until **1952**, with the complete **Revised Standard Version (RSV)** coming out on **September 30, 1952**.

The translation committee was said to have used the 17th edition of the **Nestle Greek text** for the New Testament and the traditional Hebrew Masoretic Text for the Old Testament, as well as the newly discovered **Dead Sea Scrolls**. However, the evidence shows that they apparently didn't follow the Masoretic text as closely as they had claimed.

Many Protestants are not aware that the **RSV** committee had Roman Catholics on it. The preface of their new revision states:

"The Revised Standard Version Bible committee is a continuing body, holding its meetings at regular intervals. It has become both ecumenical and international, with Protestant and Catholic active members who come from Great Britain, Canada and the United States."

In fact, most of the citations in the **1994** Catechism of the Catholic Church are from the **RSV**, showing that Rome at least to some degree, approves of the **RSV**. The **RSV** is both Protestant and Catholic theology oriented and is sponsored by the National Council of Churches.

Sword Unsheathed

Dr. Luther Weigle, chairman of the **RSV** revision committee stated that a person could not use the **KJV** and **RSV** together as the use of one with the other would cause confusion.

Interestingly, **RSV** key member Weigle was connected with some other sinister powers. *"Another person involved in the National Council of Churches' Communist-front organizations was the Revised Standard Version's Luther A. Wiegle[sic] who was found by the House Un-American Activities Committee to belong to six Communist-front organizations."* (Assault on the Remnant, p.242)

As an example of the mindset of the translators of this version, consider what two of the well-known translators, Edgar Goodspeed and James Moffatt, state about the Bible. *(James Moffatt not to be confused with missionary Robert Moffat)*

Edgar Goodspeed, in *How to Read the Bible* stated:
"The little idyl of Ruth follows the Book of Judges in the Bible, only because its story falls in the days of the Judges. But it <u>belongs to Israel's fiction</u>, rather than to its history, and should be read among its tales and stories." (p.51)

"We must think of the books of the Bible which are fiction, that is, short stories. The Book of Job is more than a novel, for it is principally drama and debate, but its <u>setting is unmistakably fiction</u>." (p.147)

James Moffatt, of the famous modern-speech **Moffatt Bible** says in the preface to the **RSV** translation that the Hebrew manuscripts from which the **King James Bible** was translated are *"desperately corrupt"*.

In his work *The Approach to the New Testament* Moffatt states: *"We also know that the New Testament writers attached a meaning to some Old Testament prophecies which was unhistorical...Historical criticism has rendered a true service to Christianity by relieving it of the necessity of accepting literally such attempts...Predictions like that of the millennium in the book of Revelation are due to some passing mood of faith in a particular age."* (p.85-86)

James Moffatt

The reader should consider the counsel of Christ regarding skeptics like this, *"And he said unto him, If they hear not Moses and the prophets, neither will they be persuaded, though one rose from the dead." Luke 16:31*

These examples are just a couple of the **RSV** translators, but these same types of sentiments were the mindset of quite a few of the translators. Case in point, the Preface to the **RSV** states the false accusations that: *"the King James Version has grave defects"* and *"The King James Version of the New Testament was based* *upon a Greek text that was marred by mistakes, containing the accumulated errors of fourteen centuries of manuscript copying."*

There are many examples of how the **RSV** translators corrupted God's Word. Just to give one example, Matthew 27:35 in the **KJV** specifies the fulfillment of the OT prophecy about the soldiers casting lots for Jesus' garment.

KJV = *"And they crucified him, and parted his garments, casting lots: That it might be fulfilled which was spoken by the prophet, they parted my garments among them, and upon my vesture did they cast lots."*

The **RSV** translation however, removes the whole sentence about fulfilling prophecy. This deletion, in addition to the quotation above, leads one to assume that they considered it "unhistorical": *"And when they had crucified him, they divided his garments among them by casting lots;"*

Also corrupted is Isaiah 7:14, which in the **KJV** clearly foretells the miraculous virgin birth of Jesus Christ. **KJV** – *"Therefore the Lord himself shall give you a sign; Behold, a virgin shall conceive, and bear a son, and shall call his name Immanuel."*

Indeed, the **RSV** attempt to change this, making Mary just a "young woman" instead of a "virgin," thereby eliminating the miracle and instead substituting a common everyday occurrence for it. *"Therefore the Lord himself will give you a sign. Behold, a young woman shall conceive and bear a son, and shall call his name Imman'u-el."*

During this time period while the **RSV** was in the making, many other key events were taking place. In **1946**, the United Bible Societies (UBS) was formed. The Papal Church is very much opposed to Bible Societies, because she does not want the Word of God freely circulated to the people.

"...the attitude of the Church toward the Bible societies is one of unmistakable opposition. Believing herself to be the divinely appointed custodian and interpreter of Holy Writ, she cannot without turning traitor to herself, approve the distribution of Scripture "without note or comment." (Catholic Encyclopedia, vol. 2, p.545)

Rome realized that if her agents (some of whom were already inside some of the member Bible societies) could infiltrate this UBS group, then they would gain much influence if not entire control of the various Bible Societies around the world, which would in turn, give them more control, not only of the comments and footnotes of the Bible translations, but also of what types of Bibles were circulated altogether. So Jesuits immediately set about to infiltrate UBS and thus "destroy" it from the inside out.

*"Bible societies and their federation in the United Bible Societies (UBS), created in **1946**, have often pioneered in interconfessional co-operation and transcultural work, where others lagged behind."* (Dictionary of the Ecumenical Movement, p.95)

Sword Unsheathed

The Trinitarian Bible Society refused to join this union of Bible Societies.

In December of **1947**, the synagogue in Aleppo, Syria was burned by rioters and the **Aleppo Codex** that was housed there mysteriously disappeared for about 10 years. It was rumored that it had been destroyed in the fire.

Then in **1958**, it reappeared in Israel except that some pages (about 40%) of the **Aleppo Codex** were found to be missing. The Jews insisted that the missing pages had been destroyed in the fire – but modern analysis show that the remaining pages were not damaged by fire but had fungus growing on them – the pages that were missing had been purposely removed. Many believe that the missing pages were torn out and are being hidden from the public. Since then, two of the pages that had supposedly been destroyed by fire reappeared, one in **1982** and the other in **2007**, which also lends credence to the torn out pages theory. Presently, the **Leningrad Codex** serves scholars as a primary source for the recovery of details in the missing parts of the **Aleppo Codex**.

Another series of events during the making of the **RSV** were taking place over in Israel. Between **1946** and **1956**, a collection of some 981 different Hebrew and Aramaic texts were discovered in caves in the ancient settlement at Khirbet Qumran close to the Dead Sea. These became known as the **Dead Sea Scrolls**. Of the ones that have been identified only about 40% of them are copies of texts from the Hebrew Scriptures, about 30% of them are texts from the Second Temple Period which were not canonized in the Hebrew Bible, and about 30% of them are sectarian manuscripts (some sources say only 25% are Biblical and 75% are not).

It is believed by some scholars that the scrolls were meticulously copied by the Essenes (a cult of Jewish mystics who were known for their strictness and abstinence and were Kabbalistic) and then hidden in the caves during the Jewish Revolt that resulted in the destruction of Jerusalem in **70 AD.**

Concerning evidence that the text of the **Dead Sea Scrolls** does not always match the Masoretic Hebrew, it is stated: *"Some of the Dead Sea Scrolls actually have more in common with the Greek Septuagint than the traditional Hebrew Masoretic Text, showing that the Greek translators must have been translating from Hebrew texts that resembled the Dead Sea Scrolls."*
(Noah Weiner, editor of *Bible History Daily*, a publication of the Biblical Archaeology Society)

In other words, while a few parts of the **Dead Sea Scrolls** do confirm some of the Masoretic readings of the **King James Version**, there are way too many Alexandrian differences, errors, and extra-Biblical additions to be able to trust the **Dead Sea Scrolls**. A larger percentage of them appear to be based in counterfeit Hebrew texts – so they are more a mixture of truth and error.

From the RV to 1979

To add even more suspicion to the **Dead Sea Scrolls** – in the year **2000**, William Kando, the son of the famous antiques dealer who originally bought the **Dead Sea Scrolls** from the bedouins who found them, opened his family's vault in Zürich – and he began to sell "authentic remnants" of the scrolls to wealthy Christian investors. The Washington D.C. Museum of the Bible, at great expense, bought 16 of these "authentic remnants" for their display in **2017**.

In what has been called *"a scandal of Biblical proportions,"* it was discovered in **2020**, much to the dismay of the museum authorities as well as many other Biblical scholars and collectors around the world, that at least 90% of these "authentic remnants" (including all 16 pieces of the museum's collection) were all forgeries!

Ironically, the reappearance of the **Aleppo Codex** and the discovery the **Dead Sea Scrolls** – both in the land of Israel, coincides very closely with the **May 14, 1948** creation of the political State of Israel – leading one to believe that their "discoveries" were "planned" and not just "coincidence."

It is said, *"Prophecies by Ezekiel, Jeremiah and Daniel not found in the Bible are written in the Scrolls."* Also, *"In the Scrolls are found never before seen psalms attributed to King David and Joshua."* It is even mentioned that, *"They show Christianity to be rooted in Judaism and have been called the evolutionary link between the two."* (Quotes from Century One Bookstore webpage – '25 Fascinating Facts about the Dead Sea Scrolls')

When the communist-front World Council of Churches (WCC) formed on **August 23, 1948**, for the ecumenical purpose of unifying all the world churches, the United Bible Societies (UBS) became their umbrella wing society to gather all the World Bible Societies under their control. The founding of the WCC is intimately linked not only the Freemasons, but also with the Jesuits and the Illuminati. (See *En Route to Global Occupation*, p.84, 94, 109 & 138)

In **1950**, the communist-front organization, the Federal Council of Churches, merged with other left-leaning church organizations to become the American arm of the World Council of Churches. Its name was then changed to the National Council of Churches (NCC).

"The NCC is known for left-wing advocacy, especially around issues of race, feminism, homosexual issues, immigration, and support for Communist dictators and left-wing revolutionary movements in the Third World."
(Conservapedia, "National Council of Churches," accessed 3-17-20)

"Who was it that founded the National Council of Churches/World Council of Churches which was also the authorizing body for the Revised Standard Version? Answer – the Jesuits." (Assault on the Remnant, p.172)

The Catholic Research Information Bureau (CRIB) warned:
"The Ecumenical movement was not founded on the free evangelical message of Christ and the outpouring of the Holy Spirit, but was spawned in the dark corridors of the Vatican by the Jesuit General Bea." (*All Roads Lead to Rome*, p.138)

In **1946**, plans for a new translation were begun in England, and in **1970** the **New English Bible (NEB)** was published. The committee for this work first met in July of **1947**. Some of the faiths represented in this group included the Presbyterian Church of England, the Society of Friends, Churches of Wales and Ireland, the Roman Catholic Church, and the British and Foreign Bible Society, as well as others. They used Kittel's **1937** edition of the **Biblia Hebraica**, **Jerome's Latin Vugate**, and the **Septuagint**, as well as the newly discovered **Dead Sea Scrolls**, for the basis of the Old Testament. For the New Testament, they used **Westcott and Hort's Greek translation**.

The New Testament of the **New English Bible** was published in **1961** with the Old Testament making up the complete Bible being added in **1970**.

One example of the corrupt changes that the **NEB** made to the Word of God would be Daniel 12:4, which in the **KJV** reads, *"But thou, O Daniel, shut up the words, and seal the book, even to the time of the end: many shall run to and fro, and knowledge shall be increased."*

But the **NEB** instead confuses the meaning of *"knowledge"* with *"punishment."* It reads, *"But you, Daniel, keep the words secret and seal the book till the time of the end. Many will be at their wits' end, and punishment will be heavy."*

In **1950**, Pope Pius XII published the dogma of the "Assumption" of Mary, entitled *Munificentissimus Deus*.

In **1952**, Kurt Aland (**1915–1994**) who was also a German theologian, evolutionist, Biblical scholar and skeptic who specialized in New Testament textual criticism, worked in cooperation with Erwin Nestle to produce the 21st edition of the **Novum Testamentum Graece**. This then became known as the theological standard work "Nestle-Aland" and it has set the standards for Biblical criticism ever since.

Kurt Aland

Eugene A. Nida was a higher critical scholar who worked with the American Bible Society (ABS) and the United Bible Societies (UBS). Nida has, on occasion been referred to by some as the father of modern Bible translation. Contrary to Protestant understanding of the Bible, Nida did not believe that the Bible was the authoritative "Word of God."

From the RV to 1979

Compare the critical type of statements Nida was known to make:
"...God's revelation involved limitations....Biblical revelation is not absolute and all divine revelation is essentially incarnational....Even if a truth is given only in words, it has no real validity until it has been translated into life....The words are in a sense nothing in and of themselves....the word is void unless related to experience"
(*Unholy Hands on God's Holy Book*, p.29)

With the true Protestant understanding:
"The creative energy that called the worlds into existence is in the word of God. This word imparts power; it begets life. Every command is a promise; accepted by the will, received into the soul, it brings with it the life of the Infinite One. It transforms the nature and re-creates the soul in the image of God." (*Education*, p.126)

Because of Nida's critically based view of the Bible, it is no surprise that it was he who coined the terms "Dynamic Equivalence" and "Formal Equivalence."
"Eugene Nida (1914-2011) is the father of the dynamic equivalency theory of Bible translation." (*Unholy Hands on God's Holy Book*, p.28)

The following is based on Nida's theory of Bible translation:
Dynamic Equivalence basically describes the "Sense-for-sense" or "Thought-for-thought" translation procedure. In other words, it means translating the meaning of each whole sentence with readability in mind, not with word accuracy. This places the accuracy of the translation solely at the discretion and whims of the translator. Conservatives warn that this method can easily create syncretism. Examples of this kind of translation would be paraphrases like the **Message Bible** or the **Living Bible**.

Formal Equivalence basically describes the "Word-for-word" translation procedure. In other words, it means translating the meanings of words and phrases in a more literal way to try to keep literal fidelity and accuracy. An example of this kind of translation would be the **King James Version**.

Optimal Equivalence basically describes the use of both translation procedures. Examples of this kind of translation would be the **New American Bible**, **Amplified Bible**, **New International Version**, or the **New Living Translation**.

In **1960**, the American Bible Society and the British and Foreign Bible Society revised the **Reina-Valera Spanish Bible** to make a more ecumenical Bible. Eugene Nida of the Bible Societies, was involved in the decision to produce this version. The six translators used, among other texts, the **English Revised Version**, the **American Standard Version**, and the International Critical Commentary. It is stated by some conservative Bible researchers that the **1960 Reina-Valera version** introduced over 70,000 changes to the **1602 Reina-Valera Bible**. It should therefore be no surprise that when it came out, the **1960 Reina-Valera** received approval from a few Roman Catholic priests.

Sword Unsheathed

In **1961**, the Watchtower Society published the **New World Translation**. It was based on several manuscripts and texts, including **Kittel's Biblia Hebraica**, the **Septuagint**, the **Latin Vulgate**, the **Aleppo Codex**, and the **Leningrad Codex**. The later editions of the **NWT** also used the **Biblia Hebraica Stuttgartensia**.

Comparing the readings from the corrupt **New World Translation** with the readings from the pure-line text is quite revealing. For example, when the **KJV** asks the simple and easily understood question in Job 6:6 *"...is there any taste in the white of an egg?"* – the **New World Translation** replaces that easy to understand question with the incorrect and rather absurd question, *"...is there any taste in the slimy juice of marshmallow?"*

Some might find this humorous, but the change in John 1:1 from the **New World Translation** is not at all laughable since it demotes Christ from His position as *"God"* to just "a god." The **NWT** reads, *"In the beginning was the Word, and the Word was with God, and the Word was a god."* Note that the same verse in the **KJV** distinctly reads, *"In the beginning was the Word, and the Word was with God, and the Word was God."*

From **1962-1965**, Vatican Council II developed plans to bring all the other religions back into unity with Rome.

"The major change in Anglican-Roman Catholic relations, however, took place during the Second Vatican Council (1962-65), at which Anglican observers were present throughout. Vatican II developed the theological principles which gave the RCC a clear dogmatic basis for its ecumenical relations with other Christians."
(*Dictionary of the Ecumenical Movement*, p.27)

"Too many people knew that the Vatican was responsible for World War II so it was time for a facelift. Time to start up smokescreens. The Vatican II Council came into existence and the mother of harlots put on a new make-up job. She wiped her mouth with her bloody hands and said, 'I've changed. Now I like the Protestants. I'm not going to call them heretics any more, but separated brethren.' She told the Protestants to forget the past. It was now time to push the love gospel. A time of healing."
(*Smokescreens*, p.45)

This demonstrated the truth of Proverbs 30:20. *"Such is the way of an adulterous woman; she eateth, and wipeth her mouth, and saith, I have done no wickedness."* One of the Vatican II Council's recommendations was that Roman Catholics cooperate with Protestant organizations to translate and distribute the scriptures.

"A movement of biblical renewal in the Roman Catholic Church was given an increased impetus by the Second Vatican Council..."
(*Dictionary of the Ecumenical Movement*, p.100)

From the RV to 1979

In the middle of this Council (**1963**) a new 'modified' **RSV** Bible came out along with a Catholic edition of it.

> *"Perhaps the most significant manifestation of the policy of the Catholic Church in this country at the present moment is her apparent trend towards Interdenominationalism."* *(Rome Stoops to Conquer, p.110)*

Just as the Jesuits had worked in the Oxford Movement in the **1860**s and **1870**s to infiltrate and corrupt the Word of God, so they were also at work in the Vatican II acceleration of the ecumenical movement.

> *"As the Greeks decked out their Trojan horse with all that would impress the enemy, so the Jesuits clothed theirs in the trappings most likely to impress their contemporaries. Even the name they gave it – "Renewal" – was an element in those trappings. Renewal of the Jesuit mission in the contemporary world, they said, was a necessary adaptation of the religious renewal demanded of all Catholics by the Second Vatican Council."*
> *(The Jesuits, p.476)*

"Renewal" Trojan Horse

This Jesuit code word "Renewal" would continue to be seen more and more in the ecumenical movement to bring the Protestant churches back to Rome. Though the word is not an evil word in itself, its use in Protestant theology, should be "red flag" to Protestants that Jesuit influence is quite possibly at work in their churches.

In **1963**, the Lockman Foundation produced the **New American Standard Bible (NASB)**, which was based on the **1901 ASV**. They used the latest edition of Kittel's **Biblia Hebraica** and the **Dead Sea Scrolls** for the Hebrew parts and the 23rd edition of **Nestle-Aland's Greek NT** for the Greek parts.

In June **1964**, a major conference (the Driebergen Conference) was held between the Bible Societies and the Roman Catholic Church. At this conference it was agreed to *"prepare a common text of the Bible in the original languages, acceptable to all churches, including Roman Catholics; and to explore the possibility of preparing a common translation in certain languages which could be used by Protestants and Roman Catholics alike."* *(Unholy Hands on God's Holy Book, p.111)*

The Trinitarian Bible Society did *not* attend this conference.

This conference also recommended that Bible Societies should consider translating and publishing the Apocrypha when Churches requested it.

Sword Unsheathed

On **October 7, 1964**, a public meeting was held between the well-known evangelist Billy Graham and the Roman Catholic Cardinal Richard Cushing. This meeting took place at Cardinal Cushing's home in the Boston Massachusetts area, and was attended by reporters for both TV and Radio.

"For forty-five minutes the Cardinal and the evangelist conversed in public. Graham spoke of the 'new day of understanding and dialogue which is going to help bring about the renewal and the revival we believe is necessary.'...Graham spoke of Cushing's long years of working for a better attitude between Protestants and Catholics, and then the two talked together about the Ecumenical Council in Rome, of a common translation of the Bible, and of Pope John and Pope Paul."
(Billy Graham, The Authorized Biography, p.264)

"...Billy Graham's crusades were sweeping aside doctrinal differences with the evangelist going out of his way to recognise 'the role in the Christian family of our Catholic brethren.'" (All Roads Lead to Rome, p.24)

"Those who 'received Christ' at the Billy Graham crusades, at which so many in the past found Christ, were told to go back to their churches. Roman Catholics who come forward in response to the message are handed over to the local clergy of the Church of Rome for follow up. This has been the standard practice of the Billy Graham Association for many years." (All Roads Lead to Rome, p.169-170)

In **1965**, the Lockman Foundation produced the **Amplified Bible (AMP)**. It was based on the newest edition of Kittel's **Biblia Hebraica**, the **Westcott and Hort Greek New Testament**, the **Septuagint**, and the 23rd edition of the **Nestle-Aland's Greek NT**.

Being based in falsehood, it might be rightfully expected that this version would also make changes to hide its deception.

The **KJV** specifies the last 5 of the 10 commandments in Romans 13:9, *"For this, Thou shalt not commit adultery, Thou shalt not kill, Thou shalt not steal, **Thou shalt not bear false witness**, Thou shalt not covet; and if there be any other commandment, it is briefly comprehended in this saying, namely, Thou shalt love thy neighbour as thyself."*

But the **AMP** version totally removes the commandment forbidding lying and dishonesty! It reads, *"The commandments, 'You shall not commit adultery, you shall not murder, you shall not steal, you shall not covet,' and any other commandment are summed up in this statement: 'You shall love your neighbor as yourself.'"*

"In 1965, the Second Vatican Council ratified the Roman Church's approval of this [the Driebergen Conference agreement]*..."* (All Roads Lead to Rome, p.200)

From the RV to 1979

In **1966**, in accord with the decisions of the Driebergen Conference, the British and Foreign Bible Society amended their constitution to remove the restrictions and to include the Apocrypha in their translation work. The UBS also adopted this policy.

Also in accord with the decisions of the Driebergen Conference, in **1966** the UBS produced a Greek Text called **The Greek New Testament** specifically for translators to use in their translation work on new versions of the Bible. This work was a tentative revision of the **1927** text of Nestle and Kurt Aland was one of the chief editors.

> *"A 'common text' was in fact produced as a result of the Driebergen Conference and the Vatican II Council. This 'common text' of the UBS (United Bible Societies) is what underlies the New Testament of the New International Version (NIV), the New Revised Standard Version (NRSV), the New American Standard Version (NASV), the Revised English Bible (REB), and the Good News Bible (GNB)."*
> (Assault on the Remnant, p.181-182)

In this same year, **1966**, the Roman Catholic Church published the **Revised Standard Version Catholic Edition (RSV-CE)** which was simply the **Revised Standard Version (RSV)** adapted with a few changes for Catholic use.

Also in **1966**, the New Testament of **Today's English Version (TEV)** was published. The whole name for this paraphrase was *Good News for Modern Man: The New Testament in Today's English Version*.

Then in **1968**, a second edition of the **TEV** was published. In the second edition, even more things were changed and more errors introduced. For example, the **KJV** tells us in Luke 1:27: *"To a virgin espoused to a man whose name was Joseph, of the house of David; and the virgin's name was Mary."*

But the **TEV** dropped the accurate term "virgin" and replaced it with the term "girl." It reads, *"He had a message for a girl...The girl's name was Mary."* This change totally undermines the concept of the miraculous virgin birth, since most any "girl" can give birth to a baby!

In **1966**, the **Jerusalem Bible** was published by Roman Catholic scholarship and within three years the Anglican Church authorized it to be used in the Church of England. The **Jerusalem Bible** is a dynamic equivalence translation, and is used as the basis for the Catholic Mass in many English speaking countries of the world.

One of the Catholic translators that contributed to the **Jerusalem Bible** was J. R. R. Tolkien. [see Note H] Tolkien translated the book of Jonah and some of the book of Job for the **Jerusalem Bible**.

A significant characteristic of this original **Jerusalem Bible** is that it is freely sprinkled with notes, many of which support Roman Catholic doctrine. Indeed, the **Jerusalem Bible** also includes the Apocrypha and has some words changed, even in the text, to make it agree more closely with Catholic theology.

For example, the **KJV** for Isaiah 58:3 reads *"Wherefore have we fasted, say they, and thou seest not? wherefore have we afflicted our soul, and thou takest no knowledge?..."* The **Jerusalem Bible** reads,*"Why should we fast if you never see it, why do penance if you never notice?..."*

This is no coincidence for the record in Daniel 10:2 also is changed to include the word "penance."

KJV – *"In those days I Daniel was mourning three full weeks."*

Jerusalem Bible – *"At that time, I, Daniel, was doing a three-week penance;"*

In addition, important symbolism is also watered down. The **KJV** specifies in Psalm 77:13 that God reveals His "way" in the sanctuary symbolism. *"Thy way, O God, is in the sanctuary: who is so great a God as our God?"*

The **Jerusalem Bible** takes the sanctuary symbolism totally out of the text. *"God, your ways are holy! What god so great as God?"*

In other places, such as the Lord's prayer in Mathew 6:13, not only is content missing, but concepts become wholly unbiblical.

KJV – *"And lead us not into temptation, but deliver us from evil: For thine is the kingdom, and the power, and the glory, for ever. Amen."*

Jerusalem Bible – *"And do not put us to the test, but save us from the Evil One."* [remainder missing]

But the plot continues to thicken, *"...in 1967, Carlo Martini joined the UBS International Editorial Committee."* (*All Roads Lead to Rome*, p.200)

Carlo Martini was a Roman Catholic Cardinal, a Jesuit Priest, and chair of textual criticism at the Pontifical Biblical Institute in Rome.

"Cardinal Carlo Maria Martini, one of the Roman Catholic Church's most influential progressive thinkers, who once was considered as a possible successor to Pope John Paul II, died in a Jesuit retreat near Milan on Friday. He was 85."

(*The New York Times*, August 31, 2012)

"Carlo Maria Martini SJ (15 February 1927–31 August 2012) was an Italian Jesuit and cardinal of the Catholic Church. He was Archbishop of Milan from 1980 to 2002 and was elevated to the cardinalate in 1983...Martini entered the Society of Jesus in 1944 and was ordained a priest in 1952." (Wikipedia – "Carlo Maria Martini" accessed 3/15/20)

In **1968**, higher critic Eugene Nida was instrumental in producing a joint effort between the United Bible Societies (UBS) and the Vatican, to create cross-denominational Bibles around the world.

From the RV to 1979

"Dr. [Eugene] Nida was also Translation Research Coordinator for the United Bible Societies from 1970 to 1980." (Billy Graham and His Friends, p.287)

In **1968**, UBS produced their second edition of **The Greek New Testament** – with important changes made to the text. The editors were Kurt Aland, Matthew Black, Bruce Metzger, Allen Wikren, and Jesuit Carlo M. Martini.

One writer comments, *"Let this sink in: The Greek New Testament that becomes required in Protestant and Baptist Bible schools and seminaries worldwide, was created by a committee that had no problem including a Roman Catholic Jesuit priest. After centuries of Catholics hating the Bible of the Christians and destroying it at every opportunity, now suddenly they had not more objections to the Greek text they would use to make new Bibles. What was so different about this Greek text?"* (Why They Changed the Bible, pg. 120,121)

Others agree, *"Now that we have seen the Jesuit roots of the 'common text' of the UBS, we can better understand why the textual changes in the modern versions are Catholic in nature."* (Assault on the Remnant, p.182)

"Thus the United Bible Societies' work is counterproductive to the work of the gospel." (Modern Bible Translations Unmasked, p.109)

In **1969**, the Catholic Church formed the *World Catholic Federation for the Biblical Apostolate*, solely for the purpose of promoting ecumenism through participation in the translation of Interconfessional Bibles. Its name was shortened in **1990** to Catholic Biblical Federation (CBF).

Several writers warn, *"The Roman Church-State in the twentieth century, however, is an institution recovering from a mortal wound. If and when it regains its full power and authority, it will impose a regime more sinister than any the planet has yet seen."* (Ecclesiastical Megalomania, p.195)

"And let it be remembered, it is the boast of Rome that she never changes. The principles of Gregory VII and Innocent III are still the principles of the Roman Catholic Church. And had she but the power, she would put them in practice with as much vigor now as in past centuries. Protestants little know what they are doing when they propose to accept the aid of Rome in the work of Sunday exaltation. While they are bent upon the accomplishment of their purpose, Rome is aiming to re-establish her power, to recover her lost supremacy. Let the principle once be established in the United States that the church may employ or control the power of the state; that religious observances may be enforced by secular laws; in short, that the authority of church and state is to dominate the conscience, and the triumph of Rome in this country is assured. God's word has given warning of the impending danger; let this be unheeded, and the Protestant world will learn what the purposes

Sword Unsheathed

of Rome really are, only when it is too late to escape the snare. She is silently growing into power. Her doctrines are exerting their influence in legislative halls, in the churches, and in the hearts of men. She is piling up her lofty and massive structures in the secret recesses of which her former persecutions will be repeated. Stealthily and unsuspectedly she is strengthening her forces to further her own ends when the time shall come for her to strike. All that she desires is vantage ground, and this is already being given her. We shall soon see and shall feel what the purpose of the Roman element is. Whoever shall believe and obey the word of God will thereby incur reproach and persecution." (Great Controversy, p.581)

"While many Evangelicals have embraced the Pope as a spiritual ally, he is only returning the favor in public. Privately, he continues to hold Bible-believing Christians in contempt." (The New World Religion, p.238)

In **1970**, the **New American Bible (NAB)**, based largely on the **Latin Vulgate**, was made in which over 97% of translators were Roman Catholic. One of the translators, Roland E. Murphy, was a Catholic priest and teacher at the Catholic University of America. He would later also participate in the translation of the **NRSV** in **1989**.

The **NAB** is an approved Bible translation by the Episcopal Church, the Anglican Church, and the only modern translation approved for use at Mass in the Roman Catholic Church. It gradually replaced the **Confraternity Bible**.

"Confraternity Bible is any edition of the Catholic Bible translated under the auspices of the Confraternity of Christian Doctrine (CCD) between 1941 and 1969. The Confraternity Bible strives to give a fluent English translation while remaining close to the Latin Vulgate. It is no longer in widespread use since it was supplanted in 1970 by the New American Bible." (Wikipedia –"Confraternity Bible", accessed 5/20/20)

However, the **NAB** continued the line of corruptions. For example, in Luke 2:14 the **KJV** specifies that the angels who heralded the Saviour's birth, declared that His birth was an action of good will toward all humanity. It reads, *"Glory to God in the highest, and on earth peace, good will toward men."* But the **NAB** makes the good will only apply to a select class. It reads, *"Glory to God in the highest and on earth peace to those on whom his favor rests."*

The **KJV** tells us in Daniel 12:4, that at the end of time, many shall be running "to and fro" throughout the scriptures (specifically the book of Daniel) and that because of this, their knowledge of the prophecies of truth will be increased. (Secondarily, this may also be seen as a reference to travel and increase of knowledge.) The **KJV** reads, *"But thou, O Daniel, shut up the words, and seal the book, even to the time of the end: many shall run to and fro, and knowledge shall be increased."*

From the RV to 1979

But the Catholic **NAB** destroys this text by changing what it says to something totally different. It reads, *"As for you, Daniel, keep secret the message and seal the book until the end time; many shall fall away and evil shall increase."*

In **1971**, the **RSV** was revised and the second edition was published.

Also, *"In 1971, Carlo Martini, extended and invitation for Eugene Nida to come speak to the Jesuits for a few weeks a year at the Pontifical Biblical Institute on the principles of translation. How could Nida say no? They both clearly believed the same (or nearly the same) about the Bible.* **That bonded a relationship between the Jesuit order and the American Bible Society that has continued to this very day."** (*Why They Changed the Bible*, pg. 120,121)

In addition, in **1971**, **The Living Bible (TLB)** was published. It is a paraphrase by Kenneth Taylor who used the **American Standard Version** for his base text.

The **KJV** tells us in Hosea 4:11,12,
"Whoredom and wine and new wine take away the heart. My people ask counsel at their stocks, and their staff declareth unto them:..."

The **TLB** says, in typical "dynamic equivalence" style,
"Wine, women, and song have robbed my people of their brains. For they are asking a piece of wood to tell them what to do. 'Divine Truth' comes to them through tea leaves!..."

 OR

Dowsing Rod or Tea Leaves?

In **1975**, UBS produced their third edition of **The Greek New Testament**, again, with many changes. The Jesuit Carlo Martini was an active editor on this edition as well. Eugene Nida was also involved with the committee. The text of the UBS third edition was so much in accordance with Kurt Aland's preferences that he chose to adopt it as the text for the 26th edition of **Nestle-Aland**.

In **1976**, the Old Testament of the **TEV** was published as the **Good News Bible: The Bible in Today's English Version.** Still officially called **Today's English Version**, the general public refer to it as the **Good News Bible**.

The following reveals the mindset of at least one of the **TEV** translators.
"In Brazil a Portuguese translation of Scripture which included the Apocrypha was produced by an ecumenical team led by Dr. Robert Bratcher, the United Bible Societies international translation consultant...Dr. Bratcher was the chief translator of the Good News Bible. In his writings this minister has denied the inerrancy of Scripture." (*Modern Bible Translations Unmasked*, p.109)

From **1966–1977** a revision of Kittel's third edition of the **Biblia Hebraica** was made and it was called the **Stuttgart Edition of the Biblia Hebraica** or **Biblia Hebraica Stuttgartensia (BHS)**. It was also based on the "older" Ben Asher text and was released in installments as they were finished, with the first complete volume being finally finished in **1977**.

The 1937 **BHK** and the 1977 **BHS** are not only based on a few minor Hebrew manuscripts which contain many erroneous footnotes like the **B19a** manuscript, but "corrections" were often made to these already inadequate and corrupt texts by referring to such things as the "**Septuagint**" or "**LXX**," which is itself corrupt and is nothing more than the Hebrew Scriptures translated into the Greek language by Origen.

The **Biblia Hebraica Stuttgartensia (BHS)** is approved by the Roman Catholic Church and printed jointly by the Vatican and Protestant Bible societies. Speaking of some of its previous releases the **BHS** states:
"...it is a welcome sign of the times that it was published jointly in 1971 by the Wurttemburg Bible Society, Stuttgart, and the Pontifical Biblical Institute, Rome...."
(Prolegomena, p. XII)

Work was started in **1960** to revise the **ASV** of **1901**. This revision was the **New American Standard Version (NASB)** which was published in **1971** and modified in **1977**. The basis for the **NASB** was the third edition of Kittel's **Biblia Hebraica**, as well as the **Dead Sea Scrolls**, and the 23rd edition of Eberhard Nestle's **Novum Testamentum Graece**.

The **NASB** is touted as the most "literal" of the modern translations. It was produced as an alternative to the **1952** edition of the **RSV** which was considered too liberal in its translation style. However, the **NASB** still contains inaccuracies. For example, Luke 2:33 in the **KJV** correctly translates the name "Iōsēph" as "Joseph" – *"And Joseph and his mother marvelled at those things which were spoken of him."* By doing this, the **KJV** clearly shows the fact that Joseph was not Jesus' biological father, but rather simply a "step-father." But the **NASB** alters this reading and incorrectly translates the word "Iōsēph" as "father" – *"And His father and mother were amazed at the things which were being said about Him."* – which undermines the fact that the "Father" of Jesus was God Himself!

And this is not an isolated reference. The **NASB** continues to make attacks on the divine character of Jesus Christ.

In 1 Timothy 3:16, the **KJV** correctly translates the word "Theos" as the word "God" – showing that Jesus Christ was God manifest in the flesh.
"And without controversy great is the mystery of godliness: God was manifest in the flesh, justified in the Spirit, seen of angels, preached unto the Gentiles, believed on in the world, received up into glory."

From the RV to 1979

But the **NASB** erroneously exchanged the word "Theos" for the nondescript pronoun "he".

"And by common confession great is the mystery of godliness: He who was revealed in the flesh, was vindicated in the Spirit, beheld by angels, proclaimed among the nations, believed on in the world, taken up in glory."

The **NASB** is clearly a corrupt and "polluted" translation.

In the late **70's**, former Jesuit Dr. Alberto Rivera stated:
"In the last eighty years we've had about eighty-one new English Bibles (all Roman Catholic) based on Origen's corrupted text, all trying to push the King James Bible out of the picture. Soon there will be an ecumenical bible (one common bible for all religions) preparing the way for the anti-Christ."
(With Cloak & Dagger, p.103)

In **1978**, the **New International Version (NIV)** was published. Work on it had begun in **1965** and the New Testament was published in **1973**. The translators were from several denominations, mainly Anglican, Assemblies of God, Baptist, Christian Reformed, Church of Christ, Evangelical Free, Lutheran, Mennonite, Methodist, Nazarene, Presbyterian, Wesleyan, and others. Virginia Mollenkott, a self-professed lesbian and editor of the NCC committee that produced the Inclusive Language Lectionary, also *"...was a consultant for the NIV translating committee."*
(Billy Graham and His Friends, p.237)

The books of the **NIV** would be translated by the scholars and then sent to the Intermediate Editorial Committee who completely revised their translation. Then it went to the General Editorial Committee which checked it and revised it again then let the Committee on Bible Translation have it, which then made more changes, and then they sent it to the printer. This enabled the entire version to go through three revisions.

The latest edition of the **Biblia Hebraica**, as well as the **Dead Sea scrolls** and the **Septuagint** were used as the basis of the Old Testament, with some reference to **Jerome's Latin Vulgate** and his other writings. The text most used for the basis of the New Testament was **The Greek New Testament** produced by UBS in **1968** – although in some cases, the Greek used was an eclectic one with the translators just choosing whatever reading best supported their ideas.

"The translators also consulted the more important early versions — the Septuagint...the Vulgate...The Masoretic O.T. is not to be followed absolutely if a Septuagint reading or other reading is quite likely correct."
(Earl Kalland, NIV committee member – quoted in New Age Bible Versions, p.139)

"Most of the New Testament citations of the O.T. are from the Septuagint...they made primary use of the LXX, even when it disagreed with the Hebrew."
(Ronald Youngblood, NIV committee member – quoted in New Age Bible Versions, p.140)

This trans-denominational version gained popularity around the world.

"Undoubtedly, this is the ecumenical Bible to which Dr. Rivera referred as 'preparing the way for anti-christ.'" (*With Cloak & Dagger, p.103*)

An example of how the **NIV** totally destroys the meaning of God's Word may be found in Numbers 11:25. The **KJV** specifies that God endowed the 70 elders with the Spirit of prophecy, and didn't remove it: *"And the LORD came down in a cloud, and spake unto him, and took of the spirit that was upon him, and gave it unto the seventy elders: and it came to pass, that, when the spirit rested upon them, they prophesied, and did not cease."*

But the **NIV** turns it around to say the exact opposite, in essence making the claim that the gift of the Spirit of prophecy was momentarily given and then just as rapidly removed: *"Then the Lord came down in the cloud and spoke with him, and he took some of the power of the Spirit that was on him and put it on the seventy elders. When the Spirit rested on them, they prophesied—but did not do so again."*

The **NIV** also went through another revision in **1984**. In **2002–2005** another revision of the **NIV** produced the **Today's New International Version (TNIV)**. And then in **2011** an updated version was released.

The book of Malachi reveals God's displeasure with His professed people. One of the reasons for this is that they are offering polluted bread on His altar. Since bread is a representation of God's word (Matthew 4:4, Luke 4:4, 1 Corinthians 5:8/John 17:17) polluted bread represents God's word that has been corrupted.

Malachi 1:6b,7 records God saying, *"O priests, that despise my name. And ye say, Wherein have we despised thy name? Ye offer polluted bread upon mine altar; and ye say, Wherein have we polluted thee? In that ye say, The table of the LORD is contemptible."*

Indeed, there are many scholarly men connected with the modern versions (polluted bread) who show contempt for the table of the Lord. Malachi 2:12 also revealed who is doing this, saying, *"The LORD will cut off the man that doeth this, the master and the scholar, out of the tabernacles of Jacob, and him that offereth an offering unto the LORD of hosts."*

Hosea reveals that this bread has been polluted by returning to Egypt and Assyria. (the Sinaiticus and the Vaticanus, etc.) *"They shall not dwell in the LORD'S land; but Ephraim shall return to Egypt, and they shall eat unclean things in Assyria. They shall not offer wine offerings to the LORD, neither shall they be pleasing unto him: their sacrifices shall be unto them as the bread of mourners; all that eat thereof shall be polluted: for their bread for their soul shall not come into the house of the LORD."* Hosea 9:3,4

From the RV to 1979

Later in the chapter, Ephraim, who is being reproved for corruption, is seen to be connected with a false prophet that is a snare of the fowler.

Hosea 9:8 says, *"The watchman of Ephraim was with my God: but the prophet is a snare of a fowler in all his ways, and hatred in the house of his God."*

Proverbs 1:17 states, *"Surely in vain the net is spread in the sight of any bird."* And indeed, a fowler works by enticing the bird a little at a time, each time putting the bait closer and closer to where the bird will be trapped and unable to escape.

So it is with Bible Versions, if one is not yet ready for a **"Message Bible"** the fowler will be happy to supply something that looks a little safer.

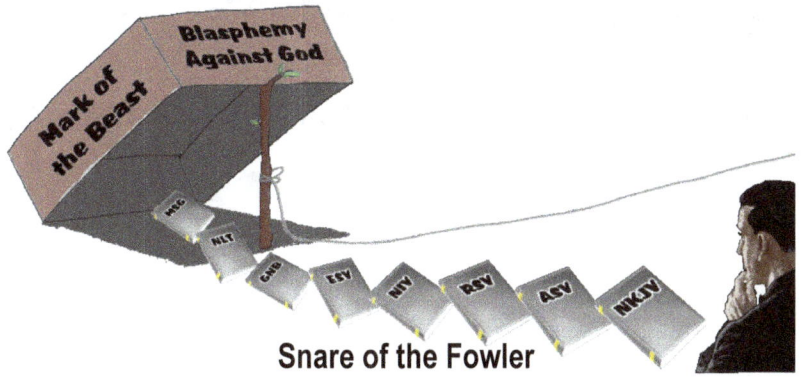

Snare of the Fowler

Proverbs 26:23 is a good example of how the devil changes God's Word, morphing it one word at a time until, while the surface appears similar, there is only a hollow crust left of what was originally there.

KJV – *"Burning lips and a wicked heart are like a potsherd covered with silver dross."*

NKJV – *"Fervent lips with a wicked heart are like earthenware covered with silver dross."*

As can be seen, the **NKJV** changed a few words, but it did keep the "silver dross." But let's continue to follow this "evil-utionary" process.

ISV – *"A clay vessel plated with a thin veneer of silver—that's what smooth lips with a wicked heart are."*

Now the "burning" lips have given place to "smooth" lips and the "dross" is totally gone, it is changed to a "veneer of silver" – totally opposite what the **KJV** stated.

ERV – *"Good words that hide an evil heart are like silver paint over a cheap, clay pot."*

Now not only have the "smooth" lips been changed to "good words" but the "veneer of silver" has become "silver paint." But the changes continue.

Sword Unsheathed

NLT – *"Smooth words may hide a wicked heart just as a pretty glaze covers a clay pot."*

ESV – *"Like the glaze covering an earthen vessel are fervent lips with an evil heart."*

GNB – *"Insincere talk that hides what you are really thinking is like a fine glaze on a cheap clay pot."*

MSG – *"Smooth talk from an evil heart is like glaze on cracked pottery"*

Note, that by the end, all the references to "silver" and to "dross" and thus any meaning included with those words has been eliminated. That is just one slick trick of the "fowler" to ensnare the reader of the modern corrupt Bibles.

Perhaps the most innocent looking of the modern versions is the **NKJV**. But beware the snare of the fowler.

The New King James Version (NKJV)

In 1975, the **New King James Version** project was begun. It was conceived by a scholar named Arthur Farstad who had been a former editor at Thomas Nelson Publishers. The **NKJV** Executive Review Committee positioned Dr. Arthur L. Farstad as the Executive Editor. It is also of interest that the body of translators for the **NKJV** included nine translators who had participated in the making of the **NIV**.

The New Testament of the **NKJV** was finished first and published in **1979**, the Psalms in **1980**, and the full **NKJV** Bible in **1982**. The **NKJV** today has two editions/versions. The original version was completed in **1982**, and a revision of that version, which was revised by a committee of 11 reviewers chaired by Farstad, was made in **1984/1985**. Since then, there have been several printings of these versions. Farstad also began yet another translation project to produce a new Bible version which he called **Logos 21**. But the **Logos 21** version was never finished. It would though, years later, give birth to the **Holman Bible**.

Arthur Farstad

The majority of Christians have been taught the misconception that the **New King James Version (NKJV)** is just an newer edition of the good old trustworthy **King James Version**. In David Daniels' book *New King James – The Bridge Bible*, is found the evidence that even Thomas Nelson Publishers promoted the **NKJV** as such. Daniels' book displays a picture of an **1979** promotional ad for the **NKJV** and states,

"When the New King James first came out, Thomas Nelson ran an ad on the back cover of the June 1979 issue of Moody Monthly. It said: '...making the King James even better.' Does that mean it's more 'King Jamesey?' [It claimed,] '...The New King James Bible isn't a new translation. It isn't another version. It is a carefully researched new edition of the King James in which some of the words, punctuation, and grammar have been changed to make it more accurate and easier to read.' So it isn't a new translation, yet it changes words? Isn't that what a new translation is? [The ad continued,] '...It restores and protects the originally intended beauty, authority, and meaning of every verse. It makes the King James even better.' If it 'protects the originally intended...meaning,' that means that Thomas Nelson claimed it doesn't change the meaning of the verse."

(New King James The Bridge Bible, p.29)

As will be shown, the claims made by **NKJV** promotional ad described here are totally false. There are quite a few people who mistakenly believe that the only difference between the **KJV** and the **NKJV** is that the **NKJV** has changed the

Sword Unsheathed

"thees" and "thous" to more modern terms like "you." But this opinion is totally erroneous, and based on bad information. Dr. Farstad himself specifically contradicted that misinformation by telling the public, *"...we didn't just 'change the thees and thous'!"* (*The New King James Version in the Great Tradition*, p.3) Nevertheless, the chapter on the **King James Version** has already covered the difficulties that result just by changing the singular "thees" and "thous" to plural forms like "you."

Many Christians are told that the **NKJV** is just an "updated" or "revised" **KJV**. In fact, Farstad himself claimed:

"The New King James Version, as the name implies, is not a completely new translation, but a conservative and careful revision of...the Authorized or King James Version." (*The New King James Version in the Great Tradition*, p.9)

But in spite of Farstad's claims, and in spite of these commonly believed misunderstandings, one finds that this concept – that the **NKJV** is not much different than the **KJV** and that both Bibles are based on the same Hebrew and Greek texts – is totally erroneous, and is simply the result of believing the false propaganda that has been used to promote the **NKJV**.

According to the **NKJV**'s own Preface, the translators even freely admitted that they based the Old Testament (approximately 2/3 of the Bible) of their **NKJV**, not strictly on the pure-line manuscripts like the **KJV** had, but rather on the (Vatican-approved) **Biblia Hebraica Stuttgartensia (BHS)**. While they say they made "comparisons" to the **Daniel Bomberg** edition, they also consulted the (corrupt) **Septuagint (LXX)**, the (Roman Catholic) **Latin Vulgate**, and the **Dead Sea Scrolls**. Also, the last line in their description, though artfully stated, brings to light the point that the **NKJV** translators saw some portions of the **KJV** as "problems."

"For the New King James Version the text used was the 1967/1977 Stuttgart edition of the Biblia Hebraica, with frequent comparisons being made with the Bomberg edition of 1524–25. The Septuagint (Greek) Version of the Old Testament and the Latin Vulgate also were consulted. In addition to referring to a variety of ancient versions of the Hebrew Scriptures, the New King James Version draws on the resources of relevant manuscripts from the Dead Sea caves.

The New King James Version (NKJV)

In the few places where the Hebrew is so obscure that the King James followed one of the versions, but where information is now available to resolve the problems, the New King James Version follows the Hebrew text. Significant variations are recorded in the footnotes." (NKJV Preface, p.xiii)

According to the Preface of the **NKJV**, its New Testament, supposedly, followed the Greek text of the **Textus Receptus** just like the **KJV** did. However, they also state that they compared it with the "**Majority Text**," the 26th edition of the **Nestle-Aland Greek New Testament**, and the **UBS Third edition of the Greek New Testament** – and it is these sources that are responsible for the many footnotes.

"...because the New King James Version is the fifth revision of a historic document translated from specific Greek texts, the editors decided to retain the traditional text in the body of the New Testament and to indicate major Critical and Majority Text variant readings in the center reference column." (NKJV Preface, p.xiv)

In other words, the **NKJV** New Testament was created to appear to have some influence from the **Textus Receptus**. However, upon closer examination, one can see that the **NKJV** translators chose to disregard many of the **Textus Receptus** readings for the readings of the corrupted Alexandrian type manuscripts which are more in agreement with the modern corrupt Bibles. In addition, the Old Testament of the **NKJV** is based primarily on on the corrupted manuscripts underlying the modern adulterated Bibles; it is not based solely on the same pure-line manuscripts that the the **King James** was based upon. Because of these facts, it is easily seen that the LIE actually begins on the front cover of the the **NKJV** – in its title. It cannot be considered a "new" or just "updated" rendition of the "**King James**" Bible like Farstad and many others claim! It is rather a separate and distinct modern adulterated translation that is, in many places, in opposition to the **King James Bible**. For example, while understanding that junk food is detrimental to health, are the "wounds" of Proverbs 26:22 actually the same thing as "tasty trifles"?

KJV – *"The words of a talebearer are as wounds, and they go down into the innermost parts of the belly."*

NKJV – *"The words of a talebearer are like tasty trifles, And they go down into the inmost body."*

The ecumenical approach of the **NKJV** translators *"whose textual policy will not offend those who differ"* at times appears to have respect for the **KJV**, while at other times, they undermine it as a firm foundation. (*The New King James Version in the Great Tradition*, pg. 114) For example, Dr. Farstad admitted that he had gained new respect for the accuracy of the **King James Bible** and said that when he had begun, he was biased toward the belief that the **KJV** contained many errors, but after working to make a new translation, he concluded that the original **KJV** translators had *"worked with extreme accuracy!"*

(*Adventist Review*, July 5, 1979, p. 13)

In fact, in Farstad's own book on the **NKJV** he even specifically states, *"Let me say, as one who has studied that grand old Bible in the light of the originals at Bible college, seminary, and graduate school, that the King James Version is very accurate."* *(The New King James Version in the Great Tradition, p.28)*

But even though Farstad admitted that the original **KJV** is "very accurate," the evidence shows that he did not uphold that statement himself, because he then went on to attack and attempt to destroy confidence in the **KJV** throughout the remainder of his book – with statements like:

"...the KJV does not even seem to be a very good guess..."(p.45)
"...two words in the KJV that are not quite correct..."(p.45)
"...the King James needed some improvement."(p.46)
"A person reading the KJV would likely get a totally false picture of what Paul meant" *(p.50)*, etc.

In addition, speaking of the translation of the original **King James Version**, Farstad sinks so low as to claim that *"even the Douai-Rheims* [Jesuit]*, also made significant contributions to the final version."*
(The New King James Version in the Great Tradition, p.22)

However, a quick reference to the **1611 KJV** translator's notes to the reader, quickly exposes Farstad's claim as a lie. It is obvious from what the **KJV** translators state, that they had no respect for the Jesuit **Douay Rheims Bible.**

"...we have shunned the obscurity of the Papists, in their azimes, tunic, rational, holocausts, praepuce, pasche, and a number of such like, whereof their late translation is full—and that of purpose to darken the sense, that since they must needs translate the Bible, yet by the language thereof, it may be kept from being understood." *(1611 KJV, The Translators to the Reader)*

In other words, Farstad apparently didn't really care for the **KJV** – and even though he claimed he did on the surface, it appears that he was only paying lip-service to the **KJV** in order not to bring opposition to his **NKJV**.

There is also something revealing about the text that the **NKJV** claims was the "**Majority Text**." In the Definitions and Terms section of this book, the difference between the **Majority Text** and the **Textus Receptus** was explained. This picture shows how it could be possible to cherry-pick so-called "**Majority Text**" manuscripts from the minority of altered manuscripts – and it is here that the **Majority Text** issue with the **NKJV** may be found. (See diagram, next page)

In **1982**, the exact same year that the completed **NKJV** was first published Farstad, in conjunction with Zane Hodges, published **The Greek New Testament according to the Majority Text**. In this work, they used Hermann Von Soden's work as representing the "**Majority Text**" - just as they

The New King James Version (NKJV)

had done in the translation of the **NKJV**. The Preface of **The Greek New Testament according to the Majority Text** states,

"In these two places, through the extensive work of von Soden and Hoskier, most of the manuscript evidence has been minutely collated. In the rest of the New Testament we were forced to rely heavily on von Soden's work, augmented by Tischendorf..." (The Greek New Testament According to the Majority Text, p.vi)

Remember, Von Soden's text only represented about 8% of the available Greek manuscripts known to exist – by far NOT the majority! In other words, the manuscripts Von Soden used were the "altered" ones from the fringes of the **Majority Text** family. And even though Von Soden's work is claimed by some to be in agreement with the **Textus Receptus (TR)** and the "**Majority Text**," it has been found to be rather Alexandrian in its makeup and it contains an abundant Alexandrian influence.

"...though von Soden's text is closer to the TR than other critical editions, yet his views and product are still firmly within the Alexandrian camp."
(When the KJV Departs from the "Majority" Text, p.24)

"Soden's text is so thoroughly Alexandrian that it falls into line with Hort, irrespective of MS evidence." (Codex B and its Allies, vol.1, p.461)

Ironically, Farstad and Hodges even admitted in their Preface: *"The Majority Text is a text that employs the available evidence of the whole range of surviving manuscripts rather than relying chiefly on the evidence of a few. To us it is unscientific to practically ignore eighty to ninety percent of the evidence in any discipline."* (The Greek New Testament according to the Majority Text, p.v)

Yet, the supposed "**Majority Text**" that Farstad and Hodges used, does this very thing – it practically ignores 80 to 90 percent of the evidence. In other words, while the term

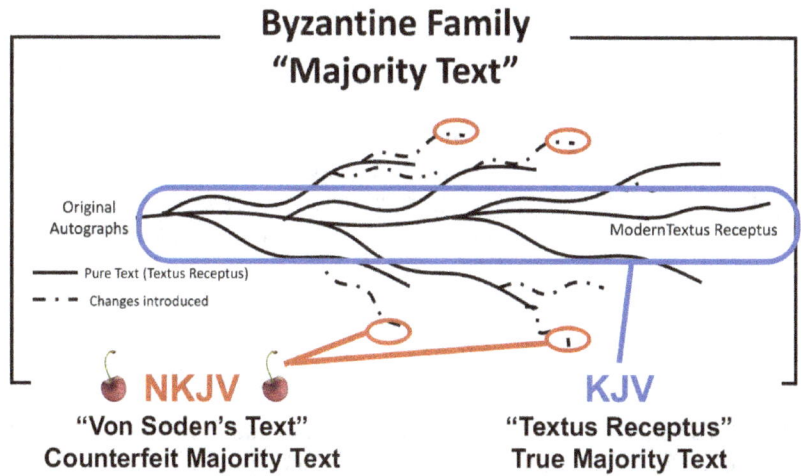

"**Majority Text**" in reality applies to all the thousands of manuscripts that agree with the **Textus Receptus**, (of which the **Textus Receptus** forms a large part), Farstad and Hodges chose to erroneously refer to Von Soden's cherry-picked Alexandrian texts as representing the **"Majority Text**." This is the **"Counterfeit Majority Text"** mentioned previously. This **"Majority Text"** they favored above the **Textus Receptus**. This is evidenced in many places in *The New King James Version – in the Great Tradition*. Indeed, it is exampled on page 111 where the book states that in the **NKJV** *"those TR readings that have weak support…are corrected."*

One Wikipedia writer has summarized the subtle tenor of doubt of the **Textus Receptus** demonstrated throughout Farstad's book. He states,
"While defending the Majority Text (also called the Byzantine text-type), and claiming that the Textus Receptus is inferior to the Majority Text, he [Farstad] *noted (p. 114) that the NKJV references significant discrepancies among text types in its marginal notes…"*   (Wikipedia – 'New King James Version'– accessed 7-2021)

Indeed, doubt-ridden footnotes and the body in the **NKJV** are given equal credence by Farstad. Instead of the expected endorsement of the **Textus Receptus** and thus the **King James** that one might expect to find in a "New" **King James Bible**, Farstad, giving some insight into the higher critical mindset of his **NKJV** translators, states:
"None of the three traditions on every page of the New Testament – Textus Receptus, critical, or majority text, is labeled 'best' or 'most reliable.' The reader is permitted to make up his or her own mind about the correct reading."
(*The New King James Version in the Great Tradition* p.114)

Contrast this critical concept of *"the Bible as you pick it"* with the biblical concept of *"by every word of God"* and not even removing one jot or tittle from the scriptures, as presented in this statement of Jesus.
"Think not that I am come to destroy the law, or the prophets: I am not come to destroy, but to fulfil. For verily I say unto you, Till heaven and earth pass, <u>one jot or one tittle shall in no wise pass from the law</u>, till all be fulfilled." Matthew 5:16,17

"We call on you to take your Bible, but do not put a sacrilegious hand upon it, and say, "That is not inspired," simply because somebody else has said so. <u>Not a jot or tittle is ever to be taken from that Word</u>. Hands off, brethren! Do not touch the ark. Do not lay your hand upon it, but let God move."   (*Sermons and Talks*, vol.1, p.73)

In addition, Farstad wrote,
"While the King James Version is very accurate in the light of its time, we don't believe that the KJV, the NKJV, or indeed any translation, is flawless!"
(*The New King James Version in the Great Tradition*, p.28)

Farstad's comments are in total contrast with the true Protestant understanding of the pure-line **KJV** Bible. Consider the following description of Protestant

The New King James Version (NKJV)

Reformer Ulrich Zwingli, *"He accepted the Bible as a first authority, an infallible rule, in contradistinction to the Church or tradition, on the one hand, and to subjectivism or spiritualism on the other. This was the great and distinguishing principle of Zwingle, and of the Reformation which he founded–THE SOLE AND INFALLIBLE AUTHORITY OF HOLY SCRIPTURE."* (History of Protestantism, vol 1, bk 8, chpt 6, p.430)

Indeed, *"No work of man can improve the great and precious truths of God's word. They are not a mixture of truth and error. They are without a flaw."*
(Review & Herald, August 8, 1899)

In other words, the **NKJV** translators views of the Bible were totally 100% opposite of the way the Bible should be viewed!

David Daniels tells his experience of being educated in "doubt" by the **NKJV.**
"I was more unsure about what God said than ever before. Placing any faith in the New King James Bible meant not trusting the King James Bible. And yet, because of the doubting footnotes, I couldn't trust the reading of the New King James either – even if it matched the King James!"
(New King James – The Bridge Bible, p.104)

Notwithstanding all the doubt and "flaws" that the **NKJV** promotes, there are yet other assertions used in support of the **NKJV**. One of the commonly heard claims used to promote the **NKJV** is that it is "simpler to understand." Amazingly, the Thomas Nelson Publishers even claimed in an ad for the **NKJV** that,
"Nothing has been changed except to make the original meaning clearer."
(Moody Monthly, June 1982, back cover)

This is a false claim as can easily be seen by comparing its verses to the **KJV** texts.

For example, in Genesis 35:4, the **KJV** uses the simple and easily understood phrase *"...the oak which was by Shechem."*
The **NKJV** on the other hand, changes what was easily understood to something much more difficult to comprehend – *"...the terebinth tree which was by Shechem."*

In Judges 8:13, the **KJV** simply states: *"And Gideon the son of Joash returned from battle before the sun was up,"*
But the **NKJV** again changes what was simple to something much more difficult and complex – *"Then Gideon the son of Joash returned from battle, from the Ascent of Heres."*

In Acts 27:17, the **KJV** states, *"...fearing lest they should fall into the quicksands, ..."*
Quicksands is a fairly easy word to understand. But the **NKJV** changes it to, *"...fearing lest they should run aground on the Syrtis Sands, ..."*
Again, definitely a more complex reading level!

Proverbs 1:12 says:
KJV: *"Let us swallow them up alive as the grave; ..."*
NKJV: *"Let us swallow them alive like Sheol, ..."*

In Daniel chapter 6, the easily understood word *"princes,"* as it reads in the **KJV**, is replaced in the **NKJV** with the more difficult and complex word *"satraps."*

But one of the most astounding differences is found in Numbers 21:14!
KJV: *"Wherefore it is said in the book of the wars of the LORD, What he did in the Red sea, and in the brooks of Arnon,"*
NKJV: *"Therefore it is said in the Book of the Wars of the LORD: WAHEB IN SUPHAH, The brooks of the Arnon."*

What happened to making it "clearer" and "easier to understand?" Here again, the **NKJV** didn't even bother translating these words. They just left the Hebrew words and transliterated them into English letters, so this phrase cannot even be looked up in an English dictionary!

Though these words are not necessarily "wrong" translations, these are just a few of the many examples of how the **NKJV** has taken what was much easier to understand from the **KJV** and made it more difficult – which is one reason why the **NKJV** is considered a more complex reading level than the **KJV**.

Yet, if the texts of the **KJV** and the **NKJV** (as well as other corrupt versions) are compared using the Flesch-Kincaid readability scale formulas, which are the internationally recognized industry-standard method of testing (used extensively throughout the field of education), the "easier to understand" argument for the **NKJV** totally collapses.

> *"As for the unsubstantiated assertion that the modern versions are easier to understand, the Flesch-Kincaid Research Company's Grade Level Indicator shows this to be a fallacy. Their research shows the language of the King James was actually easier to understand in 23 out of 26 comparisons. In their study they compared the first and last chapters of the first and last books of the Bible (Genesis and Revelation), one Gospel (John), one Pauline epistle(Galatians), and one General epistle (James). The result of their research can be seen on the following chart."* **(opposite page)**
> (*The Men, Motive, and Malicious Mutilations behind the Modern Bible Versions*, p. 44,45)

In fact, Rudolf Flesch, the leading authority on the readability subject and developer of those readability formulas, declared in his own book:
"The best example of VERY EASY prose (about 20 affixes per 100 words) is the King James Version of the Bible..." (*The Art of Plain Talk*, p. 43, emphasis in the original)

Using these industry standard formulas, it is revealed that the **KJV,** on

The New King James Version (NKJV)

average, reads between the 4th–6th grade reading level, while the **NKJV**, on average, reads between the 7th–8th grade reading level.

In fact, speaking of the **NKJV**, the official Thomas Nelson **NKJV** history page specifically states, *"The reading level is eighth grade..."*
(https://www.thomasnelsonbibles.com/about-nkjv-history/)

Bible Books	KJV Grade Level	NIV Grade Level	NASB Grade Level	TEV Grade Level	NKJV Grade Level
Gen. 1	4.4	5.1	4.7	5.1	5.2
Mal. 1	4.6	4.8	5.1	5.4	4.6
Matt. 1	6.7	16.4	6.8	11.8	10.3
Rev. 1	7.5	7.1	7.7	6.4	7.7
John 1	3.6	3.6	4.2	5.9	3.9
Gal. 1	8.6	9.8	10.4	6.7	8.9
James 1	5.7	6.5	7.0	6.0	6.4
Grade Level Average	5.9	7.6	6.6	6.8	6.7

However, the real "dangers" begin not with reading level, but when the changes in the **NKJV** begin to change, counterfeit, and warp the meaning of verses and the Biblical doctrines of the verses – in many cases, changing the meaning completely, sometimes to the exact opposite of the original. There are hundreds upon hundreds of examples that could be given, but there is not room here to list more than just a few examples.

(More listed in the chapter Examples of Modern Bible Changes Affecting Doctrine)

Numbers 11:25
KJV: *"...when the spirit rested upon them, they prophesied, and did not cease."*
NKJV: *"...when the Spirit rested upon them, that they prophesied, although they never did so again."*

Proverbs 25:23
KJV: *"The north wind driveth away rain: so doth an angry countenance a backbiting tongue."*
NKJV: *"The north wind brings forth rain, And a backbiting tongue an angry countenance."*

Yet, the **1898** book *Bible Manners & Customs* has a whole chapter describing the climate and weather patterns of Israel, and it specifically states:
"The north wind is remarkable for its power of arresting rain and dispersing clouds." (p.24)

In other words, the **KJV** is the Bible that accurately represents the true weather – the **NKJV** has its facts wrong and changes the verse to read incorrectly.

Zechariah 13:6 – shadowing forth the manner of Christ's death and the marks of His crucifixion
KJV: *"And one shall say unto him, What are these wounds in thine hands?..."*
NKJV: *"And one will say to him, 'What are these wounds between your arms?'..."*

Revelation 19:8
KJV: *"...for the fine linen is the righteousness of saints."*
NKJV: *"...for the fine linen is the righteous acts of the saints."*
No longer a "faith-based" religion, the **NKJV** totally changes the doctrine taught in this text!

It also appears that, for all practical purposes, the majority of the **NKJV** committee did not really believe that the Bible was the pure unadulterated Word of God and they sought to "correct" the "supposed errors" that they found.

The Preface of the **NKJV** makes the claim that they followed the "Complete Equivalence" (also called Formal Equivalence –"Word-for-word") method. However, a careful reading of the **NKJV** shows that in many places, the translators rather appear to have followed more the "Sense-for-sense" or "Thought-for-thought" concept (Dynamic Equivalence method).

For example, in the **KJV** Psalm 146:4 reads, *"His breath goeth forth, he returneth to his earth; in that very day his thoughts perish."* But the **NKJV** changes the Hebrew word for "thoughts" to the incorrect word "plans." It reads thus, *"His spirit departs, he returns to his earth; in that very day his plans perish."*

The Hebrew word used in this text is "'eshtônâh" which literally means "thoughts" – it does not mean "plans" and it is never translated in the **KJV** as "plans." "Thoughts" and plans are two totally different concepts. A person can have all their "plans" perish and still be alive. Not so with "thoughts" – when "thoughts" perish, the person is dead.

The prophecy of Christ, the "Desire of all nations" coming to the temple in Haggai 2:7 has been totally adulterated in the **NKJV**.
KJV: *"And I will shake all nations, and the desire of all nations shall come: and I will fill this house with glory, saith the LORD of hosts."*
NKJV: *"and I will shake all nations, and they shall come to the Desire of All Nations, and I will fill this temple with glory,' says the LORD of hosts."*

The New King James Version (NKJV)

The **NKJV** totally changes the text to the complete opposite – now it's not Christ coming to the temple, it is all nations coming to Christ (teaching of Universalism). This alteration also removes the connection with Haggai 2:9 – a prophecy of the man Christ Jesus' personal presence in the temple, *"The glory of this latter house shall be greater than of the former, saith the LORD of hosts: and in this place will I give peace, saith the LORD of hosts."*

The **KJV** shows in Genesis 22:8 that Abraham recognized the symbolism of the lamb was pointing to Christ who was "God manifested in human flesh."

KJV: *"And Abraham said, My son, God will provide himself a lamb for a burnt offering..."*

But the **NKJV** takes that symbolism out of the verse.

NKJV: *"And Abraham said, 'My son, God will provide for Himself the lamb for a burnt offering.'..."*

Through centuries of the English Bible, from **Tyndale** to the **KJV**, Bible readers have had the *"sure word of prophecy."* But now that "sure word" is literally marginalized in the **NKJV**, so that the "sure word" appears "unsure" of its meaning.

KJV: *"We have also a more sure word of prophecy;..."* 2 Peter 1:19
NKJV: *"And so we have the prophetic word confirmed;..."* 2 Peter 1:19

In verses like Revelation 9:4; 13:16; 14:1,9; 22:4 the **KJV** specifically uses the word "in" to designate the "frontal lobe of the mind" where our decisions for moral right or wrong and worship (see Revelation 14:9) are made, but the **NKJV** changes it to "on."

KJV: *"...in their foreheads"*
NKJV: *"...on their foreheads"*

In other words, the **NKJV** removes the "mark of the beast" from the person's frontal lobe of their mind, and places it on the surface of the skin – so the "mark" has been changed from a conscious mental decision to follow and obey the beast, to just a tattoo or bar code which could be forced and would have no bearing on a person's "character."

It is significant that even in places where the **NKJV** translates the verses correctly, it adds critical footnotes making various claims that the reading is not in the oldest manuscripts or that it doesn't read that way in the **Nestle-Aland** or the **UBS texts**, or that the **Majority Text** (Soden's) doesn't have it. These footnotes, in essence, effectively strike thorough portions of scripture, such as those found accompanying Matthew 5:44.

KJV: *"But I say unto you, Love your enemies, bless them that curse you, do good to them that hate you, and pray for them which despitefully use you, and persecute you;"*

NKJV: *"But I say to you, love your enemies, ~~bless those who curse you, do good to those who hate you~~, and pray for those who ~~spitefully use you and~~ persecute you,*

Footnote – **NU But I say to you, love your enemies and pray for those who persecute you"*

In other words, the process that the snare of the fowler uses many times is not at first a direct denial of what God has said, but rather a question to cause "doubt" as to whether certain words –"*bless them that curse you, do good to them that hate you,*" etc. are actually included in the Bible. By adding "questioning footnotes" – the **NKJV** is casting the exact same type of doubt on the authority of God's Word that Satan did in Eden, *"Yea hath God said?"*

Indeed, *"a prominent feature of the NKJV is the addition, in the study editions, of extensive textual footnotes which constantly cast doubt on the Scripture text and call into question the authenticity of many passages."*
(*Urgent Plea for Christian Fervency in these 'Last Days'*, p.1682)

Each of these "doubts" then becomes a "seed" that gradually grows in the reader's mind until they begin to doubt the accuracy and authority of the Word of God!

All through the **NKJV**, changes have been made to cast subtle doubt on God. For example, Luke 1:34 states:
KJV: *"Then said Mary unto the angel, How shall this be, seeing I know not a man?"*
NKJV: *"Then Mary said to the angel, 'How can this be, since I do not know a man?'"*

The Greek word ἔσομαι (esomai) [translated "shall" in this **KJV** verse] comes directly from the **Textus Receptus** and is a future tense verb in the third person sense. The **NKJV** ignores the original Greek text and translates the word as "can" [which in Greek would be δύναμαι (dunamai) – but that word is not in this text].

This seemingly insignificant change is much more sinister than the surface reader may realize. Not only is the **KJV** word "shall" the correct translation, while the **NKJV** word "can" is not in agreement with the **Textus Receptus** – but Webster's dictionary defines the word SHALL – *"...In the second and third persons, shall implies a promise, command or determination."* While it defines the word "CAN" – *"to be able, to be possible."*

In other words, in the **KJV**, Mary's question is just wondering how this is going

The New King James Version (NKJV)

to happen. She is not doubting the truth of what the angel has stated, but is merely wondering about the manner in which it is going to happen. In the **NKJV**, Mary's question has been changed to express "doubt" about the ability or capability of God to be able to do this thing which the angel has said.

Simply put, this little supposed insignificant change, by just changing "shall" to "can" – altered Mary's question from a "faith-filled" expression of wonder, to a subtle "doubt" of God's Word. And these type of changes can be found all through the **NKJV**.

Concerned Christians have also pointed out that the:
"Analysis of the NKJV text reveals the translators' wanton disregard and disrespect for God's name. Based on the Logos Research Systems computer program:
1. The word 'LORD' is thrown out 56 times out of the 6,668.
2. The word 'God' is ejected 35 times out of the 3,878.
3. The word 'JEHOVAH' is altogether missing."
(*Urgent Plea for Christian Fervency in these 'Last Days'*, p.1681)

Another aspect to recognize is that different editions of the **NKJV** translate things differently, adding instability and error at random. For example, just looking at Hebrews 9:3-4, the **1982** edition translated the object in the most holy place as *"censer,"* the **1984** edition translated it as *"altar"*, and the **1990** edition translated it as "censer." These facts, along with many others, make the **NKJV** confusing and a dangerously subtle mixture of truth and error. [see the chapter entitled *Examples of Modern Bible Changes Affecting Doctrine*]

The Word of God, in Titus 1:9 directs that men who work for God are to be, *"Holding fast the faithful word as he hath been taught, that he may be able by sound doctrine both to exhort and to convince the gainsayers."* By God specifying the *"faithful word,"* He clearly implies that there will also be *"unfaithful words."* And if *"sound doctrine"* is what comes from the *"faithful word"* – then it would suggest that the *"unfaithful words"* would produce *"unsound doctrine!"*

Kirk DiVietro

Dr. Kirk DiVietro, Pastor of Grace Baptist Church in Franklin, Massachusetts, attended a pre-publication meeting about the **NKJV**. This meeting was at a conference that was hosted by Hackman's Bible Book Store. He stated that the Thomas Nelson representative who was promoting the **NKJV** to the room full of Bible college scholars and pastors, said something to the effect of:
"We're educators here; and we would never admit this to our people or congregations. But we all know that the King James Bible is an inferior translation, coming from

inferior manuscripts. But every time we've tried to give your people a better Bible, they've just refused to take it. So what we've done is we've taken the King James Bible, and we've revised it as little as we could, changed it here and there, to give you (and he used the phrase) '*a transitional bridge*' to get your people away from the King James Bible, so that ultimately you can move them to a better, more accurate Bible." (The Real Reason They Made the NKJV, *Battle Cry*, 2019, p.2)

Dr. DiVietro stated that from that point, he was *"done with the NKJV"* – he would never use it anymore.

Dr. DiVietro's story is confirmed by reading the back of the Thomas Nelson **KJV/NKJV** Parallel Bible itself. The description on the back specifically states: *"And this is the perfect transition Bible if you are thinking about moving from the classic King James to a modern translation."*

So according to this representative of Thomas Nelson publishing, and the description on the back of the **NKJV** itself, the **NKJV** was designed to be the "transitional bridge" to wean people off of the **KJV** and get them into the modern corrupt Bibles!

And that is exactly what has been seen over and over again in many Christian churches – the **KJV** is changed out for the **NKJV**, and before long, they gradually migrate from using the **NKJV** into using other modern even more corrupt versions.

An additional point worth investigating is that the statement that the publishers of the **NKJV** made asserting, *"we've revised it as little as we could, changed it here and there,"* This appears to be a gross understatement at best, if not a complete lie. In actuality, a close investigation finds, as David Cloud states: *"There are an estimated 100,000 changes, averaging 80 per page. This was probably done for copyright purposes."* (Answering the Myths on the Bible Version Debate, p.203)

Copyright laws state: *"To be copyrightable, a derivative work must be different enough from the original to be regarded as a 'new work' or must contain a substantial amount of new material. Making minor changes or addition of little substance to a preexisting work will not qualify the work as a new version for copyright purposes."*
(https://en.wikipedia.org/wiki/Derivative_work, accessed 10/7/2021)

The New King James Version (NKJV)

In other words, one cannot make a new translation and make money off of it, without making lots of changes to it. It is not possible to just change two or three words in the Bible and make a new translation out of it. Every single "new" translation has to have a certain percentage of changes made to the text, in order to be able to copyright it and market it.

Dr. William Grady, in his book *Final Authority*, also points out that the **NKJV** makes over 100,000 estimated translation changes to the text. That averages to 82 changes per page and about three changes per verse! Obviously the **NKJV** was not revised *"as little as"* possible.

"Conservative estimates of the total translation changes in the NKJV are generally put at over 100,000! This is an average of 82 changes for each of the 1219 pages in the NKJV... the most shocking revelation about the 'New' King James Version is that it is literally laced with 'old' readings from the Revised Standard and New American Standard Versions. This revival of Alexandrian readings is one of the best-kept secrets of the decade. Whenever there is a marked departure from the text of the KJV, the alternative reading is frequently taken from either the RSV, NASV, or oftentimes, both. For instance, in the first chapter of John's Gospel, there are 51 verses. Of this total, 45 (or 88%) have been altered by the NKJV. Among this number, 34 (75%) exhibit a distinct RSV or NASV reading while 6 show a partial reading. Only 5 (15%) appear unique to the NKJV." (Final Authority, p. 305)

And what have Christians been told about God's Word? *"My son, fear thou the LORD and the king: and meddle not with them that are given to change:"* Proverbs 24:21 *"For I am the LORD, I change not..."* Malachi 3:6

Remember the purpose of the "fifth column"? It was inside elements, infiltrators of the enemy, whose purpose was to undermine their opponents from inside their own ranks. It seems rather interesting that:*"The NKJV was originally advertised as the fifth revision of the Authorized Version, 'carefully updated so that it will once again speak God's eternal truths with clarity,' subtly insinuating that the King James Bible did not speak God's eternal truths with clarity. (Why the NKJV, Thomas Nelson Publishers). The Publishers claim that the purpose of publishing the NKJV was to preserve the authority and accuracy of the original King James Bible while making it understandable to 20th Century readers by updating the grammar, punctuation, archaic words, etc. Smoke-screens!"* (Urgent Plea for Christian Fervency in these 'Last Days', p.1680)

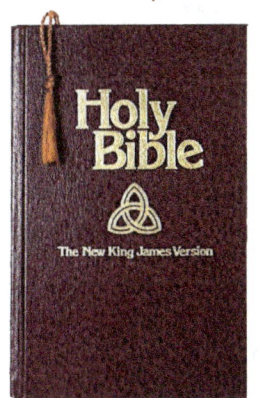

Indeed, even the symbol that was chosen as the "brand" to represent the **NKJV** is found to be sinister. The symbol found on the cover and front page of the majority of the **NKJV** editions is known as the triquetra.

Sword Unsheathed

It is claimed by ignorant Christians that this symbol represents the Godhead – however, this is not the case – they have been deceived. *"...we ought not to think that the Godhead is like unto gold, or silver, or stone, graven by art and man's device."* Acts 17:29

The triquetra's connections with paganism and with the occult predate its use in Christian circles. In some pagan traditions, it is used as a symbol of the three realms of earth, sea, and sky. Some sources also claim that it has ties to the triple goddess.

This symbol actually comes from the occult and is in reality comprised of three interlocking sixes (# 666 – Revelation 13:18).

This exact same occult triquetra symbol can be found on the covers of many rap, heavy metal rock, Techno, Trance, and New Age electronic punk albums, as

well as on the front covers of well-known New Age books such as Marilyn Ferguson's *The Aquarian Conspiracy*.

This comes as no surprise since the **NKJV** makes the same changes that many spiritualist books and New Age books do; it changes "end of the world" to "end of the age." For example, in Matthew 13:39-40

KJV: *"...end of the world...end of this world."*
NKJV: *"...end of the age... end of this age."*
in Matthew 28:20
KJV: *"... end of the world. ..."*
NKJV: *"...end of the age. ..."*
in Luke 18:30
KJV: *"...and in the world to come life everlasting."*
NKJV: *"...and in the age to come eternal life."*
and in Hebrews 6:5
KJV: *"And have tasted the good word of God, and the powers of the world to come,"*
NKJV: *"and have tasted the good word of God and the powers of the age to come,"*

The New King James Version (NKJV)

What "age" is that? Was that the end of the Jewish Age, the end of the Dark Ages, the arrival of the Age of Aquarius, the New Age, maybe the Millennial Age – what "age?"

As previously stated, known spiritualist and prolific occult writer, Alice A. Bailey writes in her book *The Reappearance of the Christ*, *"The final words of the Christ to His apostles were, 'Lo, I am with you all the days, even unto the <u>end of the age</u>' or cycle. (Matt. 28.20.)"* Bailey continues by stating that this *"means the end of the time period, with another immediately following after (what would be called the end of a cycle)."* (*The Reappearance of the Christ*, Alice A. Bailey, PDF pg. 11)

In addition, high level occultist, Helena Blavatsky, also uses this phrase, stating, *"Both Jesus and St. John the Baptist preached the <u>end of the Age</u> which proves their knowledge of the secret computation of the priests and <u>kabalists</u>, who with the chiefs of the <u>Essene communities</u> alone had the secret of the duration of the cycles."* (*Isis Unveiled*, Blavatsky, vol. 2, p.144)

In other words, the changes the **NKJV** makes in these various texts match the teachings of the occult New Age movement which is also tied with the kabalists & Essenes (the cult of Jewish mystics connected with the **Dead Sea Scrolls**). Is it possible that the **NKJV** and other modern Bibles are a fulfillment of occultist Manly P. Hall's intentions to make a more "occult-friendly" Bible? Hall made this startling statement, *"To make things right* [for occultists] *we will have to undo much that is cherished error. The problem of revising the Bible shows how difficult it is to do this. For the last hundred years we have been trying to get out an edition of the Bible that is reasonably correct* [for occultists] *but nobody wants it. What's wanted is the good old King James version, every jot and tittle of it, because most people are convinced that God dictated the Bible to King James in English."*
(*'Asia in the Balance of the Scales'*, Horizon, Vol.4, No.1, Spring 1944, p.13)

What method did Hall say occultist would use to undermine God's pure word? He states,*"We will discover numerous errors and alternative renderings, and slowly recover from the infallibility complex which so many orthodox Bible readers seem to suffer.* (*'The Secret Doctrine in the Bible'*, The Students Monthly Letter, Fourth Year, Letter 12, p.8)

With all of these occult connections, it should be no surprise that the triquetra symbol used on the cover of the **NKJV** is also often prominently displayed in witchcraft and occult ritual and spell books, wiccan altars and various occult paraphernalia, as well as on some Ouija boards and Occult movies.

Furthermore, the use of the triquetra, besides being linked to the blatant occult, is also linked with the deception of "spiritual formation." For example, in **1988**, Spiritual Formation guru, Richard J. Foster, founded the Renovaré Institute to promote the mysticism of "Spiritual Formation" to the Christian world. The Renovaré Institute also uses the triquetra in the center of its official symbol.

With all these pagan and spiritualistic connections, finding that the **NKJV** alters texts to hide Satan's identity, to point the finger away from him, to portray him as already destroyed, or to depict him in the best possible light should be no surprise. Texts like Psalm 109:6 and Ezekiel 28:16,18

KJV: *"Set thou a wicked man over him: and let Satan stand at his right hand."*
NKJV: *"Set a wicked man over him, And let an accuser stand at his right hand."*

KJV: *By the multitude of thy merchandise they have filled the midst of thee with violence, and thou hast sinned: therefore I will cast thee as profane out of the mountain of God: and I will destroy thee, O covering cherub, from the midst of the stones of fire... Thou hast defiled thy sanctuaries by the multitude of thine iniquities, by the iniquity of thy traffick; therefore will I bring forth a fire from the midst of thee, it shall devour thee, and I will bring thee to ashes upon the earth in the sight of all them that behold thee....* Note the destruction is future tense.

NKJV: *"By the abundance of your trading You became filled with violence within, And you sinned; Therefore I cast you as a profane thing out of the mountain of God; And I destroyed you, O covering cherub, From the midst of the fiery stones...You defiled your sanctuaries by the multitude of your iniquities, by the iniquity of your trading; Therefore I brought fire from your midst; It devoured you, and I turned you to ashes upon the earth in the sight of all who saw you."* Note the destruction portrayed here is past tense depicting Satan already burnt to ashes.

Thus, regardless of the claims made of its accuracy and faithfulness to the **Textus Receptus**, the **NKJV** has, in many ways, shown itself to be nothing but a subtle design by skeptics and critics to undermine the inspired Word of God as given in the **Authorized King James Bible**. And, like it's witchcraft symbol reveals, the **NKJV** artfully weaves its *spell* of skepticism over the people. Oh, that men would heed God's admonition found in Jeremiah 6:16, *"Thus saith the LORD, Stand ye in the ways, and see, and ask for the old paths, where is the good way, and walk therein, and ye shall find rest for your souls. But they said, We will not walk therein."*

From the NKJV to Today

In **1981**, Kurt and Barbara Aland published *The Text of the New Testament* in which they introduced their new system of categorizing Greek NT manuscripts. It consisted of five categories.

Category I – <u>Alexandrian</u> text type manuscripts and papyri.
Category II – <u>Egyptian</u> text type – manuscripts similar to category one but that contain influences from other categories.
Category III – <u>Eclectic</u> text type – manuscripts with independent readings with distinctive character.
Category IV – <u>Western</u> text type manuscripts
Category V – <u>Byzantine</u> text type manuscripts

In **1985**, the **New Jerusalem Bible (NJB)** was published. It's basis was the 25th edition of **Novum Testamentum Graece**, **Codex Bezae**, the **Biblia Hebraica Stuttgartensia**, the **Septuagint**, and the **Latin Vulgate**. It is an updated version of the **Jerusalem Bible** and it is also an approved Catholic Bible.

Among the many errors in this version are places where the text has been altered to agree with Papal doctrine. For example, the **KJV** states in Matthew 6:7:
"But when ye pray, use not vain repetitions, as the heathen do: for they think that they shall be heard for their much speaking."
But since Catholicism uses many "vain repetitions" in their rituals, the **NJB** changed this verse to read in a way that doesn't as distinctly condemn the Catholic religion: *"In your prayers do not babble as the gentiles do, for they think that by using many words they will make themselves heard."*

In **1987**, the **New Century Version (NCV)** was released. The **NCV** was based on the **UBS third edition of the Greek New Testament**, the **Biblia Hebraica Stuttgartensia**, and the **Septuagint**. The **NCV** was replaced by a gender-neutral edition in **1991** which was then updated in **2007**.

Many modern Bibles change the text to say the exact opposite of what the original said. The **NCV** contains many good examples of this foolishness. For example, Proverbs 29:21 in the **KJV** states:
"He that delicately bringeth up his servant from a child shall have him become his son at the length."
But the **NCV** changes the text to make it say the opposite:
"If you spoil your servants when they are young, they will bring you grief later on."

In **1988**, the **Word Made Fresh (WMF)** paraphrase was published. It added humour and familiar names and places for those who have no desire to read the Bible and just want to treat the Bible as a joke.
While the **KJV** clearly states in Judges 6:20:

"And the angel of God said unto him, Take the flesh and the unleavened cakes, and lay them upon this rock, and pour out the broth. And he did so."

According to internet sources (since the writer didn't want to waste money buying a copy of this paraphrase for himself) – the **WMF** claims that the angel told Gideon to: *"Bring an uncooked TV dinner and place it on the rock before me,"*

The **WMF** also changes Biblical names to foolish names. For example, Eglon is instead called the *"Evil king of New Orleans,"* Ehud is named *"Mac the Knife,"* and Sisera is called *"Jesse James."*

In **1989**, the National Council of Churches published a revision of the **Revised Standard Version** called the **New Revised Standard Version (NRSV)**. The **NRSV** was made supposedly for the purpose of serving the needs of the broadest possible range of religious people, and it is regarded as a leading force of the ecumenical movement. The full translation includes not only the books of the regular Protestant Bibles, but also the Deuterocanonical or Apocryphal books of Roman Catholicism. Three editions of the **NRSV** were made: the common edition (Protestant Bible); one with Apocryphal books added; and the Catholic Edition with the OT books arranged in the order of the **Vulgate**.

The translation committee's stated rule was to make their translation, *"As literal as possible, as free as necessary."* They used the same corrupt sources that the **RSV** translators did, the **BHS**, the **Septuagint**, the **Greek by Theodotion**, as well as the Jesuit-influenced **Greek NT produced by the UBS**.

Members of the **NRSV** committee included not only Protestant and Orthodox representatives, but also feminists and Catholic priests.

The **NRSV** contains many errors and changes in doctrine. It also attacks and undermines the eternal pre-existence of Jesus Christ.

For example, the **KJV** clearly states that the Son of God existed from all eternity – Micah 5:2 *"But thou, Bethlehem Ephratah, though thou be little among the thousands of Judah, yet out of thee shall he come forth unto me that is to be ruler in Israel; whose goings forth have been from of old, from everlasting."*
But the **NRSV** takes eternity totally out of Micah 5:2 and implies that the Son of God was a created being with an origin. *"But you, O Bethlehem of Ephrathah, who are one of the little clans of Judah, from you shall come forth for me one who is to rule in Israel, whose origin is from of old, from ancient days."*

In **1993**, Eugene Peterson published the New Testament of his free paraphrase, **The Message Bible (MSG)**. It is an idiomatic, sometimes eccentric paraphrase that resorts to using contemporary slang and street language throughout its text.

For example, in Luke 9:27 in the **KJV**, Jesus tells His disciples, *"But I tell you of a truth, there be some standing here, which shall not taste of death, till they see the kingdom of God."*

The **MSG** takes the solemnity out of the text and makes it sound like street language with, *"This isn't, you realize, pie in the sky by and by. Some who have taken their stand right here are going to see it happen, see with their own eyes the kingdom of God."*

The **KJV** states in Mark 13:9: *"But take heed to yourselves: for they shall deliver you up to councils; and in the synagogues ye shall be beaten: and ye shall be brought before rulers and kings for my sake..."*

The **MSG** says: *"And watch out! They're going to drag you into court. And then it will go from bad to worse, dog-eat-dog, everyone at your throat because you carry my name..."*

In **1989–1996**, the **Living Bible** paraphrase was revised and the new edition became the **New Living Translation (NLT)** which was published in **1996**. It is rather odd to call a revision of a paraphrase a "translation." The revision project originally starting out as an effort to revise the **Living Bible**, but then evolved into producing a new English translation from Hebrew and Greek texts. But the **NLT** Bible was based on the **BHS**, **LXX**, and **Jerome's Latin Vulgate** as well as 27th edition of **Novum Testamentum Graece** and the fourth **UBS Greek New Testament**.

While there was some influence from the Hebrew and Greek, the **NLT** was still translated based on the Dynamic Equivalence theory of "Thought-for-thought" instead of the more accurate "Word for Word" process. Yet, *"When the New Living Translation came out, [Billy] Graham said: 'The Living Bible has been used by God around the world for many years to introduce people to the Scriptures. Now I am pleased to recommend the New Living Translation for even greater readability and accuracy.'"* (Billy Graham and His Friends, p.461)

Some examples of the inaccuracy of the **NLT** can be seen by comparing Mark 10:24 to the **KJV** which says, *"And the disciples were astonished at his words. But Jesus answereth again, and saith unto them, Children, <u>how hard is it for them that trust in riches</u> to enter into the kingdom of God!"*

But the **NLT** removes the qualifier, thereby making it very hard for anyone to enter heaven: *"This amazed them. But Jesus said again, "Dear children, <u>it is very hard</u> to enter the Kingdom of God."*

The **KJV** clearly identifies who the voice is that is speaking behind John in Revelation 1:11: *"<u>Saying, I am Alpha and Omega, the first and the last</u>: and, What thou seest, write in a book..."* But the **NLT** totally leaves that phrase out, stating only: *"<u>It said</u>, "Write in a book everything you see..."*

Sword Unsheathed

The **NLT** is a standard "Spiritual Formation" Bible designed to promote the mysticism of Spiritual Formation. One internet site states,
"...we have a case of New Believer's Bibles available to gift. A great resource, this Bible is translated into the New Living Translation. It's easy to read and offers insets that help provide context around important spiritual formation themes."
(www.2riverschurch.com/going-deeper/tools-first-steps-bible, accessed 5/18/20)

Another site reiterates, *"SPIRITUAL FORMATION RESOURCES... Bible Translations To Consider... New Living Translation (NLT) ...Books...In Celebration of Discipline by Richard Foster..."* (popmn.org/worship/spiritual-resources/, accessed 5/18/20)

The second revision of the **NLT** came out in **2004** with a third revision in **2007**.

Interestingly enough, the scholar who translated the book of Daniel in the **NLT** is a professor at the Catholic University of America. Then in **2015**, the "Protestant" **NLT** edition was changed to read exactly like the Roman Catholic edition. A Catholic blog tells about the response they got from Tyndale House publishers.
"I was excited to receive the following response from Tyndale:
'The changes suggested by the Conference of Catholic Bishops of India were reviewed by Tyndale and incorporated into the 2015 edition of the translation for all Bibles, Catholic and Protestant. Going forward any NLT with a copyright of 2015 incorporates these changes. We were very pleased with the suggestions made by the Conference and felt the suggested changes made the NLT better.'
This is joyous news! It means that the NLT is now in a similar category to the NRSV: the only difference between Catholic and protestant* versions are the deuterocanonical books. The translation is identical!" (*missing capitalization in original)
(catholicbibletalk.com/2018/09/tracking-down-the-revisions-in-the-nlt-ce-and-the-esv-ce/, accessed 5/18/20)

Meanwhile, in **1994**, down in Monterrey, Mexico, a Baptist congregation and their pastor, Raul Reyes, who were tired of dealing with corrupt Spanish versions of the Bible, began work on a new revision of the Spanish Bible. They wanted to translate a pure Spanish Bible that would be to the Spanish-speaking world what the **King James** was to the English-speaking world. They recognized the corruption in the Bible societies and instead of entrusting the work to the societies, they chose to do the work themselves. They also recognized the problems with having a single person doing it, so they made it a united work among the whole congregation. They even learned Greek and Hebrew so that they could work from the original manuscripts.

They referenced quite a few of the Spanish Bibles in their translation work, but the sources used for the basis of their translation was the **Ben Chayyim Masoretic text**, the **Greek Textus Receptus**, the **1556 Pineda New Testament**, the **1553 Ferrara Old Testament**, the **1569 Reina Bear Bible**, and the **1602 Valera Revision**.

From the NKJV to Today

Their first NT was printed in **1999**, but had many spelling mistakes, and had to be printed again in **2002** to fix the spelling mistakes. They named their finished translation the **1602 Purificada** [Purified], sometimes just referred to as **1602P**. This Bible corrected many of the errors that were present in the Bible Societies Spanish versions, so that the **Purificada** would read much closer to the **KJV**. There were, however, still a few incorrect translation issues in this Bible.

For example, the **KJV** states in Numbers 31:39 *"...of which the LORD'S tribute was threescore and one."* (that is 61) The **1602P** reads *"...y de ellos el tributo para el SEÑOR, setenta y uno."* (that is 71)

Thankfully, some of these errors and mistakes have been corrected in newer editions of the **1602 Purificada.**

In **1994**, Jack Blanco published the **Clear Word Bible**. The **Clear Word Bible** was not actually a translation, but rather a paraphrase of the Bible that contains much material that was added by the author. It was written as a personal devotional exercise by Blanco, to be an additional study tool and devotional for himself. After his friends and family had seen it, they encouraged him to publish it. Its original purpose was never intended to be used in place of the Bible but rather as a sort of commentary on the Bible, though many people have mistakenly taken it as a new Bible translation. Many sources were used by Blanco for his "inspiration" – some of truth, some of error, making this paraphrase a dangerous mixture of truth and error.

For instance, the **Clear Word Bible** uses the incorrect word *"eagle"* in Revelation 8:13, and *"washed their robes"* in Revelation 22:14. [see these texts in the chapter *Examples of Modern Bible Changes Affecting Doctrine*]

In 1995, the **NASB** was "updated" and called **NASB95**. For this update, they used the **Biblia Hebraica Stuttgartensia** and the 26th edition of **Nestle-Aland**.

To give an example of the way this Bible is changed, compare Matthew 9:13 from the **KJV**: *"But go ye and learn what that meaneth, I will have mercy, and not sacrifice: for I am not come to call the righteous, but sinners to repentance."*

Now see how the **NASB** removes key words: *"But go and learn what this means: 'I DESIRE COMPASSION, AND NOT SACRIFICE,' for I did not come to call the righteous, but sinners."* This corrupt **NASB** takes out "to repentance"!

In **1997**, because of the trend of the modern Bibles to gender-inclusive and non-Christian issues, James Dobson and other evangelicals called a meeting and it was decided to create a new version without the new-age, homosexual, gender-inclusive agenda. With permission from the National Council of Churches, it was decided to build their new evangelical version on the **1971** revision of the **RSV**. This was the birth of the four year project that would produce the **English Standard Version (ESV)** in **2001**.

Sword Unsheathed

The basis for the **ESV** was the fifth edition of **Biblia Hebraica Stuttgartensia**, the fifth corrected edition of the **Greek New Testament by UBS**, and Nestle-Aland's 28th edition of **Novum Testamentum Graece**.

The **ESV** committee tried to stay "essentially literal" in their translation, and as a result, the **ESV** is more "literal" than the **NIV**.

However, the **ESV**, like many other modern versions, totally throws out entire texts of scripture. For example, the **KJV** clearly shows what the requirements are for baptism in Acts 8:37.

"36 And as they went on their way, they came unto a certain water: and the eunuch said, See, here is water; what doth hinder me to be baptized?
37 And Philip said, If thou believest with all thine heart, thou mayest. And he answered and said, I believe that Jesus Christ is the Son of God.
38 And he commanded the chariot to stand still: and they went down both into the water, both Philip and the eunuch; and he baptized him."

Philip and the Ethiopian Eunuch who Believed

This is why Protestants believe that a person must make a knowledgeable decision to follow Christ before they are baptized.

But the **ESV** totally removes the whole 37th verse.

"36 And as they were going along the road they came to some water, and the eunuch said, "See, here is water! What prevents me from being baptized?"
38 And he commanded the chariot to stop, and they both went down into the water, Philip and the eunuch, and he baptized him."

This change shows the influence of Roman Catholic manuscripts, because the doctrine of the Papal Church teaches that there is no requirement for baptism, which is why they baptize babies.

But the **ESV** also contains several ludicrous errors. The **KJV** clearly states in 1 Samuel 13:1 that Saul was an adult when he took the throne and began to reign. *"Saul reigned one year; and when he had reigned two years over Israel,"*

But the **ESV** makes this foolish statement in 1 Samuel 13:1, *"Saul lived for one year and then became king, and when he had reigned for two years over Israel,"*

So in spite of the fact that 1 Samuel 10:23 states that Saul was head and shoulders taller than all the people, the **ESV** portrays Saul as a baby (he must have been a huge baby!).

In **1998**, the **International Standard Version (ISV)** was produced to provide an exclusive textual apparatus comparing the text of the **Dead Sea Scrolls** with the **Masoretic text** of the Hebrew.

However, the **ISV** is just another corrupted version that makes incorrect changes and adds errors to the Biblical text.

For example, if one checks Mark 10:21 in the **KJV** it states: *"Then Jesus beholding him loved him, and said unto him, One thing thou lackest: go thy way, sell whatsoever thou hast, and give to the poor, and thou shalt have treasure in heaven: and come, take up the cross, and follow me."*

The **ISV** ignores the original text and takes the cross totally out of the verse.

"Jesus looked at him and loved him. Then he told him, 'You're missing one thing. Go and sell everything you own, give the money to the destitute, and you will have treasure in heaven. Then come back and follow me.'"

And the **ISV** doesn't seem to mind taking things out of the Word of God, because the **ISV** leaves Luke 17:36, as well as other verses, totally out of the text.

In the year **1998**, the **Revised King James New Testament (RKJNT)** was produced. The makers of it did not return to the original languages, but instead incorporated the readings of the **modern corrupt versions** into the **King James**. Because of this fact, the **RKJNT** contains many of the same errors that the **NIV**, the **ISV**, and other corrupt Bibles contain.

For example, in Galatians 5:12, as it reads in the **KJV**, Paul expresses the desire that those who were causing the church of Galatia trouble, would be "cut off" – in other words, removed from church fellowship. He said, *"I would they were even cut off which trouble you."* But the **RKJNT** reads just the same as many of the corrupted Bibles – *"I wish those who trouble you would even emasculate themselves."*

The **ISV**, **GNB**, and the **MSG** all use the word *"castrate"* in this text. Needless to say, this self-mutilation concept was never in the original text of the pure-line Bibles (but rather the concept of wickedness being "cut off" or brought to nought as found in Isaiah 29:20).

In **1999**, the **Holman Christian Standard Bible (HCSB)** was produced. This version originated in **1984** as the **Logos 21 version**, an independent project of Arthur Farstad, former general editor for the **New King James Version**. Farstad's original concept was to produce a modern English translation of the New Testament based on the **counterfeit Greek Majority Text (MT)** which he had edited and published in **1982**. However, Farstad died in **1998** only five months after work on the new translation was started, and the committee dropped Farstad's **MT** and used the 27th edition of **Nestle-Aland Novum Testamentum Graece**, the **UBS fourth edition Greek New Testament**, and the fifth edition of the **Biblia Hebraica Stuttgartensia**. The New Testament was published in **1999**, and the whole **HCSB** was published in **2004**.

The **HCSB** is filled with all sorts of errors and rejected text. It also uses the word *"castrated"* in Galatians 5:12.

In addition, the **KJV** tells us in Romans 8:1 that: *"There is therefore now no condemnation to them which are in Christ Jesus, who walk not after the flesh, but after the Spirit."*
But the **HCSB** drops the defining characteristics off of the end of the verse: *"Therefore, no condemnation now exists for those in Christ Jesus,"*

During the time that the congregation in Monterrey, Mexico was working to produce the Spanish **1602 Purificada**, Humberto Gomez, a Baptist missionary in Mexico, also tired of the errors of the Bible Societies versions, began working in **2000**, on his own revision of the **Reina-Valera Bible**.

In 2001, the **TEV** was officially renamed the **Good News Bible (GNB)** or the **Good News Translation (GNT)**.

Another example of Papal influence can be seen by comparing Matthew 16:18 in the **GNB** to the Protestant **KJV**. The **KJV** says, *"And I say also unto thee, That thou art Peter, and upon this rock I will build my church; and the gates of hell shall not prevail against it."*

Protestantism correctly recognizes that Christ was talking about Himself to Peter (whose name *"petros"* means "a piece of rock") and Christ showed the contrast between Himself and Peter by referring to Himself as *"this rock"* (*"petra"* meaning "a mass of rock")

on which the church was to be built. The original Greek terms "Petros" and "Petra" refer to two very different things, a fact which the **KJV** translators correctly recognized and showed in their translation.

But the Papal Church teaches that Peter was the rock that the church was to be built on, and the **GNB** changes the meaning of this text to promote Catholic doctrine.

The **GNB/GNT** says, *"And so I tell you, Peter: you are a rock, and on this rock foundation I will build my church, and not even death will ever be able to overcome it."*

The **ESV** was finally finished and published on **September 24, 2001**. When comparing the **ESV** to its foundational **RSV** version, only about five to ten percent of the **RSV** text was changed in the **ESV**. Not surprisingly, the **ESV** contains many of the same errors that the **NIV**, the **CEV**, and the **NKJNT** all contain. The **ESV** also translates Galatians 5:12 as *"I wish those who unsettle you would emasculate themselves!"*

In 2002, the **Today's New International Version (TNIV)** was published. It was a revision of the **NIV**. The **TNIV** used gender-neutral or gender-inclusive language. Many sources were used for the basis of this Bible, including the **Dead Sea Scrolls**, the **Septuagint**, the **Greek of Aquila, Symmachus and Theodotion** from **Origen's Hexapla**, the **Latin Vulgate**, and the United Bible Societies **Nestle-Aland Greek New Testament** text.

Amazingly, even the publisher, Zondervan, as well as the CEO of the International Bible Society (now called Biblica) later admitted that producing the **TNIV** had been a mistake.

"...decisions surrounding the release of the NIV inclusive language edition and the 2002 revision, Today's New International Version (TNIV), were mistakes."
(www.christianitytoday.com/news/2009/september/correcting-mistakes-of-tniv-and-inclusive-niv-translators.html, accessed 3/21/20)

Revelation 3:20 in the **KJV** states an individual call: *"Behold, I stand at the door, and knock: if any man hear my voice, and open the door, I will come in to him, and will sup with him, and he with me."*

The **TNIV** changes the text to incorrect, impersonal, gender-inclusive language: *"I stand at the door and knock. If anyone hears my voice and opens the door, I will come in and eat with them, and they with me."*

In the year **2002**, Eugene Peterson published his complete **Message Bible** paraphrase with both the Old and New Testaments. It has many defects.

For example, the beautiful verse talking about Christ answering questions about the nail scars in His hands in Zechariah 13:6 states in the **KJV**: *"And one shall say unto him, What are these wounds in thine hands? Then he shall answer, Those with which I was wounded in the house of my friends."*

The **Message Bible** totally destroys the meaning by writing it as, *"And if someone says, 'And so where did you get that black eye?' they'll say, 'I ran into a door at a friend's house.'"*

Humberto Gomez was still working to finish his Spanish translation when the **1602 Purificada** was published in 2002. Gomez used the **1909 Version Antigua**, the Greek **Textus Receptus**, the **Masoretic Hebrew**, and the **King James Bible** for his translation.

In **2004**, Gomez published the first edition of his revision of the **Reina-Valera Bible**, known as the **Reina-Valera Gomez (RVG)** version. Copies were sent out to many other Spanish speaking authorities in over 12 countries, the text was carefully examined for accuracy with the **Textus Receptus** and **King James**, and corrections were submitted. The text was also submitted to Spanish and English linguists as well as Greek and Hebrew experts who also examined and corrected Gomez' work. The first edition had some printing mistakes and errors, so these were corrected and the **RVG** was republished in **2010**.

The **Reina-Valera Gomez (RVG)** reads more with today's more common vernacular Spanish. This is the main difference between the the **RVG** and the **Purificada** which was translated in the old Castilian Spanish of the original **Reina-Valera**.

Gomez stated this about the **RVG**:

"To accomplish this work we have put parallel the Textus Receptus, the 1909 Spanish Bible, and King James. We have gone verse by verse making sure first of the purity of the text and then comparing the 1909 with the Authorized KJV. Every single verse that did not line up with the TR or the KJV we immediately corrected. Because not all the words mean the same in every language we have used the best words available in our Spanish language, the words that have the most meaning, never contradicting the TR or the KJV...We have attempted to correct every mistranslation. We have attempted to correct every verse that was not in line with the TR and the KJV. We added all the words that were omitted, and we have removed all the words that were added, and we feel we have a perfect text."

(Dr. Humberto Gomez, December 18, 2004)

In **2005**, mystic Richard Foster along with other key spiritual formation leaders like Dallas Willard, Eugene Peterson and Walter Brueggemann, using the **New Revised Standard Version (NRSV)**, produced a "Spiritual Formation" Bible incorporating the Jesuit "Renewal" theology. It is called the **Renovaré Spiritual Formation Study Bible**, or **The Life with God Bible**.

"In reality The Renovaré Spiritual Formation Bible is an amalgamation of doctrinal pluralism, Romanism, higher criticism, mysticism, spiritualistic theories, and philosophical speculation with Satan as its editor."

(Assault on the Remnant, p.281)

The **Renovaré Spiritual Formation Bible** also promotes pantheism.
For example, in the **KJV**, Ephesians 4:6 states that God lives in His people, *"One God and Father of all, who is above all, and through all, and in you all."*
But the **Renovaré Spiritual Formation Bible** drops the word "you" out of the text, which shows the pantheistic teaching that God is in everyone and in everything. *"one God and Father of all, who is above all, and through all and in all."*

From the NKJV to Today

In October of **2010**, a new edition of the **New Revised Standard Version (NRSV)** was released with quotes from the writings of author C.S. Lewis interwoven throughout it. It's called the **C.S. Lewis Bible**. [see Note H]

In 2012, the **Queen James Bible (QJV)** also called the **"Gay Bible"** was published. In it all negative references to homosexuality have been removed. It is based on the **KJV** text but it is edited by changing and by adding things in the name of preventing "homophobic interpretations." A good example is found in Leviticus 18:22. Here the **KJV** specifically condemns homosexuality as an abomination saying, *"Thou shalt not lie with mankind, as with womankind: it is abomination."*

But the **QJV** totally nullifies God's Word by inserting a phrase to take the meaning out of the text. *"Thou shalt not lie with mankind as with womankind in the temple of Molech; it is an abomination."* Here the **QJV** makes it appear that it is not the act of homosexuality that is the abomination, it is the act done in the temple of Molech that is the abomination. This obviously does not agree with God's pure word.

On **June 22, 2015**, the world was shocked by the headlines:
"Pope asks pardon from Waldensian Protestants for past persecution" – "On behalf of the Catholic Church, I ask forgiveness for the un-Christian and even inhumane positions and actions taken against you historically," he said. "In the name of the Lord Jesus Christ, forgive us!" (www.reuters.com)

Pope Francis even held and kissed the Waldensian Bible in front of thousands of viewers worldwide, which convinced many ignorant viewers to believe that Francis was admitting that the Papacy's persecution of the Waldensians was being repented of. But the viewers were not aware that the language of the Pope's "confession" was carefully worded with amphibology so as not to really admit to any wrong on the part of the papacy; and the supposed Waldensian Bible that he kissed was not the original Protestant version of their Bible that their ancestors fought and died for, but in actuality, it was a modern interconfessional and Vatican-approved Bible that the Waldensian church now uses.

History specifically states:
"Leo XIII was candid enough to tell us what is really going on when the Roman Church-State seems to be adopting a less violent or less totalitarian position. Leo XIII wrote: 'And although in the extraordinary condition of these times the Church usually acquiesces in certain modern liberties, not because she prefers them in themselves, but because she judges it expedient to permit them, she would in happier times exercise her own liberty...' Thus, happier times for the Roman Church-State mean sadder times for everyone else. Then the Roman Church-State will be able to put into practice its own principle, and it will not have to acquiesce in certain modern liberties for expedient reasons." (Ecclesiastical Megalomania, p.181)

Another writer, in even plainer English, expounds thus,

"The Romish Church now presents a fair front to the world, covering with apologies her record of horrible cruelties. She has clothed herself in Christ-like garments; but she is unchanged. Every principle of popery that existed in past ages exists today. The doctrines devised in the darkest ages are still held. Let none deceive themselves. The popery that Protestants are now so ready to honor is the same that ruled the world in the days of the Reformation, when men of God stood up, at the peril of their lives, to expose her iniquity. She possesses the same pride and arrogant assumption that lorded it over kings and princes, and claimed the prerogatives of God. Her spirit is no less cruel and despotic now than when she crushed out human liberty, and slew the saints of the Most High.

"Popery is just what prophecy declared that she would be, the apostasy of the latter times. [2 Thessalonians 2:3, 4.] It is a part of her policy to assume the character which will best accomplish her purpose; but beneath the variable appearance of the chameleon, she conceals the invariable venom of the serpent. 'We are not bound to keep faith and promises to heretics,' She declares. Shall this power, whose record for a thousand years is written in the blood of the saints, be now acknowledged as a part of the church of Christ?

"It is not without reason that the claim has been put forth in Protestant countries, that Catholicism differs less widely from Protestantism than in former times. <u>There has been a change; but the change is not in the papacy. Catholicism indeed resembles much of the Protestantism that now exists, because Protestantism has so greatly degenerated since the days of the reformers.</u>

"As the Protestant churches have been seeking the favor of the world, false charity has blinded their eyes. They do not see but that it is right to believe good of all evil; and as the inevitable result, they will finally believe evil of all good. Instead of standing in defense of the faith once delivered to the saints, they are now, as it were, apologizing to Rome for their uncharitable opinion of her, begging pardon for their bigotry." (Great Controversy, p.570-571)

In 2017, the **Christian Standard Bible (CSB)** was published. It is a revision of the **Holman Christian Standard Bible (HCSB)**.

In July of 2019, the **Revised New Jerusalem Bible (RNJB)** was released. Like its predecessor, the **Jerusalem Bible**, it is a Roman Catholic Bible that is based on the **Biblia Hebraica Stuttgartensia**, the **Septuagint**, and the 27th edition of the **Novum Testamentum Graece**.

The reader can see how since the revision of the **King James Bible** in the **1880's**, there has been a literal flood of Bibles produced, numbering well over several hundred different versions. It can also be seen how the vast majority of them have all been based, either totally or largely, on the contaminated manuscripts from the corrupt stream.

Producing a new edition of the Bible is so commonplace today; it is as easy as making a new product for the consumer market. Yet to avoid copyright issues, each time there is a new English Bible made, more and more of the word of God "must be" changed. Bible publishers appear more interested in the profits to be made and catering to what the populous wants, than they are about Scriptural accuracy – forgetting that Jesus said *"Ye cannot serve God and mammon."* (Matthew 6:24).

Some of these modern Bibles are versions, some are translations, some are translations of translations, some are revisions and revisions of revisions, and some are paraphrases and paraphrases of paraphrases.

But with all, it would be well to heed the Biblical admonition and warning, *"For I am the LORD, I change not..."* (Malachi 3:6) therefore, *"...meddle not with them that are given to change:"* (Proverbs 24:21)

Note where these changes are leading.
"What the Roman Church-State accomplished on a small scale during the Middle Ages is what it desires to achieve on a global scale in the coming millennium." (Ecclesiastical Megalomania, p.187)

Warning has been given about the higher criticism of the Bible and where it is leading: *"Through form criticism and oral tradition Protestantism is marching back to Rome."* (Assault on the Remnant, p.289)

Interestingly enough, even the scholars of the Islamic religion refer to and quote from the modern Bible versions – as proof that the Bible cannot be the truth of God – since it has had to change so many times. This should cause missionary-minded people to sit up and take notice. The corrupted versions of the Bible are giving the enemies of Christianity "fuel" for their arguments!

It can be noted that today there is a Bible edition for every sort of religious belief or type of personal preference that exists. No matter if a person wants to believe that the world is the result of evolution, or that God is a woman, or that homosexuality is endorsed in the Bible – the various Bible publishers have produced a Bible just for them!

Here is just a small non-exhaustive list of Bibles that have been published from the **1611 KJV** to today (**2022**). Notice the rapid multiplication of Bibles from the late 1800's through today!
1611 - King James Version (KJV) a.k.a. the Authorized Version (AV)
1615 - Barker Bible

Sword Unsheathed

1666 - Armenian Bible
1729 - Daniel Mace English Translation of the Bible
1755 - Dodderidge Family Expositor
1755 - John Wesley New Testament (JWNT)
1764 - Purver's Bible
1790 - Clementine Edition
1797 - Geddes Holy Bible
1799 - David Macrae Translation
1808 - Thomson Holy Bible
1812 - Fry Holy Bible
1818 - Bellamy Holy Bible
1833 - Webster's Holy Bible with Amendments
1836 - Book of the New Covenant Penn
1841 - Conquest Holy Bible
1849 - Whiting's Good News of Our Lord Jesus, the Anointed
1850 - Bible Revised Barham
1850 - Commonly Received Version of the N.T. Cone
1850 - Forshall Holy Bible
1850 - Madden Holy Bible
1855 - Leeser Holy Scriptures
1858 - English Version of the Polyglot Bible (EVPB)
1859 - Wellbeloved Holy Scriptures
1862 - Sawyer Bible
1865 - Common English New Testament (CENT)
1867 - Joseph Smith's Inspired Version (IV)
1876 - Julia Smith Holy Bible
1885 - English Revised Version (RV)
1885 - Wordsworth Holy Bible
1905 - Godbey Translation of the New Testament (GTNT)
1905 - Holy Scriptures Leeser (HSL)
1906 - Ferrar Fenton Holy Bible In Modern English (FFHB)
1909 - University New Testament (UNT)
1912 - American Bible Union Holy Bible: An Improved Edition
1912 - The American Baptist Publication Society Bible (ABPS)
1913 - Literary Man's New Testament (LMNT)
1914 - Bible Numerics New Testament (BNNT)
1914 - The New Covenant New Testament (CNT)
1914 - Restored New Testament (PRNT)
1916 - Alexander Harkavy Holy Scriptures (AHHS)
1917 - New Translation Jewish (NTJ)
1917 - Jewish Publication Society Bible (JPS)
1917 - Wisdom Books in Modern Speech (WBMS)
1921 - A Plain Translation of New Testament (PTNT)
1922 - Moffatt New Translation (MNT)

1922 - Shorter Bible Kent (SBK)
1923 - Darby Holy Bible (DHB)
1923 - Modern Reader's Bible (MRB)
1923 - Riverside New Testament (RNT)
1924 - Centenary Translation of the New Testament (CTNT)
1924 - Older Children's Bible (OCB)
1924 - The Everyday Bible (TEB)
1925 - People's New Covenant (PNC) meta-physical
1926 - Concordant Literal New Testament (CLNT)
1926 - Western New Testament (WNT)
1928 - Christian's Bible Lefevre (CBNT)
1929 - Westminster Version of the Sacred Scriptures (WVSS)
1930 - Bible Designed to Be Read as Literature (BDRL)
1931 - American Translation Smith-Goodspeed (SGAT)
1934 - Documents of the New Testament (DNT)
1935 - The Moffatt Bible
1937 - Pulpit Bible (PB)
1937 - Williams New Testament (WNT)
1941 - Spencer New Testament (SCM)
1942 - Emphatic Diaglott (EDW)
1945 - Knox Translation from the Latin Vulgate (KNX)
1945 - Berkley Version of the New Testamant (BVNT)
1947 - Swann New Testament (SNT)
1948 - Letchworth Version in Modern English (LVME)
1949 - Bible In Basic English (BBE)
1950 - Basic Bible (TBB)
1951 - Holy Scriptures Harkavy (HSH)
1952 - Revised Standard Version (RSV)
1952 - Revised Standard Version, Ecumenical (RSVE)
1953 - Confraternity of Christian Doctrine Translation (CCDT)
1954 - The Story Bible (TSB)
1956 - Kleist-Lilly New Testament (KLNT)
1956 - Knox Translation (KTC)
1957 - Jewish Bible for Family Reading (JBFR)
1957 - Lamsa Bible (LBP)
1958 - Authentic New Testament (ANT)
1958 - J.B. Phillips New Testament In Modern English (JBP)
1959 - Emphasized Bible (EBR)
1960 - New American Standard Bible 1960-1973 (NASB)
1961 - Dartmouth Bible (TDB)
1961 - Noli New Testament (NNT)
1961 - Norlie's Simplified New Testament (NSNT)
1961 - Wuest Expanded Translation (WET)
1962 - Jerusalem Bible Koren (JBK)

1962 - Lattimore New Testament (LNT)
1962 - Modern King James Version (MKJV)
1963 - New Testament in Plain English (WPE)
1963 - Holy Name Bible (HNB) a.k.a. Holy Name Version HNV
1965 - Amplified Bible (AB)
1966 - Jerusalem Bible (TJB) (Catholic)
1967 - New Berkeley Version in Modern English (NBV)
1968 - Cotton Patch Version (CPV)
1969 - William Barclay New Testament (WBNT)
1969 - Bible Reader (TBR)
1969 - New Life Version (NLV)
1970 - Cotton Patch New Testament Jordan
1970 - New American Bible (NAB) (Catholic)
1970 - New English Bible (NEB)
1971 - Abbreviated Bible (TAB)
1971 - Living Bible (LB)
1972 - Bible in Living English Byington
1972 - Phillips Revised Student Edition (PRS)
1972 - Today's English New Testament (TENT)
1973 - Holy Scriptures Menorah (HSM) a.k.a. Jewish Family Bible
1976 - American Translation Beck (AAT)
1976 - Interlinear Bible Green (IB)
1976 - Restoration of Original Sacred Name Bible (SNB)
1976 - Today's English Version (TEV) a.k.a. Good News Bible
1977 - New American Standard Version (NASB)
1978 - New International Version (NIV)
1978 - Easy-to-Read Version (ERV)
1979 - King James II Version (KJII)
1980 - Reese Chronological Bible (RCB)
1980 - The Distilled Bible (TDB)
1980 - The Easy Bible (TEB)
1980 - Versified Rendering of the Complete Gospel Story (VRGS)
1981 - Sacred Scriptures, Bethel Edition (SSBE)
1982 - New King James Version (NKJV)
1982 - Reader's Digest Bible (RDB)
1984 - New World Translation (NWT)
1985 - New Jerusalem Bible (NJB) (Catholic)
1985 - Original New Testament (ONT)
1987 - Aramaic Bible Targums (ABT)
1987 - New Century Version (NCV)
1988 - New JPS Version (NJPS)
1988 - Word Made Fresh (WMF)
1989 - Cassirer New Testament (CNT)
1989 - Complete Jewish Bible (CJB)

From the NKJV to Today

1989 - Dramatized Bible Perry (DBP)
1989 - English Version for the Deaf (EVD)
1989 - McCord's New Testament Translation (MCT)
1989 - New Revised Standard Version (NRSV)
1989 - Revised English Bible (REB)
1989 - William Tindale Newe Testament (WTNT)
1990 - New King James Version (NKJ)
1991 - Recovery Version (RcV)
1991 - New Century Version (NCV)
1991 - Unvarnished New Testament (UNT)
1992 - Contemporary English Version (CEV)
1992 - New Evangelical Translation (NET)
1993 - Black Bible Chronicles McCary
1993 - The Message (TM or MSG)
1993 - Scholars Version (SV)
1994 - 21st Century King James Version (KJ21)
1994 - The Clear Word (CW)
1995 - Christian Community Bible Grogan
1995 - God's Word (GW) a.k.a. Today's Bible Translation
1995 - Inclusive Version (AIV)
1995 - New Testament: An Understandable Version (NTUV)
1996 - Aramaic New Covenant (ANCJ)
1996 - New Living Translation (NLT)
1996 - New International Version Inclusive Language (NIVI)
1996 - Orthodox Jewish Brit Chadasha (OJBC)
1996 - Stone Edition of the Tanach (SET)
1997 - Dead Sea Scrolls Bible (DSSB)
1998 - International Standard Version (ISV)
1998 - Revised King James New Testament (RKJV)
1998 - Scriptures (ISR) (SISR)
1998 - King James Clarified New Testament (KJCNT)
1998 - New Authorized Version (NAV)
1999 - New Millennium Bible (NMB)
1999 - American King James Version (AKJV)
1999 - Holman Christian Standard Bible (HCSB)
2000 - English Jubilee Bible (EJB)
2000 - King James 2000 Version, (KJ2000)
2000 - Updated King James Version (UKJV)
2001 - English Standard Version (ESV)
2001 - Today's New International Version (TNIV)
2003 - Comfort-able King James Version (CKJV)
2003 - New Simplified Bible (NSB)
2003 - Plain English Bible (PEB)
2003 - Updated Bible Version (UPDV)

2003 - Word of Yahweh (WOY)
2004 - Defined King James Bible (DKJB)
2005 - De Nyew Testament in Gullah (NTG)
2005 - Easy English Bible Translation (EEB)
2005 - Translator's New Testament (TNT)
2007 - New Century Version (NCV) updated
2008 - Comprehensive New Testament (CNT)
2008 - The Free Bible (TFB)
2008 - Modern American Standard Version (MASV)
2008 - Transparent English Bible (TEB)
2009 - Restored Name King James Version (RNKJ)
2010 - LOLCat Bible (LOL)
2011 - Common English Bible (CEB)
2011 - Easy Study Bible (ESB)
2011 - New American Bible Revised Edition (NABRE)
2011 - New EVersion (NEV)
2012 - Mirror Bible (MB)
2012 - Queen James Bible (QJV)
2012 - Tree of Life Bible Version (TLV)
2013 - Wilton Translation of the New Testament (WTNT)
2014 - Modern English Version (MEV)
2014 - The Passion Translation (TPT)
2014 - Revised English Version (REV)
2016 - Modern Evangelical Version (MEV)
2017 - Christian Standard Bible (CSB)
2019 - Revised New Jerusalem Bible (RNJB)

In actually, this list only includes a couple hundred of the various Bibles versions – there are hundreds more that are not listed!

Truly, the enemy has come in like a flood. It is time to lift up God's standard. *"So shall they fear the name of the LORD from the west, and his glory from the rising of the sun. When the enemy shall come in like a flood, the Spirit of the LORD shall lift up a standard against him."* Isaiah 59:19

Examples of Modern Bible Changes Affecting Doctrine

The following are just a few examples of how changing one or more words can change the doctrinal meaning – from the truth of God in the **KJV** – into a lie in the corrupted versions. Apparently, others have noted the same thing:

"Consider something very important. <u>There may be many translations, but there are only two Bibles. One is the Bible of Catholicism and the other is the Bible of the apostolic church, the Waldenses and the Reformation</u>. One has been in the continual possession of God's faithful, the other in the possession of the "great whore." One presents the clear teaching of God's word and is doctrinally sound, while the other presents the confusing concepts of pagan philosophy and mingles the truth with "doctrines of devils."
(*The Diabolical Dangers and Doctrinal Destruction in the Modern Bible Versions*, pg. 46)

Only Two Bibles
The Bible of the Faithful or the Bible of the Great Whore

It is past time for God's people to wake up, because *"Form criticism and its corollary, oral tradition, along with historical criticism, have made a mighty move against Adventism and its central doctrines, thus diminishing the authority of Scripture and the Spirit of Prophecy and yet going largely unnoticed."*
(*Assault on the Remnant*, p.251)

Take note of how the old pure-line Bible versions agree and harmonize with the **KJV** and then compare this with the discrepancies and dissonance that the modern versions create. Also observe how the modern versions, in many cases, are creeping back, not only to match Papal doctrines, but in many cases to actually match the **Papal Douay Rheims/Latin Vulgate Version** decreed at the council of Trent (held in defiance of the Protestant Reformation) to be the only authentic Bible.

"The argument was hailed in the council as of Inspiration only; the party for "Scripture alone," surrendered; and the council at once unanimously condemned

Protestantism and the whole Reformation as only an unwarranted revolt from the communion and authority of the Catholic Church; and proceeded, April 8, 1546 'to the promulgation of two decrees, the first of which enacts, under anathema, that Scripture and tradition are to be received and venerated equally, and that the deutero-canonical {the apocryphal} books are part of the cannon of Scripture. <u>The second decree declares the Vulgate to be the sole authentic and standard Latin version, and gives it such authority as to supersede the original texts</u>; forbids the interpretation of Scripture contrary to the sense received by the Church, 'or even contrary to the unanimous consent of the Fathers,' etc."

(*Rome's Challenge: Why Do Protestants Keep Sunday?* p. 22-23)

It would be well to remember the counsel of the Reformer, Martin Luther.

"<u>No greater mischief can happen to a Christian people than to have God's word taken from them, or falsified so that they no longer have it pure and clear.</u> God grant the we and our descendants be not witnesses of such a calamity."

(Kepler, the *Table Talk of Martin Luther*, pg. 10 quoted in *The Men, Motives & Malicious Mutilations behind the Modern Bible Versions*, pg. 4)

How Modern Bibles differ from the Pure-line Bibles

History testifies that, *"Almost immediately after the Revised Version was released, an official Catholic publication declared: 'It (Protestantism) has also been robbed of its only proof of Bible inspiration by the correct rendering of 2 Timothy 3:16.' They continued by saying that 'perhaps the most surprising change of all is John 5:39. It is no longer "Search the Scriptures," but "Ye search;" and thus Protestantism has lost the very cause of its being.' (Dublin Review, July 1881)"*
(*The Diabolical Dangers and Doctrinal Destruction in the Modern Bible Versions*, pg. 46)

Note how the changes in 2 Timothy 3:16 (which actually make it incorrect, not correct) leave room for picking and choosing which Scriptures are inspired by God and which are not:

KJV – 2 Timothy 3:16
"<u>All scripture</u> *is given by inspiration of God, and is profitable for doctrine, for reproof, for correction, for instruction in righteousness:*"

RV – 2 Timothy 3:16
"<u>Every scripture inspired of God</u> *is also profitable for teaching...*"
ASV – 2 Timothy 3:16
"<u>Every scripture inspired of God</u> *is also profitable for teaching…*"

Many remove the COMMAND to search the Scriptures by subtly changing it into a statement:

KJV – John 5:39
"<u>Search the scriptures</u>; *for in them ye think ye have eternal life: and they are they which testify of me.*"

Examples of Modern Bible Changes Affecting Doctrine

1534 Tyndale – John 5:39
"*Searche the scriptures* for in them ye thinke ye have eternall lyfe: and they are they which testify of me."

1568 Bishops Bible – John 5:39
"*Searche the scriptures*, for in them ye thynke ye haue eternall lyfe: and they are they which testifie of me."

1587 Geneva – John 5:39
"*Searche the Scriptures*: for in them ye thinke to haue eternall life, and they are they which testifie of me."

Note how the command, in the Protestant Bibles, to search the Bible more thoroughly (in order to see that the Bible testifies of Christ) progresses, in the modern versions, to a statement where Bible reading has almost a negative connotation.

Jerusalem Bible (Catholic) – John 5:39
"*You pore over the scriptures*, believing that in them you can find eternal life; it is these scriptures that testify to me"

NKJV – John 5:39
"*You search the Scriptures*, for in them you think you have eternal life; and these are they which testify of Me."

ESV – John 5:39
"*You search the Scriptures* because you think that in them you have eternal life; and it is they that bear witness about me,"

Phillips – John 5:39
"*You pore over the scriptures* for you imagine that you will find eternal life in them. And all the time they give their testimony to me!"

NLV – John 5:39
"*You do read the Holy Writings*. You think you have life that lasts forever just because you read them. They do tell of Me."

MSG – John 5:39
"*You have your heads in your Bibles constantly* because you think you'll find eternal life there. But you miss the forest for the trees. These Scriptures are all about me!"

Changes the doctrine of hell:

KJV – 2 Peter 2:4,9
" For if God spared not the angels that sinned, but cast them down to hell, and delivered them into chains of darkness, to be *reserved unto judgment*…The Lord knoweth how to deliver the godly out of temptations, and to *reserve the unjust unto the day of judgment to be punished*:"

1534 Tyndale Bible – 2 Peter 2:4,9
"For yf god spared not the angels that synned but cast them doune into hell and delyuered them in chaynes of darknes *to be kept vnto iudgement*…The lorde

knoweth how to deliver the godly out of temptacion and how <u>to reserve the vniuste vnto the daye of iudgement for to be punisshed</u>:"

1568 Bishop's Bible – 2 Peter 2:4,9
"For if God spared not the angels that sinned, but cast them downe into hell, and delyuered them into chaynes of darknesse, <u>to be kept vnto iudgement</u>.... The Lorde knoweth howe to delyuer the godly out of temptation, and to <u>reserue the vniust vnto the day of iudgement for to be punished</u>":

According to the **KJV** and other pure-line Bibles, these verses are "future tense" – in other words, Hell is a once-for-all-time destruction of the wicked at the end of time when God pours out fire on the wicked. This also agrees with the rest of the Bible texts that describe this future event. (Malachi 4:1-3; Revelation 20:9-15; Ezekiel 28:18-19; 2 Peter 2:6; Jude 1:7)

Notice however, that the modern corrupted versions change the sense to "present tense" in order to teach that Hell is burning now and the wicked are being punished now. They are teaching the false Roman Catholic doctrine of eternally burning hell-fire, in agreement with the Roman Catholic Bibles.

1582 Douay Rheims (Catholic) – 2 Peter 2:4,9
"For if God spared not angels sinning: but with the ropes of hel being drawen downe into hel, <u>delivered them to be tormented</u>, that they should reserved unto judgment...Our Lord knoweth to deliver the godly from tentation, but to reserve the unjust unto the day of judgment to be tormented:"

1899 Douay Rheims (Catholic) – 2 Peter 2:4,9
" For if God spared not the angels that sinned, but <u>delivered them, drawn down by infernal ropes to the lower hell, unto torments,</u> to be reserved unto judgment:...The Lord knoweth how to deliver the godly from temptation, but to reserve the unjust unto the day of judgment to be tormented:"

NAB (Catholic) – 2 Peter 2:9
"...<u>to keep the unrighteous under punishment for the day of judgment</u>,"

NKJV – 2 Peter 2:9
"Then the Lord knows how to deliver the godly out of temptations and to <u>reserve the unjust under punishment for the day of judgment</u>."

ESV – 2 Peter 2:9
"then the Lord knows how to rescue the godly from trials, and <u>to keep the unrighteous under punishment until the day of judgment</u>,"

RSV – 2 Peter 2:9
"then the Lord knows how to rescue the godly from trial, and <u>to keep the unrighteous under punishment until the day of judgment</u>,"

NIV – 2 Peter 2:9
"If this is so, then the Lord knows how to rescue godly men from trials and <u>to hold the unrighteous for the day of judgment, while continuing their punishment</u>."

Examples of Modern Bible Changes Affecting Doctrine

(Note: The writer has occasionally updated spelling for easier reading)

Changes who rebelled against God:

KJV – Hebrews 3:16
"For some, when they had heard, did provoke: howbeit not all that came out of Egypt by Moses."

1535 Coverdale Bible – Hebrews 3:16
"For some whan they herde, prouoked. Howbeit not all they yt came out of Egipte by Moses."

Geneva Bible – Hebrews 3:16
"For some when they heard, prouoked him to anger: howbeit, not all that came out of Egypt by Moses."

According to the **KJV** and other pure-line Bibles, this verse is a "statement" declaring that "some" of Israel provoked God by their rebellion, but that not all of those who came out of Egypt were involved in this rebellion (ie: Caleb, Joshua, Moses, etc.)

According to the modern corrupt versions, they change this "statement" into a "question" and word it in such a way that they make it into a lie, including Godly men such as Caleb and Joshua in the rebellion of Israel.

NKJV – Hebrews 3:16
"For who, having heard, rebelled? Indeed, was it not all who came out of Egypt, led by Moses?"

ESV – Hebrews 3:16
"For who were those who heard and yet rebelled? Was it not all those who left Egypt led by Moses?"

NLT – Hebrews 3:16
"And who was it who rebelled against God, even though they heard his voice? Wasn't it the people Moses led out of Egypt?"

NIV – Hebrews 3:16
"Who were they who heard and rebelled? Were they not all those Moses led out of Egypt?"

Changes location of Christ when He ascended to Heaven:

KJV – Hebrews 9:12
"… by his own blood he entered in once into the holy place, having obtained eternal redemption for us."

1549 Matthews Bible – Hebrews 9:12
"neyther by the bloude of gotes and calues, but by hys owne bloude he entred once for al into the holye place…"

According to **KJV** and other pure-line Bibles, after Christ had been offered as the sacrifice in the "Outer Court" of this world, He then took His blood into the "Holy Place" of the heavenly sanctuary to officiate as the Mediator for mankind in the "Daily Service." In doing this, Christ is in perfect harmony with His own object lesson for this is exactly the sequence of events that is portrayed in the service of the earthly sanctuary in the Old Testament. The word "once" is a reference back to Hebrews 10:10-12 speaking of "the offering of the body of Jesus Christ once for all."

NKJV – Hebrews 9:12
"... with His own blood He entered the Most Holy Place once for all, having obtained eternal redemption."

ESV – Hebrews 9:12
"... he entered once for all into the holy places, not by means of the blood of goats and calves but by means of his own blood, thus securing an eternal redemption."

GNB – Hebrews 9:12
"... entered once and for all into the Most Holy Place, he did not take the blood of goats and bulls to offer as a sacrifice; rather, he took his own blood and obtained eternal salvation for us."

NIV – Hebrews 9:12
"... he entered the Most Holy Place once for all by his own blood, having obtained eternal redemption."

According to the modern corrupted versions, Christ skipped the "Daily Ministration" of the sanctuary service upon His ascension to heaven and went straight to the Most Holy Place for the "Day of Atonement" judgment. This is a very attractive teaching to those who want to discredit the precise symbolism pointing to Christ as our High Priest and the correct process of the judgment.

There is also absolutely no justification for this change in the modern versions. The original Greek word "hagion" that is translated in English as "holy place" is listed once for "Holy Place" or twice (repeated) for "Most Holy Place" (as in Heb. 9:3) – and in this verse, the original Greek only lists "hagion" once!

Changes the fallen angel from Satan to Jesus Christ:

According to the **KJV** and other pure line Bibles, it was Lucifer who fell from heaven and Jesus is the Day Star and Morning Star. Lucifer is the "son of the morning," not the morning or "daystar."

KJV – Isaiah 14:12
"How art thou fallen from heaven, O Lucifer, son of the morning! how art thou cut down to the ground, which didst weaken the nations!"

KJV – Revelation 22:16
"I Jesus have sent mine angel to testify unto you these things in the churches. I am the root and the offspring of David, and the bright and morning star."

Examples of Modern Bible Changes Affecting Doctrine

KJV – 2 Peter 1:19
"We have also a more sure word of prophecy; whereunto ye do well that ye take heed, as unto a light that shineth in a dark place, until the day dawn, and the <u>day star</u> arise in your hearts:"

1568 Bishops Bible – Isaiah 14:12
"Howe art thou fallen from heauen O <u>Lucifer</u>, thou faire mornyng chylde? Howe hast thou gotten a fall euen to the grounde, which didst weaken the nations?"

1568 Bishops Bible – Revelation 22:16
" I Iesus sent myne angell, to testifie vnto you these thynges in ye Churches. I am the roote and the generation of Dauid, and the bryght <u>mornyng starre</u>."

1568 Bishops Bible – 2 Peter 1:19
"We haue also a ryght sure worde of prophesie, wherevnto yf ye take heede, as vnto a lyght that shyneth in a darke place, ye do well, vntyll the day dawne, and the <u>day starre</u> arise in your heartes."

According to the modern corrupted versions, if one cross-references this text with 2 Peter 1:19 and Revelation 22:16, they find that it was not Lucifer, but rather Jesus, who fell from heaven. Sadly, this has caused confusion to many readers.

ESV – Isaiah 14:12
"How you are fallen from heaven, O <u>Day Star</u>, son of Dawn! How you are cut down to the ground, you who laid the nations low!"

NIV – Isaiah 14:12
"How you have fallen from heaven, O <u>morning star</u>, son of the dawn! You have been cast down to the earth, you who once laid low the nations!"

RSV – Isaiah 14:12
"How you are fallen from heaven, O <u>Day Star</u>, son of Dawn! How you are cut down to the ground, you who laid the nations low!"

ASV – Isaiah 14:12
"How art thou fallen from heaven, O <u>day-star</u>, son of the morning! how art thou cut down to the ground, that didst lay low the nations!"

If one traces this back to the **Olivetan Bible** (a gift from the Waldensian church in the Wilderness to the Protestant Reformation) renders Isaiah 14:12 thus *"Cos ment es tu cheute du ciel o estoille tournale, sortont de matin?"* Written modernly, *"Comment es tu chute du ciel o étoile tournaillé, sortant du matin?"* This translates out to mean something like *"How are you falling from the heaven o star twirled/wandering round and round, coming out/outgoing of the morning?"* Thus, while the **Olivetan** does not use the word Lucifer as the **Latin Itala** probably did, it does distinctly differentiate this being from Jesus Christ, the morning star – unlike the modern versions.

Also the **1607 Italian La Bibbia Diodati** (the one that the Waldensian historian Ledger treasured) reads, *"Como sei caduto dal cielo, o Lucifero, figliuol (modern – figliol) dell' aurora?"* meaning *"How did you fall from heaven, O Lucifer, son of the dawn?"* Again, this distinctly differentiates that this being is not the same as the "day star" referred to in 2 Peter 1:19. So why is it being confused today?

Changes Prophetic Time:

KJV – Revelation 10:5-6
"And the angel which I saw stand upon the sea and upon the earth lifted up his hand to heaven, And sware by him that liveth for ever and ever, who created heaven, and the things that therein are, and the earth, and the things that therein are, and the sea, and the things which are therein, that there should be time no longer:"
Tyndale – Revelation 10:6b - *"that there shulde be no lenger tyme:"*
Coverdale – Revelation 10:6b - *"that there shalbe nomore tyme:"*
Bishops – Revelation 10:6b - *"that there shoulde be no longer tyme."*
Geneva – Revelation 10:6b - *"that time should be no more."*

According to the **KJV** and other pure-line Bibles, the Angel of Revelation 10 specifies the end of prophetic time. The use of the term "time" linking the reader to the other Bible verses specifically dealing with "time" prophecies. This was confirmed in the Advent movement of the **1840**'s.

"This time which the angel declares with a solemn oath, is not the end of this world's history, neither of probationary time, but of prophetic time, which should precede the advent of our Lord." (Manuscript Releases, vol. 1, p.100)

"This message announces the end of the prophetic periods." (Selected Messages, vol.2, p.108)

NKJV – Revelation 10:6
"...that there should be delay no longer,"
NIV – Revelation 10:6
"...There will be no more delay!"
ESV – Revelation 10:6
"...there would be no more delay,"
NLT – Revelation 10:6
"...There will be no more delay."

According to the corrupted versions, this end of prophetic time has now been removed and replaced with a no more delay reading. Delay of what? This change, among other sinister aspects, takes the doctrine from teaching that God had specified certain time prophecies that had to reach their complete fulfillment first, down to the incorrect concept that God has been, as it were, dragging His feet or wasting His time – delaying the results.

Examples of Modern Bible Changes Affecting Doctrine

Changes Resurrection of Jesus Christ:

KJV – Romans 4:25
"Who was delivered for our offences, and was raised again for our justification."
1549 Matthews Bible – Romans 4:25
"Whiche was deliuered for oure synnes and rose agayne for to iustifye vs."

According to **KJV**, Christ was raised from the dead "for" our justification – meaning that repentant sinners can be justified because He had paid the price and He overcame the power of death.

NKJV – Romans 4:25
"Who was delivered up because of our offenses, and was raised because of our justification."
LITV – Romans 4:25
"who was delivered because of our deviations, and was raised because of our justification."

According to some of the corrupted versions, Christ was not raised "for" our justification, but "because" of our justification. This changes the meaning of the verse substantially!

Changes status of Christ's coming:

KJV – John 10:10
"The thief cometh not, but for to steal, and to kill, and to destroy: I am come that they might have life, and that they might have it more abundantly."
Coverdale Bible – John 10:10b
"I am come, yt they might haue life, and haue it more abundauntly."
1568 Bishops Bible – John 10:10b
"I am come, that they myght haue lyfe, and that they myght haue it more aboundauntly."

According to the **KJV**, Christ uses the phrase *"I am come"* – which not only links the statement with Jehovah through its use of the name "I Am"; but it also is worded in a way to show past, present, and future tense (not only that Christ came 2,000 years ago, but that His presence is still with us and He will also come again.) All of this meaning is embraced with the term *"I am come."*

NKJV – John 10:10
"The thief does not come except to steal, and to kill, and to destroy. I have come that they may have life, and that they may have it more abundantly."
ESV – John 10:10
"The thief comes only to steal and kill and destroy. I came that they may have life and have it abundantly."

Sword Unsheathed

NIV – John 10:10
"The thief comes only to steal and kill and destroy; I have come that they may have life, and have it to the full."
NLT – John 10:10
"The thief's purpose is to steal and kill and destroy. My purpose is to give them a rich and satisfying life."

According to the corrupt versions, Christ coming was past tense only, or, in the case of the **NLT**, Christ' coming is totally removed.

Changes location of the Altar of Incense:

KJV – Hebrews 9:3-4
"And after the second veil, the tabernacle which is called the Holiest of all; Which had the golden censer, and the ark of the covenant overlaid round about with gold,…"
Tyndale – Hebrews 9:3-4
"But with in the secode vayle was ther a tabernacle which is called holiest of all which had the golden senser and the arcke of the testamet overlayde round about with golde…"
1568 Bishops Bible – Hebrews 9:3-4
"But after the seconde vayle [was] a tabernacle, which is called holyest of al: Which had the golden senser, and the arke of the couenaunt ouerlaide rounde about with golde…."

According to the **KJV** and other pure-line Bibles, it was the golden censer that the High Priest carried with incense in it that was in the Most Holy Place. This is in perfect agreement with the Old Testament that specifically tells that the Altar where the incense was burned was in the Holy Place but the High Priest would carry the censer into the Most Holy when he entered there.

NKJV (1984 edition) – Hebrews 9:3-4
"And behind the second veil, the part of the tabernacle which is called the Holiest of All, which had the golden altar of incense and the ark of the covenant overlaid on all sides with gold…"

Examples of Modern Bible Changes Affecting Doctrine

ESV – Hebrews 9:3-4
"Behind the second curtain was a second section called the Most Holy Place, having the golden altar of incense and the ark of the covenant covered on all sides with gold, ..."

RSV – Hebrews 9:3-4
"Behind the second curtain stood a tent called the Holy of Holies, having the golden altar of incense and the ark of the covenant covered on all sides with gold..."

NIV – Hebrews 9:3-4
"Behind the second curtain was a room called the Most Holy Place, which had the golden altar of incense and the gold-covered ark of the covenant..."

According to many of the modern corrupted versions, it wasn't the censer but rather the Altar of Incense that was in the Most Holy Place. In Exodus, the Bible distinctly states that this altar was in the Holy Place (Exodus 28:43). This altar was where the priests performed the "daily service" of mediation between God and the sinner – and the Bible specifies that the High Priest only entered the Most Holy Place "ONCE" each year (Leviticus 16:34) – so by placing the altar of incense in the Most Holy Place, there is a very subtle attack on the sanctuary symbolism of the judgment as well as an undermining of the consistency of the Bible.

Changes promise of Christ's second coming to statement by wicked:

KJV – Isaiah 66:5
"Hear the word of the LORD, ye that tremble at his word; Your brethren that hated you, that cast you out for my name's sake, said, Let the LORD be glorified: but he shall appear to your joy, and they shall be ashamed."

Geneva – Isaiah 66:5
"Heare the worde of the Lorde, all ye that tremble at his worde, Your brethren that hated you, and cast you out for my Names sake, said, Let the Lord be glorified: but he shall appeare to your ioy, and they shall be ashamed."

According to the **Geneva Bible** and the **KJV** this verse promises that there will be false-hearted brethren who throw God's people out while claiming that they are glorifying God – but then it states that when Jesus comes, it will be revealed that His people were in the right and those who turned against them and threw them out will be confused by the consciousness of their guilt and error. This is an encouraging promise to those who have been persecuted because they stood for the truth.

NKJV – Isaiah 66:5
"Hear the word of the Lord, You who tremble at His word: Your brethren who hated you, Who cast you out for My name's sake, said, Let the LORD be glorified: that we may see your joy, but they shall be ashamed."

ESV – Isaiah 66:5
"Hear the word of the LORD, you who tremble at his word: 'Your brothers who hate

you and cast you out for my name's sake have said,"'Let the LORD be glorified, that <u>we may see your joy</u>"; but it is they who shall be put to shame."
ISV – Isaiah 66:5
"Hear this message from the LORD, you who tremble at his words: 'Your own brothers who hate you and exclude you because of my name have said:"Let the LORD be glorified; <u>he will see your joy</u>," yet it is they who will be put to shame."
RV – Isaiah 66:5
"Hear the word of the LORD, ye that tremble at his word: Your brethren that hate you, that cast you out for my name's sake, have said, Let the LORD be glorified, that <u>we may see your joy</u>; but they shall be ashamed."

Here the corrupted versions are backtracking from the wisdom of a multitude of counselors consulted in the translation of the **KJV** and **Geneva Bible**. According to these modern translations, the wicked ones throwing out God's people, while making the claim that they are glorifying God, are the ones who state they are casting them out so that they may see the joy of God's people. This totally changes the meaning of the verse.

Changes nature of Jesus Christ:

KJV – Hebrews 2:16
"For verily he <u>took not on him the nature of angels</u>; but he took on him <u>the seed of Abraham</u>."
Tyndale – Hebrews 2:16
"For he in no place taketh on him the angels: but <u>the seede of Abraham</u> taketh he on him."
1568 Bishops Bible – Hebrews 2:16
"For he in no place taketh on hym the Angels: but <u>the seede of Abraham</u> taketh he on hym."

According to the **KJV** and other pure-line Bibles, Jesus Christ didn't take on a supernatural nature but rather the human nature.

NKJV – Hebrews 2:16
"For indeed He <u>does not give aid to angels</u>, but He does give aid to the seed of Abraham."
ESV – Hebrews 2:16
"For surely it is <u>not angels that he helps</u>, but he helps the offspring of Abraham."
ASV – Hebrews 2:16
"For verily not to <u>angels doth he give help</u>, but he giveth help to the seed of Abraham."

According to the modern corrupted versions, this verse is no longer talking about the kind of nature Jesus had, but rather who He helps. They totally destroy the meaning of the verse.

Examples of Modern Bible Changes Affecting Doctrine

> "Many say that Jesus was not like us, that He was not as we are in the world, that He was divine, and that we cannot overcome as He overcame. But Paul writes, **'Verily he took not on him the nature of angels; but he took on him the seed of Abraham...'"** (Selected Messages, volume 3, p. 197)

Changes being superstitious to being religious:

KJV – Acts 17:22
"Then Paul stood in the midst of Mars' hill, and said, Ye men of Athens, I perceive that in all things ye are <u>too superstitious</u>."

Coverdale – Acts 17:22
"Paul stode on the myddes of the comon place, and sayde: Ye me of Athens, I se that in all thinges ye are <u>to supersticious</u>."

Geneva – Acts 17:22
"Then Paul stoode in the mids of Mars streete, and sayde, Yee men of Athens, I perceiue that in all things yee are <u>too superstitious</u>."

According to the **KJV**, the men of Athens were a superstitious people who worshiped many pagan gods.

NKJV – Acts 17:22
"Then Paul stood in the midst of the Areopagus and said, 'Men of Athens, I perceive that in all things you are <u>very religious</u>;"

ESV – Acts 17:22
"So Paul, standing in the midst of the Areopagus, said: 'Men of Athens, I perceive that in every way you are <u>very religious</u>."

GNB – Acts 17:22
"Paul stood up in front of the city council and said, 'I see that in every way you Athenians are <u>very religious</u>."

ISV – Acts 17:22
"So Paul stood up in front of the Areopagus and said, 'Men of Athens, I see that you are <u>very religious</u> in every way."

According to the modern corrupted versions, the men of Athens were just very religious – which of course, changes the meaning of the verse extensively!

Changes the messenger:

KJV – Revelation 8:13
"And I beheld, and heard an <u>angel</u> flying through the midst of heaven, saying with a loud voice, Woe, woe, woe, to the inhabiters of the earth by reason of the other voices of the trumpet of the three angels, which are yet to sound!"

According to the **KJV** and ALL pure-line Bibles from **Tyndale** to the **Geneva Bible**, from the **French Olivetan** and the **German Luther** to the **Italian Diodati**, the messenger that flies through the sky at the end of the first four trumpets and proclaims the three woes of the last three trumpets is ALWAYS an **angel**. From where did the **eagle** in the modern versions come?

Douay Rheims (Catholic) – Revelation 8:13
"And I beheld: and heard the voice of one eagle flying through the midst of heaven, saying with a loud voice: Woe, Woe, Woe to the inhabitants of the earth, by reason of the rest of the voices of the three angels, who are yet to sound the trumpet!"

NKJV- Revelation 8:13 footnote – *"NU,M eagle"*

ESV – Revelation 8:13
"Then I looked, and I heard an eagle crying with a loud voice as it flew directly overhead, "Woe, woe, woe to those who dwell on the earth, at the blasts of the other trumpets that the three angels are about to blow!"

RSV – Revelation 8:13
"Then I looked, and I heard an eagle crying with a loud voice, as it flew in midheaven, "Woe, woe, woe to those who dwell on the earth, at the blasts of the other trumpets which the three angels are about to blow!"

NIV – Revelation 8:13
"As I watched, I heard an eagle that was flying in midair call out in a loud voice: "Woe! Woe! Woe to the inhabitants of the earth, because of the trumpet blasts about to be sounded by the other three angels!"

NLT – Revelation 8:13
"Then I looked, and I heard a single eagle crying loudly as it flew through the air, "Terror, terror, terror to all who belong to this world because of what will happen when the last three angels blow their trumpets."

According to the corrupted versions, this messenger is no longer an **angel**, it is now an **eagle**.

There is no excuse for that mistake! The Greek word in this text is "angelos" and is translated "angel" in all the Bibles which were influenced by the pure line of manuscripts. But the corrupt lines that come through the corrupt **Sinaiticus** and the corrupt **Latin Vulgate** all falsely claim that the Greek word is "aetos" which they translate as "eagle."

The writer has followed this use of the word "eagle" back as far as possible with available sources. The earliest reference found to this "eagle" is in Eusebius' corrupt **Sinaiticus** which he made for Emperor Constantine from Origen's work. It is interesting that Eusebius was good friends with Constantine and he places an "eagle" in as the messenger of the woes since the symbol for both Rome and Babylon was the eagle. **Does this effectively place the Roman standard in the holy place of God's Word?** What is dead? Has the Protestant Bible fallen prey to its persecutors (Lamentations 4:19)? Why did Jesus say in His list of last day events, *"For wheresoever the carcase is, there will the eagles be gathered together."* (Matthew 24:28)?

Examples of Modern Bible Changes Affecting Doctrine

Changes "do his commandments" to "wash their robes":

KJV – Revelation 22:14
"Blessed are they that do his commandments, that they may have right to the tree of life, and may enter in through the gates into the city."

Tyndale – Revelation 22:14
"Blessed are they that do hys commaundmentes that their power maye be in the tree of lyfe and maye entre in thorow the gates into the cite."

Geneva – Revelation 22:14
"Blessed are they, that doe his commaundements, that their right may be in the tree of life, and may enter in through the gates into the citie."

According to the **KJV**, in order to have right to the tree of Life, the redeemed have to be living up to all the light they have had the opportunity to learn, and they must be doing everything in their power to remain faithfully obedient to the Law of God – the righteous keep God's Law – all ten commandments of it.

Douay Rheims (Catholic) – Revelation 22:14
"Blessed are they that wash their robes in the blood of the Lamb: that they may have a right to the tree of life and may enter in by the gates into the city."

NIV – Revelation 22:14
"Blessed are those who wash their robes, that they may have the right to the tree of life and may go through the gates into the city."

NLT – Revelation 22:14
"Blessed are those who wash their robes. They will be permitted to enter through the gates of the city and eat the fruit from the tree of life."

ESV – Revelation 22:14
"Blessed are those who wash their robes, so that they may have the right to the tree of life and that they may enter the city by the gates."

Clear Word – Revelation 22:14
"I, John, understand that those who are blessed are those who have washed their robes in the blood of the Lamb. This is what gives them the right to the Tree of Life and to enter through the gates into the City."

Almost all the modern corrupt Bibles change this verse to read something about washing robes. There is no excuse for such error, other than in this day and age when sin is so popular and telling people that they need to obey God's Law is so "politically incorrect." It seems that people are choosing an erroneous reading that doesn't condemn their sinful lifestyles.

The original Greek term used in this verse is "ποιουντες τας εντολας αυτου" which translated literally means *"doing the commands of Him."* This phrase is translated as *"do his commandments"* in all the **pure-line manuscripts** and all the **pure-line Bibles**. The phrase *"wash their robes"* in this text only appears in **Jerome's Latin Vulgate** and the corrupt-Greek line promoted by the **Westcott and Hort text** where the phrase "πλυνοντες τας στολας αυτων" (washed the robes of them) is used.

Sword Unsheathed

For many years writers have reiterated strongly the words of Revelation 22:14, "Says the Saviour, "<u>Blessed are they that do his commandments, that they may have right to the tree of life</u>, and may enter in through the gates into the city. <u>These are the words of God;</u> they are not my words. Keep the commandments of God, and you will have a right to the tree of life." (Review & Herald, April 30, 1889)

As may be seen by these examples, changing just a few words can cause major doctrinal changes to the text – and these were just a few of the many hundreds of examples that could be given.

Notice also, how changes in the modern Bibles, move them backwards from the Protestant doctrine shown in the **KJV** to make the Bibles more closely agree with the false Roman Catholic doctrine in Catholic Bibles. The following are a few examples.

Changes Protestant "faults" to Catholic "sins":

KJV – James 5:16
"Confess your <u>faults</u> one to another, and pray one for another, that ye may be healed..."

Bishops Bible – James 5:16
"Knowledge your <u>faultes</u> one to another, and pray one for another, that ye may be healed: For ye feruent prayer of a ryghteous man auayleth much."

The Protestant pure-line Bibles all use the word "faults" in reference to what is to be *confessed* to any other man.

Douay/Rheims (Catholic) – James 5:16
"Confess therefore your <u>sins</u> one to another: and pray one for another, that you may be saved..."

Jerusalem (Catholic) – James 5:16
"So confess your <u>sins</u> to one another, and pray for one another, and this will cure you..."

NAB (Catholic) – James 5:16
"Therefore, confess your <u>sins</u> to one another and pray for one another, that you may be healed."

ASV – James 5:16
"Confess therefore your <u>sins</u> one to another, and pray one for another, that ye may be healed..."

ESV – James 5:16
"Therefore, confess your <u>sins</u> to one another and pray for one another, that you may be healed..."

NIV – James 5:16
"Therefore confess your <u>sins</u> to each other and pray for each other so that you may be healed..."

Examples of Modern Bible Changes Affecting Doctrine

NLT – James 5:16
"Confess your sins to each other and pray for each other so that you may be healed..."

NKJV – James 5:16
"Confess your trespasses to one another, and pray for one another, that ye may be healed." with discrediting margin note: *"5:16 NU Therefore confess your sins"*

Modern corrupt Bibles change the word "faults" to "sins" in order to promote Papalism's claims to be able to "forgive sins."

"Says the apostle: 'Confess your faults one to another, and pray one for another, that ye may be healed.' This scripture has been interpreted to sustain the practice of going to the priest for absolution; but it has no such application. Confess your sins to God, who only can forgive them, and your faults to one another." (5T, p. 639)

Changes Protestant "Bible Study" to a Catholic Generic Works Term

Note how the modern versions put Protestants back on the Road to Rome by matching closely the Counter-Reformation's **Douay Rheims** and eliminating the command to study the Bible (which would expose any false doctrine).

KJV – 2 Timothy 2:15
"Study to shew thyself approved unto God, a workman that needeth not to be ashamed, rightly dividing the word of truth."

1549 Matthews – 2 Timothy 2:15
"Studye to shewe thy selfe laudable vnto God a workeman that nedeth not to be ashamed dyuydynge the worde of truste iustelye."

Geneva – 2 Timothy 2:15
"Studie to shewe thy selfe approued vnto God, a workeman that needeth not to be ashamed, diuiding the worde of trueth aright."

1582 Douay/Rheims – 2 Timothy 2:15
"Carefully prouide to present thy self approued to God, a worke-man not to be confounded, rightly handling the word of truth."

Jerusalem *(Catholic)* – 2 Timothy 2:15
"Do all you can to present yourself in front of God..."

NAB *(Catholic)* – 2 Timothy 2:15
"Be eager to present yourself as acceptable to God..."

ASV – 2 Timothy 2:15
"Give diligence to present thyself approved unto God... handling aright..."

NKJV – 2 Timothy 2:15
"Be diligent to present yourself approved to God..."

ESV – 2 Timothy 2:15
"Do your best to present yourself to God..."

NIV – 2 Timothy 2:15
"Do your best to present yourself to God..."

NLT – 2 Timothy 2:15
Work hard so God can approve you...

The modern corrupt Bibles remove the word "study" and replace it with any generic works term. In addition, they change the correct term "dividing" to the incorrect term "rightly handling" (which could refer to doing it the way directed by the priest).

Completely removes text in order to support false doctrine of infant baptism:

KJV – Acts 8:36-38
"And as they went on their way, they came unto a certain water: and the eunuch said, See, here is water; what doth hinder me to be baptized? And Philip said, If thou believest with all thine heart, thou mayest. And he answered and said, I believe that Jesus Christ is the Son of God. And he commanded the chariot to stand still: and they went down both into the water, both Philip and the eunuch; and he baptized him."

Jerusalem (Catholic) – Acts 8:37
omitted
NAB (Catholic) – Acts 8:37
omitted
ASV – Acts 8:37
omitted
(some editions contain it in italics with discrediting footnote)
NKJV – Acts 8:37
contains it but contains a discrediting margin note: "NU, M omit v.37"
NASB – Acts 8:37
contains this discredit "[many mss do not contain this verse]"
ESV – Acts 8:37
omitted
RSV – Acts 8:37
omitted
NIV – Acts 8:37
omitted
NLT – Acts 8:37
omitted

Modern corrupt Bibles, in order to promote the Catholic practice of baptizing infants, remove this text that shows that a person has to make an intelligent choice to believe in Jesus.

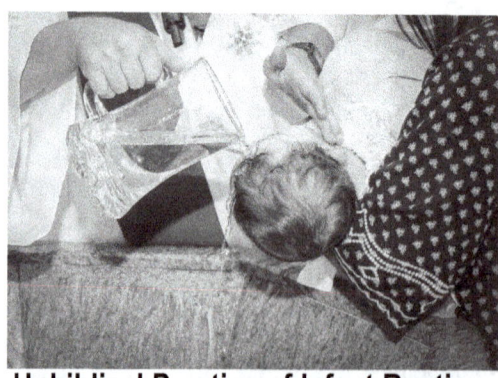

Unbiblical Practice of Infant Baptism

Examples of Modern Bible Changes Affecting Doctrine

Demotes God and Christ by removing the word "wise":

KJV – 1 Timothy 1:17
"Now unto the King eternal, immortal, invisible, the only wise God, be honour and glory for ever and ever. Amen."

Coverdale – 1 Timothy 1:17
"So then vnto God kynge euerlastinge, immortall and invisible, and wyse onely, be honoure and prayse for euer and euer Amen."

Jerusalem (Catholic) – 1 Timothy 1:17
"...invisible and only God..."

NAB (Catholic) – 1 Timothy 1:17
"...the only God..."

ASV – 1 Timothy 1:17
"...the only God..."

NKJV – 1 Timothy 1:17
contains it but with a discrediting margin note: *"NU the only God"*

NASB – 1 Timothy 1:17
"...the only God..."

ESV – 1 Timothy 1:17
"...the only God,..."

RSV – 1 Timothy 1:17
"...the only God..."

NIV – 1 Timothy 1:17
"...the only God..."

NLT – 1 Timothy 1:17
"...he alone is God..."

Modern corrupt Bibles remove God's "wise" characteristic, His omniscience.

Removes Jesus Christ as Creator:

KJV – Ephesians 3:9
"And to make all men see what is the fellowship of the mystery, which from the beginning of the world hath been hid in God, who created all things by Jesus Christ:"

Tyndale – Ephesians 3:9
"...in God which made all thynges thorow Iesus Christ"

Douay/Rheims (Catholic) – Ephesians 3:9
"...in God who created all things:"

Jerusalem (Catholic) – Ephesians 3:9
"...in God, the creator of everything."

NAB (Catholic) – Ephesians 3:9
"...in God who created all things"
ASV – Ephesians 3:9
"...in God who created all things"
NKJV – Ephesians 3:9
margin: *"NU omits through Jesus Christ"*
NASB – Ephesians 3:9
"...in God, who created all things;"
ESV – Ephesians 3:9
"...in God who created all things,"
RSV – Ephesians 3:9
"...in God who created all things;"
NIV – Ephesians 3:9
"...in God, who created all things."
NLT – Ephesians 3:9
"...God, the Creator of all things"

Removes the specification of Christ as the gospel:

KJV – Romans 1:16
"For I am not ashamed of the gospel of Christ: for it is the power of God unto salvation to every one that believeth; to the Jew first, and also to the Greek."
1549 Matthews Bible – Romans 1:16
"For I am not ashamed of the Gospel of Christ, because it is the power of God vnto saluacion to all that beleue, namely to þe Iewe and also to the gentyle."

Douay/Rheims (Catholic) – Romans 1:16
"...not ashamed of the gospel. For it is the power of God..."
Jerusalem (Catholic) – Romans 1:16
"...not ashamed of the Good News:..."
NAB (Catholic) – Romans 1:16
"...am not ashamed of the gospel. It is the power of God..."
ASV – Romans 1:16
"...not ashamed of the gospel: for it is the power of God..."
NKJV – Romans 1:16
margin: *"NU omits of Christ"*
NASB – Romans 1:16
"...not ashamed of the gospel, for it is the power of God..."
ESV – Romans 1:16
"...not ashamed of the gospel, for it is the power of God..."
RSV – Romans 1:16
"...not ashamed of the gospel: it is the power of God..."
NIV – Romans 1:16
"...not ashamed of the gospel, because it is the power of God..."

Examples of Modern Bible Changes Affecting Doctrine

Takes "God" out of the flesh removing the deity of Christ:

KJV – 1 Timothy 3:16
"And without controversy great is the mystery of godliness: <u>God</u> was manifest in the flesh, justified in the Spirit, seen of angels, preached unto the Gentiles, believed on in the world, received up into glory."

Geneva – 1 Timothy 3:16
"And without controuersie, great is the mysterie of godlinesse, which is, <u>God</u> is manifested in the flesh, iustified in the Spirit, seene of Angels, preached vnto the Gentiles, beleeued on in the world, and receiued vp in glorie."

Note: The Greek word used here is "Theos," meaning God, NOT just a generic term like "he."

Douay/Rheims (Catholic) – 1 Timothy 3:16
"And manifestly it is a great sacrament of pietie, <u>which</u> was manifested in flesh..."

Jerusalem (Catholic) – 1 Timothy 3:16
"Without any doubt, the mystery of our religion is very deep indeed: <u>He</u> was made visible in the flesh..."

NAB (Catholic) – 1 Timothy 3:16
"Undeniably great is the mystery of devotion, <u>Who</u> was manifested in the flesh..."

ASV – 1 Timothy 3:16
"...<u>He</u> who was manifested in the flesh.."

NKJV – 1 Timothy 3:16
margin: *"NU <u>Who</u>"*

NASB – 1 Timothy 3:16
"...<u>He</u> who was revealed in the flesh..."

ESV – 1 Timothy 3:16
"...<u>He</u> was manifested in the flesh..."

RSV – 1 Timothy 3:16
"...mystery of our religion: <u>He</u> was manifested in the flesh.."

NIV – 1 Timothy 3:16
"...<u>He</u> appeared in a body,..."

Takes out "Christ is come in the flesh" – making modern corrupt antichrist Bibles?

KJV – 1 John 4:3
"And every spirit that confesseth not that <u>Jesus Christ</u> is come in the <u>flesh</u> is not of God: and this is that spirit of antichrist, whereof ye have heard that it should come; and even now already is it in the world"

Tyndale – 1 John 4:3
"And every sprete which cofesseth not yt <u>Iesus Christ</u> is come in the <u>flesshe</u> is not of God. And this is that sprete of Antichrist of whom ye have hearde howe that he shuld come: and even now alredy is he in the worlde."

Geneva – 1 John 4:3
"And euery spirit that confesseth not that <u>Iesus Christ</u> is come in the <u>flesh</u>, is not of God: but this is the spirit of Antichrist, ..."

Despite the fact that the word for Jesus (Ἰησοῦς – Iēsous) and Christ (Χριστός – Christos) are included in the Greek, the word "Christ" has been eliminated in this verse in the following versions. This is of significance because the word "Christ" means "anointed," that is, the "Messiah," more closely specifying the Jesus of the Bible.

Douay/Rheims (Catholic) – 1 John 4:3
"every spirit that dissolveth Jesus is not of God..."
Jerusalem (Catholic) – 1 John 4:3
"any spirit which will not say this of Jesus is not from God,..."
NAB (Catholic) – 1 John 4:3
"and every spirit that does not acknowledge Jesus does not belong to God...."
ASV – 1 John 4:3
"and every spirit that confesseth not Jesus is not of God..."
NKJV – 1 John 4:3
margin: *"NU omits that Christ has come in the flesh"*
NASB – 1 John 4:3
"and every spirit that does not confess Jesus is not from God..."
ESV – 1 John 4:3
"and every spirit that does not confess Jesus is not from God..."
RSV – 1 John 4:3
"and every spirit which does not confess Jesus is not of God..."
NIV – 1 John 4:3
"but every spirit that does not acknowledge Jesus is not from God..."

Removes "Christ" as our source of strength replacing it with a generic term:

KJV – Philippians 4:13
"I can do all things through <u>Christ</u> which strengtheneth me."
Coverdale – Philippians 4:13
" I can do all thinges thorow <u>Christ</u>, which stregtheth me."
1549 Matthews Bible – Philippians 4:13
"I can do al thinges thorowe the helpe of <u>Christe</u> whiche strengtheth me."

The word for Christ (Χριστός – Christos) is included here in the Greek, but the word "Christ" has been replaced with a generic (New Age acceptable) term in this verse in the following versions.

Douay/Rheims (Catholic) – Philippians 4:13
"I can do all things in <u>him</u> who strengtheneth me"

Examples of Modern Bible Changes Affecting Doctrine

Jerusalem (Catholic) – Philippians 4:13
"There is nothing I cannot master with the help of the One who gives me strength."
NAB (Catholic) – Philippians 4:13
"I have the strength for everything through him who empowers me."
ASV – Philippians 4:13
"I can do all things in him that strengtheneth me."
NKJV – Philippians 4:13
margin: *"NU him who"*
NASB – Philippians 4:13
"I can do all things through Him who strengthens me."
ESV – Philippians 4:13
"I can do all things through him who strengthens me."
RSV – Philippians 4:13
"I can do all things in him who strengthens me."
NIV – Philippians 4:13
"I can do everything through him who gives me strength."

Sadly, when a vague, generic term is used here in this verse, this promise/phrase could refer to a patron saint, a false prophet, or the pope, etc.

Removes the "mark" of the beast:

In pure-line Bibles there are three separate & distinct identifiers that the righteous are counseled to avoid.

KJV – Revelation 13:17
"And that no man might buy or sell, save he that had the mark, or the name of the beast, or the number of his name."
Tyndale – Revelation 13:17
"And that no ma myght by or sell save he that had the marke or the name of the beest other the nombre of his name."

Note that the "mark" is missing in the Catholic/corrupted Bibles

Douay/Rheims (Catholic) – Revelation 13:17
"And that no man might buy or sell, but he that hath the character, or the name of the beast, or the number of his name."
Jerusalem (Catholic) – Revelation 13:17
"and made it illegal for anyone to buy or sell anything unless he had been branded with the name of the beast or with the number of its name."
NAB (Catholic) – Revelation 13:17
"so that no one could buy or sell except one who had the stamped image of the beast's name or the number that stood for its name."

Sword Unsheathed

Notice how these corrupt Bibles cleverly make it look as if they are listing three characteristics while they are actually narrowing it down to two.

ESV – Revelation 13:17
"so that no one can buy or sell unless he has the mark, that is, the name of the beast or the number of its name."

NIV – Revelation 13:17
"so that no one could buy or sell unless he had the mark, which is the name of the beast or the number of his name."

This is no accident for it is repeated in Revelation 15:2, again in contrast to the pure-line Bibles.

KJV – Revelation 15:2
"And I saw as it were a sea of glass mingled with fire: and them that had gotten the victory over the beast, and over his image, and over his mark, and over the number of his name, stand on the sea of glass, having the harps of God."

Tyndale – Revelation 15:2
"And I sawe as it were a glassye see mingled with fyre and the that had gotten victory of the beest and of his ymage and of his marke and of the nombre of his name stode on the glassye see havinge ye harpes of God"

Geneva – Revelation 15:2
"And I sawe as it were a glassie sea, mingled with fire, and them that had gotten victorie of the beast, and of his image, and of his marke, and of the number of his name, stand at the glassie sea, hauing the harpes of God,"

Douay/Rheims (Catholic) – Revelation 15:2
"And I saw as it were a sea of glass mingled with fire: and them that had overcome the beast and his image [?missing "mark"] and the number of his name, standing on the sea of glass, having the harps of God:"

NAB (Catholic) – Revelation 15:2
"Then I saw something like a sea of glass mingled with fire. On the sea of glass were standing those who had won the victory over the beast and its image [?missing "mark"] and the number that signified its name. They were holding God's harps,"

ESV – Revelation 15:2
"And I saw what appeared to be a sea of glass mingled with fire—and also those who had conquered the beast and its image [?missing "mark"] and the number of its name, standing beside the sea of glass with harps of God in their hands"

NIV – Revelation 15:2
"And I saw what looked like a sea of glass mixed with fire and, standing beside the sea, those who had been victorious over the beast and his image [?missing "mark"] and over the number of his name. They held harps given them by God"

Examples of Modern Bible Changes Affecting Doctrine

Indeed, there seems to be a deliberate attempt to change the word of God and create a clever counterfeit by slowly removing and changing select words and phrases to culminate in a more generic, ecumenical, unsharpened sword.

Is this fulfilling the sinister plot that atheist, Dr. Richard Day, an insider of "the Order," revealed in his **March 20, 1969** Speech to the Pittsburgh Pediatric Society?

"But the major religions of today have to be changed because they are not compatible with the changes to come…In order to do this, the Bible will be changed. It will be rewritten to fit the new religion. Gradually, key words will be replaced with new words having various shades of meaning. Then, the meaning attached to the new word can be close to the old word. And as time goes on, other shades of meaning of that word can be emphasized, and then gradually that word replaced with another word. I don't know if I'm making that clear.

"But the idea is that everything in Scripture need not be rewritten, just key words replaced by other words. And the variability in meaning attached to any word can be used as a tool to change the entire meaning of Scripture, and therefore

New World Order Insider Exposes Planned Bible Corruption in 1969

Dr. Richard Day (1927-1989) was a professor of Pediatrics the University of Pittsburgh and Mount Sinai Medical School in NY and National Medical Director of Planned Parenthood (1965-1968) which is funded, by the government, the Rockefeller Foundation (since its inception in 1921) and private donors.

Dr. Lawrence Dunegan (1923–2004) was Practicing Pediatrician in Mt. Lebanon, PA for over 34 years. The following is quoted from his recollections of a lecture he attended on March 20, 1969 at a meeting of Pediatricians.

The transcribed document titled ,NWO PLANS EXPOSED BY INSIDER in 1969, outlines the complete destruction of the world based on the "New World System."1

"**In order to do this, the Bible will be changed.** It will be rewritten to fit the new religion. Gradually, **key words will be replaced with new words having various shades of meaning.** Then the meaning attached to the new word can be close to the old word - and as time goes on, other shades of meaning of that word can be emphasized and then gradually that word replaced with another word.

1 http://www.stopthecrime.net/docs/NWO%20Plans%20Exposed%20By%20Insider%20in%201969.pdf

make it acceptable to this new religion. Most people won't know the difference; and this was another one of the times where he said, 'the few who do notice the difference won't be enough to matter.'

"Then followed one of the most surprising statements of the whole presentation: He said, 'some of you probably think the churches won't stand for this,' and he went on to say, 'The churches will help us!'" (Shadow Government – The New Order of the Barbarians – 1988 reminiscences by Dr. Lawrence Dunegan)

Consider what Fenton Hort, one of the original authors of this *"dastardly deed,"* had to say about the effect of their changes to the Bible. *"I do not think the significance of their existence is generally understood. It is quite impossible to judge the value of what appears to be trifling alterations merely by reading them one after another.*

<u>*Taken together they often have important bearings which few would think of at first.*</u>*"* (*The Life and Letters of Fenton John Anthony Hort*, Vol II, pg. 102 quoted in *The Men, Motives & Malicious Mutilations behind the Modern Bible Versions*, pg. 29)

It is time to follow the counsel in Jude which *"exhort[s] you that ye should earnestly contend for the faith which was once delivered unto the saints."* Jude 1:3

God's people are to have discernment. As Charles Spurgeon once said, *"Discernment is not knowing the difference between right and wrong. It is knowing the difference between right and almost right."*

Without a doubt then, God's true people will treasure the *unadulterated* word of God for it is written, *"<u>Blessed is he that readeth</u>, and they that hear the words of this prophecy, <u>and **keep** those things which are written therein</u>: for the time is at hand."* Revelation 1:3

What about Foreign Bibles?

Whan looking for a well-translated Bible, especially that in a foreign language, the words of Martin Luther should be kept in mind. *"Translating [the Bible] is certainly not everybody's business, as the mad saints imagine; it requires a genuinely pious, faithful, diligent, God-fearing experienced, practiced heart. Therefore, I hold that a false Christian or a sectarian spirit is unable to give a faithful translation."* (Green, Unholy Hands on the Bible, Vol. II, pg. 313, quoted in The Men, Motives and Mutilations behind the Modern Bible Versions, pg. 42)

Historically, despite many sincere missionaries best efforts at translating the Bible accurately into a foreign language, they can be at a distinct disadvantage. Because often they are new to the language, they have to depend heavily on others, who may not be even be Christians, for translation help. There are also many other obstacles and challenges to translation. Although there are currently a few, rarely, has the writer or his family found foreign Bibles that are perfectly translated and that match up to the standard of the **KJV**. Thus, missionaries in the field must ask for some extra guidance from the Holy Spirit for their readers and God's special blessing on these **"Wycliffe Bibles"** while the missionaries continue to work toward a **"Tyndale"** or a **"King James"** equivalent.

However, all the inaccuracies, especially in more recent foreign Bibles are not accidental. It is a sad state of affairs that the majority of Bible translation being carried on today, is done by the various Bible Societies which are, to a great extent, controlled in some degree by the Papal Church and use the critical texts. This unfortunate fact means that the vast majority of foreign language Bibles are based in the corrupt texts and manuscripts. This means that many times words are changed to something else that they don't mean.

For example, in Revelation 12 in the **KJV**, there are several references to the "dragon" (which is Satan – Rev. 12:9, 20:2). But in the African **Kwangali Bible**, published in **1987**, the word "dragon" has been replaced with the word for "rainbow." So from this corrupt Bible, readers are taught that it is a rainbow (the symbol for God's covenant – Genesis 9:13,16) that is waging war against God and His people.

African Kwangali Bible uses the word "Rainbow" in Revelation 12 instead of *"Dragon"*

Sword Unsheathed

"Even more sinister is it, that in Latin America the distribution of these modern Bible versions, approved of Rome, is seen as a powerful weapon in the Roman Catholic counterattack against the inroads of Protestantism in that part of the world. 'Ecumenical cooperation...which includes the distribution of the over one million Bibles a year, has been successful in minimizing the divisive inroads of sectarian proselytizing.'" (Modern Bible Translations Unmasked, p.109)

"In 1984 the Burundi Bible Society arranged to print '40,000 copies of the traditional Catholic version of the New Testament in Kirundi...The UBS signed an agreement with the Roman Catholic bishopric in Burundi regarding the production of this edition, which will be printed until the new interconfessional translation is completed." (UBS Report 1984.21)

"...the General Secretary of the Bible Society of Cameroun reported: The visit of the Pope to Cameroun was an opportunity for distribution of Scriptures among Roman Catholics. We supplied a summary of our activities to the Holy See and the Pope mentioned it with satisfaction during his visit to our country... Many of our translation projects, most of which are interconfessional, are progressing extremely well." (Modern Bible Translations Unmasked, p.110)

In some cases, places that had a good pure-line Bible in the past, have lost it, because the language has changed so much (in some cases changing from a Roman script to an Arabic script) that the old language cannot be read or understood anymore. Often the only translations into the language of today are from the corrupt versions. This is true of the Chinese and the Urdu languages. For example, Missionary Robert Morrison translated the pure-line Bible into Chinese and it was published in **1823**. Traditionally, Chinese, Japanese, and Korean were written vertically in columns going from top to bottom and ordered from right to left, with each new column starting to the left of the preceding one. The front of the book was what we would consider the back of the book. But modern Chinese has changed from Morrison's day. Instead of reading like it used to, right to left like Hebrew, it now reads left to right like English. It also uses simplified characters instead of the traditional ones. Thankfully, a group called Bible Believers of Washington have now, as of **2019**, produced a better **KJV**-equivalent **Chinese Bible**.

1813 Morrison Chinese Bible (John 1) reading in columns right to left

What about Foreign Bibles?

In some cases, Bibles in other languages have a lot of changes or missing text. The pure-line **KJV** states in Psalm 19:1 *"The heavens declare the glory of God; and the firmament sheweth his handywork."* But in the Telegu Bible and in several Hmong Bibles, this text only says, "The heavens declare the glory of God" – the rest of the text is missing, the same thought is not even repeated for emphasis (which might indicate a lack of different characters for the thought).

Another aspect, that makes foreign Bible translation a rather difficult task, is the differences in languages. Martin Luther realized this when he stated: *"I have undertaken to translate the Bible into German. This was good for me; otherwise I might have died in the mistaken notion that I was a learned fellow."*

Sometimes the language is more complex in grammar and words are more specific to number, gender, or other details than in English. For example, early missionaries to the Nama people (then called Bushman), who lived in parts of South Africa and Namibia, found that *"these Bushmen are so precise that, as in many other tongues, they wanted to know whether more than two shepherds were abiding in the field at St. Luke ii, 8; and which was the elder brother of St. Luke xii, 13, in order that they might use the term appropriate, in their language."*

(*The Bible Throughout the World*, pg. 65)

Missionaries to India in the Bengal region found that *"Santali is one of the many tongues throughout the world which use inclusive and exclusive pronouns. The word for the first person plural must be either in the one form or the other. How then are we to translate "our trespasses" in the Lord's Prayer; or "Carest thou not that we perish" in the storm on the lake? The Prayer as said by Jesus would have to be different from that said by us, for He had no trespasses to be forgiven. And did the Disciples mean to suggest that He would save himself during' the storm and let them perish?"* (*The Bible Throughout the World*, pg. 118)

Other missionaries encountered a most unique translation problem among natives. *"Kele is one of the languages of which there are many examples in South Africa, in India and other parts of the world, where 'women's words' abound. This means that certain terms are used by women, but not by men, and vice versa. It is stated that at one time the Parable of the Lost Sheep could not be put into this Congo tongue in a version which could be used by both sexes. It appears that there was some taboo associated with the Kele word for ninety-nine."*

(*The Bible Throughout the World*, pg. 89)

In addition, it is found that many native languages use a whole phrase for a "simple" English word. Consider the story of a South American language in Paraguay and *"R. J. Hunt, who reduced the language to writing. As one illustration of the difficulty of this achievement, he tells how the Lengua word for 'eighteen',* **sohog-emek-wakthlamok-eminik-antanthlama**, *is literally made up by a combination of 'finish my hands, pass to my other foot, three', for fingers and toes are their only numerators."* (*The Bible Throughout the World*, pg. 166)

Sword Unsheathed

In the translation process, sometimes you will find that there are not any equivalent words in the target language. The reader my better understand this problem by reading about Rachel Saint, the sister of Nate Saint, one of the five missionaries who was killed by the Auca Indians. She translated the Bible into the Waodani language.

"The task before Rachel was a daunting one. How to tell the parable of the lost sheep, when they had never seen a sheep? How to say Jesus rode on a donkey when they had never seen a donkey? How to describe a manger when they had no hay, no ox, shepherds or angels? How to describe the desert when they knew only jungle? How to describe the Sea of Galilee when they knew only the river? The problems were endless." (A Saint among Savages, p.122)

Sometimes a translator might need a whole sentence to explain a concept that the English and Greek language contains in a single word. This explanation might make perfectly good sense within the culture of the target language, but it might not make sense to someone from outside that culture, so it can be rather difficult for an outsider to figure out some things about a Bible's accuracy.

A good story to illustrate this point is of a missionary translating the phrase "God redeemed us" in Bambara, which is spoken in Mali, West Africa. *"The literal translation for the phrase is 'God took our heads out.' The Africans had memories of Arab slave traders forcing men and women to walk in chains with heavy iron collars around their neck. If a chief or king saw someone in the line he wanted to free, he would have to pay the slave trader for the person and then take his head out of the iron collar. ...'God saw us in slavery to sin and self, being driven under the lash of Satan, and so He sent His Son to die that men might live. He took our heads out.'"* (The Story of the Bible, p.92-93)

Much like the **Tyndale Bible's** coined word "Passover," sometimes the creation of compound words are needed for translation, sometimes a whole phrase. *"The Moskito Indian language, like many others, lacks words for several ethical ideas. Yet their New Testament contains a term for 'forgiveness' which rendered literally would mean 'take a man's fault out of your heart'. Heart is evidently a familiar word to them. 'Anger' is described as a 'burst heart' and 'the law of God's white heart' is their way of translating 'God's mercy'."* (The Bible throughout the World, pg.162)

A preacher in Samoa worked with a *"language* [that] *had only thirteen letters, and not a single original word to describe many of the Christian's commonest religious thoughts. It had to coin* **akavangakam**, *literally 'heart-judge', for 'conscience'. Faith is* **akarongo**, *'listening to God speaking'. To trust in God became 'leaning upon God'. Heaven is 'the day or light of God'. Abundant grace was described as 'even running over'. For ever and ever became 'time on, on, still on'."* (The Bible throughout the World, pg. 171)

Of interest also is the story of John Patton's translation work: *"From his early boyhood,*

What about Foreign Bibles?

John Paton wanted to be a missionary. Before studying theology and medicine, Paton served for ten years as a Glasgow City Missionary. After graduation, he was ordained and set sail for the New Hebrides as a Presbyterian missionary. Three months after arriving on the island of Tanna, Paton's young wife died, followed by their five-week-old son. For three more years, Paton labored alone among the hostile islanders, ignoring their threats, seeking to make Christ known to them, before escaping with his life. Later, he returned and spent fifteen years on another island.

"Paton was working one day in his home on the translation of John's Gospel - puzzling over John's favorite expression pisteuo eis, to 'believe in' or to 'trust in' Jesus Christ, a phrase which occurs first in John 1:12. 'How can I translate it?' Paton wondered. The islanders were cannibals; nobody trusted anybody else. There was no word for 'trust' in their language. His native servant came in. 'What am I doing?' Paton asked him. 'Sitting at your desk,' the man replied. Paton then raised both feet off the floor and sat back on his chair. 'What am I doing now?' In reply, Paton's servant used a verb which means 'to lean your whole weight upon.' That's the phrase Paton used throughout John's Gospel to translate to "believe in."

(Trials of a Missionary, Morning Glory, Sept./Oct., 1997, p. 50)

A good example, of how additional words maybe needed to achieve the same sense, can be seen in John 3:16 in the **Tok Pisin King Jems Baibel** (King James equivalent in the Papua New Guinea Tok Pisin language).

Long wanem, God i laikim tru ol manmeri bilong dispela graun olsem, inap long Em i givim dispela wanpela Pikinini Man tasol Em i kamapim, long husat man i bilip long Em i no ken lus, tasol em i ken gat laip i stap gut oltaim oltaim. Jon 3:16

The first line in English reads *"For God so loved the world,"* but in the Pidgin English translation the word *"manmeri,"* meaning *"people,"* is added for clarity. It is obvious to English speakers what the text means, but if one looks up the word for *"world"* in pidgin, it also means *"earth, ground, and clay."* In other words, adding the word for *"people"* is probably a necessary requirement to distinguish it from saying *"God so loved the ground."*

If one is trying to check out a foreign language Bible to see if it is accurate, they can check the various texts that the writer has shown are altered and changed in many modern Bibles. For example, the **Chinese Union Bible** is very similar to the **NIV**. If someone does not know how to read the foreign language, here is a fairly simple test that can be used. It works well at least in any Bible that has a Latin-based alphabet (Latin-based alphabets are used by about 70% of the world's population).

Look for the three angels' messages in Revelation 14 in the foreign Bible. This is fairly easy since as in most cases Revelation is the last book of the Bible. If the Bible in question has numbered chapters, finding the chapter is simple – just look at verses 6,8,9 – and figure out what the word "angel" looks like – because it is used numerous times in this chapter.

Here is an example using the pure-line **Olivetan Bible**, which is old French, and does not include regular verse numbers. One can soon notice, that even though they cannot necessarily read the text, they can still make out some words. This is because the English language is made up of thousands of words collected from many other different languages.

In this example, it is not very difficult to make out the word "throne." And from the distance that this word is into the chapter, it is fairly obvious that this is the reference in Revelation 14:5. This indicates that the next sentence should have the word "angel" in it, and "angel" should be found three times here.

Once one figures out what the word *"angel"* looks like (in this case "ange"), then they can turn to Revelation 8:13. Even if the verses are not numbered, if they can find chapter 8, the 13th verse is just the last verse in the chapter. In this verse, the phrase *"woe, woe, woe"* is used (some Bibles only have "woe" twice). It is fairly easy to see what word is repeated two or three times. Now one can look before this phrase and see if the word for "angel" is used – it should be used twice in this text (once as singular and once as plural).

As already pointed out in the chapter "Examples of Modern Bible Changes Affecting Doctrine," if the first part of this text uses the word for "angel," then it is a sign that the Bible translation was based on the pure-line manuscripts (or at least influenced by them.) If the word is not the same word used for "angel" in Revelation 14, then chances are, it is the word for "eagle" – which is a good sign that the Bible translation is based either totally or at least in part, in the corrupted manuscripts.

What about Foreign Bibles?

To date, the writer has never found a pure-line Bible that uses the word "eagle" in this text! Here is an example of a corrupt Italian text pulled at random from the internet – notice the word "aquila" (eagle).

> terzo della luna e un terzo degli astri fu colpito e si oscurò: il giorno perse un terzo della sua luce e la notte ugualmente. ¹³ Vidi poi e udii u**'aquila** he volava nell'alto del cielo e gridava a gran voce: «Guai, guai, guai agli abitanti della terra al suono degli ultimi squilli di tromba che i tre **angeli** stanno per suonare!».

As mentioned above, often, there is no modern pure-line Bible in many languages. In this case, one must move forward with a **"Wycliffe"** Bible until a **"Tyndale"** Bible (accurate, but translated by one man) or better yet a **"KJV"** (accurate & proofed by many) can be translated. In the meantime, if another pure-line Bible can be understood by the person, use it as the standard, but allow them to compare with the Bible in their "heart language." Extra prayer and personal labor needs to attend these situations.

Consider the lessons from Acts 8:26-35 when God sent Philip specifically to help the Ethiopian eunuch understand what he was reading in Isaiah.

In this instance is found an illustration of the care of God for his children. He called Philip from his successful ministry in Samaria, to cross the desert and go to Gaza, to labor for a single inquiring soul. In addition, the story encourages Christians that God often especially links His divine power to human effort where mission work is concerned. Acts 8:39 records the end of the story, *"And when they were come up out of the water, the Spirit of the Lord caught away Philip, that the eunuch saw him no more: and he went on his way rejoicing."* The hope for miracles, however, in no way diminishes the Christian's duty to put forth decided efforts toward making available pure-line Bibles in languages where they are not now available.

Here the writer adds an additional note, on the human effort side of things, for those who may be meeting the challenge of translating pamphlets or books using a potentially inaccurate foreign Bible. One suggestion, and our ministries' practice, is to use the most accurate Bible translation available in a particular language. However, on occasion, where the translation is either extremely corrupted, or the particular point we are trying to make from the scripture is obscure or entirely missing out of the foreign text, the writer and his family typically just insert a reference back to the **KJV** and then simply translate the scripture, or portion of scripture, directly from the English (with Greek and Hebrew input from Strong's Concordance, where available). The pictured sample is from an Afrikaans tract.

> *"Nou moet jy weet en verstaan: van die uitgang van die woord af om Jerusalem te herstel en op te bou tot op 'n Gesalfde, 'n Vors, is sewe sewetalle; en twee en sestig sewetalle lank sal dit herstel en opgebou word, met pleine [strate – KJV] en slote [mure – KJV], maar in tye van benoudheid."* – **Daniël 9:25**

Christians must ever keep in mind that God is not limited by language barriers. In spite of a faulty Bible translation and language difficulties, it has been demonstrated that when human agents have done their best, God sends the power of His Spirit to work on the human heart, to convict of sin, and to guide into truths never thought possible. Consider the promise of the Holy Spirit to help overcome language barriers in Acts 2:1-11.

"And when the day of Pentecost was fully come, they were all with one accord in one place. And suddenly there came a sound from heaven as of a rushing mighty wind, and it filled all the house where they were sitting. And there appeared unto them cloven tongues like as of fire, and it sat upon each of them. And they were all filled with the Holy Ghost, and began to speak with other tongues, as the Spirit gave them utterance. And there were dwelling at Jerusalem Jews, devout men, out of every nation under heaven.

"Now when this was noised abroad, the multitude came together, and were confounded, because that every man heard them speak in his own language. And they were all amazed and marvelled, saying one to another, Behold, are not all these which speak Galilaeans? And how hear we every man in our own tongue, wherein we were born? Parthians, and Medes, and Elamites, and the dwellers in Mesopotamia, and in Judaea, and Cappadocia, in Pontus, and Asia, Phrygia, and Pamphylia, in Egypt, and in the parts of Libya about Cyrene, and strangers of Rome, Jews and proselytes, Cretes and Arabians, we do hear them speak in our tongues the wonderful works of God."

Today, we see God working again to aid all in hearing His word. A new "language" called Symbolic Universal Notation (SUN) has been created recently by Wycliffe Bible Translators. Originally, it's purpose was to help those who are both blind and deaf. Since only a small portion of these people, especially those in foreign countries, are actually literate, this symbol/picture language was made so the illiterate could also learn to read. Technology is now making it possible to both 3-D print materials and to provide tactile-type tablet readers with raised bumps so that all can read God's word.

Although the New Testament and portions of the Old Testament that have currently been translated into SUN are a "Wycliffe" Bible paraphrase (also, sadly, completely missing some verses), the good news is the "language" is easy to learn. Because there are only about

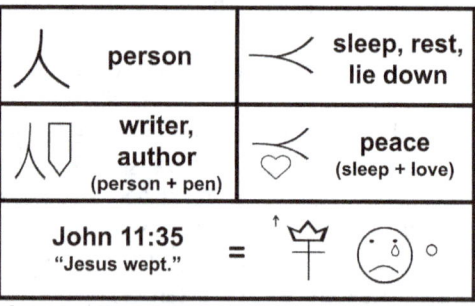

Symbolic Universal Notation (SUN)

100 characters in SUN, (that can then be combined to create extensions or compound words) some people have been able to "read" it in as little as four days. Efforts are already being made to make a pure-line translation in this language. Where now only corrupt-line Bibles are available, a Bible like this could soon be used, as a stand alone or as a "pure-line" point-of-reference, to bring God's pure word to language groups all around the world. (SUN pure-line Bible updates available at biblepicturepathways.com)

An Unrelenting Plot

Throughout history, the Word of God has had many enemies, both in the pagan/occult/atheistic world and in the apostate Christian world. The pagan world just tried to destroy it all together, but the apostate Christian world has tried to corrupt it and destroy its ability to accurately portray the Creator.

"Satan's warfare against God's Word has continued unabated and will increase until the end of time. Since Eden Satan has been saying "Yea hath God Said?" (Gen. 3:1). He has inspired "many" to "corrupt the word of God" (2 Cor. 2:17), to "handle the word of God deceitfully" (2 Cor. 4:2), to "pervert the words of the living God" (Jer. 23:36), to steal the words of God (Jer. 23:30), to "wrest" or twist and misapply the Word of God (2 Pet. 3:16), to "make the word of God of none effect" (Mark 7:13), to "change the truth of God into a lie" (Rom. 1:25), to "take away the word" (Luke 8:12), to "cast down the truth to the ground" (Dan. 8:12), to "make war" against the Word of God (Rev. 11:7), and to kill God's people "for the word of God" (Rev. 6:9, 20:4).

"To the very end of time Satan will carry on his warfare against the Word of God. Every device will be used, every angle artfully applied, including as Paul says, corrupting the Word. God has promised, however, to preserve His Word. Matt. 24:35; 1 Pet. 1:24, 25; Psalm 119:89; Isa. 40:8.

"He says, also, that His Word is incorruptible (1 Pet. 1:23) and that the Scripture cannot be broken (John 10:35). By the testimony of Scripture, we understand there are both a "corrupt" and an "incorruptible" line of Bibles."

(Assault on the Remnant, p.5)

One of the common reasons claimed for changing and corrupting the Word of God, is the supposed "new discoveries" of old manuscripts. Critics like to use these "new discoveries" as an excuse to alter the parts of the Word of God that they do not like. But it should be pointed out, that there have been supposed "discoveries" of manuscripts and papyrus fragments that were promoted as true originals that were later found to be nothing but forgeries.

For example, in **2011**, a piece of papyrus manuscript was "discovered" that promoted the idea that Jesus had a wife. It is known as the *"Gospel of Jesus' Wife."* Many scholars and professionals examined it and ran many scientific tests on it, including micro-Raman spectroscopy tests, which supposedly "proved" that the papyrus and the ink were authentic.

Forgery – "The Gospel of Jesus' Wife"

Many scholars began promoting it as a real artifact. Even the Harvard Theological Review, in **2014**, published articles showing its authenticity. Then in **June of 2016**, it was discovered that the papyrus was a cunning forgery by a pornography businessman and his clairvoyant wife, who produces forgeries by channeling spirits.

In other words, just because there is a "new find" in the realm of Bible manuscripts and papyrus – does not mean that it is something good or accurate. And just because "scientific tests" claim to "prove it," does not mean anything at all – it can still easily be a forgery.

Could the warning found in Revelation 16:13-14 of *"three unclean spirits like frogs"* that *"come out of the mouth of the dragon...the beast, and...the false prophet,"* that are *"the spirits of devils, working miracles"* be, in part, referring to corrupted Bibles that are translated or made by skeptics, non-believers, and people under the influence of spiritualism?

Another circumstance that the writer has unearthed is that in many cases, in countries that used to have a pure-line Bible, it has become obvious that the devil and his agents have gradually replaced the good Bibles with counterfeit Bibles. For example, one missionary found as recently as **1980**, the Herero people of Africa had a good Bible from the pure stream of manuscripts. But in the last 40 years the pure-line Bible has mysteriously disappeared and the Herero population now have only corrupt-stream Bibles. For a Bible to "disappear" in this short amount of time it is obvious that the devil's agents have been working over-time to replace God's Word with the corrupted word.

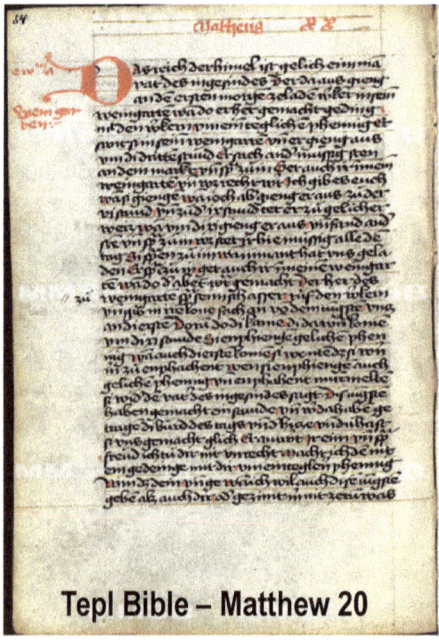

Tepl Bible – Matthew 20

In addition, during the course of his research the writer has found the history of old Bibles to be purposely "erased" and not only unappreciated, but actually disdained in areas where it should have been appreciated. For example, upon contacting a certain Waldensian cultural center in reference to the Waldensian **Tepl Bible**, the writer was told in no uncertain terms by a high official (who his letter had been forwarded to by several kind staff members) that he knew nothing of what he referred to as the *"so-called Tepl Bible."* Yet, later the writer was able to find a manuscript of the **Tepl Bible**. Furthermore, the writer has discovered that some old Bibles seem to be "locked away" where only those with certain credentials are allowed to access them.

An Unrelenting Plot

Down through the last two millennia, the Papal Church has sought to control and destroy, not only all the historical records that were not pro-Catholic, but also to destroy the pure copies of God's Holy Word. The Jesuits today have their people placed in key positions to watch for old history books and other old books and Bibles that would be detrimental to their plans, and when any are located, they are obtained and disposed of or hidden away in secret Vatican archives where the public will never see them.

"...the Jesuits always have a man, either a priest or a layman, on the committee of almost every public library in Great Britain. 'The Jesuits' man comes provided with two lists, a black list, which includes every well-known book, ancient and modern, adverse to Romanism; and a white list of new books especially favourable to Romanism which he submits beforehand to the librarian, and eventually succeeds in getting placed in the library.' It is quite evident from our investigation of the facts that the Jesuits are the same in America as in England." (Facts of Faith, p.252)

Library in Great Britain

Another example might be cited is the fact that some historians *"...estimated the number of books written about the Jesuits over the years to be around 6000 at the end of the 18th century. In the 19th century books and sermons countering the Jesuits and their activities were published in profusion. Nowadays they are few and far between. It seems that innumerable such works have gone out of print and disappeared from the bookshelves. In theological colleges and public libraries, it is now hard to find any history of the Jesuits beyond the beginning of the 17th century. Most books on the counter-reformation are written by Roman Catholics, many by the Jesuits themselves...Protestant watchmen believe that the Jesuits have accomplished a remarkable feat in a relatively short time span in ridding schools, universities and theological colleges of almost all historical literature written from a Protestant viewpoint."*

(All Roads Lead to Rome, p.130)

In this work, the writer has attempted to include quotations, not only from commonly recognized sources, but also from many old, rare, and less well-known historical works. Even this, is only a scratch on the surface. There are many more old works that the enemy would like for modern society to forget about. It is the writer's purpose to remind the readers of these forgotten books, so that they can research and discover them and truth for themselves.

Today, it is possible to buy any number of Bibles from a huge selection of the modern versions from a Roman Catholic bookstore – such as the **NIV**, **RSV**, **TEV**, et cetera, but one will not likely find the **King James Bible** – most Catholic bookstores do not even stock them! Papal sources condemn, sometimes openly, other times more subtly and secretly, the **King James Bible**.

Why does the devil hate the pure Bibles so much? Consider this statement:
"It is impossible to enslave, mentally or socially, a Bible-reading people. The principles of the Bible are the groundwork of human freedom." (Horace Greeley)

But before sitting back and resting confident that one has a **KJV** so there is no cause for concern, please take note. Modern copyright laws did not exist back in **1611**, so to protect the **King James Bible** from being changed and corrupted by unscrupulous printers and enemies, they chose to protect it by a Royal Prerogative that restricts publication and distribution of it solely to the crown of England. This was a perfect way to protect it back then. But, that Royal Prerogative is still in place. So, while today, the **KJV** is in the public domain everywhere else around the world, in England, ONLY the Crown's publishing houses can print and distribute the **KJV**. The Crown holds the sole right to publish, license, or sell the **KJV**.

Why is this significant? Because due to the actions of King John in **1215**, the Vatican secretly owns the Crown of England – which in turn, owns the rights to the **KJV**. This little known fact sets the stage for a possible future "confiscation and banning" of the **KJV Bibles** around the world. Whether such a thing will happen or no one cannot say, but it could be a possibility whenever Rome decides to make her move to bring the world back under her control.

But at the moment, she feigns indifference, allowing everyone to take their **KJV Bibles** for granted, while her agents secretly and quietly remove, erase, or hide the history of all the good old pure-line manuscripts that the **KJV** was based on, and deceive the population into believing the lie that there is really no difference between all the modern versions and the pure-line Bibles. It is time to put into practice, Psalm 119:11 *"Thy word have I hid in mine heart, that I might not sin against thee."*

"Let us put away the foolish reading-matter, and study the Word of God. Let us commit its precious promises to memory, so that, when we are deprived of our Bibles, we may still be in possession of the Word of God." (Review & Herald, January 6, 1910)

The issue, between the Pure-line **Textus Receptus**/True **Majority Text** based Bibles such as the **Geneva**, **Olivetan**, **Tyndale**, and **KJV**, and the Corrupt-line **Alexandrian/Minority Text** based Bibles such as the vast bulk of the modern versions, boils down to a very simple matter:
"It is simply a matter of divine inspiration and preservation versus philosophic, scholastic textual criticism and man's reasoning." (Ed Branch)

An Unrelenting Plot

Yet, this simple fact is a life or death matter!

In 2 Timothy 3:15-17 the scriptures state, *"And that from a child thou hast known the holy scriptures, which are able to make thee wise unto salvation through faith which is in Christ Jesus. All scripture is given by inspiration of God, and is profitable for doctrine, for reproof, for correction, for instruction in righteousness: That the man of God may be perfect, throughly furnished unto all good works."*

Because of the importance of a pure Bible to pure doctrine and a pure life, Satan and his agents have sought to rid Christians of the pure word. In a battle, if a soldier loses his sword, he also typically loses the battle. God's Word is our sword and it is necessary to correct discernment in these last days.

"For the word of God is quick, and powerful, and sharper than any twoedged sword, piercing even to the dividing asunder of soul and spirit, and of the joints and marrow, and is a discerner of the thoughts and intents of the heart." Hebrews 4:12

Indeed, it also must be necessarily sharp. Like the Philistines of old, Satan would love to have everyone come to him for any sword sharpening. 1 Samuel 13:19-22 records, *"<u>Now there was no smith found throughout all the land of Israel: for the Philistines said, Lest the Hebrews make them swords or spears: But all the Israelites went down to the Philistines, to sharpen every man his share, and his coulter, and his axe, and his mattock</u>. Yet they had a file for the mattocks, and for the coulters, and for the forks, and for the axes, and to sharpen the goads. So it came to pass in the day of battle, that there was neither sword nor spear found in the hand of any of the people that were with Saul and Jonathan: but with Saul and with Jonathan his son was there found."*

Sometimes Satan's plan is more subtle, changing only a word or two at a time, as when he tempted Christ in the wilderness. The devil cleverly quotes scripture leaving out the parts that might expose his plot. Matthew 4:5-7 records, *"Then the devil taketh him up into the holy city, and setteth him on a pinnacle of the temple, And saith unto him, If thou be the Son of God, cast thyself down: for it is written, He shall give his angels charge concerning thee: and in their hands they shall bear thee up, lest at any time thou dash thy foot against a stone. Jesus said unto him, It is written again, Thou shalt not tempt the Lord thy God."*

"It is written, Man shall not live by bread alone, but by <u>every word</u> that proceedeth out of the mouth of God."

Here, to support presumption, Satan quoted only a portion of Psalm 91 instead of quoting *"every word"* which presents faith in its proper connection with obedience to God's will. The words he left out, and their connecting texts, make clear that God's promise of protection is for those who walk in His ways, *"Because thou hast made the LORD, which is my refuge, even the most High, thy habitation; There shall no evil befall thee, neither shall any plague come nigh thy dwelling. For he shall give his angels charge over thee, to keep thee in all thy ways. They shall bear thee up in their hands, lest thou dash thy foot against a stone."* Psalm 91:9-12

"In all thy ways acknowledge him, and he shall direct thy paths." Proverbs 3:6

Indeed, *"All should become familiar with God's Word; because Satan perverts and misquotes Scripture, and men follow his example by presenting part of God's Word to those whom they wish to lead in false paths, withholding the part which would spoil their plans. All have the privilege of becoming acquainted with a plain "Thus saith the Lord." ...There are false shepherds who will say and do perverse things. Children should be so instructed that they will be familiar with God's Word, and be able to know when part of a Scripture is read and part left unread in order to make a false impression."* – Manuscript 153, 1899.   (Evangelism, p.591)

Consider how difficult it is to recognize a misquotation of the Bible today with all the different versions. Little by little and almost imperceptibly, Satan has changed words over years and even centuries, so that one can find a supposed Bible that will uphold almost any desired position, especially if they mix and match versions. Accepting plastic butter knives, offered by one's opponent – in exchange for a real sword, can be dangerous in battle.

Thankfully, in the pure-line Bibles, handed down through the generations, God has preserved for his people a divinely sharpened sword that will help them *"earnestly contend for the faith which was once delivered unto the saints."* Jude 1:3

Contending for the faith in this battle being fought over the Bible versions, is much more important than the majority of people realize. Just as the devil convinced the majority of the inhabitants of planet earth to unite with him in rebellion against God by building the city Babylon with its tower of Babel (Genesis 11:1-9), so the evil forces that are working today to establish their New One World Order system of Religion, in rebellion against the God of heaven, are in the process of completing the modern "spiritual" Babylon of Bible prophecy.

Throughout the Bible, the term "Babylon" is used to represent a system of false worship. The symbolism of a "tower" is also used to represent a church (Jeremiah 6:26,27, Micah 4:8) – so the symbolism of the Tower of Babel shows us a representation of a worldwide system of false religion that is united in a war of rebellion against God's truth. As God confused the words of the people at Babel slowing the progress of the synagogue of Satan, so the devil, as Babylon's ultimate leader, is now seeking, in retaliation, to confuse God's word in order to tear down

God's church. Indeed, as the Reformer Calvin reiterated, *"Every addition to His [God's] word is a lie."* The modern corrupt Bibles are subtly planting the seeds of false doctrines in people's minds, which will then spring up and bear the fruit of rebellion against God's true doctrines.

"The Forbidden Reading"

"From the fourth century the corruptions of the Christian Church continued to make marked and rapid progress. <u>The Bible began to be hidden from the people</u>. And in proportion as the light, which is the surest guarantee of liberty, was withdrawn, <u>the clergy usurped authority over the members of the Church. The canons of councils were put in the room of the one infallible Rule of Faith; and thus the first stone was laid in the foundations of "Babylon</u>, that great city, that made all nations to drink of the wine of the wrath of her fornication." (History of the Reformation, vol 1, bk 1, chpt 2, p.4)

God's Last Day message is an urgent call to all those honest souls that have been deceived into being in that false religious system, and of drinking of the "wine" of her false doctrines to "come out" of her.

"And after these things I saw another angel come down from heaven, having great power; and the earth was lightened with his glory. And he cried mightily with a strong voice, saying, Babylon the great is fallen, is fallen, and is become the habitation of devils, and the hold of every foul spirit, and a cage of every unclean and hateful bird. For all nations have drunk of the wine of the wrath of her fornication, and the kings of the earth have committed fornication with her, and the merchants of the earth are waxed rich through the abundance of her delicacies. **And I heard another voice from heaven, saying, Come out of her, my people, that ye be not partakers of her sins, and that ye receive not of her plagues.**" Revelation 18:1-4

It is the prayer of the writer that not just his Protestant brothers and sisters, but also his Catholic, New Age, and Islamic brothers and sisters, as well as many others, will heed God's last day warning to *"come out"* of Babylon. Come out of the secret societies. Come out of all the false systems of worship. It is his prayer that each one will choose to take the pure *"sword of the Spirit, which is the word of God"* that they may valiantly *"fight the good fight of faith,"* and by a well-sharpened, time-tested *"it is written"* forever vanquish the foe. (Ephesians 6:17, 1 Timothy 6:12, Matthew 4:7,10)

Cutting Edge Facts – Building Faith in God's Word

Seven Scientific Statements of the Bible that have been Proven to be True

Earth is Suspended in Space *"He stretcheth out the north over the empty place, and <u>hangeth the earth upon nothing</u>."* Job 26:7

Blood Sustains Life *"<u>For the life of the flesh is in the blood</u>: and I have given it to you upon the altar to make an atonement for your souls: for it is the blood that maketh an atonement for the soul."* Leviticus 17:11

Cover body waste with dirt, a septic system thousands of years ahead of its time *"Thou shalt have a place also without the camp, whither thou shalt go forth abroad: And thou shalt have a paddle upon thy weapon; and it shall be, when thou wilt ease thyself abroad, thou shalt dig therewith, and shalt turn back and <u>cover that which cometh from thee</u>:"* Deuteronomy 23:12,13

The Stars Cannot be Numbered *"As the host of heaven cannot be numbered, neither the sand of the sea measured: so will I multiply the seed of David my servant, and the Levites that minister unto me."* Jeremiah 33:22

The Universe is Made of Invisible Things *"Through faith we understand that the worlds were framed by the word of God, so that things which are seen were not made of things which do appear."* Hebrews 11:3

Stars Differ in Magnitude *"There is one glory of the sun, and another glory of the moon, and another glory of the stars: for one star differeth from another star in glory."* 1 Corinthians 15:41

The Water Cycle keeps the land Watered *"'All the rivers run into the sea; yet the sea is not full; unto the place from whence the rivers come, thither they return again." Ecclesiastes 1:7*

Conclusion

In this work, the reader has taken a journey that covers a little over 2,000 years. This has not been an exhaustive work, the writer has only briefly mentioned some of the highlights of this history. But even as brief as it has been, many new insights have been revealed of this much-forgotten history of the Bible.

Through the ages, two distinct lines of Bibles have been seen – the pure line and the corrupt line.

The corrupt line of Bibles "has been preserved" largely by philosophers and higher critics, many of whom do not even believe the miracles, the creation story, and even class whole books of the Bible as fiction. In addition, in this line are found many who did not adhere to the testimony of the Bible itself – in some cases their goal was to unite paganism and Christianity, in others they embraced spiritualism, or even actively created forgeries and persecuted those who wanted to read the Bible in their own language.

In direct contrast, are those who preserved the pure-line Bibles; those who valued the Word of God above friends and family, money, comfort and even life itself. Many died at the martyr pile for refusing to conform to worldly customs that were in opposition to the Word of God. They lived and died that the Word might be preserved in its purity. They recognized that,

"Truth mixed with error is equivalent to all error, except that it is more innocent looking and, therefore, more dangerous. God hates such a mixture! Any error, or truth-and-error mixture, calls for definite exposure and repudiation. To condone such is to be unfaithful to God and His Word and treacherous to imperiled souls for whom Christ died." (Harry A. Ironside)

The question for the reader is this: "Which line of Bibles correctly represents the Biblical description in Revelation 12:17 *'And the dragon [Satan] was wroth with the woman [God's people], and went to make war with the remnant of her seed, which keep the commandments of God, and have the testimony of Jesus Christ.'"*?

Is the Bible of the reader, the testimony of Jesus Christ, or only a counterfeit?

Which Bible? A Scriptural Walk through the History

All scripture is given by inspiration of God... 2Timothy 3:16
For the prophecy came not in old time by the will of man: but holy men of God spake as they were moved by the Holy Ghost. 2 Peter 1:21

The Corrupted Line -- "Yea, hath God said?..." Gen. 3:1
"many, which corrupt the word of God..." 2 Cor. 2:17

Origen's Septuagint
"The Scriptures are of little use to those who understand them as they are written." -- Origen. (Quoted in Maclaine's Mosheim, Century iii, part ii, chap. iii, par. 5, note)
Rev. 2:8,9 And unto the angel of the church in Smyrna write...I know the **blasphemy** of them which say they are Jews, and are not, but are **the synagogue of Satan**.

Codex Alexandrinus (A)
This Alexandrian manuscript is an early 5th century manuscript of the Greek Bible whose OT is based on Origen's Septuagint.
"The original founders of the ecclesiastical college at Alexandria strove to exalt tradition.....Clement, most famous of the Alexandrian college faculty and a teacher of Origen, boasted that he would not teach Christianity unless it were mixed with pagan philosophy."
(Truth Triumphant, PDF pg. 42)
Colossians 2:8 Beware lest any man spoil you through philosophy and vain deceit, after the tradition of men, after the rudiments of the world, and not after Christ.
Matt. 15:9 But in vain they do worship me, teaching for doctrines the commandments of men.

The Pure Line– "by every word of God." Luke 4:4

The Second Rabbinical Bible or Ben Chayyim Masoretic Text of the OT
Hebrew preserved by the Levites and meticulous Masorites until compiled by a Jew converted to Protestantism Ezra 7:12 Ezra the priest, a scribe of the law of the God of heaven... 1Chr. 24:6 Nethaneel the scribe, one of the Levites, wrote them ... Deut. 4:2 Ye shall not add unto the word which I command you, neither shall ye diminish ought from it, that ye may keep the commandments of the LORD your God which I command you.

Lucian of Antioch's Greek Vulgate New Testament
Lucian gathered all the writings of the apostles together (at least the ones not already gathered by Polycarp and John) and produced the **Greek Vulgate** New Testament used by the Christians in the capital, Constantinople, and in most of the Near East for centuries. When Constantinople fell, this was carried to the West and became the foundation for the **Textus Receptus** compiled by Erasmus.
"Erasmus had published his Greek and Latin version of the New Testament.... In this work many errors of former versions were corrected, and the sense was more clearly rendered." {GC 245.1}
Rev. 1:9 I John, ...your brother, and companion in tribulation... was in the isle that is called Patmos, **for the word of God, and for the testimony of Jesus Christ.**
Titus 1:9 Holding fast the faithful word....

Conclusion

The Corrupted Line -- *"Yea, hath God said?..."* Gen. 3:1

The Pure Line – *"by every word of God."* Luke 4:4

Bibles of the Great Whore who persecuted God's People

Jerome's Latin Vulgate— *"The second decree [of the council of Trent] declares the Vulgate to be the sole authentic and standard Latin version, and gives it such authority as to supersede the original texts..."* Rome's Challenge.. p. 22-23

"Wycliffe's Bible had been translated from the Latin text, which contained many errors." {GC 245.1}

Douay Rheims– Purpose was the Counter Reformation and to *"challenge English Protestants for corrupting the text"* 1582 Preface

Siniaticus—Found in a trashcan in a monastery at Mt. Sinai. Some parts of it had been erased and rewritten 70 times. Kept in the Vatican Archives

Vaticanus—Found in the Vatican Archives

Rev.19:2 *"For true and righteous are his judgments: for he hath judged the great whore, which did corrupt the earth with her fornication...* Rev 17:5,6 *And upon her forehead was a name written, MYSTERY, BABYLON THE GREAT, THE MOTHER OF HARLOTS AND ABOMINATIONS OF THE EARTH. And I saw the woman drunken with the blood of the saints, and with the blood of the martyrs of Jesus...*

Waldensian "Church in the Wilderness"

The Latin Itala and Romaunt

"The Waldenses were among the first of the peoples of Europe to obtain a translation of the Holy Scriptures. Hundreds of years before the Reformation they possessed the Bible in manuscript in their native tongue. They had the truth unadulterated, and this rendered them the special objects of hatred and persecution." {GC 65.2}

Rev. 12:14,17 *And to the woman were given two wings of a great eagle, that she might fly into the wilderness, into her place, where she is nourished for a time, and times, and half a time, from the face of the serpent... And the dragon was wroth with the woman, and went to make war with the remnant of her seed, which keep the commandments of God, and have the testimony of Jesus Christ.* John 5:39 *Search the scriptures; for in them ye think ye have eternal life: and they are they which testify of me.*

Sword Unsheathed

Wescott and Hort were spiritualists who didn't believe the Bible, even creation, and hated the *Textus Receptus*:
HORT wrote to John Ellerton, December 29, 1851:
"Westcott,... etc., and I have started a society for the investigation of ghosts ["The 'Ghostly Guild,"] and all supernatural appearances and effects, being all disposed to believe that such things really exist, and ought to be discriminated from hoaxes and mere subjective disillusions."
(Life of Hort, Vol. I. p. 211)
Isaiah 8:19,20 And when they shall say unto you, Seek unto them that have familiar spirits, and unto wizards that peep, and that mutter: should not a people seek unto their God? for the living to the dead? To the law and to the testimony: if they speak not according to this word, it is because there is no light in them.
WESTCOTT wrote... March 4, 1890: *"No one now, I suppose, holds that the first three chapters of Genesis, for example, give a literal history -I could never understand how anyone reading them with open eyes could think they did."*
(Life of Westcott, Vol. II. p. 69)
Hort wrote, *"Think of that vile Textus Receptus."*
(Life of Westcott, Vol. I, p. 393)
Isaiah 5:20 Woe unto them that call evil good, and good evil; that put darkness for light, and light for darkness...!

Modern Bibles based on this Line **NIV, RSV, NLT, ESV, ASV**, etc. *Ezekiel 4:13 "defiled bread"*	Hybrid Bible based in part on corrupt line **NKJV** *Is.1:22 "thy wine mixed with water."*

French Olivetan Bible/Protestant Bibles, The Two Witnesses prophecy, and the French Revolution
The Olivetan, a gift from the Waldensians to the Protestant Reformation was pronounced *"entire and pure.. It is by the means of the Vaudois ...that France today has the Bible in her own language."* (Our Authorized Bible Vindicated, pg. 32 quoting Waldensian historian Ledger)
Note: only the pure-line Bibles prophesied in sackcloth
Rev. 11:3,4, 7,8, 11,12 And I will give power unto my two witnesses, and they shall prophesy a thousand two hundred and threescore days, clothed in sackcloth. These are the two olive trees, and the two candlesticks standing before the God of the earth. ...And when they shall have finished their testimony, the beast that ascendeth out of the bottomless pit shall make war against them, and shall overcome them, and kill them. And their dead bodies shall lie in the street of the great city, which spiritually is called Sodom and Egypt, where also our Lord was crucified.. ...And after three days and an half the Spirit of life from God entered into them, and they stood upon their feet; and great fear fell upon them which saw them. And they heard a great voice from heaven saying unto them, Come up hither. And they ascended up to heaven in a cloud; and their enemies beheld them.
[Shows Bible is complete and no longer in sackcloth]

The **King James Bible** was translated by 54 learned men over a period of 7 years. *The words of the LORD are pure words: as silver tried in a furnace of earth, purified seven times. Psalm 12:6*

ADDITIONAL NOTES

Note A
Royal Line Compared to Counterfeit Line

Lineage of the pure stream, the "Royal Line," compared to the Lineage of the Counterfeit Line. **All dates are Anno Domini (AD)**

Pure Line

The Old Testament in Hebrew
1524-25 Bomberg Edition of the Masoretic Text also known as the Ben Chayyim Text – based on the vast majority of ancient Hebrew manuscripts from antiquity and well-known for its superior accuracy.

The Old Testament in Greek
270 Lucian of Antioch's translation from the original manuscripts – used by the Christians in the capital, Constantinople, and in most of the Near East for centuries.

The New Testament
30-95 Original Autographs
95-150 Greek Vulgate (Copy of Originals)
1535 Erasmus's Fifth Greek Textus Receptus
1551 Stephanus Fourth Textus Receptus
1599 Nuremberg Polyglot

Old & New Testaments
120-157 The Old Latin Vulgate (Itala Bible)
150 Peshitta (Syrian Copy)
177 The Gallic Bible
330 The Gothic Version of Ulfilas
400 The Armenian Bible
400 The Old Syriac
450 The Palestinian Syriac Version
1180 Waldensian Romaunt Version
1525 Tyndale Bible
1534 Luther's German Bible
1534 Tyndale's Corrected Version
1535 Coverdale Bible
1535 Olivetan's French Bible
1537 Matthew's Bible
1539 The Great Bible
1541 Swedish Uppsala Bible

1550 Danish King Christian III Bible
1558 Biestken's Dutch Bible
1560 The Geneva Bible
1565 Theodore Beza's 1st Textus Receptus
1568 The Bishop's Bible
1569 Reina's Spanish Translation
1587 Geneva Bible
1602 Czech Kralice Bible
1602 Reina-Valera Bible
1607 Diodati Italian Version
1611 The King James Bible
1769 4th update of the KJV; Non-copyright KJV Bibles today are from this **1769** edition.
1602 Spanish Purificada
2010 Reina-Valera Gomez Bible

Counterfeit Line

The Old Testament in Hebrew
895 The Ben Asher text based on only a small few corrupt manuscripts like B19a, Codex Cairensis, and Aleppo manuscripts and some have changed numerous times while other's authenticity is doubtful.

The Old Testament in Greek
240 Origen's Hexapla Septuagint – written by a Neo-Platonist Greek philosopher and based on lies, forgeries, and works of fiction.

The New Testament
100-200 Numerous corrupted versions which were changed by different heretics and apostates, then followed by those from the Gnostics.
160 Tatian's corrupt Diatessaron

Old & New Testaments
331 Eusebius produces 50 Origen-based Bibles, for the baptized pagan emperor Constantine who was seeking to amalgamate Christianity and Paganism. These were later lost.
404 Jerome's corrupt Latin Vulgate
410 Codex Alexandrinus the Eusebius & Septuagint-based manuscript.
450 Codex Ephraemi (C) which is a rescript which was erased and written over.
1448 Vaticanus, which is one of the lost Constantine Bibles
1609 the Jesuit Douay-Rheims Bible which was an attempt to destroy the Protestant Reformation.
1862 Codex Sinaiticus, also one of Constantine's lost Bibles
1885 Revision of KJV done by Catholic influenced critics and spiritualists like Westcott and Hort.
1885-2022+ All the flood of modern English versions.

Additional Notes

Bible Family Tree

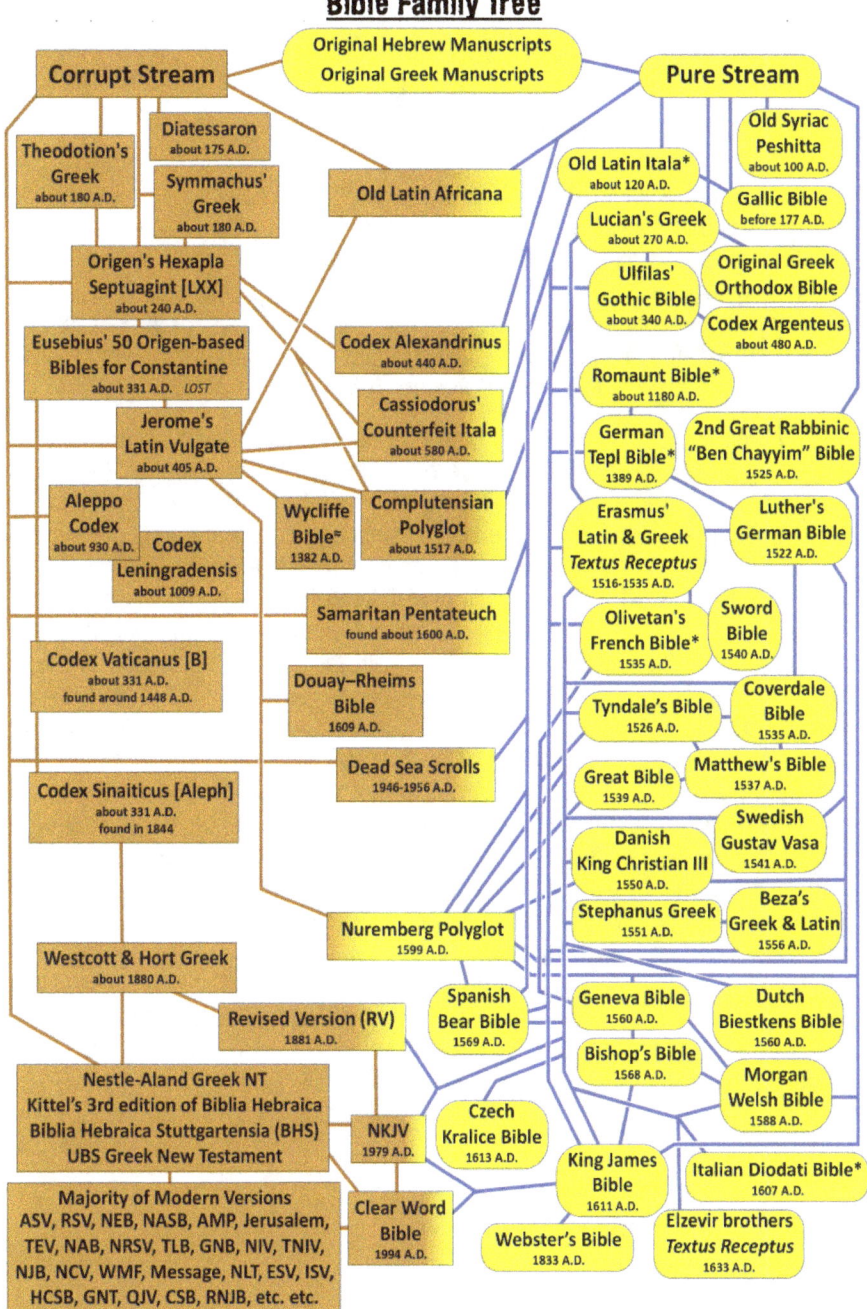

≈ Wycliffe did a good work for Protestantism by translating the Bible into English for the common people, but he used the only Bible he knew, Jerome's Latin Vulgate, to base his translation on.

* Waldensian Bibles

Note B
The Beauty of Classic Bibles

"God in His wisdom had invested these Latin versions by His Providence with a charm that outweighed the learned artificiality of Jerome's Vulgate. This is why they persisted through the centuries. A characteristic often overlooked in considering versions, and one that cannot be too greatly emphasized, needs to be pointed out in comparing the Latin Bible of the Waldenses, of the Gauls, and of the Celts with the later Vulgate. To bring before you the unusual charm of those Latin Bibles, I quote from the Forum of June, 1887:

"'The old Italic version into the rude Low Latin of the second century held its own as long as Latin continued to be the language of the people. The critical version of Jerome never displaced it, and only replaced it when the Latin ceased to be a living language, and became the language of the learned. The Gothic version of Ulfilas, in the same way, held its own until the tongue in which it was written ceased to exist. Luther's Bible was the first genuine beginning of modern German literature. In Germany, as in England, many critical translations have been made, but they have fallen stillborn from the press. The reason of these facts seems to be this: that the languages into which these versions were made, were almost perfectly adapted to express the broad, generic simplicity of the original text. Microscopic accuracy of phrase and classical nicety of expression may be very well for the student in his closet, but they do not represent the human and divine simplicity of the Scriptures to the mass of those for whom the Scriptures were written. To render that, the translator needs not only a simplicity of mind rarely to be found in companies of learned critics, but also a language possessing in some large measure that broad simple, and generic character which we have seen to belong to the Hebrew and to the Greek of the New Testament. It was partly because the low Latin of the second century, and the Gothic of Ulfilas, and the rude, strong German of Luther had that character in a remarkable degree, that they were capable of rendering the Scriptures with faithfulness which guaranteed their permanence.'"

(*Our Authorized Bible Vindicated*, p.27-28)

Additional Notes

Note C
The "Johannine Comma" – 1 John 5:7,8

The "Johannine Comma" is a Latin term used to refer to a portion of 1 John 5:7-8. "Johannine" meaning *"of, relating to, or characteristic of the apostle John or the New Testament books ascribed to him,"* And "comma" meaning *"a short clause of words cut off or isolated as a single group."*

The below underlined portion of verse 7 and 8 of 1 John 5 is known as the "Johannine Comma".
"For there are three that bear record <u>in heaven, the Father, the Word, and the Holy Ghost: and these three are one. And there are three that bear witness</u> in earth, the Spirit, and the water, and the blood: and these three agree in one." 1 John 5:7-8

The legitimacy of the "Johannine Comma" in the Bible is hotly debated by modern critical scholars today. In fact, many modern Bibles remove the Johannine Comma leaving behind only a hollow crust of the verses.
"For there are three that bear record, the Spirit, and the water, and the blood: and these three agree in one." 1 John 5:7-8

However, as the reader will see, one can trust God's word for He has given us *"sufficient evidence upon which to base our faith."* Proofs for the Johannine Comma include:
- Its agreement with other Bible testimony
- Its mention by early writers
- Greek manuscripts that indeed contain it
- Erasmus inclusion has been vindicated
- Its inclusion in numerous Old Latin manuscripts
- Internal Evidence for its inclusion

The Johannine Comma Agrees with other Bible Testimony
First of all, one must ask the question, does the Johannine Comma agree with the testimony of the Bible itself? Yes it does!

The three persons of the Godhead are confirmed in both the Old and New Testaments (Hebrew and Greek) with texts such as Isaiah 48:16 (a prophecy of Jesus) *"Come ye near unto me, hear ye this; I have not spoken in secret from the beginning; from the time that it was, there am I: and now <u>the Lord GOD</u>, and <u>his Spirit</u>, hath sent <u>me</u>."* and texts such as the Great Commission in Matthew 28:19: *"Go ye therefore, and teach all nations, baptizing them in the name of <u>the Father</u>, and of <u>the Son</u>, and of <u>the Holy Ghost</u>:"*

Therefore, the "Johannine Comma" passes the *"to the law and to the testimony"* test (Isaiah 8:20). That means that the Johannine Comma agrees with the Bible itself.

The Johannine Comma is Cited by Several Early Writers

Critics claim that the Johannine Comma was not added to 1 John until sometime during the 5th century (**400–500 AD**). However, those who study history find a trail of evidence from several writers in the early centuries who quote from, allude to, or reference to this text as early as the 2nd century. While these men were by no means infallible, their cumulative testimony is still strong evidence for the existence of the Comma at this time.

Around the year **177 AD**, Athenagoras alluded to the Comma. *"...what is the oneness of the Son with the Father, what the communion of the Father with the Son, what is the Spirit, what is the unity of these three, the Spirit, the Son, the Father, and their distinction in unity;..."*
(Ante-Nicene Fathers, vol. 2, ch. 12)

Athengoras

Around **200 AD** Tertullian, alluding to the verse, spoke of the three members of the Godhead as being one.

"Thus the connection of the Father in the Son, and of the Son in the Paraclete [Spirit], produces three coherent Persons, who are yet distinct One from Another. These Three are, one..."
(Ante-Nicene Fathers, vol. 3, ch. 25)

Tertullian

Around **250 AD**, Cyprian of Carthage actually quoted from the Johannine Comma. In fact, Cyprian specifically says "it is written" and then quotes "and these three are one." *"The Lord says, 'I and the Father are one;' (John 10:30) and again it is written of the Father, and of the Son, and of the Holy Spirit, 'And these three are one.' (1 John 5:7)"*
(Ante-Nicene Fathers, vol. 5, Treatise I. – On the Unity of the Church)

About **350 AD**, Athanasius, an anti-Arian, directly alluded to the Comma. By "Athanasius," it is meant Athanasius (c. **296–373 AD**) or Pseudo-Athanasius (c. **350 – c. 600 AD**). Athanasius quoted the Comma in *Disputatio Contra Arium*:

"Τί δὲ καὶ τὸ τῆς ἀφέσεως τῶν ἁμαρτιῶν παρεκτικὸν, καὶ ζωοποιὸν, καὶ ἁγιαστι κὸν λουτρὸν, οὗ χωρὶς οὐδεὶς ὄψεται τὴν βασιλείαν τῶν οὐρανῶν, οὐκ ἐν τῇ τρισμα καρίᾳ ὀνομασίᾳ δίδοται τοῖς πιστοῖς; Πρὸς δὲ τούτοις πᾶσιν Ἰωάννης φάσκει· «<u>Καὶ οἱ τρεῖς τὸ ἕν εἰσιν</u>.»"
(*Disputatio Contra Arium*, PDF, pg. 21)

"But also, is not that sin-remitting, life-giving and sanctifying washing [baptism], without which, no one shall see the kingdom of heaven, given to the faithful in the Thrice-Blessed Name? In addition to all these, John affirms, '<u>and these three are one</u>.'"
(Translation by KJV Today, the portion in question double-checked by this writer of *SU*)

Additional Notes

Also around **the year 350 AD**, the Spanish bishop Priscillian wrote in his Liber Apologeticus:

"...sicut Iohannes ait, tria sunt quae testimonium dicunt in terra aqua caro et sanguis et haec tria in unum sunt, et tria sunt quae testimonium dicunt in caelo pater uerbum et spiritus et haec tria unum sunt in Christo Iesu."

translated, Priscillian's quote reads,

"...as John says, there are three things which bear witness on earth, water, flesh, and blood, and these three are one, and there are three things which bear witness in heaven, the Father, the Word, and the Spirit; and these three are one in Christ Jesus." (Corpus Scriptorum Ecclesiasticorum Latinorum, vol.18, p.6)

About **360 AD**, Idacius Clarus also quotes it as well.

In **380 AD**, the written Christian document called *Varimadum* specifically stated: *"And John the Evangelist says,... 'And there are three who give testimony in heaven, the Father, the Word, and the Spirit, and these three are one'."*

Around **398 AD**, Aurelius Augustine was also referring to the Bible text.

As one can see, it is obvious that the early Christians were well aware of the existence and authenticity of the Johannine Comma – and these references are all from the early centuries long before the modern critics supposed "5th century addition" lie. Notice again, all these sources confirm the Johannine Comma, in one way or another, in the centuries prior to when the modern critics claim the Johannine Comma came into existence.

It can also be seen that in **484** or **485 AD**, Eugene of Carthage quoted 1 John 5:7 as evidence,*"Et ut luce clarius unius divinitatis esse cum Patre et Filio Spiritum Sanctum doceamus, Joannis Evangelistae testimonio comprobatur. Ait namque: Tres sunt qui testimonium perhibent in coelo: Pater, Verbum et Spiritus Sanctus et hi tres unum sunt."* – which means, in English, *"And as a shining light teaching the unity of the divinity of the Father and Son and Holy Spirit, the testimony of John the Evangelist demonstratively testifies: 'There are three who bear witness in heaven, the Father, the Word, and the Holy Spirit, and these three are one.'"*

(Victor Vitensis quoted in Maynard's *The History of the Debate over 1 John 5:7*, pg. 43)

The Council of Carthage endorsed the Johannine Comma in its official document, which was endorsed by hundreds of church representatives. *"Between three and four hundred prelates attended the Council which met at Carthage; and Eugenius, as bishop of that see, drew up the Confession*

Council of Carthage

of the orthodox, in which the contested verse is expressly quoted. That a whole church should thus concur in quoting a verse which was not contained in the received text is wholly inconceivable; and admitting that 1 John v 7 was thus generally received, its universal prevalence in that text is only to be accounted for by supposing it to have existed in it from the beginning."

(Inquiry Into Integrity of the Greek Vulgate, p.296-297)

Of this piece of evidence one man stated *"In my mind, <u>this is absolutely convincing evidence all by itself</u>. Even if there was no other evidence (and there is more evidence) this single piece of evidence is extremely convincing."*

More evidence could be shared, but an evidence from the Vaudois Line will suffice. Indeed, from the Waldensians may be found external evidence of the truth of the three persons of the Godhead or Heavenly Trio. This is found in the "Noble Lesson" written in the language of the ancient inhabitants of the Valleys (The Waldenses); in the year **1100 AD**. The following is extracted out of a most authentic manuscript, the true original whereof is to be seen in the public library of the famous University of Cambridge.

The Noble Lesson

"Wherefore every one that will do good works, The honour of God the Father ought to be his first moving principle.

He ought likewise to implore the aid of His glorious Son, the dear Son of the Virgin Mary*,
And the Holy Ghost which lightens us in the true way.

These three (the holy Trinity*) as being but one God, ought to be called upon.
Full of power, wisdom, and goodness."

(Translation from "The History of the Evangelical Churches of the Valleys of Piemont." by Samuel Morland. 1658. CHRAA. 1982. p.100)

*NOTE: "Santa" can mean "blessed" which is still Biblical. (Luke 1:28) The Waldensians did not worship Mary. Also note "Trineta" can also mean triad. *"A triad is three things or people considered as one unit. A triad is a trio."* https://www.vocabulary.com › dictionary › triad

As was shown on pages 66 through 68 there are two different ways to understand the 3/1 characteristics of the Godhead – a false way, and a true way. When the Godhead is viewed as three separate individuals who are united in one purpose – 1 John 5:7 makes perfectly good sense – and does not support the false concept of the Papal Trinity.

Additional Notes

A Biblical View on "Original" Manuscript Evidence

Skeptics and critics like to claim that they will only believe the "original manuscripts" and since the "original manuscripts" are all long gone, they will only accept the "oldest" existing manuscripts.

But contrary to their ideas, God is not as interested in preserving the "original manuscripts" as He is interested in "preserving" His word. *"The words of the LORD are pure words: as silver tried in a furnace of earth, purified seven times. Thou shalt keep them, O LORD, thou shalt preserve them from this generation for ever."* Psalm 12:6-7

When "original manuscripts" are burned in fires, torn up, sunken in the sea, eaten by beasts, erased, buried, or destroyed in any other way, God can "preserve" His word through memory, through copying, or through any number of other methods.

For example, when God told Jeremiah to write his book, and then king Jehoiakim cut up Jeremiah's "original manuscript" and threw it in the fire – that was the end of the "original manuscript" of Jeremiah (Jeremiah 36:23). But God had Jeremiah make a copy, a second manuscript of Jeremiah (Jeremiah 36:28). It wasn't about preserving the "original manuscript" – it was about "preserving God's word."

Then later, in Jeremiah 51:63, one finds that Jeremiah's manuscript was tied to a stone and thrown into the Euphrates river – again, another manuscript destroyed. But today, the whole book of Jeremiah exists, because God has preserved it – by having His people copy it through the years!

This same principle was also illustrated at Sinai. God wrote His Law on tables of stone (the original "manuscript") and when Moses reached the foot of the mountain, by God's direction, He threw down the "original" and broke it – end of "original manuscript." Then God had Moses make a second set of tables of stone (second "manuscript") and God wrote the same information on them. Years later, this second set of tables (second "manuscript") was taken and buried in a cave, where it still remains to this day. The complete record of it listed in Exodus 20:1-17.

Here again, it wasn't about "preserving the original manuscript" – it was about "preserving the words of God"! God's word is not some old cracked, broken, moldy "dead" fragment of an "original manuscript" – God's word is *"quick and powerful"* (Hebrews 4:12 'quick' = 'alive/living'). God "preserves" His word, by the "Power" that is "in" His word.

God's pure word contains in itself the power to preserve itself and to explain itself. That is why Christians are to let the Bible be its own interpreter! As the reader has seen God's pure word has been "preserved" down through the centuries in many languages (ex. in English – the King James Bible).

But back to the manuscript issue.

There are Greek Manuscripts that contain the Comma

The most prominent argument used against the Johannine Comma is that it is not contained in some Greek manuscripts. While containing some truth, the writer will demonstrate that this argument is often exaggerated. It is true that there are some early Greek manuscripts that do not contain the Johannine Comma, but when one understands what was happening in the first few centuries in the Greek speaking church and the battles that were raging, they can better understand this supposed "lack" of the text in some of those early manuscripts.

Despite less manuscript evidence many diligent Bible students have placed their faith in the Johannine Commas authenticity. For example, John Wesley wrote concerning the Johannine Comma that one Bible commentator's *"doubts were removed by three considerations: (1.) That though it is wanting in many copies, yet it is found in more; and those copies of the greatest authority: — (2.) That it is cited by a whole gain of ancient writers, from the time of St. John to that of Constantine. This argument is conclusive: For they could not have cited it, had it not been in the sacred canon: — (3.) That we can easily account for its being, after that time, wanting in many copies, when we remember that Constantine's successor was a zealous Arian, who used every means to promote his bad cause, to spread Arianism throughout the empire; in particular the erasing this text out of as many copies as fell into his hands. And he so far prevailed, that the age in which he lived is commonly styled, Seculum Aranium, — "the Arian age;" there being then only one eminent man who opposed him at the peril of his life. So that it was a proverb, Athanasius contra mundum: "Athanasius against the world."*

(John Wesley, Sermon 55)

Indeed, the Bible reveals there were many corrupting the word. Paul wrote to the Corinthians *"For we are not as many, which corrupt the word of God..."* 2 Cor. 2:17

So it is likely that some manuscripts do not contain the Comma because they were altered by Sabellists (who denied the plurality of persons in God), Nicolaitans (Rev. 2:6,15), Gnostics, or others.

During the 2nd and 3rd centuries, there was a large movement to "worship knowledge" which was called Gnosticism, and because the Johannine Comma undermines the error of Gnosticism, the Gnostics would have had motivation to remove it from every manuscript that they had any control over. In other words, it is

Additional Notes

possible that the various manuscripts that have been discovered that lack the Johannine Comma, could very well be manuscripts that the Gnostics had altered to match their false belief systems. Also, *"With respect to 1 John v. 7,8 it has been already observed, that it was directed against the peculiar errours of the Nicolaitans and Cerinthians. Of those sects it has been likewise observed, that they respectively denied that Jesus was "the Son of God," and "came in the flesh," though they mutually expressed their belief in a Trinity. Such are the fundamental errours which the apostle undertakes to refute, while at the same time he inculcates a just notion of the Trinity, distinguishing the Persons from the substance by opposing τρεις in the masculine to εν in the neuter."*

(Inquiry Into Integrity of the Greek Vulgate, p.276)

It is important to realize first of all, that for many of the manuscripts, the origin is unknown. Did they come from a Bible-believing Christian or were they copies and counterfeits made by skeptics or Gnostics? Common sense suggests that if a Bible manuscript was "translated" by an unbelieving skeptic, that manuscript would not be trustworthy. Also there is no way of knowing what manuscripts have been discovered – did archeologists stumble across several libraries of manuscripts from a Christian society, or from a pagan/occult society? What if some of the manuscripts found today, originated as "fakes" or "counterfeits" produced by pagans to lead Christians astray?

Bring this thought down to today – what if modern society was suddenly "lost" and a thousand years in the future, some archeologist was to "dig up" a "Christian" bookstore from the year **2022**. What would they find? Hundreds if not thousands of Bibles (manuscripts) that were translated by skeptics and higher critics (ex. NIV, ESV, NLT, etc.) – while only a very few, if any, that were translated from the pure-line of manuscripts (example: KJV, Tyndale, Erasmus, Waldensian, etc.) See the point? Who was involved with the translation will determine, in a great degree, whether it is accurate to the original or not.

However, the promise of God is that He will guide His people (those who love and obey Him) into all truth.

John 16:13 *"Howbeit when he, the Spirit of truth, is come, he will guide you into all truth:"*

Acts 5:32 *"And we are his witnesses of these things; and so is also the Holy Ghost, whom God hath given to them that obey him."*

John 7:17 *"If any man will do his will, he shall know of the doctrine, whether it be of God..."*

In addition, it should be pointed out, that just because some Greek manuscripts do not contain the text, that does not in any way discredit the text itself. To claim that the Commas absence in some manuscripts is proof that it doesn't belong there, is what is known as a logical fallacy, very similar to claiming that *"since Joe didn't visit the grocery store in Denver, that means he wasn't hungry"* – when in reality, the facts reveal that Joe lives in Atlanta, so he wasn't anywhere near Denver to go to any store.

For example, the critics like to claim that out of the 140+ papyrus fragments and the 5,800+ Greek manuscripts that are extant today, very few actually contain the Johannine Comma, which, they claim as "proof" that it shouldn't be there. But that reasoning is using skewed numbers and logical fallacies to attempt to "prove" itself.

Papyrus Fragment Argument Exposed

The fact of the matter is, any knowledgeable person should never be so foolish as to make any claims against the Johannine Comma based on papyrus fragments, as there are only two known fragments in the entire world that even contain a fragment of 1 John. Papyrus #9, which only contains part of six verses from chapter four, it doesn't contain any of the fifth chapter, and Papyrus #74, which is missing more than 76% of the fifth chapter (including verses 1, 2, 5-8,11-16,18-21).

Papyrus 9

In other words, Papyrus fragments have absolutely no bearing on the Johannine Comma at all.

Greek Manuscript Arguments Unmasked

With the Greek New Testament manuscripts, is found a somewhat similar situation as the papyrus. Of all the various 5,800+ Greek manuscripts that have been discovered to date, the vast majority of them actually do not contain the whole New Testament from beginning to end (remember these had to be hand copied, there were no printers available).

In other words, whether the manuscripts were partial copies from someone's personal study endeavors or were originally complete New Testament copies that have just had parts of them lost through the centuries, what they are today are only partial manuscripts which many times only contain a few of the New Testament books.

This means that well over 91% of those 5800+ Greek manuscripts do not even contain the book of 1 John. So here again, **all those fragmentary manuscripts that make up that 91+% have absolutely no bearing on the Johannine Comma and can not be used as evidence for or against it!**

Additional Notes

There are, in reality, only about 8.5% of the existing Greek manuscripts that even contain part of the book of 1 John, and quite a few of those, being fragments themselves, do not contain the fifth chapter, so they cannot be used as evidence for or against it either.

This means, that instead of having thousands of manuscripts being contrasted to the few, like the skeptics and critics claim – because only 8.5% contain the book in question, and an even smaller percentage contains the chapter under question – all the thousands of manuscripts that do not contain both the book and chapter under question, cannot be used as any kind of evidence either for or against 1 John 5:7.

One of the arguments of the critics is that there are not any "early" manuscripts that have been found that contain it but rather that all the manuscripts that contain it are what they call "late" manuscripts from the 10th century or later. But what they fail to point out is that among the Greek manuscripts which do contain the book of 1 John but omit the Johannine Comma, 97% are what the critics admit are "late manuscripts."

In fact, it should be noted too that Michael Maynard, author of *The History of the Debate over 1 John 5:7*, significantly points out that there are only five remaining Greek manuscripts that even contain the epistle of 1 John in whole or in part that date from the 7th century or before. This means 97% of the discovered manuscripts that the critics use for "proof" against the Johannine Comma are not from the early centuries either but rather from the 10th century or later, so in essence, their arguments are basically pitting "late manuscripts" against "late manuscripts."

And contrary to what the critics want people to believe, there are Greek manuscripts that do contain the Johannine Comma. Some known Greek Manuscripts that do contain the Johannine Comma in their text include,

Date	Designation #	Name	Contents
1300 - 1400	629	Codex Ottobonianus	Acts - Jude
1480 - 1520	61	Codex Montfortianus (Britannicus)	Entire NT
1500 - 1600	918	Codex Escurialensis	Romans - Jude
1634	2473	Minuscule 2473	Acts, James - Jude
1700 - 1800	2318	Minuscule 2318	Romans - Jude

Here are some Greek Manuscripts that contain the Johannine Comma in the their margin,

Date	Designation #	Name	Contents
900 - 1000	221	Minuscule 221	Acts - Jude
1000 - 1100	635	Codex Regius Neapolitanus	Acts - Jude
1000 - 1100	177	BSB Cod Graec. 211	Acts - Revelation
1100 - 1200	88	Codex Regis	Acts - Revelation
1200 - 1300	429	Guelferbytanus XVI. 7	Acts - Revelation
1400 - 1500	636	Minuscule 636	Acts - Jude

Erasmus Inclusion of the Johannine Comma Vindicated

One of the commonly used stories promoted by the critics to try to undermine the Johannine Comma is the story they relate of the Greek text of Erasmus.

The story they relate basically claims that *Erasmus didn't include the Johannine Comma in the first couple editions of his Greek text, because he believed that since he didn't have any Greek manuscript that contained it, that meant the comma was false, so he left it out. But then he haphazardly made the rash promise that if anyone could produce a Greek manuscript with that text, that he would then add it to his New Testament, whereupon someone forged a Greek manuscript with this text and Erasmus, not wanting to break his promise, then added the text to his third edition even though he knew the manuscript was false.* **But this commonly circulated story is totally fictitious and was concocted in the attempt by the critics to discredit Erasmus.**

The part of the story that is true, is that Erasmus had not included the text of 1 John 5:7 in his first two editions of the New Testament. This was because it was Erasmus' desire to provide the best translation that he could, and, of the Greek manuscripts that he had available to him at the time of his translation of his first two editions, none of them contained this text, so he just left it out of his translation.

"If he had had a Greek manuscript with the Comma Johanneum then he would have included the Comma but he had not found a single such manuscript and consequently he omitted the Comma Johanneum."
(Erasmus and the Comma Johanneum, H.J. DE JONGE)

Additional Notes

But the part of the story claiming Erasmus made a rash promise and someone forged a manuscript and Erasmus compromised to save face, is total **fiction**. There is not one shred of evidence to support this part of the story, and not one single historian of that time period ever mentioned anything about it.

Evidence shows that this false story first originated with Westcott, Hort, Tregelles, and the other higher critics that began attempting to change the Bible in the middle of the 19th century, and this lie has been continued and promoted by Nestle, Kenyon, Bruce Metzger, and various other higher critics ever since.

The renowned historian, H. J. de Jonge, who is known worldwide as the "authority" on the life and writings of Erasmus, completely debunked this fictitious story on Erasmus. So much so, that even Princeton Theological Seminary professor and textual critic Bruce M. Metzger, who was one of the most outspoken critics that was promoting this fictitious story, was forced to retract it.

"'Erasmus promised that he would insert the Comma Johanneum, as it is called, in future editions if a single Greek manuscript could be found that contained the passage. At length such a copy was found—or made to order.' (Bruce Metzger)

However, on pg 291 (n2) of the (new) third edition of *The Text of the New Testament* Bruce Metzger writes: *'What is said on p. 101 above about Erasmus' promise to include the Comma Johanneum if one Greek manuscript were found that contained it, and his subsequent suspicion that MS.61 was written expressly to force him to do so, needs to be corrected in the light of the research of H.J. de Jonge, a specialist in Erasmian studies who finds <u>no explicit evidence that supports this frequently made assertion</u>; see his "Erasmus and the Comma Johanneum', Ephemerides Theologicae Lovanienses, lvi (1980), pp 381-9."*

(https://www.theopedia.com/johannine-comma)

The clear facts show that, rather than 1 John 5:7 just being "added" because of some rash promise like the critics claim, Erasmus wisely chose to include this important verse in his third edition because he was constantly trying to improve his Greek New Testament to remove any flaws. By the time that his third edition came out, there were other Greek manuscripts containing the Johannine Comma that had been discovered and brought to his attention.

Codex Montfortianus

349

The Johannine Comma is included in Numerous Old Latin Manuscripts

It is also important to understand that the original Old Latin manuscripts were translated directly from the Greek originals, and there are many more Latin manuscripts that date earlier than the Greek manuscripts that are extant.

The original **Itala Bible** was translated by the Christians in Antioch within the first couple decades of the 2nd century. It was proven to be in existence by **157 AD**, with some evidence pointing to as early as around **120 AD**.

Scrivener points out this early date from which Latin copies were first made by stating:
"*The Old Latin version was likely translated from the Greek in roughly 157 AD.*"
(A Plain Introduction to New Testament Criticism, II, 1894; p.42-42)

This **Itala** is the "Old Latin" Italic Bible that was used by the early Christian missionaries to Italy and Europe and the very Bible of the early Waldensian church that arose in the 2nd century. Beza himself stated that the Waldenses could trace their church back to **120 AD**.

"*The Bishop of Meaux highly chargeth Beza for saying, that the Waldenses, time out of mind, had stiffly opposed the abuses of the Romish Church, and that they held their doctrine from father to son, ever since the year 120, as they had heard and received it from their elders and ancestors.*"
(Some Remarks Upon the Ecclesiastical History of the Ancient Churches of Piedmont, p. 193)

The **Itala** traced from Asia Minor to Northern Italy, Europe, and the British Isles during the first three centuries, is the pure Bible manuscripts from which the later Waldensian church translated all their various **Romaunt Bibles**.
"*The Waldenses were the first of all the peoples of Europe to obtain a translation of the Holy Scriptures. Hundreds of years before the Reformation, they possessed the Bible in manuscript in their native tongue. They had the truth unadulterated, and this rendered them the special objects of hatred and persecution.*"
(Great Controversy, 1888, p.65)

In other words, the **Old Latin Itala** that the early Christian church used, has the same antiquity and the same authority as the early Greek manuscripts! And since the Latin speaking areas were not having the same extent of the Sabellianism and Gnosticism heresies to deal with that the Greek church was, there was not the same temptation to leave out the Johannine Comma from the Latin translations.

Speaking of the **Itala Bible**, well known theologian and linguist Frederick Nolan tells us: "*The Scripture was not less committed to the keeping of the Latin than of the Greek church, as the witnesses of its authenticity, and the guardians of its*

Additional Notes

purity; and the knowledge of the languages spoken by those churches, was nearly commensurate with the Roman and Macedonian conquests. The former church possessed a translation, which, as generally quoted by the Latin fathers previously to the council of Nice, was consequently, made previously to any alterations which the original might have undergone under Constantine. This translation has been celebrated for its literal fidelity, and we have this security of its having long continued unaltered..." (Inquiry Into Integrity of the Greek Vulgate, p.56-57)

In the 5th century AD, Augustine refers to the faithful purity & accuracy of the **Itala** by stating, *"Now among translations themselves the Italian (Itala) is to be preferred to the others, for it keeps closer to the words without prejudice to clearness of expression."* (Augustine of Hippo, *On Christian Doctrine*, Book II, ch. 15)

It has been stated that even though there are currently about 6,000 Latin manuscripts that have not been examined yet, because of the sheer amount that have been examined that contain the Johannine Comma, it is estimated that about 95% of the roughly 10,000 Latin manuscripts available today, contain the Johannine Comma. What is known for sure, from the ones that have been examined so far, is that at least 12 Old Latin manuscripts from the 7th century, 21 Old Latin manuscripts from the 8th century, & 189 Old Latin manuscripts from the 9th century, all contain the Johannine Comma.

For example, here are just a few of the many Old Latin manuscripts extant (available) today that contain the Johannine Comma.

Date	Designation #	Name	Contents
400	m	Codex Speculum	New Testament
500	r	Codex Frisingensis	Romans-Phil. /Tim./Heb./1John
750	l	León Palimpsest (Codex Legionensis)	James/1Pet./1-3John
1150	p	Codex Perpinianus	New Testament

Interestingly, here are a couple of Old Latin manuscripts that were confirmed in the past to contain the Johannine Comma, but, either through carelessness or purposeful intent, they have gotten "Lost" through the years and researchers can now no longer find them.

1250	dem	Codex Demidovianus	Acts - Revelation
1250	div	Codex Divionensis	Romans - Revelation

Sword Unsheathed

Besides the **Itala Bible** from **157 AD** and all those other old Latin manuscripts, the Johannine Comma can also be found many other sources, such as:

- the Old Syriac – **170 AD**
- the **1350** Tepl Bible, a translation of Old Latin into ancient German
- the Waldensian Romaunt Bibles
- Waldensian and Albigensian writings from the 12th century
- the **1526** Tyndale NT
- the **1534** Luther Bible in German
- the **1535** Olivetan Bible in French
- the **1565** Greek text of Theodore Beza
- the **1568** Bishop's Bible
- the 12 language **1599** Nuremberg Polyglot
- the **1607** Diodati in Italian
- the Geneva Bible
- the **1611** King James

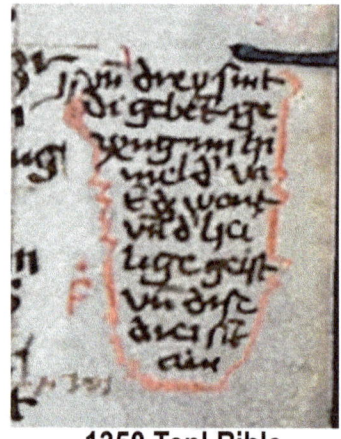

1350 Tepl Bible

> cause the sprete ys trueth. For there are thre whych beare recorde in heven / the father / the worde / and the wholy goost. And these thre are one. And there are thre which beare recorde in

1526 Tyndale NT

In addition, other English Bibles such as the: **1535** Coverdale Bible / **1537** Matthew's Bible / **1539** Taverner Bible / **1539** Great Bible, as well as Spanish Bibles, Dutch Bibles, Bohemian Bibles, Danish Bibles, the old Russian Synodal Bible, the old Gaelic Bible, the Czech Kralicka (**1613**), even Morrison's Chinese Bible (**1814**) etc. – in other words, many other Bibles and manuscripts from all over the world.

Luther Bible 1534 AD

French **Olivetan Bible** *(Waldensian)* **1535 AD**

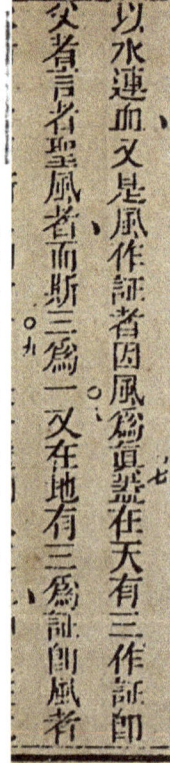

Robert Morrison's 1814 Chinese Bible

Additional Notes

Hutter's Nuremburg Polyglot
1599 AD

But even with all the various old manuscripts for evidence, those manuscripts are not the "foundation of proof," but rather are only further evidence for "confirmation purposes."

Internal Evidence of the Johannine Comma

Christians must realize that it is "Faith in God's word" that is our true foundation. The word of God specifically states *"Now faith is the substance of things hoped for, the evidence of things not seen."* Hebrews 11:1 God also didn't leave mankind any room to doubt. Instead He gave sufficient evidence on which to base their faith. He confirmed His "witness" by the way He had the original Greek written – a fact that can be confirmed by anyone who understands Greek grammar.

One question to ask the skeptics and critics might be, *"If 1 John 5:7 is mysteriously missing in some of the Greek manuscripts, and that is why you claim it shouldn't be included – why did renowned and scholarly men of learning like Erasmus, Beza, and the 54 King James translators choose to include this text in their Bible translations?"*

Certainly, these well-educated men would have been aware of the serious warnings against tampering with God's Word, such as Revelation 22:18,19, *"For I testify unto every man that heareth the words of the prophecy of this book, If any man shall add unto these things, God shall add unto him the plagues that are written in this book: And if any man shall take away from the words of the book of this prophecy, God shall take away his part out of the book of life, and out of the holy city, and from the things which are written in this book."*

For anyone who has done in-depth research into these translators of both the Greek text and the English **KJV**, the answer is obvious. These scholarly men were not just some random ignorant people off the street. Both Erasmus and Beza were top scholars in the known world. In fact, all of Europe and England vied for Erasmus' attention. Kings pleaded with him to make their country his home.

Also, as already pointed out in a previous chapter, the 54 **KJV** translators were the top scholars of the 16th & 17th centuries and every single one of them was fluent in at least four languages – English, Latin, Hebrew, and Greek. In fact, some of them knew many more languages (one of them knew 21 languages), and another one of them, John Reynolds, had a photographic memory and had studied all the ancient writings of the early church fathers and all the old manuscripts. It was shown that he could readily at any time, turn to any sentence in any manuscript or writing from the early centuries. He was so intelligent that he was known all over Europe as *"The Living Library."*

As scholars that were all extremely knowledgeable of the original Greek language, they would obviously recognize a detail about the Johannine Comma that many modern day critics either don't recognize or just chose to willfully ignore. They would recognize that the "internal evidence" of the Bible's Greek confirms the authenticity of the Johannine Comma.

When reference to the original Greek text is made, it is discovered that if the Johannine Comma is left out (like the modern critics want to claim), it leaves this Greek sentence, which all the **KJV** translators would easily recognize – is grammatically impossible!

οτι τρεις εισιν οι μαρτυρουντες το πνευμα και το υδωρ και το αιμα και οι τρεις εις το εν εισιν

The problem with leaving the Johannine Comma out of the text is that the nouns translated as "Spirit" "Water" and "Blood" in verse eight are 'neuter gender' in the Greek language, and as such, they require accompanying words that are also neuter gender. But the words and phrases that accompany them, such as the phrase *"there are three"* (οτι τρεις εισιν) and *"that bear witness"* (οι μαρτυρουντες) are masculine gender, as they would naturally be if they were accompanying masculine gender nouns. But only the nouns "heaven" "Father" and "Word" in the Johannine Comma in verse seven are "masculine" gender. This means that the Johannine Comma had to have been included in the original Greek manuscript as written by the apostle John.

If the Johannine Comma is left out (such as what is promoted by the modern critics and done in the text or footnotes of all the modern corrupted Bible versions) then the sentence in the original Greek doesn't make logical or grammatical sense.

Additional Notes

To give a simple example of this in the English language, it would be like writing the sentence, "He agrees with themselves."

This is why Dr. Gaussen in his famous book "The Inspiration of the Holy Scriptures" uses the grammatical argument and concludes basically:
Remove it, and the grammar becomes incoherent.
"Cette irrégularité, qui se justifie pleinement par ce qu'on nomme en Grammaire le principe d'attraction, le passage demeure dans son entier, devient inexplicable lorsque vous en voulez retrancher les paroles contestées."
(Théopneustie ou Pleine Inspiration des Saintes Écritures, pg. 281)

Also John Calvin wrote,
"the passage flows better when this clause is added, and as I see that IT IS FOUND IN THE BEST AND MOST APPROVED COPIES, I am inclined to receive it as the true reading."

So the Johannine Comma has not only been included in the line of Bibles that have been demonstrated to bear good fruit over the centuries – fruit like the Protestant Reformation – it also is required for the original Greek to make grammatical sense. Therefore, it is obvious to the honest, thinking mind, that 1 John 5:7 is a true rendering of the original text as written by John.

Likewise, it becomes quite obvious who the powers and individuals are behind the scenes that might want to tear down the Bibles that include it. Therefore, it would be well to heed the inspired counsel of Paul to Timothy and *"Hold fast the form of sound words... in faith and love which is in Christ Jesus."* 2 Timothy 1:13

Note D
Authenticity of Matthew 28:19 and the Godhead

Another verse which some modern skeptics are claiming that someone "added" to the Bible is Matthew 28:19. However, a simple examination of the facts reveal that this verse can be traced all the way back to the time period just after the time of the apostle John through the pure stream of Bibles.

Every surviving manuscript that contains the final pages of the book of Matthew, contains this verse. In other words, there is a 100% unanimous agreement in the manuscript evidence that Matthew 28:19 existed in the original. Anyone wishing to assert the theory that this text was added later has to go against the actual physical evidence.

Tertullian, quoting from the original Itala Bible (120–157 AD):
"Go," He saith, "teach the nations, baptizing them into the name of the _Father_, and of the _Son_, and of the _Holy Spirit_."
(Ante-Nicene Fathers, Vol. 3, book 1, The Writings of Tertullian, Chap. 13)

Irenaeus (the first missionary to the Waldensian area and a disciple of Polycarp who was personal friends with John the Revelator) **wrote around 182 AD:**
"He said to them," Go and teach all nations, baptizing them in the name of the _Father_, and of the _Son_, and of the _Holy Ghost_." (Mat 28:19)"
(Ante-Nicene Fathers, Vol. 1, section 8, book 3, Chap. 17)

Lucian of Antioch (compiler of the complete NT – finishing the work that Polycarp started) **in 300 AD:**
"We believe... in the Holy Ghost given for consolation and sanctification and perfection to those who believe; as also our Lord Jesus Christ commanded his disciples, saying, 'Go ye, teach all nations, baptizing them in the name of the Father, and of the Son, and of the Holy Ghost;' clearly of the Father who is really a _Father_, and of a _Son_ who is really a Son, and of the _Holy Ghost_ who is really a Holy Ghost; these names being assigned not vaguely nor idly, but indicating accurately the special personality, order, and glory of those named, so that in Personality they are three, but in harmony one."   (Creeds of Christendom, 1896, Vol.2, p.26)

995 Anglo-Saxon Bible
"Faraþ witodlice and læraþ ealle Þeoda, and fulligeaþ hig on naman _Fæder_, and _Suna_, and dæs _Hálgan Gástes_;"

Matthew 28:19 in Anglo-Saxon Bible

1522 Luther NT – "darumB geet hyn / vnd leren alle vólcter / vnd teusst sy in den namen des _vatters_ vnd des _suns_ vnd des _heyligen geysts_ /"

Additional Notes

1526 Tyndale Bible – *"Goo therefore and teache all nacions, baptisynge them in the name of the Father, and the Sonne, and the Holy Goost"*

1535 Coverdale Bible – *"Go ye youre waye therefore, and teach all nacions, and baptyse them in the name of the father, and of the Sonne, and of the holy goost"*

1535 Olivetan French Bible (Waldensian) – *"Allez donc & enseignez toutes jens / les baptizant au nom du pere & du filz & du sainct esperit."*

Matthews 28:19 in the French Olivetan Bible

1535 Erasmus Greek NT – "Πορευθέντες οὖν μαθητεύσατε πάντα τὰ ἔθνη, βαπτίζοντες αὐτοὺς εἰς τὸ ὄνομα τοῦ πατρὸς καὶ τοῦ υἱοῦ καὶ τοῦ ἁγίου ωνοὺματσ"

1556 Beza Greek NT - "Πορευθέντες οὖν μαθητεύσατε πάντα τὰ ἔθνη, βαπτίζοντες αὐτοὺς εἰς τὸ ὄνομα τοῦ πατρὸς καὶ τοῦ υἱοῦ καὶ τοῦ ἁγίου πνεύματος"

Matthew 28:19 in Erasmus Greek NT

1560 Geneva Bible – *"Go therefore, & teache all nacions, baptizing them in the Name of the Father, and the Sonne, and the holie Gost"*

1611 KJV Bible – *"Goe ye therefore, and teach all nations, baptizing them in the Name of the Father, and of the Sonne, and of the holy Ghost:"*

1633 Elzevir brothers Greek NT – "πορευθεντες ουν μαθητευσατε παντα τα εθνη βαπτιζοντες αυτους εις το ονομα του πατρος και του υιου και του αγιου πνευματος"

1769 KJV Bible – *"Go ye therefore, and teach all nations, baptizing them in the name of the Father, and of the Son, and of the Holy Ghost:"*

Sword Unsheathed

Note E
How to Study the Bible from the Bible

Believe in the inspiration of the Bible

"All scripture is given by inspiration of God, and is profitable for doctrine, for reproof, for correction, for instruction in righteousness: That the man of God may be perfect, throughly furnished unto all good works."
2 Timothy 3:16,17

"Knowing this first, that no prophecy of the scripture is of any private interpretation. For the prophecy came not in old time by the will of man: but holy men of God spake as they were moved by the Holy Ghost."
2 Peter 1:20, 21

Pray for the leading of the Holy Ghost after turning one's back on all known sin

"If I regard iniquity in my heart, the Lord will not hear me:" Psalm 66:18

"If ye then, being evil, know how to give good gifts unto your children: how much more shall your heavenly Father give the Holy Spirit to them that ask him?"
Luke 11:13

"Howbeit when he, the Spirit of truth, is come, he will guide you into all truth: for he shall not speak of himself; but whatsoever he shall hear, that shall he speak: and he will show you things to come."
John 16:13

"For every one that useth milk [the first principles of the oracles of God] *is unskillful in the word of righteousness: for he is a babe. But strong meat belongeth to them that are of full age, even those who by reason of use have their senses exercised to discern both good and evil."*
Hebrews 5:12-14

"If any man will do his will, he shall know of the doctrine, whether it be of God, or whether I speak of myself."
John 7:17

Dig Deep, Put Forth Quality Time and Effort

"Ask, and it shall be given you; seek, and ye shall find; knock, and it shall be opened unto you:"
Matthew 7:7

"I love them that love me; and those that seek me early shall find me."
Proverbs 8:17

Additional Notes

"Yea, if thou criest after knowledge, and liftest up thy voice for understanding; If thou seekest her as silver, and searchest for her as for hid treasures; Then shalt thou understand the fear of the LORD, and find the knowledge of God."
Proverbs 2:3-5

"But this I say, He which soweth sparingly shall reap also sparingly; and he which soweth bountifully shall reap also bountifully."
2 Corinthians 9:6

"For even when we were with you, this we commanded you, that if any would not work, neither should he eat."
2 Thessalonians 3:10

New Light Will Never Counteract Old Light
(Hidden Truths will NEVER contradict Surface Truths)

"To the law and to the testimony: if they speak not according to this word, it is because there is no light in them."
Isaiah 8:20

"Thus saith the LORD, Stand ye in the ways, and see, and ask for the old paths, where is the good way, and walk therein, and ye shall find rest for your souls..."
Jeremiah 6:16

"And thine ears shall hear a word behind thee, saying, This is the way, walk ye in it, when ye turn to the right hand, and when ye turn to the left."
Isaiah 30:21

Biblical Methods of Study

Proof-texting – *"Whom shall he teach knowledge? and whom shall he make to understand doctrine? them that are weaned from the milk, and drawn from the breasts. For precept must be upon precept, precept upon precept; line upon line, line upon line; here a little, and there a little: For with stammering lips and another tongue will he speak to this people."*
Isaiah 28:9-11

"Which things also we speak, not in the words which man's wisdom teacheth, but which the Holy Ghost teacheth; comparing spiritual things with spiritual. But the natural man receiveth not the things of the Spirit of God: for they are foolishness unto him: neither can he know them, because they are spiritually discerned."
1 Corinthians 2:12-14

Types – *"Now all these things happened unto them for ensamples: and they are written for our admonition, upon whom the ends of the world are come."*
1 Corinthians 10:11

"Howbeit that was not first which is spiritual, but that which is natural; and afterward that which is spiritual."
1 Corinthians 15:46

Hidden Manna/Prophecy/Sanctuary Studies – *"A wise man will hear, and will increase learning; and a man of understanding shall attain unto wise counsels: To understand a proverb, and the interpretation; the words of the wise, and their dark sayings."*
Proverbs 1:5,6

"Thy way, O God, is in the sanctuary: who is so great a God as our God?"
Psalm 77:13

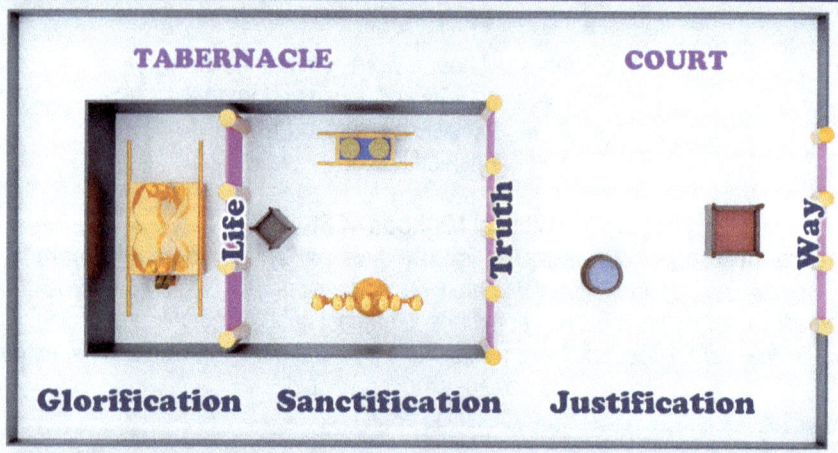

Additional Notes

Note F
Papal vs. Protestant Bibles & Bible Study Methods

Papal Principle of Higher Criticism shown in the Corrupt Bibles

- Bible verses have only one meaning
- Laypersons need someone more intelligent to interpret the Bible for them.

"A fundamental principle in grammatico-historical exposition is that the words and sentences can have but <u>one significance in one and the same connection</u>. The moment we neglect this principle we drift out upon a <u>sea of uncertainty and conjecture</u>." (Biblical Hermeneutics, p.103)

All counterfeit methods of Bible study attempt to use some outside source to define what the Bible teaches – whether the writings of some scholar, the arguments of some theologian, or the traditions of some church hierarchy. This is Roman Catholic doctrine – *you can't understand the Bible for yourself, only the "Church" can interpret the Bible.*

"Therefore, the Church is the divinely appointed Custodian and Interpreter of the Bible. For, her office of infallible Guide were superfluous if each individual could interpret the Bible for himself." (Faith of Our Fathers, p.63)

"In 1994, the Vatican officially criticized a literal interpretation of the Bible and said the fundamentalist approach to Scripture was 'a kind of intellectual suicide.'" (Billy Graham and His Friends, p.418)

Protestant Principle of the Pure-Line Bibles

- The Bible is inexhaustible
- The Bible is its own interpreter and the Holy Spirit your guide, thus it is equally as understandable to the common man as to the scholar

"In what light so ever we regard the Bible, whether with reference to revelation, to history, or to morality, it is an invaluable and inexhaustible mine of knowledge and virtue." (J.Q. Adams)

"Nobody ever outgrows Scripture: the book widens and deepens with our years." (Spurgeon)

"<u>It is impossible for any human mind to exhaust even one truth or promise of the Bible</u>. One catches the glory from one point of view, another from another point; yet we can discern only gleamings. The full radiance is beyond our vision. As we contemplate the great things of God's word, we look into a fountain that broadens and deepens beneath our gaze. Its breadth and depth pass our knowledge. As we

gaze, the vision widens; stretched out before us we behold a <u>boundless, shoreless sea</u>. Such study has vivifying power. The mind and heart acquire new strength, new life. This experience is the highest evidence of the divine authorship of the Bible."
(Education, p.171)

The Protestant principle is that the Holy Spirit is the Author of the Bible, and therefore – **only the Holy Spirit has the right and the ability to "interpret" the Word of God** – and this is done by allowing the Bible to interpret itself, by its own "internal evidence"!

"The Bible was not written for the scholar alone; on the contrary, it was designed for the common people. The great truths necessary for salvation are made as clear as noonday; and none will mistake and lose their way except those who follow their own judgment instead of the plainly revealed will of God."
(Steps to Christ, p.89)

Martin Luther wrote:
"It is very certain, that we cannot attain to the understanding of Scripture either by study or by the intellect. Your first duty is to begin by prayer. Entreat the Lord to grant you, of his great mercy, the true understanding of his Word. <u>There is no other interpreter of the Word of God than the Author of this Word</u>..."
(History of the Reformation, Vol. 1 Book 3, p.106)

History tells of Wycliffe:
"Wycliffe accepted the Holy Scriptures with implicit faith as the inspired revelation of God's will, a sufficient rule of faith and practice. ...he taught not only that the Bible is a perfect revelation of God's will, but that <u>the Holy Spirit is its only interpreter</u>, and that every man is, by the study of its teachings, to learn his duty for himself. Thus he turned the minds of men from the pope and the Church of Rome to the word of God."
(The Great Controversy, p.93)

The Protestant method of Bible study is to let the Bible interpret itself. (The Bible always interprets itself!)

"Observe system in the study of the Scriptures... <u>Make the Bible its own expositor</u>, bringing together all that is said concerning a given subject at different times and under varied circumstances."
(Counsels for the Church, p. 87)

"I believe the Bible is to be understood and received in the plain and obvious meaning of its passages; for I cannot persuade myself that a book intended for the instruction and conversion of the whole world should cover its true meaning in any such mystery and doubt that none but critics and philosophers can discover it."
(Protestant Statesman Daniel Webster)

Additional Notes

"When you search the Scriptures with an earnest desire to learn the truth, God will breathe His Spirit into your heart and impress your mind with the light of His word. The Bible is its own interpreter, one passage explaining another. <u>By comparing scriptures referring to the same subjects, you will see beauty and harmony of which you have never dreamed</u>. There is no other book whose perusal strengthens and enlarges, elevates and ennobles the mind, as does the perusal of this Book of books. Its study imparts new vigor to the mind, which is thus brought in contact with subjects requiring earnest thought, and is drawn out in prayer to God for power to comprehend the truths revealed." (*Testimonies*, vol.4, p. 499)

Allowing the Bible to be it's own interpreter means that if one wants to understand the Biblical teaching on the subject of death – then they must look up every verse that talks about "death," "dying," "die," "dead," etc. throughout the whole Bible. Each text will give the Bible doctrine more detail until one has the complete picture of that Bible doctrine. Though many times a single text that summarizes the correct Bible doctrine can be found, the reader must always take every text into account.

In other words, if the Bible has ten verses that talk about the subject, and eight of them seem to say one thing and two of them say something else – then one is not understanding the issue correctly. They must go back and see how ALL the verses agree – and only when they have an understanding of the doctrine in which every single text matches – then they will have the correct understanding of that Bible doctrine.

If a single text contradicts what the reader thinks is the correct doctrine, then their interpretation of that Bible doctrine is not quite correct, and they need to reexamine the Bible to understand the doctrine correctly.

Another "layer of meaning" that one can find, by allowing the Bible to interpret itself, is to first, locate a text. Then use a concordance to look up each "real" word and see everywhere that that particular word is used throughout the Bible. Consider all of these references to discover the "spiritual meaning" of each "real" word. Then one can read the verse inserting the spiritual meaning in place of the "real" word.

*"Thy **word** is a **lamp** unto my feet, and a light unto my path."* Psalm 119:105

For example: Ecclesiastes 11:1

***"Cast thy bread upon the waters:
for thou shalt find it after many days."***

Real Word	Spiritual Meaning	Proof-Text
Bread	Bible, Word of God	Amos 8:11, Matthew 4:4
Waters	People, Nations, Inhabited areas	Revelation 17:15
Days	Years	Ezekiel 4:6, Numbers 14:34

Now one can substitute the "spiritual meanings" back into the verse:

"Cast (spread) the Word of God to the people and nations: for you shall find (see the results of) it after many years."

This method makes the Bible "come to life"! Once the reader gets the spiritual definition memorized, they will discover that the spiritual definition "holds true" throughout the entire Bible! In this verse, the word "Bread" represents the "Word of God," the "Scriptures." So one may recognize that every story in the Bible that talks about bread, is referring to the Word of God. All the stories of the Old and New Testaments, are "Acted Parables" talking about the "Last Days"! The reader may also notice also the characteristics listed by the condition of the bread. If it is moldy or defiled bread, it is talking about Bibles that have been contaminated by the doctrines of man. If it is good and pure bread, it is the pure, unadulterated Bible.

Here is another example: Isaiah 7:15

"Butter and honey shall he eat, that he may know to refuse the evil and choose the good."

Now one may note that this is a prophecy about Christ (see verse 14).

Question – "How much butter and honey does a person have to eat in order to know the difference between good and evil?" Obviously, eating lots of butter and honey will not make one more intelligent, it will only make them fat! So this text must have a spiritual meaning.

Additional Notes

It is helpful to always think of the "physical" in order to understand the "spiritual"! Butter comes from churning milk. The components of the butter are always in the milk, but unless it is churned, one will never find the butter. Also the more it is churned, the more butter may be found.

Real Word	Spiritual Meaning	Proof-Text
Milk	Basic principles (surface reading) of God's Word	Hebrews 5:12-14
Churn Milk (go back and forth)	Compare Scripture with Scripture	Isaiah 28:10-13; 1 Corinthians 2:13
Butter	The hidden treasure found in God's Word	Proverbs 30:33; Job 20:17
Honey	The Words of God, 10 Commandments	Psalm 119:103; Psalm 19:7-10
Eat	To read (to gain knowledge or understanding)	Jeremiah 15:16

Now one can substitute the spiritual meaning back into the verse:

"The hidden treasure (hidden knowledge of God) and God's Law shall he gain understanding of, that he may know to refuse the evil and choose the good." Isaiah 7:15 Hidden Treasure Paraphrase

As the reader get these spiritual meanings learned and memorized, they will start to see things in the Bible that they did not see before.

In other words, whenever one sees a text that uses the word "butter," they can automatically realize that it has a "spiritual layer" that is talking about the "hidden treasure and meaning in the Word of God!"

This is one of the things the Bible is talking about when it says:

"For precept must be upon precept, precept upon precept; line upon line, line upon line; here a little, and there a little:" Isaiah 28:10

Note G
William Miller's Rules of Bible Interpretation

"Those who are engaged in proclaiming the third angel's message are searching the Scriptures upon the same plan that Father Miller adopted."
(Review & Herald, Nov. 25, 1884)

"His manner of studying the Bible is thus described by himself:

'I determined to lay aside all my prepossessions, to thoroughly compare Scripture with Scripture, and to pursue its study in a regular, methodical manner. I commenced with Genesis, and read verse by verse, proceeding no faster than the meaning of the several passages should be so unfolded as to leave me free from embarrassment respecting any mysticisms or contradictions. Whenever I found anything obscure, my practice was to compare it will all collateral passages; and, by the help of Cruden, I examined all the texts of Scripture in which were found any of the prominent words contained in any obscure portion. Then, by letting every word have its proper bearing on the subject of the text, if my view of it harmonized with every collateral passage in the Bible, it ceased to be a difficulty. In this way I pursued the study of the Bible, in my first perusal of it, for about two years, and was fully satisfied that it is its own interpreter. I found that by a comparison of Scripture with history, all the prophecies, as far as they have been fulfilled, had been fulfilled literally; that all the various figures, metaphors, parables, similitudes, etc., of the Bible, were either explained in their immediate connection, or the terms in which they were expressed were defined in other portions of the word; and when thus explained, are to be literally understood in accordance with such explanation. I was thus satisfied that the Bible is a system of revealed truths, so clearly and simply given, that the wayfaring man, though a fool, need not err therein.'

In pursuing his study of the Holy Scriptures, Mr. Miller adopted the following rules of interpretation:"

"1. Every word must have its proper bearing on the subject presented in the Bible." Proof, Matt. 5:18; Matt. 4:4.

"2. All Scripture is necessary, and may be understood by a diligent application and study." Proof, 2 Tim. 3:15-17.

"3. Nothing revealed in the Scriptures can or will be hid from those who ask in faith, not wavering." Proof, Deut. 29:29; Matt. 10:26,27; 1 Cor. 2:10; Phil. 3:15; Isa. 45:11; Matt. 21:22; John 4:13,14; 15:7; James 1:5,6; 1 John 5:13-15.

Additional Notes

"4. To understand doctrine, bring all the scriptures together on the subject you wish to know; then let every word have its proper influence; and if you can form your theory without a contradiction, you cannot be in error." Proof, Isa. 28:7-29; 35:8; Prov. 29:27; Luke 24:27,44,45; Rom.16:26; James 5:19; 2 Pet.1:19,20.

"5. Scripture must be its own expositor, since it is a rule of itself. If I depend on a teacher to expound to me, and he should guess at its meaning, or desire to have it so on account of his sectarian creed, or to be thought wise, then his guessing, desire, creed, or wisdom, is my rule, and not the Bible." Proof, Ps. 19:7-11; 119:97-105; Matt. 23:8-10; 1 Cor. 2:12-16; Eze. 34:18,19; Luke 11:52; Matt. 2:7,8.

"6. God has revealed things to come, by visions, in figures and parables; and in this way the same things are oftentime revealed again and again, by different visions, or in different figures and parables. If you wish to understand them, you must combine them all in one." Proof, Ps. 89:19; Hos.12:10; Hab. 2:2; Acts 2:17; 1 Cor. 10:6; Heb. 9:9,24; Ps. 78:2; Matt. 13:13,34; Gen. 41:1-32; Dan. 2,7, and 8; Acts 10:9-16.

"7. Visions are always mentioned as such." 2 Cor. 12:1.

"8. Figures always have a figurative meaning, and are used much in prophecy to represent future things, times and events – such as mountains, meaning governments, Dan. 2:35,44; beasts, meaning kingdoms, Dan. 7:8,17; waters, meaning people, Rev. 17:1,15; day meaning year, etc. Eze. 4:6."

"9. Parables are used as comparisons, to illustrate subjects, and must be explained in the same way as figures, by the subject and Bible." Mark 4:13.

"10. Figures sometimes have two or more different significations, as day is used in a figurative sense to represent three different periods of time, namely: first, indefinite, Eccl. 7:14; and second, definite, a day for a year, Eze.4:6; and third, a day for a thousand years, 2 Pet. 3:8. "The right construction will harmonize with the Bible, and make good sense; other constructions will not."

"11. If a word makes good sense as it stands, and does no violence to the simple laws of nature, it is to be understood literally; if not, figuratively." Rev. 12:1,2; 17:3-7.

"12. To learn the meaning of a figure, trace the word through your Bible, and when you find it explained, substitute the explanation for the word used; and if it make good sense, you need not look further; if not, look again."

Sword Unsheathed

"13. To know whether we have the true historical event for the fulfillment of prophecy: If you find every word of the prophecy (after the figures are understood) is literally fulfilled, then you may know that your history is the true event; but if one word lacks a fulfillment, then you must look for another event, or wait its future development; for God takes care that history and prophecy shall agree, so that the true believing children of God may never be ashamed." Ps. 22:5; Isa. 45:17-19; 1 Pet. 2:6; Rev. 17:17; Acts 3:18.

"14. The most important rule of all is, that you must have faith. It must be a faith that requires a sacrifice, and, if tried, would give up the dearest object on earth, the world and all its desires – character, living, occupation, friends, home, comforts, and worldly honors. If any of these should hinder our believing any part of God's word, it would show our faith to be vain. Nor can we ever believe so long as one of these motives lies lurking in our hearts. We must believe that God will never forfeit his word; and we can have confidence that He who takes notice of the sparrow's fall, and numbers the hairs of our head, will guard the translation of his own word, and throw a barrier around it, and prevent those who sincerely trust in God, and put implicit confidence in his word, from erring far from the truth."

(1868 J.W., *Life Incidents*. p. 34-38)

For fourteen years, from 1816–1831, Miller diligently studied the Bible before going forth to promote his views on prophecy.

Additional Notes

1850 Prophecy Chart
Demonstrating how Miller and those who were part of the Millerite Movement Studied "Line Upon Line"

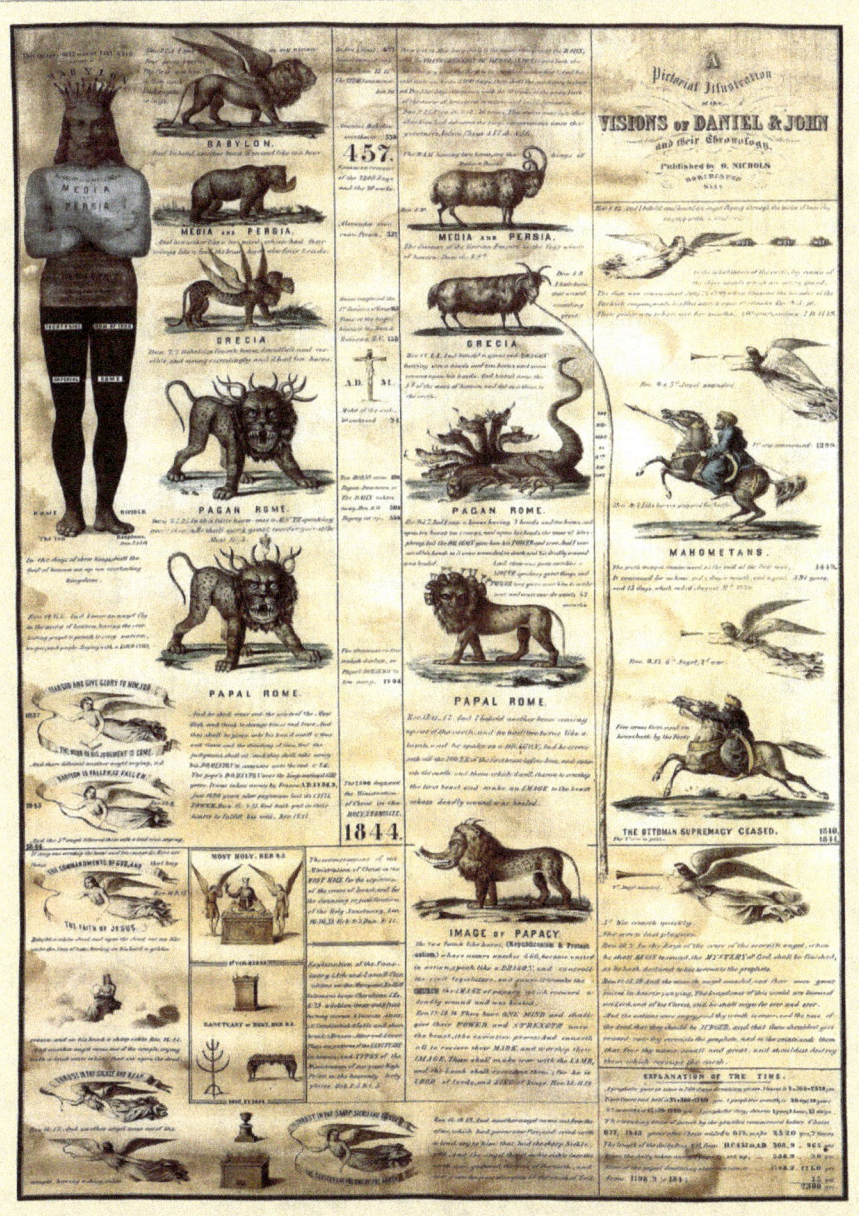

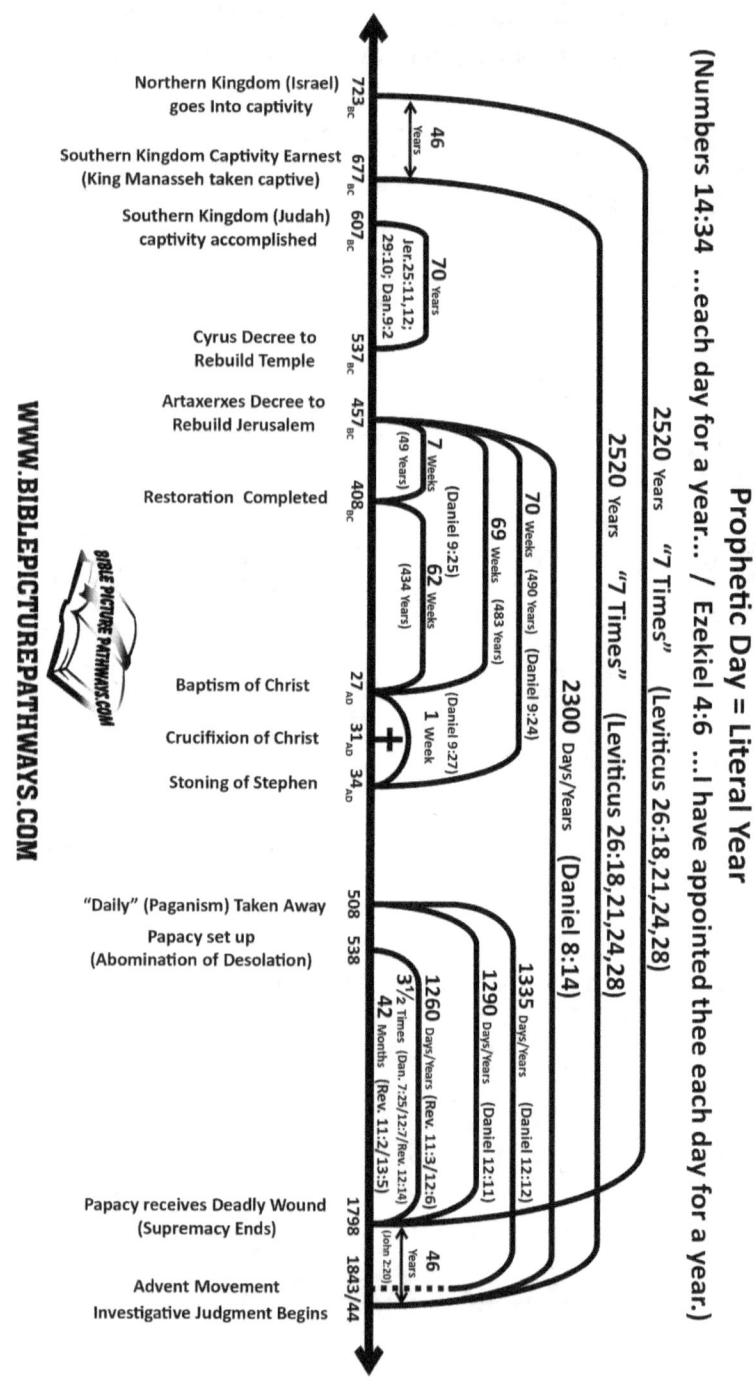

Additional Notes

Note H
"Christian" Fiction

The infiltration of Christianity by fantasy, mythology, and the occult!

Universalist George MacDonald (**1824-1905**), was considered the pioneer in the field of fantasy novels. He wrote a dozen or so fantasy novels as well as many other works of fiction.

His fantasy novels such as "Phantastes" and "Lilith" explored the world of the occult, mythology, magic and other spiritualistic themes. Lilith, is in fact, the name occultists give as Adam's (mythical) evil first wife.

MacDonald's writings were the inspiration behind many other fantasy writers such as Lewis Carroll, J.R.R. Tolkien, C.S. Lewis, and J.K. Rowling.

Charles Dodgson (aka Lewis Carroll) (**1832-1898**) was good friends with MacDonald and when Carroll wrote his mystical fantasy "Alice in Wonderland," it was MacDonald who encouraged his work and persuaded him to lengthen the story.

Roman Catholic J.R.R. Tolkien (**1892-1973**), was the author of several fantasy/mythology novels such as "Lord of the Rings" and "Hobbit." He spent his childhood reading MacDonald's novels and grooming his mind for fantasy. His writings are filled with spiritualism and sorcery. (It has been claimed by some that Tolkien even copied some material for his novels from the Wiccan text called "The Book of Shadows.")

C.S. Lewis (**1898-1963**) was a good friend and convert of J. R. R. Tolkien. He was also a large fan of MacDonald's novels. Lewis wrote several introductions and prefaces to some of MacDonald's republished books. In MacDonald's Lilith, C.S. Lewis wrote of MacDonald:

"I have never concealed the fact that I regarded him as my master; indeed I fancy I have never written a book in which I did not quote from him."

C.S. Lewis was also a fantasy/mythology novelist whose supposed "Christian" writings contain pagan gods, witchcraft, magic spells, and occult themes.

Sadly, many Christians and Christian bookstores have been duped into believing the lie that Lewis' novels are "Christian Allegories" and somehow constitute good reading material, when in reality, they are not. They are occult sorcery disguised as "Christian." There are even modern day witches that state that they got into witchcraft by reading C.S. Lewis' novels.

Lewis himself reveals his twisted unChristian mindset:

"I have the deepest respect even for Pagan myths, still more for <u>myths in the Holy Scripture</u>."   (C.S. Lewis, *The Problem of Pain*, p. 66)

"I have therefore no difficulty in accepting, say, the view of those scholars who tell us that the account of <u>Creation in Genesis is derived from earlier Semitic stories which were Pagan and mythical</u>."   (C.S. Lewis, *Reflections on the Psalms*, p. 110)

"Their Master had told them so. He shared, and indeed created, their delusion. He said in so many words, 'this generation shall not pass till all these things be done' And he was wrong. He clearly knew no more about the end of the world than anyone else." It is certainly the most embarrassing verse in the Bible... The one exhibition of error and the one confession of ignorance grow side by side. That they stood thus in the mouth of Jesus himself, and were not merely placed thus by the reporter, we surely need not doubt...<u>The facts, then, are these: that Jesus professed himself (in some sense) ignorant, and within a moment showed that he really was so.</u>"   (C.S. Lewis, *The World's Last Night and Other Essays*, p.98-99)

The names of characters and places in Lewis' Chronicles of Narnia come from a combination of places. Some are the names of real demons and occult sources, some are pagan gods and goddesses, some are from Roman Catholic mysticism, and the name Narnia is from the real town in Italy where his character "Lucy" was born as a real Roman Catholic mystic and a stigmatic.

J.K. Rowling, the author of the sorcery/witchcraft fantasy novel series on Harry Potter, was also influenced by the fantasy/occult themes of C.S. Lewis.

"As a child, Rowling has said her early influences included The Lion, The Witch and The Wardrobe by C.S. Lewis..."   (Wikipedia)

And today, many ignorant Christians allow their children to read these novels, or to watch movies based on these novels – and the world of Satan marches into these Christian homes and takes control!

Additional Notes

Note I
Law of God and the Law as Changed by Rome

Exodus 20:2-17

The Law of God in the Bible	Law as Changed by Rome
1) *I am the LORD thy God, which have brought thee out of the land of Egypt, out of the house of bondage. Thou shalt have no other gods before me.*	1) *I am the Lord thy God, thou shalt not have strange gods before me.*
2) *Thou shalt not make unto thee any graven image, or any likeness of any thing that is in heaven above, or that is in the earth beneath, or that is in the water under the earth: Thou shalt not bow down thyself to them, nor serve them: for I the LORD thy God am a jealous God, visiting the iniquity of the fathers upon the children unto the third and fourth generation of them that hate me; And shewing mercy unto thousands of them that love me, and keep my commandments.*	2) *Thou shalt not take the name of the Lord thy God in vain.*
3) *Thou shalt not take the name of the LORD thy God in vain; for the LORD will not hold him guiltless that taketh his name in vain.*	3) *Remember that thou keep holy the Sabbath-day.*
4) *Remember the sabbath day, to keep it holy. Six days shalt thou labour, and do all thy work: But the seventh day is the sabbath of the LORD thy God: in it thou shalt not do any work, thou, nor thy son, nor thy daughter, thy manservant, nor thy maidservant, nor thy cattle, nor thy stranger that is within thy gates: For in six days the LORD made heaven and earth, the sea, and all that in them is, and rested the seventh day: wherefore the LORD blessed the sabbath day, and hallowed it.*	4) *Honor thy father and thy mother.*

| **The Law of God in the Bible** | **Law as Changed by Rome** |
| Continued | Continued |

5) *Honour thy father and thy mother: that thy days may be long upon the land which the LORD thy God giveth thee.*

5) *Thou shalt not kill.*

6) *Thou shalt not kill.*

6) *Thou shalt not commit adultery.*

7) *Thou shalt not commit adultery.*

7) *Thou shalt not steal.*

8) *Thou shalt not steal.*

8) *Thou shalt not bear false witness against thy neighbor.*

9) *Thou shalt not bear false witness against thy neighbour.*

9) *Thou shalt not covet thy neighbor's wife.*

10) *Thou shalt not covet thy neighbour's house, thou shalt not covet thy neighbour's wife, nor his manservant, nor his maidservant, nor his ox, nor his ass, nor any thing that is thy neighbour's.*

10) *Thou shalt not covet thy neighbor's goods.*

Bibliography

This book has been the result of over seven years of research carried out by the compiler. Originally begun simply as a personal study, after many requests for him to share what he was learning, it was compiled into book format.

In the compilation of this work, literally thousands of Bible history pages on the internet were examined in addition to researching through the following list of books and documents. The compiler has tried his best to track quotes back to their original sources, though sometimes this was not possible.

Please note again, this is just a list of the different source materials referenced, it should not be considered a "blanket endorsement" for every single one of these works. Some are from good and excellent sources, some are not; some are Protestant, others are Catholic; some of these resources are rare or hard to find and contain priceless information, while some are a mixture of truth and error. The compiler wishes to state that NOT all the information one finds while researching through some of these resources is correct. It takes much prayer for guidance from the Holy Spirit and much study, to differentiate between the true facts and the disinformation; to gather the truth and weed out the lies.

Resources

ADENEY, WALTER F., *The Greek and Eastern Churches*, Charles Scribner's Sons, 1908

ALLIX, PETER, *Remarks upon the Ecclesiastical History of the Ancient Churches of the Albigenses*, Oxford Clarendon Press, 1831

ALLIX, PETER, *Some Remarks upon the Ecclesiastical History of the Ancient Churches of the Piedmont*, Oxford Clarendon Press, 1821

ALLEY, FREDERICK, *The Dignity of Man*, Gorham Press, 1919

ANDERSON, CHRISTOPHER, *The Annals of the English Bible*, Volumes 1-2, William Pickering, 1845

ANDERSON, JAMES, *Royal Genealogies*, James Bettenham, 1732

ANDREWS, JOHN N., *History of the Sabbath*, Review & Herald Publishing Association, 1887

ARNAUD, HENRI, & ACLAND, HUGH D., *The Glorious Recovery by the Vaudois of their Valleys, London*, 1827

BAGSTER, SAMUEL, *Ecclesiastical Historians of the First Six Centuries*, Samuel Bagster & Sons, 1844

BAGSTER, SAMUEL, *The Bible in Every Land*, Samuel Bagster & Sons, 1860

BAGSTER, SAMUEL, *The Holy Scriptures by Miles Coverdale*, Samuel Bagster & Sons, 1847

BARRETT, E. BOYD, *Rome Stoops to Conquer*, Orion Publishing, 2004

BARRETT, WILLIAM T., *The Defiled Bread; Which Version of the Bible Shall I Use?*, Barrett, 2007

BAYBROOK, GAR, *The S.D.A Bible*, Leaves of Autumn, 1994

BEACH, BERT B., *Vatican II: Bridging the Abyss*, Review & Herald Publishing, 1968
BLAIR, ADAM, *History of the Waldenses*, Vol. 1 & 2, Adam Black, Edinburgh, 1832
BLISS, SYLVESTER, *Analysis of Sacred Chronology*, Publish by Joshua Himes, 1850
BOEHMER, EDWARD, *Bibliotheca Wiffeniana: Spanish Reformers of Two Centuries*, Karl J. Trubner, 1904
BOMPIANI, SOPHIA V., *A Short History of the Italian Waldenses*, A. S. Barnes & Co., 1897
BOSWORTH, JOSEPH, *The Gothic and Anglo-Saxon Gospels with the Versions of Wycliffe and Tyndale*, Oxford University Press, 1865
BRANDT, GERARD, *The History of the Reformation & other Ecclesiastical Transactions in & about the Low Countries*, Volumes 1-4, Timothy Childe London, 1720
BRAUER, JERALD C., *The History of Protestantism in America*, A Narrative History, Philadelphia, Westminister Press, 1953
BRIGGS, CHARLES A., *The Authority of Holy Scripture*, Charles Scribner's Sons, 1891
BROWNLEE, WILLIAM CRAIG, *Sketch of History of the Western Apostolic Churches from which the Roman Church Apostatized*, American Protestant Society, 1857
BUCKLEY, JOHN W., *Prophecy Unveiled*, Xulon Press, 2007
BURGON, JOHN WILLIAM, *Causes of the Corruption of the Traditional Text*, George Bell & Sons, 1896
BURGON, JOHN WILLIAM, *The Revision Revised*, William Clowes & Sons, 1883
BURGON, JOHN WILLIAM, *The Last Twelve Verses of the Gospel According to S. Mark*, James Parker and Co., 1871
BURGON, JOHN WILLIAM, *Traditional Text of the Holy Gospels Vindicated and Established*, George Bell & Sons, 1896
BURNS, CATHY, *Billy Graham and His Friends*, Sharing, 2001
BURNS, CATHY, *Masonic & Occult Symbols Illustrated*, Cathy Burns, 2009
BURNSIDE, GEORGE, *The Falling Away from Truth*
CATHCART, WILLIAM, *The Ancient British and Irish Churches*, Charles H. Banes, 1894
CHEETHAM, S., *A History of the Christian Church During the First Six Centuries*, Cambridge University Press, 1894
CHEETHAM, S., *A History of the Christian Church Since the Reformation*, Cambridge University Press, 1907
CHICK, JACK, *Smokescreens*, Chick Publications, 1983
CHICK, JACK, *The Prophet*, Chick Publications, 1988
CHINIQUY, CHARLES, *Fifty Years in the Church of Rome*, S. R. Briggs, 1886
CLOUD, DAVID, *Unholy Hands on God's Holy Book*, Way of Life Literature, 2012

Bibliography

COLLETT, SIDNEY, *All About the Bible*, Fleming H. Revell Company
COMMITTEE ON PROBLEMS IN BIBLE TRANSLATION, *Problems in Bible Translation*, Review and Herald Publishing, 1954
CONDIT, BLACKFORD, *The History of the English Bible*, A.S Barnes & Company, 1882
CORNWELL, JOHN, *Hitler's Pope, The Secret History of Pius XII*, Penguin Books, 1999
COULTON, G. G., *The Roman Catholic Church and the Bible*, Simpkin, Marshall, Hamilton, Kent & Co., 1921
CREWS, SHARON THOMAS, *The Faithful Witness*, Amazing Facts, Inc., 1986
CURRENT, FREIDEL, BRINKLEY, WILLIAMS, *American History: A Survey*, Alfred Knopf Inc., 1987
D'AUBIGNE, J. H. MERLE, *A Discourse Against Modern Oxford Theology*, Wm. Wooddy, 1843
D'AUBIGNE, J. H. MERLE, *History of the Reformation of the Sixteenth Century*, Baker Book House, 1976
DANIELS, DAVID W., *New King James The Bridge Bible*, Chick Publications, 2020
DANIELS, DAVID W., *Why They Changed the Bible*, Chick Publications, 2014
DE JONGE, H.J., *Erasmus and the Comma Johanneum*, Extrait des Ephemerides Theologicae Lovanienses, 1980
DE ROSA, PETER, *Vicars of Christ, The Dark Side of the Papacy*, Crown Publishers, Inc., 1988
DE THOYRAS, RAPIN, (French) [English Translated by TINDAL, N.], *The History of England*, Volume 1, John & Paul Knapton, London, 1743
DEVENS, R.M., *The Great Events of Our Past Century*, Hugh Heron, 1881
DIBDIN, THOMAS FROGNALL, *An Introduction to the Knowledge of Rare and Valuable Editions of the Greek and Latin Classics*, Harding and Lepard, 1827
DOBSHUTZ, ERNST VON, *The Influence of the Bible on Civilisation*, Charles Scribner's Sons, 1914
DRAPER, JOHN WILLIAM, *A History of the Intellectual Development of Europe*, Vol. 1, George Bell & Sons, London, 1875
EDWARDS, TRYON, *The New Dictionary of Thoughts*, Standard Book Company, 1963
EDWARDSON, CHRISTIAN, *Facts of Faith*, Southern Publishing Assoc. 1943
EPPERSON, A. RALPH, *The New World Order*, Publius Press, 2008
EPPERSON, A. RALPH, *The Unseen Hand*, Publius Press, 1995
FABER, GEORGE STANLEY, *The History of the Ancient Vallenses and Albigenses*, Hartland Publications, 1997
FARRER, J. A., *Literary Forgeries, Longmans*, Green and Co., 1907
FARSTAD, ARTHUR L., *The Greek New Testament according to the Majority Text*, Thomas Nelson Publishers, 1985
FARSTAD, ARTHUR L., *The New King James Version in the Great Tradition*, Thomas Nelson, Inc., 1989
FERRELL, VANCE, *The Fabulous First Centuries of Christianity*, Harvestime Books, 2006
FLESCH, RUDOLF, *The Art of Plain Talk*, Harper & Brothers Publishers, 1946

FOX, JOHN, *Fox's Book of Martyrs*, John Winston Company, 1926
FROOM, LEROY, *The Prophetic Faith of Our Fathers*, Review & Herald Publishing Assoc. 1948
FULLER, DAVID OTIS, *Which Bible?*, Grand Rapids International Publications, 1975
GIBBONS, JAMES CARDINAL, *The Faith of our Fathers*, Tan Books, 1980
GILLY, W. S., *Vigilantius and His Times*, Seeley, Burnside, & Seeley, 1844
GILLY, WILLIAM, *Waldensian Researches*, Gilbert & Rivington, 1831
GIPP, SAMUEL C., *An Understandable History of the Bible*, Gipp, 2000
GIPP, SAMUEL C., *The Answer Book*, Gipp, 1989
GOODSPEED, EDGAR J., *How Came the Bible?*, 1940
GRADY, WILLIAM, *Final Authority*, Grady Publications, 1993
GRESHAM, JOE, *The Men, Motives & Malicious Mutilations Behind the Modern Bible Versions*, Fourth Angel Publishing, 2017
GRESHAM, JOE, *The Diabolical Dangers and Doctrinal Destruction in the Modern Bible Versions*, Fourth Angel Publishing, 2017
GUINNESS, H. GRATTAN, *Romanism and the Reformation*, Hartland Publications, 2008
HALL, MANLY P., 'Asia in the Balance of the Scales', *Horizon: The Magazine of Useful & Intelligent Living*, Vol.4, No.1, Horizon Publishing Co., Spring 1944
HALL, MANLY P., 'The Secret Doctrine in the Bible:The Revelation of St. John', *The Students Monthly Letter*, Fourth Year, Letter 12, Philosophical Research Society, Inc.
HASKELL, STEPHEN N., *The Story of Daniel the Prophet*, South Lancaster Printing Co., 1908
HASKELL, STEPHEN N., *The Story of the Seer of Patmos*, Southern Publishing Association, 1905
HESCHEL, SUSANNAH, *The Theological Faculty of the University of Jena during the Third Reich*, Dartmouth College, 2000
HILLS, EDWARD F., *The King James Version Defended*, Christian Research Press, 1984
HISLOP, ALEXANDER, *The Two Babylons*, S.W. Partridge & Company, 1871
HODGKIN, THOMAS, *Italy and Her Invaders*, Oxford University Press, 1892
HORE, A.H., *Eighteen Centuries of the Orthodox Greek Church*, James Parker & Co., 1899
HORNE, THOMAS HARTWELL, *An Introduction to the Critical Study and Knowledge of the Holy Scriptures*, Longman, Brown, Green, Longmans, & Roberts, 1856
HORNE, THOMAS HARTWWELL, *An Introduction to the Critical Study and Knowledge of the Holy Scriptures*, T. Cadwell, Strand, 1828
HORT, ARTHUR FENTON, *Life and Letters of Fenton John Anthony Hort*, Macmillan and Co., 1896
HOSKIER, H.C., *Codex B and its Allies*, William Clowes and Sons London, 1914
HOSKIER, H.C., *Von Soden's Text of the New Testament*, Journal of Theological Studies Vol. 15, APRIL, 1914

Bibliography

JONES, ALONZO T., *The Two Republics*, Review and Herald Publishing Co.,1891
JONES, FLOYD NOLEN, *The Septuagint: A Critical Analysis*, Kings Word Press, 2000
JURASINSKI, STEFAN, *The Old English Penitentials and Anglo-Saxon Law*, Cambridge University Press, 2015
KAH, GARY H., *En Route to Global Occupation*, Huntington House Publishers, 1992
KAH, GARY H., *The New World Religion*, Hope International Publishing, 1998
KENYON, FREDERIC G., *Our Bible and the Ancient Manuscripts*, Eyre and Spottiswoode, London, 1895
KILGOUR, ROBERT, *The Bible throughout the World*, World Dominion Press, 1939
KING JAMES I, *Basilikon Doron*, Cambridge University Press, 1599
KOHLENBERGER, JOHN, *All About Bibles*, Oxford University Press, 1985
LAMPE, G. W. H., *The Cambridge History of the Bible*, Cambridge University Press, 1969
LOUGHBOROUGH, J. N., *Heavenly Visions*, Leah Schmitke, 1984
LAUGHRAN, DAVID B., *Bible Versions*, Stewarton Bible School, Scotland,
LIGHTFOOT, NEIL R., *How We Got The Bible*, Sweet Publishing Co., 1962
MACFARLAND, CHARLES S., *Federal Council of Churches Quadrennial Report* "Christian Cooperation & World Redemption," Missionary Education Movement, 1917
MACKIE, G.M., *Bible Manners and Customs*, Fleming H. Revell Co., 1898
MARTIN, MALACHI, *The Jesuits*, Simon & Schuster, Inc., 1987
MCCABE, JAMES DABNEY, *Cross and Crown*, National Publishing Company, 1874
MCCARTY, BURKE, *The Suppressed Truth about the Assassination of Abraham Lincoln*, Burke McCarty, 1922
MCCLURE, A.W., *The Translators Revived*, Charles Scribner, 1853
MCCOMB, SAMUEL, *The Making of the English Bible*, Moffat, Yard and Company, 1909
MEIER, J. H., *What Catholics and Protestants Should Know*, Pacific Press Publishing, 1953
MEYERS, H. H., *With Cloak & Dagger*, Hartland Publications, 3rd Ed. 2006
MEYERS, H. H., *Battle of the Bibles*, New Millennium Publications, 1997
MIDDLETON, CONYERS, *A Letter from Rome Showing the Exact Conformity between Popery and Paganism*, William Innys and Richard Manby, London, 1733
MONTEITH, STANLEY, *Brotherhood of Darkness*, Hearthstone Publishing, 2000
MOORMAN, JACK, **When the KJV Departs from the "Majority" Text**, Dean Burgon Society, 2010
MORLAND, SAMUEL, *The History of the Evangelical Churches of the Valleys of the Piemont*, Henry Hills, London, 1658
MORRIS, HENRY M., *Defending the Faith: Upholding Biblical Christianity and the Genesis Record*, Master Books, 1999
MUSTON, ALEXIS, *The Israel of the Alps - A Complete History of the Waldenses of Piedmont*, Volumes 1 & 2, Blackie And Son London, 1866

NEVIN, ALFRED, et. al., ***The Parallel Bible***, The Authorized and Revised Versions, A.J. Holman & Co., 1888
NOLAN, FREDERICK, ***Inquiry into the Integrity of the Greek Vulgate***, F. C. & J. Rivington, 1815
NORTON, PETER B., et. al., ***Encyclopedia Britannica 15th Edition***, Encyclopedia Britannica Inc., 1994
ORR, JAMES, ***The International Standard Bible Encyclopaedia***, The Howard-Severance Company, Chicago, 1915
PARIS, EDMOND, ***The Secret History of the Jesuits***, Chick Publications, 1975
PHELPS, ERIC JON, ***Vatican Assassins***, Halycon Unified Services, 2001
PIPER, KEITH, ***Serious Omissions in the NIV Bible***, Keith Piper, 2005
POLANO, PIETRO SOAVE, ***The History of the Council of Trent***, J. Macock London, 1676
POLLOCK, JOHN, ***Billy Graham: The Authorized Biography***, Zondervan, 1967
RIPLINGER, GAIL, ***Hazardous Materials, Greek & Hebrew Study Dangers***, A.V. Publications, 2008
RIPLINGER, GAIL, ***In Awe of Thy Word***, A.V. Publications, 2003
RIPLINGER, GAIL, ***New Age Bible Versions***, A.V. Publications, 2008
RIPLINGER, GAIL, ***The Hidden History of the English Scriptures***, A.V. Publications, 2010
RIPLINGER, GAIL, ***The Language of the King James Bible***, A.V. Publications, 1998
ROBBINS, JOHN W., ***Ecclesiastical Megalomania***, The Trinity Foundation, 1999
ROBERTSON, A.T., ***An Introduction to the Textual Criticism of the New Testament***, Broadman Press, 1925
SCHAFF, PHILIP, ***History of the Christian Church***, Vol. 1-8, Charles Scribner, 1859-1905
SCHAFF, PHILIP, ***Schaff-Herzog Encyclopedia of Religious Knowledge***, Funk & Wagnalls Company, 1952
SCHAFF, PHILIP, ***The Creeds of Christendom***, Volumes 1-3, 1919
SCHULTZ, TED, ***Assault on the Remnant***, Dog Ear Publishing, 2016
SCHWANTES, SIEGFRIED J., ***The Biblical Meaning of History***, Pacific Press, 1970
SEMLYEN, MICHAEL DE, ***All Roads Lead to Rome***, Dorchester House Publications, 1993
SIME, WILLIAM, ***History of the Inquisition***, Presbyterian Board of Publication, 1840
SMITH, WILLIAM, ***A Dictionary of the Bible***, John C. Winston Company, 1884
SOCRATES, ***The Ecclesiastical History of Socrates Scholasticus***, Henry Bohn London, 1853
STANDISH, RUSSELL R. & COLIN D., ***Modern Bible Translations Unmasked***, Hartland Publications, 1993
STEED, ERNEST H.J., ***Two Be One***, Logos International, 1978
STOKES, GEORGE T., ***Ireland and the Celtic Church***, Hodder and Stoughton, 1888

Bibliography

SUTTON, WILLIAM J., *The Illuminati 666*, Institute of Religious Knowledge, 1983

SUTTON, WILLIAM J., *The Antichrist 666*, Workers for God Inc., 1983 (Revised Edition)

SUTTON, WILLIAM J., *UFO's and the New World Order Connection*, Institute of Religious Knowledge, 1999 (2nd Edition)

SUTTON, WILLIAM J., *Mysticism, Hollywood, and the Music Industry*, Institute of Religious Knowledge, 1998

SUTTON, WILLIAM J., *The Dragon, the Beast, and the False Prophet*, Institute of Religious Knowledge, 2005 edition

SWETE, HENRY B., *An Introduction To The Old Testament In Greek*, Cambridge University Press, 1900

TAN, PAUL LEE, *Encyclopedia of 7700 Illustrations*, Nordica International LTD, 1991

TERRY, MILTON S., *Biblical Hermeneutics*, Eaton and Mains, New York, 1890

TISCHENDORF, CONSTANTINE, *When were our Gospels Written?*, American Tract Society, 1866

TOW, S.H., *"An Urgent Plea for Christian Fervency in these 'Last Days' and a Defense of the Authorized King James Bible"* - *The Defined King James Bible*, Bible for Today Press, 2011

TOWNLEY, JAMES, *Illustrations of Biblical Literature*, Vol. 1 & 2, Lane & Tippett, 1842

VANCE, MURL, *The Trail of the Serpent*, Oriental Watchman Publishing, 1991

VANCE, MURL, *Breaking the Code of the Secret Societies*, Teach Services, 2002

VOERMAN, JAN, *The Hidden Agenda*, Teach Services, 2007

WACE, HENRY; PIERCY, WILLIAM, *A Dictionary of Christian Biography and Literature*, John Murray London, 1911

WALKER, WILLISTON, *A History of the Christian Church*, Charles Scribner's Sons, 1950

WALSH, MARY E., *The Apocrypha*, Southern Publishing Assoc., 1968

WALSH, MARY E., *The Wine of Roman Babylon*, Southern Publishing Assoc., 1945

WALSH, WALTER, *The Secret History of the Oxford Movement*, Swan Sonnenschein & Co., 1899

WESTCOTT, ARTHUR, *Life and Letters of Brooke Foss Westcott*, Macmillan And Co., 1903

WHITE, ELLEN G., *Education*, Pacific Press Publishing Association, 1952

WHITE, ELLEN G., *Sermons and Talks*, vol.1, Ellen G. White Estate, 1990

WHITE, ELLEN G., *The Spirit of Prophecy*, 4 Volumes, Review and Herald Publishing Association, 1870-1884

WHITE, ELLEN G., *Testimonies for the Church*, Vol. 1-9, Pacific Press Publishing Association, 1948

WHITE, ELLEN G., *The Great Controversy between Christ and Satan*, Review and Herald Publishing Association, 1888

WHITE, ELLEN G., ***Acts of the Apostles***, Review and Herald Publishing Association, 1911
WHITE, ELLEN G., ***Letters and Manuscripts***, Ellen White Estate Files
WHITE, ELLEN G., ***Sketches from the Life of Paul***, Review and Herald Publishing Association, 1883
WHITE, JAMES, ***Sketches of the Christian Life of William Miller***, SDA Publishing Association, 1875
WILKINSON, BENJAMIN G., ***Our Authorized Bible Vindicated***, Benjamin Wilkinson, 1930
WILKINSON, BENJAMIN G., ***Our Authorized Bible Vindicated – Answers to Objections***, Teach Services, 2008
WILKINSON, BENJAMIN G., ***Truth Triumphant***, Hartland Publications, 2004
WILKINSON, ROWLAND F., ***The New Revised Standard Version of the Bible***, Wilkinson, 1953
WISSE, FREDERIK, ***The Profile Method for the Classification and Evaluation of Manuscript Evidence***, William Eerdmans Publishing Co., 1982
WOLFF, JOSEPH, ***Journal of the Rev. Joseph Wolff***, R. Perring, 1839
WYLIE, JAMES AITKEN, ***History of the Waldenses***, CHJ Publishing, 1880
WYLIE, JAMES AITKEN, ***History of Protestantism***, Volumes 1-3, Cassell Petter & Galpin, 1878
-------, ***Adventist Review***, July 5, 1979
-------, ***Ante-Nicene Fathers*** Volumes 1-9, E-Sword Reference, 1867
-------, ***Catechism of the Catholic Church***, Ignatius Press, 1994
-------, ***Dictionary of the Ecumenical Movement***, Eerdmans Publishing Company, 1991
-------, ***Encyclopedia Britannica 9th Edition***, Edinburgh: Adam and Charles Black, 1880
-------, ***Encyclopedia Britannica 10th Edition***, The Werner Co., 1898
-------, ***Handbook for Bible Students***, Review & Herald Publishing Association, 1922
-------, ***Moody Monthly***, June 1982
-------, ***Review & Herald***, August 8, 1899
-------, ***Rome's Challenge: Why Do Protestants Keep Sunday?*** From the *Catholic Mirror*, 1893
-------, ***Source Book for Bible Students***, Review & Herald Publishing Association, 1919
-------, "The Real Reason They Made the NKJV" ***Battle Cry Newsletter*** from Chick Publications, Sept.-Oct. 2019
-------, ***The Catholic Encyclopedia***, Encyclopedia Press, 1907
-------, ***The World Book Encyclopedia***, Field Enterprises Education Corporation, 1966
-------, ***1611 KJV***, *The Translators to the Reader*

Bibliography

Image Credits

Images taken from
Public Domain, Roberts' collection, Screenshots and Fair Use

Images on p.42, 47, 72, 103, 190
by Joe Maniscalco

Image of Waldo on p.105
© Alexander Hoernigk
(via Wikimedia Commons) Creative Commons 3.0 & 4.0

Sword Unsheathed

Index

Abomination 71, 86, 87, 186, 208, 216, 281
Abyssinia 77, 83, 145, 201
Acrostic 139
Adams, John 361
Adolphus, Archbishop 116
Adoptionism 50, 59
Advent Movement, Adventist 67, 201, 203, 204, 205, 255, 289, 296
Æthelstan, King 96
Afghanistan 23
Africa 22-24, 44-45, 52, 64, 70, 76-78, 81, 90, 92, 117-118, 209, 315, 317
Agape 63
Alamanni 57
Aland, Kurt 238, 243, 245, 247, 271
Alans 81
Alaric, King 87
Albigenses 73, 76, 97, 102, 103, 106, 110
Alboin, King 91
Alcazar, Luis De 189
Alden, John 189
Alemanni 85
Alexander the Great 42
Alexandria 13-14, 19, 26, 34, 36-38, 40, 41, 48-53, 56-61, 70, 76, 82, 84-85, 92, 166, 178, 191, 211-212, 218, 222, 227, 231, 236, 255, 257-258, 267, 271, 326, 332
Algeria 24, 76, 81
Alice (in Wonderland) 371
Allah 91-92
Alps 71-74, 97, 103, 131, 190, 357
Amalasuntha, Queen 93
Ambrose 69, 73, 125
America/American 119, 155, 163, 177, 187, 197, 199, 200, 203, 205, 209-211, 218-219, 224-225, 234, 237, 246, 274, 284, 285-288, 316, 325
Amish 191
Ammann, Jakob 191
Amsdorf, Nicolaus von 102
Amsterdam 170
Anabaptist 131, 132, 141, 170, 191
Anastasius, Emperor 87
Angel 1, 223, 264, 265, 272, 294, 296, 301, 302, 319-321, 329
Angles 57, 81, 83
Anglican 240, 243, 246. 249
Anglo-Saxon 64, 66, 81, 83, 94, 96, 111, 113, 142, 143, 182, 356
Angrogna, valley of 134
Anne, Queen 134, 142

Index

Ante-Nicene Fathers 52, 340, 356
Antinomian 131, 132
Antioch 14, 24-25, 45, 58-59, 68-69, 79, 82, 83, 92, 117, 120, 177,335, 350, 356
Antiochus Epiphanes 178
Apocrypha 19-20, 34-35, 99, 116, 130, 145, 148, 159, 166, 173,177-178, 180, 199-200, 224, 241, 243, 244, 247, 272, 290
Aqua Tofana (poison) 193
Aquarian Conspiracy book 268
Arabic 91-92, 95, 171-172, 174, 316
Aramaic 7, 22, 42-43, 95, 121, 146, 160, 231, 236, 286-287
Arcadius, Emperor 69
Arianism 57, 62, 65, 68, 82, 123, 230, 344
Aristeas (letter of) 34, 36, 40, 56
Aristocles (see Plato)
Armenian 23, 52, 57, 69, 83, 85
Arnold of Brescia 104, 106
Arsenic 193
Arundel, Thomas 115
Asia 14, 22-24, 42, 51-53, 58, 62, 64, 69, 78, 80, 201, 269, 322, 350
Assyria 38, 250
Astrology 40, 55, 194
Athanasius 340, 344
Atheism 194-196, 313, 323
Athenagoras 340
Athens 52, 301
Atlantis (lost civilization) 39
Attila the Hun 85
Auca Indians 318
Augsburg 129
Augustine, Aurelius 341
Augustine of Canterbury 94-95
Augustine of Hippo 63, 76-77, 125, 351
Augustinians 136
Aurelian, Emperor 59
Austria 57, 80, 147, 189
Auto-da-fe 119
Autographs 8, 42, 335
Auxentius 69, 73

Babel 160, 215, 328
Babington Plot 162
Babylon 23-24, 31-32, 38, 40, 41, 49, 75, 97, 98, 100-101, 210, 225, 302, 328-329, 333
Bailey, Alice 3, 269
Ballard, John 162
Bambara 318

Baptism 23, 49, 50, 53, 67, 72, 103, 131, 170, 221, 276, 306, 340,336
Baptist 100, 107, 112, 170, 228, 245, 250, 265, 269, 274, 278, 284
Baradai, Jacob 87
Barker, Christopher 155
Becket, Thomas Archbishop 110
Belgium 81
Ben Asher, Aaron Moses 32, 98-99, 101, 232-233, 248, 336
Ben Chayyim, Jacob 119, 127-128, 228, 232-233, 274, 332, 335, 337
Benedictines 89, 94, 136
Bengal 317
Benigno, (Father) 203
Blayney, Benjamin 180
Ben Naphtali, Moses 32, 98
Bernard (abbot) 103
Berthier, Louis-Alexandre (General) 197
Bethlehem 70, 272
Beza, Theodore 47, 126, 153, 156, 166, 168, 177, 190, 336, 350,352-354, 357
Bible Societies
    American (ABS) 122, 182, 198-200, 203, 212, 229, 238-239, 247
    American & Foreign (AFBS) 203, 208
    United Bible Societies (UBS) 122, 235, 237-238, 243-245, 247,249, 255, 263,
        271-273, 276-277, 316, 337
Bible, manuscripts & codices
    Africana 45, 337
    Aleppo 99, 101, 236, 237, 240, 336-337
    Alexandrinus 56, 84-85, 204, 207, 222, 332, 336-337
    Ambrosianus 231
    Antehieronymian (Itala) 47, 79
    Argenteus 65, 88-89, 337
    Babylonicus Petropolitanus 98
    Bezae (Beza) 156, 222, 271
    Brixianus 46-47, 65, 76, 104, 114
    Cairensis 98, 336
    Carolinus 65
    Claromontanus 156
    Complutensis I 98
    Curetonian 13
    Demidovianus (dem) 351
    Diatessaron 13, 51, 336-337
    Divionensis (div) 351
    Ephraemi 85, 207, 222, 336
    Escurialensis 347
    Frisingensis (r) 351
    Guelferbytanus 348
    Itala (Vetus Italica) 45, 47, 52, 70, 74-76, 79, 89, 93-94, 97, 99,106-107, 114, 123,

Index

153, 157, 159, 177, 295, 333, 335, 337, 339, 350-352, 356
Jerome's Latin Vulgate 39, 69-71, 74-76, 93-94, 97-98, 106,111-112, 116, 118, 121, 123, 125, 130, 132, 136, 145, 148-149, 153, 159-161, 164, 197, 203, 212, 219-220,240, 246, 249, 254, 271, 273, 279, 285, 289-290, 302,333, 336-338
Legionensis (l) 351
Leningradensis (B19a) 101, 232-233, 236-337, 240

Montfortianus 347, 349
Mortimer-McCawley 223
Ottobonianus 347
Perpinianus (p) 351
Peshitta 14, 43, 44, 57, 83, 155, 223, 313, 337, 339
Philoxenian 44
Regis 348
Regius Neapolitanus 348
Septuagint 20, 33
Lucianic 38, 58-60, 62, 65, 70, 332, 335, 337
LXX 34-39, 56, 58, 60, 84, 93, 160, 199, 204, 207, 212, 230, 236, 238, 240, 242, 248, 249, 254, 271-272, 279, 282,332, 336, 337
Hesychius 60
Sinaitic Syriac 13, 215, 337
Sinaiticus (Aleph) 13, 56, 62, 85, 125,177, 197, 199-201, 204, 206-208,211-213, 218-219, 222, 230, 250, 302, 333, 336-337
Speculum (m) 351
Textus Receptus 14, 15, 17, 58, 85, 123, 125, 128, 159, 164, 190, 212, 213, 218, 219, 222, 224, 228, 229, 255, 256-258, 264, 270, 274, 279, 280, 326, 332, 334-337
Erasmus 121, 123, 125, 129, 141, 144, 150, 156, 335, 337
Stephanus 123, 149-150, 156, 228, 335, 337
Vaticanus 56, 62, 85, 115-116, 204, 207, 212, 213, 218, 222, 250, 333, 336-337

Bibles

AMP (Amplified) 239, 242, 286, 337
Antigua 229, 279
Antwerp Polyglot 159
Armenian 69, 83, 190, 284, 335
ASV (American Standard) 225, 233, 241, 248, 290, 295, 300, 304-311, 334, 337
Bear (Reina's) 158-159, 161, 164, 166, 274, 336-337
Biestkens 156, 336-337
Bishop's 3, 157, 163, 174-175, 183, 208, 291-292, 295-298, 300,304, 336-337
Bomberg (2nd Great Rabbinic Bible) 127-128, 254, 332, 335, 337
Breeches (Britches) 155
CEV (Contemporary English) 279, 287
Chinese Union Bible 319
Complutensian Polyglot 99, 121, 123, 337

387

Confraternity 246, 285
Coverdale 3, 141, 142, 150, 175, 293, 296-297, 301, 307, 310, 335, 337, 352, 357
Cranmer 144
C.S. Lewis 281
Diodati 168, 169, 170, 198, 295, 336-337, 352
Douay-Rheims 160-161, 191-192, 256, 289, 292, 302-305, 307-312, 333, 336-337
ERV 251, 286
ESV (English Standard) 252, 275-276, 279, 287, 291-297, 299-312, 334, 337, 345
Ferrara 152, 159, 274
Gallic 51, 164, 335, 337
Geneva 3, 146, 153-157, 160-161, 163-164, 166, 171, 175, 180, 189, 291, 293, 296, 299-301, 303, 305, 309-310, 312, 326, 336-337, 352, 357
GNB (Good News) 243, 252, 277-278, 294, 301, 337
Great Bible (Wilchurch) 143-144, 153, 164, 175, 335, 337, 352
Gustav Vasa 144
HCSB (Holman Christian Standard) 253, 277-278, 282, 287, 337
Hutter Polyglot (Nuremberg) 163-165, 335, 337, 352, 353
ISV (International Standard) 251, 277, 287, 300, 301, 337
Jerusalem 243-244, 271, 282, 285-286, 291, 304-311, 337
KJV (King James) 3, 33, 112, 123, 128, 167, 171-187, 189, 192, 197-199, 201, 203-205, 208, 212-213, 217-221,223-225, 229, 231, 234-236, 238-240, 242-244, 246-248, 250-251, 253-283, 289-301, 303-312, 314-317, 319, 321, 326, 334, 336-337, 344-345, 352-354, 357
Kralice (Kralicka) 164, 167, 336-337
Lamsa 231, 285
Liesveldt 134
Luther's 121, 129-132, 134, 141, 144, 150, 164, 301, 335, 337-338, 352, 356
Matthew's 3, 142-144, 175, 293, 297, 305, 308, 310, 335, 337, 352
Mentel 118
Moffatt 234, 284
MSG (Message) 239, 251-252, 272-273, 277, 279, 287, 291, 337
NAB (New American) 246-247, 286, 292, 304-312, 337
NASB (New American Standard) 241, 248-249, 275, 285-286, 306-311, 337
NCV (New Century) 271, 286-288, 337
NEB (New English) 238, 286, 337
NIV (New International) 239, 243, 249-250, 253, 276-277, 279, 286-287, 292-296, 298-299, 302-312, 319, 325, 334, 337, 345
NJB (New Jerusalem) 271, 282, 286, 288
NKJV (New King James) 3, 251-270, 286, 291-294, 296-302, 305-311, 334, 337
NLT (New Living) 239, 252, 273-274, 287, 293, 296, 298, 302-303, 305-308, 334, 337, 345
NRSV (New Revised Standard) 243, 246, 272, 274, 280-281, 287, 337
Olivetan 137-141, 153, 196, 198, 295, 301, 319, 326, 334-335, 337, 352, 357
Pineda NT 152, 157, 159, 166, 274
Pinel 152

Index

    Plantin Polyglot 159
    PNC (People's New Covenant) 229, 285
    1602 Purificada 275, 278-280, 336
    QJV (Queen James) 281, 288, 337
    REB (Revised English) 243, 287
    Reina-Valera 161, 166, 229, 239, 274, 278, 280, 336
    Renovaré 280
    RKJNT (Revised King James New Testament) 277
    RSV (Revised Standard) 233-237, 241, 243, 247, 248, 267, 272, 279, 285, 292, 295, 299, 302, 306-311, 334, 337
    RVG (Reina-Valera Gomez) 280, 336
    Robert Aitken 197
    SBK (Shorter) 229, 285
    Sword 140-141, 337
    Taverner 144, 352
    Tepl 114, 129, 324, 352
    TEV (Today's English) 243, 247, 278, 286, 325, 337
    TLB (The Living) 21, 239, 247, 273, 286, 337
    Tok Pisin King Jems Baibel 319
    TNIV (Today's New International) 250, 279, 287, 337
    Tyndale 3, 121, 133-135, 141-142, 149-150, 153, 175, 183, 263, 291, 296, 298, 300-301, 303, 307, 309, 311-312, 315, 318, 321, 326, 335, 337, 345, 352, 357
    Valencia 118
    Webster 3, 201, 284, 337
    Welsh 163, 337
    Weymouth 227-228
    WMF (Word Made Flesh) 271-272, 286, 337
Bibles (list of modern) 283-288
Biblia Hebraica (BHK) 228, 233, 238, 240, 241, 242, 248, 249, 337
Biblia Hebraica Stuttgartensia (BHS) 240, 248, 254, 271, 275, 276, 277, 282, 337
Biblion/Biblios 7
Blahoslav, Jan 167
Blanco, Jack 275
Blavatsky, Helena Petrovna 214, 223, 269
Blayney, Benjamin 180
Bohemia 106, 111, 114-115, 119, 134, 164, 167, 189, 352
Bois, John 173, 180
Boleyn, Anne 134, 142
Bomberg, Daniel 127-128
Booth, John Wilkes 210
Brescia (city) 47, 72, 88, 104, 119
Britain 44, 51-52, 66, 76, 81, 94, 101, 109-110, 233, 325
British 24, 44, 51, 78, 198-201, 225, 228-229, 238-239, 243, 350
Brueggemann, Walter 280
Bruys, Peter de 103, 104, 106

Sword Unsheathed

Bulgaria 97-98
Burgon, John (Dean) 45, 207, 222-223
Burgundians 57, 81, 86
Burundi 316
Bushmen 317
Byzantine 13-14, 17-18, 24, 47, 58, 60, 69, 84, 98, 219, 222, 258, 271

Cabbala (Kabbalah) 49-50, 91-92, 236
Caesarea 37, 56-57, 61, 70, 212, 205
Calpurnius 78
Calvin, John 126, 137, 140-141, 153, 166, 355, 329
Cambridge 37, 107, 121, 146, 156, 172-173, 175, 177, 179-180, 217, 228, 342
Cameroun 316
Canada 199, 233
Canterbury 94, 109-110, 142, 173, 224
Cardinal 49, 96, 99-110, 121, 124, 159, 192, 197, 202, 215, 232, 242, 244
Carolingian 95-96
Carroll, Lewis 371
Carthage 23, 52, 81, 340-341
Cassiodorus 93-94
Castilian 152, 280
Castro 195
Catalaunian Fields (battle of) 85
Cathari 105
Catholic 20, 26-27, 39, 44, 56, 58, 61, 64, 66-67, 69-70, 74, 76, 79-82, 86-87, 90, 92-96, 98, 101-102, 104-106, 108, 110, 114, 117-118, 120, 123, 126, 132, 134, 141, 147-148, 150-151, 156-163, 166, 178, 186, 189, 191-193, 195, 197, 200, 202, 204, 209-210, 212, 214-215, 220-221, 224, 230-233, 235, 238-249, 254, 271-272, 274, 276, 278, 281-282, 286, 290-292, 302-312, 316, 325-326, 329, 336, 361, 371-372, 375
Catholicism 26, 58, 64, 77, 78, 80, 86, 87, 91, 94, 102, 109, 120, 136, 137, 163, 194, 202, 212, 271, 272, 282, 289
Catholic Biblical Federation (CBF) 245
Catholic Research Information Bureau (CRIB) 238
Confraternity of Christian Doctrine (CCD) 246
Celts/Celtic 24-25, 51, 70, 76, 78, 79, 94, 95, 104, 338
Cerulanius, Michael 101
Chalcedon (Counsel of) 85
Chaldee/Chaldean 91, 97, 145, 171-172, 174
Challoner, Bishop 192
Chameleon 282
Chamforan (Synod of) 134
Charlemagne 95-96
Charles I, King 84
China/Chinese 8, 23, 44, 153, 316, 352
Chiniquy, Charles 210

Index

Christmas 63
Chronicles of Narnia 372
Chrysographia 89
Chrysostom 14, 58, 68-69, 125, 177, 190
Cicero 97
Claude, Bishop 97
Claudius, Emperor 44
Clement of Alexandria 41, 51-54, 332
Clermont (monastery of) 156
Clovis, King 86-87
Colón, Cristóbal (see Columbus, Christopher)
Colophon 9, 101, 211
Columba 89-90, 104
Columbus, Christopher 119
Comet (Great, 1843) 204
Commandment(s) 2, 4, 49, 59, 63, 73, 77, 96, 97, 242, 303, 304, 331, 373
Communism 39, 195, 229, 234, 237
Conchessa 78
Confederacy 209
Constance (Council of) 113
Constantine the Great 37, 41, 61-63, 66, 68, 70, 96, 101, 115, 207, 211, 302, 336, 344, 351
Constantinople 14, 24, 42, 58, 60, 68-70, 82, 84, 90, 92, 96, 117, 332, 335
Consubstantial 67
Coptic 13, 40, 85
Coronavirus 200
Cottian Alps 72, 97
Cottius, King 71
Counter-Reformation 136, 147, 163, 199, 305, 325, 333
Coverdale, Miles 141, 143, 153
Cranmer, Thomas 142-144, 151
Croatia 80
Cromwell, Thomas 141-143
Crusades 93, 102
Culdee 90
Cushing, Richard 242
Cyril of Alexandria 82, 125

Dacia 64
Da Gama, Vasco 120
Damascus 92, 98
Danes 99
Danish 150, 164, 336, 352
Dark Day 195
Darwin, Charles 209, 217
Davidson, A.B. 217

Death (state of) 53-54
Demiurge 49
Denmark 99
Diamper (synod at) 145
Diaprax 199
DiVietro, Kirk 265-266
Dobson, James 275
Docetism 50
Dodgson, Charles 371
Dominicans 110, 136, 195
Donation of Constantine 96, 101
Donatists 76
Dragon 2, 73, 195, 208, 315, 324, 331, 333
Drama 189-190, 234, 287
Driebergen Conference 241-243
Druidic 200
Dublin 106-107, 221, 290
Duodecimo 19
Dum Diversas 117
Dutch 2, 108, 134, 141, 156, 171, 336, 352

Eagles 133, 275, 301-302, 320, 321
Easter 53, 59
Ebionites 50, 55-56
Edessa 44, 87
Edward, King 150, 151
Egypt 14, 18, 23-24, 34, 38, 40-41, 49, 52-53, 56-57, 60, 83, 85, 92, 100, 113, 166, 196, 201, 227-228, 230, 232, 250, 271, 293, 322, 373
Eisleben, Germany 118
Elamites 52, 322
Elizabeth I, Queen 146, 151-152, 156, 157, 162, 163, 167, 174
Elvira (Council of) 61
Elzevir 190, 337, 357
Emasculate 277, 279
"End Justifies the Means" 27
England 51, 57, 78-79, 84, 89, 96, 105-106, 109-112, 114, 124, 133-134, 142, 146, 149,151, 153, 160, 162-163, 167, 171-173, 176, 182, 187, 189, 192, 197, 199, 201-204, 209-212, 217, 224-225, 338, 243, 325-326, 338, 354
English (Engle) 1-3, 8, 16, 18, 45, 65, 67, 70, 83, 96, 99, 101, 106, 111-113, 115, 117, 125, 133, 135, 139, 141-142, 146, 155, 160-162, 164, 170, 174-175, 177-178, 180, 182-185, 189-190, 197, 199, 201, 203, 219-225, 228, 238-239, 243, 246-247, 249, 260, 263, 269, 273-275, 277, 280, 282-288, 294, 316-320, 322, 324, 336, 341, 344, 352, 354-355
Eons 49
Ephesus (Council of) 83

Index

Erasmus 121-125, 129, 132-133, 136-137, 141, 144, 150, 156, 168, 190, 332, 335, 339,
 345, 348-349, 353-354, 357
Esdras 19, 212
Essenes 236, 269
Ethelbert, King 94-95
Ethelfrid, King 95
Ethiopia 23, 77, 85, 201, 276, 320
Eucharist 97
Eudoxia, Aelia 69
Europe 22, 24, 44-45, 57, 64, 66, 75-76, 78, 80, 83, 86, 90, 92-93, 95,102-104, 106, 108,
 111, 113, 116-117, 121, 124, 132-134, 137, 141, 146, 153, 160-161, 163, 166,
 189-190, 196-198, 204, 210-211, 350, 354
Eusebius 37, 61-62, 70-71, 115, 211, 213, 302, 336-337
"Evilutionary" 251
Evolution/Evolutionary 3, 11, 209, 237, 283
Evolutionist/Evolutionism 217, 225, 227, 228, 238
Excommunication 53, 55-57, 59, 82, 98, 101, 103-104, 108-109, 115,120

Facsimile 135, 155, 212
Faith/Faithful 4, 12, 22, 24-26, 28, 30-31, 36, 41, 44, 48, 50, 53, 55-58, 61-62, 64-66, 69,
 74-79, 86, 90, 95-96, 100, 102-106, 114-115, 119-120, 126, 128, 131, 134, 136-137,
 141, 145-147, 149, 155, 157-158, 160, 166, 168, 174, 183-184, 188-189, 191-193,
 198, 200, 202-203, 205, 208-209, 214-216, 226, 229, 234, 238, 259, 262, 265,
 270, 282, 289, 303, 314-315, 325, 327-331, 338-340, 344, 351, 353, 355, 361-362,
 366, 368
Fanatical/Fanaticism 77, 131-132
Fantasy 371-372
Farel, William 126
Farrara (Council at) 115
Farstad, Arthur 253-258, 277
Fascism 39, 195
Fawkes, Guy 167
Fayyum 38, 228
Federal Council of Churches 229, 237
Feminists/Feminism 237, 272
Fiction/Fictitious 19, 36, 40, 74, 79, 122, 178, 222, 231, 234, 331, 336, 348-349, 371
Fifth-Column 232, 267
Fire 77, 102-103, 120, 167, 204, 206, 221, 236, 270, 292, 312, 322, 343
Flaming Heart 135, 136
Folio 19, 106, 128, 137, 142
Footnotes 130, 219, 235, 248, 255, 258-259, 263-264, 354
Forged/Forgery 2, 27, 36, 44, 93-94, 96, 101, 102, 105, 122, 206, 213, 237, 323-325, 331,
 336, 348-349
Forgiveness 78, 106, 109, 281, 305
Fort Scott 199

Sword Unsheathed

Fox sisters 207-208
France 23, 24, 51, 57, 70-73, 78, 80-81, 86, 92, 102-103, 105-106,110-111, 124, 126, 130, 134, 138, 144, 147, 156, 160, 172, 193, 195-198, 203, 209
Francis I, King 147
Franciscans 110, 203
Franco, General 232
Franks 57, 70, 81, 92
Freemasonry 109, 194-195, 200, 237
French 2, 8, 24, 28, 73, 99, 101, 103, 106, 108, 111, 126, 130-131,133-135, 137-141, 147, 164, 171-172, 174, 177, 182, 191, 193, 195-197, 301, 319, 335, 352, 357
Fundamental(ist) 5, 27, 76, 147, 345, 361
Fust 116
Future 121, 122, 155, 163, 187, 228, 264, 270, 292, 297, 326, 349, 367-368
Futurism 163

Galatians 24, 51, 78, 260, 277-279
Galilaeans 322
Galilee 32, 100, 317
Gaul(s) 24-25, 48, 51-52, 71, 76, 78, 80-81, 85, 338
Geneva 134-135, 137, 141, 146, 150, 152-153, 155, 166, 168, 190
German 2, 8, 18, 106, 108, 113-114, 118, 121, 126, 129, 131-133, 141, 164, 195, 205-206, 208, 227-228, 230, 238, 317, 338, 352
Germany 57, 69-70, 80, 85, 89, 106, 116, 118, 124, 126, 131-133, 134, 141, 146-147, 150, 172, 179, 187, 194, 200, 205, 230, 232, 338
Geronimo 70
Ghostly Guild 208, 218, 334
Gibbons, James Cardinal 214-215
Gnostic/Gnosticism 14, 37, 48-53, 58, 67, 336, 344-345, 350
Godhead 49, 66, 67, 68, 268, 339, 340, 342, 356
Gold 35, 47, 89, 106, 116, 124, 137, 195, 298-299
Gomez, Humberto 278-280, 336
Goodspeed, Edgar 234, 285
Gospel 7, 9, 14, 19-20, 23-25, 42-44, 48, 51-52, 57, 59, 64, 66, 69, 71-72, 84, 89, 103, 113, 116, 124, 130, 133, 135, 138, 142-143, 160, 170, 173-174, 206, 213, 215, 227, 240, 245, 260, 267, 286, 308, 318, 323
Gothic/Goths 14, 57, 64-66, 70, 80, 83, 85-93, 110-111, 113, 140, 142-143, 179, 182, 335, 338
Graecina, Pomponia 44
Graham, Billy 110, 242, 245, 249, 273, 361
Great Disappointment 205
Great Schism 101
Greece 23, 24, 40, 41, 52, 53, 121
Greek 1-3, 7-8, 10, 13-16, 19, 22, 24, 33-43, 45, 47, 49, 51-53, 55-56, 58, 60, 64-71, 77-79, 81-84, 89, 93-94, 97-98, 101, 112, 115, 117-118, 121-125, 129, 132-133, 135-136, 141, 146, 149-150, 152-153, 156, 159-161, 163-167, 171-175, 177, 183-185, 190, 191, 201, 206, 211-213, 218-224, 227-230,233, 235-236, 238, 241-243, 245,

Index

       247-249, 254-257, 264, 271-274, 276-280, 294, 302-303, 308-310, 317, 321,
       335-336, 338-339, 342, 344-355, 357
Greeley, Horace 326
Gregory the Illuminata 57
Grey, Lady Jane 151
Griesbach, M. 13, 14
Gunpowder Plot 167
Gutenberg, Johannes 116

Haldane, Robert 200
Hamburg, Germany 133
Hand(s) 7-8, 15, 47, 50-52, 54, 56, 61, 72-73, 89, 95, 107, 111-112,116, 130, 142, 147, 157,
       159, 168, 175-176, 179, 193-194, 199, 202, 209, 211-212, 215-216, 222-225,
       228, 239-242, 258-259, 262, 270, 279, 296, 305-306, 312, 314-315, 323,
       327-328, 344-346, 359
Harlot 20, 240
Harmony 289, 294, 356, 363, 366-367
Harold, David 210
Harris, General Thomas, 210
Haskell, Stephen 40, 41
Heart 1, 9, 12, 20, 24, 78, 103, 107, 111, 114, 124, 126, 135-136, 186, 192, 209-210, 221, 246-
       247, 251-252, 276, 295, 299, 306, 315, 320, 322, 326-327, 358, 362-363, 368
Heathen(ism) 25-26, 43, 50-51, 53, 60-61, 66-67, 186-187, 271
Heaven 4, 20, 28, 31, 54, 56, 63, 67-68, 81, 112, 124, 196, 198, 205, 213-215, 221, 258,
       273, 277, 293-296, 301-302, 317, 322, 328-330, 339-342, 354, 358, 373
Hebrew 1, 2, 7, 8, 16, 19, 22, 31-37, 39, 42-43, 48, 55-56, 58, 81, 92, 98, 101, 112, 117-119,
       121, 127-128, 133, 135, 141,146-147, 152, 155, 159-161, 163-164, 166, 171-175,
       177-178, 183-185, 201, 223-224, 228, 232-234, 236, 241, 248-249, 254-255, 260,
       262, 273-274, 277-280, 316, 321, 327, 335-336, 338-339, 354
Hegelian Dialectic 199-200
Hegira 91
Hellenistic 34, 56
Helvidius 69, 71, 73
Henry of Lausanne 103-104
Herero 324
Heresy 48, 51, 53, 74, 82, 97, 104, 109-110, 113, 115, 142-143, 146, 225, 350
Heretics(al) 28, 48, 50, 58, 66-67, 70, 87, 103, 106, 142, 161, 214, 224, 240, 282, 336
Herrnhut 192
Heruli 57, 85, 91
Hesychian Text 14
Hesychius 38, 60
Hexapla 36, 55, 56, 62, 211, 212, 279, 336
Hierarchy(ical) 50, 68, 70, 74, 171, 210, 230, 261
Hieronymus (see Jerome)
Hindustan 69

Historical-Critical 11
Historical-Cultural 11
Historical-grammatical 11, 12, 361
Hitler 200, 230
Hmong 317
Hodges, Zane 256-258
Holland 124, 150
Homer 41
Homoiousian 67-68
Homoousian 67
Homosexual 237, 275, 281, 283
Honey 158, 364
Hort, F.J.A. 15, 122, 192, 208, 210-212, 217-220, 222, 224, 227-228, 238, 242, 257, 303, 313-314, 334, 336-337, 349
Hospitallers 109
House(d) 8, 50, 99, 110, 130, 133, 142, 182, 205, 207, 220, 227, 234, 236, 243, 250-251, 262-263, 274, 279, 322, 326, 373-374
Hungary 57, 80, 85, 111, 115, 121, 189
Huns 57, 80, 85
Huss 114-115, 167, 192
Hunt, R.J. 317
Hutter, Elias 163-165

I-H-K 227
IHS 144
Illuminati 194-195, 237
Image 75, 95, 97, 239, 311-312, 373
Immersion (Baptism by) 131, 170
Immortal(ity) 53, 54, 67, 307
India 23, 120, 145-146, 153, 201, 274, 317
Indulgences 109, 128
Infallible(ility) 4, 103, 148, 149, 191-192, 214, 259, 269, 329, 340, 361
Infiltrate(d)(ing) 62, 157, 160, 194, 199, 209, 235, 241
Infiltration/Infiltrators 200, 232, 267, 371
Inquisition/Inquisitors 28, 77-78, 106, 109-110, 114, 118-119, 136, 143, 145-146, 152, 157-160, 232
Insabbati 74
Inspiration/Inspired 9, 11-12, 19-20, 35-36, 52, 148, 166, 178, 213, 218, 223, 258, 270, 275, 284, 289-290, 323, 326-327, 355, 358, 362, 371
Interconfessional 235, 245, 281, 316
International 45, 182, 233, 239, 244, 247, 260, 279
International Council of Religious Education 229
Iona 89
Iran 23
Iraq 23

Index

Ireland 51, 76, 78-80, 89, 105, 109, 238
Irenaeus 48, 72, 356
Irish 24, 76, 79, 94, 105
Ironside, Harry 331
Isis 214, 223, 269
Islam(ic) 91-93, 101, 102, 283, 329
Israel 23, 35, 38, 56, 74, 100, 113, 234, 236-237, 262, 272, 276, 293, 327
Italy 24-25, 45, 47-48, 57, 60, 66, 70-72, 76, 80-81, 85, 89, 90-91, 101, 104, 106, 110-111, 119, 140, 144, 152, 172, 187, 193, 350, 372
Jacobin Club 195
Jacobites 83, 87
Jansenists 203
Japanese 316
Jehovah 3, 33, 92, 183, 225, 265, 297
Jerome of Prague 114-115
Jerome (pope' secretary) 45, 58, 69-71, 76, 333
Jerusalem 23-24, 49-50, 52, 64, 92, 100, 102, 108, 129, 232, 236, 320, 322
Jesuit(s) 27-28, 109, 120, 135-136, 144-145, 147-148, 153, 160-163, 166-167, 189, 191-195, 197, 199, 202-203, 209-211, 217, 220, 230-232, 235, 237-238, 241, 244-245, 247, 249, 256, 272, 280, 325, 336
Jesus 1-4, 7, 21-23, 35, 44, 48-50, 54-55, 57, 61, 66, 73, 80, 82, 100, 126, 135, 137, 139, 144-145, 147, 172, 179, 180, 184, 193, 195, 201, 204-205, 216, 219-220, 235, 248, 258, 263, 269, 272, 273, 276-278, 281, 283-284, 294-295, 297, 299-302, 306-310, 317-318, 321, 323, 327, 331, 339, 341, 345, 355-356, 372
Jews/Jewish 7, 14, 19-20, 23, 31, 32, 34, 35, 37-43, 49-50, 52, 54-56, 63-65, 81, 91, 92, 98, 100, 110, 119, 127-128, 145-147, 152, 161, 178, 201, 216, 221, 230, 232-233, 236, 269, 284-287, 308, 322
Johannine Comma 122, 123, 339-355
Jovinian 71, 73
Jupiter 59
Justinian 86, 90

Kabbalah/Kabalist 49-50, 91-92, 223, 269
Kando, William 237
Kazakhstan 23
Ka'ba 91-92
Kele 317
Kirundi 316
Kittel, Rudolph 228, 230, 232-233, 238, 240-242, 248
Kittel, Gerhard 230, 233
KJV Translators (List) 171-174
Knights of Malta 195
Knights Templars 105, 108-109, 119, 195
Knox, John 146, 153, 156
Koran 91-92

Korean 316
Kwangali 315

Ladino 152
Laodicea 69
Lateran Council (3rd) 106
Lateran Council (4th) 110, 230
Latin 2, 7-8, 19, 42, 44-45, 47, 52, 56, 64-65, 70-71, 74, 76, 78-79, 88-89, 94, 98-99, 111-112, 121, 123, 125, 129, 133, 135,141, 145-146, 148, 153, 156, 164-165, 171-174, 177, 182, 190, 216, 316, 319, 333, 338-339, 350-352, 354
Laurentius 144
Lectionary 15, 249
Lefevre, Jacques 125-126, 130-131
Leger, Jean 73, 138, 168
Leipzig 129, 163, 211
Lengua 317
Leo, Vigilantius 48, 71-73, 97
Leonists 72-73
Lesbian 249
Lewis, C.S. 281, 371-372
Library(ies) 2, 8, 28-29, 37, 56-57, 61, 70, 89, 95, 107, 117, 121, 146, 149, 156, 173, 206, 211-212, 227-228, 325, 342, 345, 354
Libya 24, 322
Liesveldt, Jacob 134
Lightfoot, J. B. 217-218, 228
Lilith 371
Lincoln, Abraham 117, 186, 209-210
Lisbon Earthquake 193
Lockman Foundation 241-242
Lollardo, Raynard 111
Lollards 111, 113
Lombards(y) 57, 85, 91, 106, 119
London 151, 155, 167, 172-173, 177, 187, 208, 228
Loyola, Ignatius 119, 135-136, 144-145
Lucar, Cyril 166
Lucian of Antioch 38, 58-60, 62, 65, 70, 125, 335, 356
Lucifer 194, 214, 223, 294-296
Lucis Trust 214
Luther, Martin 102, 118, 121, 125, 128-132, 134, 150, 290, 315, 317, 338, 362
Lyons 48, 51, 72, 73, 105-107, 156

Maccabees 19, 178
MacDonald, George 371
Madrid 232
Magna Carta 109
Magus, Simon 24, 49, 59

Index

Maimonides 232
Majuscules 18
Malcolm III, King 104
Mali 318
Manichaeism 58, 77, 103
Marcionites 48
Marcion of Sinope 48
Margaret of Wessex 104-105
Marshmallow 240
Martini, Carlo 244-245, 247
Martyr, Justin 50-52
Marx, Karl 195
Mary-worship/Mariolatry 53, 68, 82-83, 219, 238
Masorah 31-32, 41, 119
Masoretes/Masoretic 31-32, 39, 98, 101, 119, 128, 159, 233, 236, 249, 274, 277, 279, 332, 335
Mass 63, 80, 81, 97, 101, 166, 243, 246
Massachusetts 189, 242, 265
Mauritania 24
Mayflower 189
Meaux 126, 130-131, 350
Mecca 91, 120
Medina 91
Melancthon 129
Mennonites 141, 156, 170, 191, 249
Mercersburg Theology 205, 225
Methodist 192, 229, 249
Metzger, Bruce 122, 245, 349
Mexico 274, 278
Miaphysitism 82-83
Milan 25, 65, 69, 72, 104, 244
Miller, William 199, 201, 203-205, 366, 368-370
Miniscules 19
Minnesota 210
Mithraism 25, 63
Moffatt, James 234, 284-285
Mohammed/Mohammedanism 91-93, 102
Molech 281
Monarchianism 56, 59, 67
Mongolia 324
Monophysite 82-83, 85, 87
Moravian 115, 119, 131, 167, 192
Mormons 200, 213
Morrison, Robert 316, 352
Moskito, Indian language 318

Mudd, Dr. 210
Muntzer, Thomas 131-132
Muslims (Moslems) 91, 95, 102, 108, 117, 120
Mysticism 39, 49, 50, 52, 55, 91, 92, 200, 236, 269, 270, 274, 280, 366, 371-372
Mythology 371-372

Napoleon 198
Narnia (Chronicles of) 372
National Council of Churches (NCC) 233-234, 237, 272, 275
Naval 162, 209
Nazi 230, 233
Nazianzen, Gregory 68
Necromancy 55, 208
Neo-Platonism 53, 77, 236
Nero 24, 59, 216
Nestle, Eberhard 122, 227, 228, 248, 349
Nestle, Erwin 228, 238, 243
Nestle-Aland 227-228, 238, 241-242, 247-248, 255, 263, 271, 273, 275-277, 279, 282, 337
Nestorian 82-83
Netherlands 81, 134, 141
New-Age 3, 37, 39, 195, 211, 249, 268-269, 310, 329
New Hampshire 205
Newman, Cardinal John Henry 49, 96, 192, 202-203, 205, 212, 217, 225
Nicaea 61, 66-67, 95
Nida, Eugene 238-239, 244-245, 247
Normans 101
Norway 115
Novum Testamentum Graece (see Nestle-Aland)

Oak 259
Obedience 50, 77, 81, 136, 190, 246, 263, 303, 327, 239, 345
Occult 49, 91, 194, 214, 218, 223, 268-269, 270, 323, 345, 371-372
Octavo 19, 133
Odoacer 85
Ohio 208
Olivetan, Pierre Robert 134, 137-138, 140
Olive (trees) 75, 334
Origen 13, 14, 36, 37, 40, 41, 52-58, 60-62, 70, 84, 93, 94, 115, 125, 207, 211, 212, 248, 249, 279, 302, 332, 336
Orthodox 37, 40, 58, 60, 66, 68, 76, 86, 101, 120, 166, 269, 272, 287, 342
Orthography 163, 180, 182, 212
Ostrogoths 57, 80, 85, 88, 90-91, 93
Oxford 115, 136, 149, 172-175, 177, 180, 202-203, 205, 209, 212, 217, 225, 227, 241

Pacelli, Eugenio 230

Index

Pagan/Paganism 14, 25-26, 39-41, 47-55, 57, 59-64, 66, 70, 72, 79-81, 86-87, 93-97, 113, 117, 187, 195, 268, 270, 289, 301,323, 331, 336, 345, 371-372
Pageantry 113, 187
Palestine 23, 31, 32, 34, 35, 42, 49, 53, 71, 100, 102, 201, 335
Palimpsest 21, 85, 207
Palladius 79
Pamphilus 57, 61, 211-212
Pandects of Cassiodorus 94
Pantheism 280
Papacy 28, 53, 61, 63, 77, 80, 86-87, 91, 96-98, 101-102, 105, 109-110, 113-114, 117-118, 147-149, 163, 194, 196, 214, 281-282
Papal 26, 28, 53, 68, 71, 74, 76-77, 79, 81-82, 90-91, 93-94, 98, 101-104, 106-107, 109-111, 114-118, 126, 128, 131, 137, 139, 140, 144, 146-149, 151, 160-162, 166-167, 187, 189-194, 196, 198, 210-211, 214, 218, 221, 223, 230, 235, 271, 276, 278, 289, 305, 315, 325-326, 342, 361
Papists 27, 112, 118, 138, 187, 256
Papua New Guinea 319
Papyrus 7, 13, 15, 18, 37, 227, 230, 271, 323-324, 346
P#9 346
P#74 346
Chester Beatty 230
"Gospel of Jesus' Wife" 323-324
Magdalene 18, 227, 313, 335
Nash 228
Rylands 38
Parable 317, 364, 366-367
Paraguay 317
Paraphrase 13, 21, 37, 239, 243, 247, 271-273, 275, 279, 283, 365
Parchment 18, 32, 33, 47, 206
Paris 106-108, 125-126, 135, 143, 149-150, 160, 195, 227
Parthians 52, 322
Passover 135, 318
Patmos 24, 201
Paton, John 318-319
Patrick 51, 78-80, 89-90
Peasant's War 132
Pedersen, Christian 150
Pella 24
Pennsylvania 205
Pentateuch 39, 98, 121, 130, 141
Pentecost 322
Pergamus 18
Persia 23-24, 41, 92, 100, 201
Peterson, Eugene 272, 279, 280
Peter the Hermit 101-102

Petra 278
Petrobrusians 103
Petros 278
Philo 40
Phocas, Emperor 95
Phylacteries 92
Piarists 197
Pidgin 319
Piedmont Easter 190
Pikinini 318
Pineda, Juan Perez de 152
Pinel, Duarte 152
Pisa, Italy 104
Plato 39-41, 52, 195, 219
Plattsburg 199
Poison(ing) 5, 140, 147, 151, 193, 223
Polycarp 44, 48, 58, 356
Pontifex Maximus (Pontiff) 56, 61, 118, 193
Pope/Popery 27, 59, 63, 70, 74, 76-77, 79, 90, 94-98, 101-105, 109-110, 113, 115, 117-120, 124, 126, 128-129, 133, 136, 144-145, 147-149, 153, 160, 166, 191, 193-194, 197, 199, 202, 211, 214, 230, 238, 242, 244, 246, 281-282, 311, 316, 362
Popes
    Adrian IV 105
    Alexander VI 119
    Boniface III 95
    Calixtus 103
    Callistus 56
    Celestine 79
    Clement VIII 148, 149, 166
    Clement XIV 193-194, 191
    Damasus I 70, 94
    Felix 59
    Francis 136, 281
    Gregory the Great 94
    Gregory VII 101, 245
    Gregory IX 76
    Honorius III 110
    Innocent II 104
    Innocent III 109-110, 245
    Innocent VIII 118
    John III 145
    John Paul II 110, 244
    Julius I 63
    Leo III 96

Index

    Leo XIII 281
    Nicholas I 98
    Nicholas V 115, 117
    Paul IV 149
    Pius VI 197
    Pius VII 199
    Pius XII 230, 238
    Sixtus V 148-149
    Urban II 102
    Victor I 53, 59, 62
Pornography 324
Portugal/Portuguese 57, 81, 117-120, 145, 187, 193, 247
Potter, Harry 372
Prague Manifesto 131
Presbyterian 229, 238, 249, 318
Preterism 189
Priests/Priesthood 22, 32, 39, 56-57, 61, 68, 71, 73, 80-81, 97, 100, 109, 120, 128-129, 133,
    141, 161-163, 187, 191, 194, 197, 200, 202, 204, 209-211, 231, 239, 244-246,
    250, 269, 272, 294, 298-299, 305-306, 325
Primacy of Peter 59, 147
Printing 2, 7, 28, 36, 43-44, 89, 116-117, 119-121, 123-124, 133, 135, 150, 155, 157, 178-180,
    197, 199, 224, 253, 280
Proof-text(ing) 9, 10, 204, 359, 366-368
Propaganda 37, 200, 232, 254
Prophecy/Prophetic 1-2, 11, 36, 55, 75, 87, 90-91, 102, 124, 130, 163, 189, 195-196, 198,
    201, 203-205, 214, 234-235, 237, 246, 250, 261-263, 282, 289, 295-296, 314,
    328, 339, 353,358, 360, 364, 366-370
Protestants/Protestantism 12, 20, 26, 68, 71, 76, 95, 97, 103-104,106, 109-110, 113-115,
    126, 128, 131-134, 136-138, 142, 144, 146-147, 151-153, 156, 159-164, 166-167,
    170, 178, 183, 186-187, 189-193, 196-197, 199, 202-205, 209-210, 212, 217-218,
    220-221, 233, 238-242, 245, 248, 258-259, 272, 274, 276, 278, 281-283, 289-291,
    295, 302, 304-305,316, 325, 329, 332-334, 336, 355, 361-362, 375
Purgatory 20, 54, 94, 103, 115
Puritans 105, 155, 171, 189
Purvey, John 112
Pusey, Dr. Edward 202
Pythagoras 53

Quaker 38
Qumran 50, 236

Rabbinic(al) 31, 37, 98, 119, 127-128, 172, 174, 230, 337
Rainbow 315
Rapping (spiritualism) 207-208
Reformation 6, 14, 28, 71, 74-75, 95, 104, 108, 111-114, 120, 124, 126, 128, 130, 134,

136-138, 141, 144, 146-147, 153, 157, 161, 166, 170, 183, 187, 190, 215, 259, 282, 289-290, 295, 329, 333-334, 336, 350, 355, 362
Reich 230
Reina, Casiodoro de 157-159, 164, 166
Reinerius 114
Reist, Hans 191
Renaissance 136
Renovaré Institute 270
Revolution (French) 195-196
Reyes, Raul 274
Ribera, Francisco 163
Rigdon, Sidney 200
Ritualism 202
Rivera, Dr. Alberto 249-250
Rogers, John 141-142, 151
Romania 64
Romanus Pontifex 118
Romaunt 74, 106-108, 333, 335, 337, 350, 352
Rosary 102
Rosicrucian 194-195
Rowling, J.K. 371-372
Russia/Russian 23, 98, 206, 208, 214, 352

Sabbath 7, 12, 20, 51-53, 59, 62-64, 67, 69, 73-75, 77, 79, 83, 89, 97, 98, 101, 104, 115, 116, 145, 147, 192, 201, 205, 373
Sabellianism 56, 67, 344, 350
Saint, Rachel 318
Samaria/Samaritan 23, 38-39, 49, 55, 321
Sanctuary 205, 244, 270, 294, 299, 360
Sandals 74
Santanli 317
Samoa 318
Satan 1-3, 5, 9, 25, 35, 41, 54-55, 128, 196, 264, 270, 280, 294, 315, 317, 323, 327-328, 331,372
Saturday 52, 61, 62, 69, 74, 105, 201
Saturnalia 63
Saxons 51, 57, 66, 81, 83, 94-95, 111, 182, 356
Scandinavian 99, 111
Scapegoat 135
Schaff, Dr. Philip 205, 214, 225
Schnoebelen, William 200
Scotland/Scottish 24, 51, 78-79, 89, 94-95, 104-105, 111, 146, 156, 162, 167, 200
Scrolls 7, 31, 50, 233, 236-237, 241, 248-249, 254, 269, 277, 279, 287
Seminary 122, 205, 214, 225, 256, 349
Serpent 1, 2, 25, 40, 54, 68, 96, 109, 185, 217, 282
Seventh-day Adventist 205

Index

Seymoure, Jane 142
Simon, Richard 191, 192, 224
Simonides, Constantine 206
Simons, Menno 141
Sinai 49, 206, 343
Skull & Bones 195
Slaves/Slavery 41, 51, 78-79, 87, 96, 117-118, 209-210, 218-219, 317, 326
Slovakia 167
Slovenia 80
Smith, Joseph 200, 213-214, 284
Smyrna 44, 54
Socialism 39, 195
Society of Jesus 144-145, 147, 244
Societas Sanctae Crucis (SSC) Society of the Holy Cross 202
Soden, Hermann Von 208, 227-228, 256-258, 263
Sorcerer/Sorcery 20, 24, 49, 59, 371-372
Spain 23-24, 47, 52, 57, 61, 70, 80-81, 92, 110, 119, 124, 151, 157, 159, 162-163, 187, 193, 197, 231-232
Spalatin 129-130
Spanish 18, 28, 47, 70, 106, 118-119, 133, 152, 157-159, 161-162, 164, 171-172, 177, 197, 212, 229, 231-232, 239, 274-275, 278-280, 336, 341, 352
Spanish Armada 162
Spiritual Formation 270, 274, 280
Spiritualism/Spiritualist 3, 39, 195, 207-208, 218, 259, 268-270, 280, 324, 331, 336, 371
Stalin 195
Star(s) 111, 171, 203, 294-296, 330
St. Bartholomew Day Massacre 160
St. Catherine's Monastery 206, 208, 215, 333
St. Peter of Montmartre (church) 135
Stephens, Robert 123, 149-150, 228
Suevi 57, 81
SUN (Symbolic Universal Notation) 322
Sunday 20, 52-53, 59, 62-63, 74, 79, 96, 98, 104-105, 147, 245, 290
Surratt, John 210-211
Surratt, Mary 210
Sweden/Swedish 65, 88-89, 144, 335
Swiss/Switzerland 57, 73, 81, 85-86, 89, 104, 126, 131-132, 134, 140-141, 153, 166, 191
Symmachus 55, 279, 337
Syria(n) 14, 23-25, 43, 45, 51, 58, 68-69, 85, 92, 99, 117, 145, 201, 207, 222, 236, 335
Syriac 8, 13-14, 42-44, 81, 120, 145-146, 160, 164, 171-172, 174, 215, 335, 337, 352

Talmud/Talmudists 31, 49
Tanach 287
Tannaim 31
Targum 121, 160, 286

Tatian 13, 51-52, 336
Telegu 317
Tertullian 13, 52, 340, 356
Text-Criticism 42
Theodoric 85-86, 88
Theodosius, Emperor 70
Theodotion 56, 272, 279, 337
Theosophical Society 214
Thomasines 50
Thomas Nelson Publishers 253, 259, 261, 265-267
Thomson, Charles 199
Tiberias(n) 32, 98, 101
Tischendorf, Constantine 115, 204, 206-208, 211-213, 227-228, 257
Tobias 19, 20
Tok Pisin language 319
Tolkien, J.R.R. 243, 271
Tractarianism 202
Translators List (KJV) 171-174
Transubstantiation 97, 101, 110
Tregelles, Samuel Prideaux 122, 211, 228, 349
Tremellius, Immanuel 146, 164
Trent (Council of) 20, 147-149, 156, 202, 289, 333
Trinity/Trinitarian 67-68, 70, 107, 172-173, 201, 225, 236, 241, 342, 345
Triquetra 267-270
Trojan Horse 241
Tudor, Mary (Bloody) 146, 151-153, 156, 162
Tunisia 23, 81
Turin 73, 97, 104, 168
Turks/Turkey 24, 82, 92, 102, 117
Turkmenistan 23
Tyndale, William 121, 132-135, 141-143

Ulfilas (Ulphilas) 64-66, 88, 111, 335, 337-338
Unical 15, 18
Unitarians 201, 220, 225
Uppsala 88, 144, 335
Urdu 316
United States 197, 203, 208-209, 211, 233, 245
Usque, Abraham 152
Utopian 39, 195

Valera, Cipriano de 159, 161, 166
Vandals 57, 66, 81, 90-91
Vigilantius 48, 71-73, 97
Vatican 84, 93, 102, 109, 115, 125, 144, 209, 211-212, 214, 217, 231-232, 238, 240-244, 248, 254, 325-326, 333, 361

Index

Vaudois 47-48, 72-74, 103-105, 118, 134, 138-139, 169, 190, 334, 342
Venerable Bede 95
Venice 127, 152
Victoria, Queen 182
Vikings 99
Visigoths 57, 80, 87, 92
Vivarium 93
Vulgate 19, 42, 45, 58, 76, 332, 335, 337

Waldenses/Waldensian 28, 48, 71-77, 94, 97, 101, 103, 105-108, 110-111, 114, 123, 134-135, 137-138, 147, 153, 157, 161, 166, 168-170, 190, 281, 289, 295, 324, 333-335, 338, 342, 345, 350, 352, 356-357
Waldo, Peter 72, 105-106, 108
Wales 95, 238
Walsingham, Sir Frances 162
Waodani 318
Washington 205, 210, 237, 316
Weigle, Luther 234
Weishaupt, Adam 194
Westcott, Brooke Foss 15, 122, 192, 208, 212, 217-218, 222, 228, 238, 242, 303, 334, 336-337, 349
Westminster 171-172, 175, 177, 285
Westminster Confession of Faith 180
Wiccan 200, 269, 371
Wine 64, 97, 101, 225, 247, 250, 329
Witch/Witchcraft 20, 200, 208, 214, 223, 269-270, 371-372
Wittenberg 128-129, 131
Wolff, Joseph 201
World Catholic Federation for the Biblical Apostolate 245
World Council of Churches (WCC) 237
Worms 133
Wurttemburg 248
Wycliffe, John 3, 111-115, 130, 132-133, 161, 315, 320, 333, 362

Xavier, Francis 145
Ximenes, Cardinal 99, 121

York 173, 199, 200, 204, 207, 214, 224-225, 244

Zinzendorf, Nikolaus 192
Zoroastrianism 49
Zouaves 211
Zurich 106-107, 132, 237
Zwingli, Ulrich 131-132, 141, 191, 259

www.ingramcontent.com/pod-product-compliance
Lightning Source LLC
Chambersburg PA
CBHW070523010526
44118CB00012B/1058